THE
WINGED
BOMB

History of 39 Squadron RAF

Flt Lt Ken Delve

DIE NOCTUQUE

THE
WINGED
BOMB

History of 39 Squadron RAF

Published in 1985 by
Midland Counties Publications (Aerophile) Ltd,
24 The Hollow, Earl Shilton, Leicester,
LE9 7NA, England.

ISBN 0 904597 56 3

Printed in the United Kingdom by
Nene Litho Limited, Irthlingborough, Northants.

Bound by Woolnough Bookbinding,
Church Street, Irthlingborough, Northants.

Contents

Abbreviations

AA	Anti-Aircraft
AD	Air Depot, RAF Drigh Road, Karachi
AG	Air Gunner
AI	Air Interception, airborne radar
ALG	Advanced Landing Ground
AOC	Air Officer Commanding
APC	Armament Practce Camp
APS	Armament Practice Shoot
ASR	Air Sea Rescue
ASV	Air to Surface Vessel, radar
ATAF	Allied Tactical Air Force
B.E.	Bleriot Experimental
BIB	Baby Incendiary Bombs, early type of cluster bomb used in India.
BLG	Base Landing Ground
DR	Dead Reckoning
ETA	Estimated Time of Arrival
F24	Camera, inter-war period, widely used
F49	Camera, Canberra era, vertical
F52	Camera, Canberra PR.3 & 7 main type of equipment
F95	Camera, low-level tactical
F96	Camera, PR.9 large-scale camera 24" or 48" lens.
F540	Official log of Squadron or unit activities both operational and admin.
F541	Official log of sorties, sometimes only operational sorties at other times all sorties. Gives date, take-off and landing time, aircraft type and number, crew, type of operation and weapon load, results and comments (including losses)
FEAF	Far East Air Force
fpm	Feet per minute, rate of climb/descent
Gardening	- Mine laying from aircraft.
hp	Horse-power
IO	Intelligence Officer
IRLS	Infra Red Line Scan, heat sensing camera system fitted to Canberra PR.9
LG	Landing ground
MAAF	Mediterranean Allied Air Force, WW2
MAC	Mediterranean Air Command
ME	Middle East
METS	Middle East Torpedo (Training) School
mph	Miles per hour, airspeed

MU	Maintenance Unit
MV	Motor Vessel
NA	North Africa
NACAF	North West African Coastal Air Force
NATO	North Atlantic Treaty Organization.
NCO	Non-commissioned Officer
NEAF	Near East Air Force
NWA	North West Africa
NWFP	North West Frontier Province, India
OCU	Operational Conversion Unit
POW	Prisoner of War
PR	Photo-Reconnaissance
RDAF	Royal Danish Air Force
RNAS	Royal Naval Air Service (WW1) or Royal Naval Air Station
RNoaF	Royal Norwegian Air Force
RP	Rocket Projectile
SAAF	South African Air Force
SE	Sopwith Experimental
SR	Strategic Reconnaissance
SRU	SR Unit, Maryland Unit, Western Desert 1940/41. Composition unknown
TANS	Tactical Air Navigation System, fitted to Canberra PR.9
TR	Tactical Reconnaissance
UN	United Nations
VC	Victoria Cross
WOP/AG	Wireless Operator/Air Gunner

Preface

On 15th April 1916, No 39 (Home Defence) Squadron was formed as the first of the specialist squadrons designed to counter the Zeppelin raids on London and East Anglia. In a short period in September/October 1916 the Squadron destroyed four Zeppelins and shot to national fame. 2nd Lieutenant William Leefe Robinson was awarded the VC for destroying the SL11 over London, the first of these monsters to be brought down over England. Since its formation 39 has been disbanded or reduced to cadre status a number of times, the latest disbandment being June 1982 - another milestone as 39 was the last operational Canberra squadron. However, present policy, as far as can be discerned, is for the Squadron to reform as a Tornado reconnaissance squadron towards the end of the decade.

During its existence, 39 Squadron has performed a wide variety of roles from night fighter, day bomber, torpedo bomber, day fighter, ground attack and, for its last twenty-five years, reconnaissance. Throughout its life, however, the Squadron has only once been equipped with single-seat aircraft, and then only for a short period - the Tempest Mk.VI in 1948/49 (although a number of single-seat B.E.12s were used in World War One). Furthermore, 39 has operated in many parts of the world and from 1929 to 1970 was stationed outside the UK. Throughout its history the Squadron has lived up to its motto 'DIE NOCTUQUE - By Day and By Night'.

Acknowledgements

This book could not have been written without the co-operation of all those ex-members of 39 Squadron who sat through interviews or filled in questionnaires. Furthermore, during the five years that I was collecting information, a very large number of photographs were loaned or given to the Squadron. The realities of book production economics have restricted the number reproduced herein to over a hundred carefully chosen examples. My thanks to all who sent photographs, credits for the photos in the book are given after each caption.

Thanks also to the staff of the MoD Air Historical Branch for obtaining and re-obtaining the official records of 39 Squadron and to Wing Commander Lyn Frame and Wing Commander Robin Phipps, two COs of 39 Squadron who encouraged this project. Last but not least, to June at the RAF Museum for helping with the typing and Anne for drawing the maps.

Special mention to the following ex-Squadron members: Ralph Barker, George Beckett, Pat Biegel, John Clemons, John Coles, ACM Sir Walter Dawson, 'Larry' Gaine, Pete Hatcher, Peter Kennedy, John Manners, Matt Roe and ACM Sir Alasdair Steedman.

July 1985
Ken Delve   Huntingdon, Cambs.

U.K. Day Bomber Squadron (DH 9a) 1921-29

Oerland

London Home Defence 1916-18

Campomarino

Alghero

Protville

Luqa

Western Desert Landing Grounds

Khartoum

Kabrit/Fayid

Sheikh Othman

Risalpur

Singapore

A9.

Map 1: Locations of 39 Squadron

North West Frontier 1929-39

Blenheim 1940-41

2+4 - Maryland 1941-42

2 - Beaufort 1942-43

1+2+3 - Beaufighter 1943-44

3 - Marauder 1945

Sudan 1946, 1948-49

Canal Zone 1949-55

2+4 - Meteor 1955-58

Pr. Canberra. Low Level Deployment Areas

This Map Is Only A General Guide And Readers Should Consult The Chapter Maps For Detailed Information.

1

The Giant Killers

'I had served with 22, 40, 54, 60 and 66 Squadrons but this was 39, the Air Defence of London, the Zeppelin destroyers, the squadron of Leefe Robinson who had destroyed the first Zeppelin and won a V.C.'

Thus wrote an officer who joined 39 (Home Defence) Squadron at North Weald in early 1918. As early as the end of 1916, the exploits of the Zeppelin destroyers - Leefe Robinson, Sowrey, Tempest and Brandon were known throughout Britain, with particular interest and affection being shown by the people of London who came to look on 39 Squadron as their personal protectors.

At the outbreak of the Great War in 1914 the fledgling Royal Flying Corps was sent to France to support the British Expeditionary Force and responsibility for the air defence of the United Kingdom was placed in the hands of the Admiralty. Throughout 1914 and 1915 this 'air defence' consisted of a small number of guns and searchlights around London and a variety of Royal Naval Air Service (RNAS) aircraft dispersed along the east coast to patrol the coastline from the Thames to the Humber. The system was soon put to the test and was proved to be totally ineffective. Britain suffered its first airship raid on 19th January 1915 when the German Naval Airships L3 and L4 attacked targets in East Anglia. L3 bombed Yarmouth killing one man, while L4 flew a course between Bacton - Cromer - Sheringham - Beeston - Thornham - Brancaster - Hunstanton - Snettisham - Kings Lynn, scattering bombs along the way. Those bombs which fell on Kings Lynn killed four people and did £7,740 worth of damage - not a great number of casualties and only a small amount of damage but a severe shock to a nation which had previously been beyond the range of European wars. This small raid by only two early model Zeppelins was in many ways just a trial while the German Airship Services (Navy and Army) re-equipped with better machines in preparation for the major effort - the aerial bombardment of London. The city received its first serious raid on 31st May 1915 when Hauptmann Linnarz in LZ38 dropped incendiary bombs and grenades killing seven people, injuring thirty-five and causing £18,596 worth of damage. The casualties and damage were again small but this attack, seemingly mounted with impunity, by a single airship, held the threat of worse to come and the terror caused far outweighed the material damage. The German press was jubilant, one newspaper in Leipzig announcing:

'England no longer an island! The City of London, the heart which pumps the life-blood into the arteries of the brutal huckster (mercenary) nation, has been sown with bombs by German Airships, whose brave pilots had the satisfaction of seeing the dislocated fragments of docks, banks and many other buildings rise up to the dark skies in lurid tongues of flame.'

Good strong propaganda, but the fact that 'England was no longer an island' was not lost on the population of London - especially after another attack on the night of 7/8th September by Kapitan-Leutnant Heinrich Mathy in LZ31. Once again, damage was slight but it infuriated the already angry and frightened people of London, who demanded to know why nothing was being done.

Earlier in 1915 the Zeppelin commander Heinrich Mathy had commented on the value of an aeroplane defence against Zeppelins:

'As to an aeroplane corps for the defence of London, it must be remembered that it takes some time for an aeroplane to screw itself up as high as a Zeppelin and by the time it gets there the airship would be gone. Then too it is most difficult for an aeroplane to land at night.'

Despite the notable success of Sub-Lieutenant Warneford who, in a Morane Monoplane, destroyed Zeppelin LZ37 near Ghent, Belgium, on 7th June 1915, it would appear that the British Admiralty agreed with Mathy's assessment and in September 1915 they concluded that the air defence of London would be best served by improvements in the system of guns and searchlights already in existence, supplemented by a few aircraft. Discussions continued at the War Office as to who was best suited to perform the task of Home Defence, the Admiralty or the RFC. Neither group wanted the responsibility and the RFC were claiming lack of equipment, pilots and landing grounds. A compromise was eventually reached with the Admiralty being formally responsible for the task but with the RFC agreeing to take a more active part. As a result, on 2nd October, Lieutenant-General W G Salmond, Commanding Officer of No 5 Wing at Gosport, was ordered to 'bring machines to the vicinity of London for the period 4-12 October' to strengthen the air defence network. This reinforcement consisted of seven B.E.2cs and one S.E.4a - two of the B.E.2cs went to each of the landing grounds at Northolt, LG II (later known as Sutton's Farm) and LG III (later known as Hainault Farm); one B.E.2 and the S.E.4a went to Joyce Green. Each landing ground was equipped with portable hangars and a number of temporary buildings as offices and working accommodation. Pilots were billeted in the nearest house with a telephone, this was essential as the duty pilot would be alerted with a telephone call from the War Office when a raid was expected. This system was supposed to allow time for the aircraft to climb to 10,000 feet and thus give the pilot some chance of catching any Zeppelin he might see. If no enemy was sighted the pilot was to land 1½ hours after take-off.

The trial period of 4-12th October was officially extended to an 'indefinite period' and a number of interception attempts were made on the increasing number of Zeppelins now raiding England, although invariably the fighters failed to get within range of their opponents. One attack, on 13th October, caused such chaos and terror in London that it led to a public meeting at Cannon Street Hotel with people demanding 'a declared policy of air reprisals for Zeppelin raids on London and other open cities and an adequate system of air defence.'

The calls of the people of London fell on deaf ears; instead of improvements in the air defences, by the 26th October all detachments were back with their unit at Gosport - despite the 'indefinite extension'. This meant that there was no aeroplane defence from the recently established landing grounds in and around the city. However, by the end of December, under continued public pressure, the Directorate of Military Aeronautics ordered that two B.E.2cs be stationed at each of ten landing grounds around London, a combination of the previous fields and a number of new locations. The organisation of each field was based on the limited experience gained from the earlier operations and each field was allocated six mechanics and a Royal Engineer party with one searchlight and a 13-pounder gun; as well as two aircraft

plus pilots. Despite this seemingly positive action to solve the problem and subdue the public outcry, there was still no firm policy decision as to who was responsible for air defence. With continued success by the German Airship Services and notable lack of success by the defences the conclusion was at last reached that the RFC should take the responsibility for an aeroplane force for the defence of London and at a War Committee meeting on 10th February official blessing was given for the formation of specialist squadrons for Home Defence.

At the beginning of April 1916 control of the ten dispersed flights was given to Major T C Higgins, 19th Reserve Squadron which, on 15th April 1916, officially became No 39 (Home Defence) Squadron, the first of these specialist squadrons, tasked to provide an effective aeroplane defence for London against the seemingly untouchable giants of the enemy.

The initial establishment of the squadron was for two aircraft at each of the ten fields around London - Hounslow, Northolt, Hendon, Chingford, Hainault Farm, Sutton's Farm, Joyce Green, Farningham, Croydon and Wimbledon Common. Higgins soon realised that this organisation was too unweildy to be effective and he decided to concentrate his resources at three fields - Hounslow ('A' Flight), Sutton's Farm ('B' Flight) and Hainault Farm 'C' Flight). Each field had six B.E.2cs plus their support facilities and additionally Hounslow was the training centre, supply depot and Headquarters. Sutton's Farm and Hainault Farm had been established in mid-1915 during the initial search for landing grounds. Sutton's Farm, near Hornchurch, Essex, was a 90-acre piece of farmland owned by Mr Tom Crawford and was an irregular slab of stubble-land which, by the time 39 Squadron took it over, had some semblance of being an airfield. Nevertheless, it was still only a rough grass strip with many hazards for day flying never mind night flying! Two portable hangars had been erected and a number of sheds and tents had been provided for the support facilities of the Flight. Hainault Farm, near Ilford in Essex, was somewhat similar with its hangars and buildings. All three airfields also had a 13-pounder gun and searchlight for 'self-defence', although the searchlights found more use as take-off and landing aids for night flying rather than in engaging enemy raiders.

The B.E.2c had seen service on the Western Front and very quickly became known as 'Fokker Fodder' due to its poor performance. It had been designed as a simple, easy to fly aircraft, which is exactly what it proved to be and in fact it was far too stable for the type of air warfare that had developed in Europe. This built-in stability proved to be a great advantage to 39

Above: **Lt Sowrey in B.E.2c 4112, probably at Suttons Farm, one of the landing grounds used by the Squadron.**

Squadron in its mode of operations in that it provided an excellent gun platform for night warfare and was also easy to handle in the hazardous occupation of night flying! It also had a tremendous number of disadvantages with a top speed of only 72 mph from the 90 hp RAF engine and a stated ceiling of about 10,000 feet, which it took 45 minutes to reach; the B.E.2c was vastly inferior to the latest German Zeppelins which, even when intercepted, were able to release ballast and quickly climb away from danger having a much higher ceiling than the fighter. To counter these disadvantages it was essential for the fighter to have sufficient warning of a raider to get airborne and climb to a reasonable height giving some chance of an interception. The duty pilot system was devised as a partial solution to this problem, whereby the duty pilot slept next to the telephone while his aircraft was kept at readiness outside the hut; at regular intervals the groundcrew would start-up the engine to make sure that there would be no delay when the warning call came. Standing Orders for 39 Squadron demanded that the duty aircraft be airborne within five minutes of receiving the warning and should then take position in the system of patrol lines. Designated patrol lines and heights were allocated to 39 Squadron and the other four Home Defence squadrons which had been formed by mid-1916 (33 Squadron at Bramham Moor and Knavesmere, 36 Squadron at Cramlington, 50 Squadron at Dover and 51 Squadron at Norwich). Patrolling aircraft had to fly above 8,000 feet, the height

of the London balloon cordon, and maintain station by reference to any ground lights visible. Identification of a raider would usually depend on their being illuminated by the searchlights. Maintaining position on the dark nights usually favoured by raiders was not always easy, as a Norwegian pilot on 39 Squadron, found out. During 1916 the Norwegian Government became increasingly concerned over the danger posed to their cities by German Zeppelins and a Norwegian officer, Trygve Gran, was seconded for service with the RFC, joining 39 Squadron on 5th December 1916. The following account by Gran is of a typical call-out - but with a somewhat unusual ending:

'The rain was pouring down in torrents and it whistled in the stove pipe as if it was blowing a hurricane outside. We were discussing the Norwegians and the part they had played in the war when suddenly the alarm went. I felt the blood rush to my head as I ran outside — Great Scott what a night — rain and hail hit me in the face and dark clouds were passing just above the tree tops.

'Captain Stammers had gone to the telephone and after taking a message he came back. 'Zepps my boy — stand by first machine', he shouted. The ground flares were lit and two searchlights endeavoured in vain to penetrate the dark drifting clouds. Like drowned rats the mechanics ran round the machine getting it ready.

'You cannot fly tonight sir, its impossible', said my fitter. Very seldom in my life have I felt my courage pass away on this dark stormy night.

'Come down again if its too bad', Stammers said. I gritted my teeth together, waved the mechanic away and let my machine rip out into the darkness. I saw the last landing flares disappear under my wings, and I felt the rain and

11

hail beating my face. Then suddenly everything turned into a chaos of fog and darkness in which only my instruments could be seen. My plane was terribly chucked about and for a moment I completely lost control.

'Suddenly I discovered under the brim of my upper plane some flaming flares - I was flying upside down and with terrible speed. With a purely mechanical reaction I did a 'half-roll' and came onto an even keel, putting the nose of my machine into wind I determined to hold that course until clear of cloud.

'The following ¾ hour seemed to me to be like years and I sat looking only at my compass and instruments. Then it became lighter, the motor seemed to get an easier breath and before I knew what had happened it was quite clear with my plane passing over a huge white ocean of cloud. It was just like coming into the land of the fairies. For a moment I was sitting in bewilderment at this wonderful splendour of nature.

'Then I remembered my orders to patrol the line between North Weald and London Colney at 12,000 feet, for three hours. This was easier said than done! An hour I had been airborne without seeing anything and I had only a vague idea of my position. My aneroid was showing 13,000 feet and I presumed that at this height the wind would be blowing almost due west. Lower down the wind was south-westerly and I had been steering that course for ¾ hour. Giving the speed of my machine to be 60 miles per hour, and a head wind of 30 miles an hour then I should be some 20 miles SSW of the airfield. Consequently I turned my machine onto North-East and kept going for a little over ¼ hour hoping to see some sign of the airfield - but there was nothing to see except the same ocean of cloud.

'Of the Zeppelins there was no sign, nor of any other aeroplanes, and as the minutes passed I started feeling rather lonely. It was cold too, and I could see the ice crystals glistening in the moonlight on my stays and wings.

'Two hours I kept going backwards and forwards and the faint colour of day started spreading over the horizon. Then everything went quiet .... the blood rushed to my head and my heart beat violently; the engine had stopped and nothing would make it start again. Downwards towards the layer of clouds I went, whilst the pressure of the wind whistled in the stays and rigging. Everything turned to cloud and fog. I arranged my landing flares and turned the aeroplane into the presumed wind. The aneroid was showing 2,000 feet and still nothing but fog - I dropped a parachute flare which fell open and lit revealing nothing but fog. Carefully, in huge circles I followed the falling star. Then

suddenly the clouds disappeared and I saw the earth - a forest, a river, a few roads. I turned my aeroplane and noticed a field within easy reach, I lit the two magnesium flares under my wing tips and glided into the grassy field.

'What a wonderful sensation to feel the earth under my wheels. I ran towards the road and met some locals in a car. 'Where's the nearest town?' I shouted.

'Hull' answered one of the locals!

Gran returned from his little 'excursion' later the same day when the weather had improved. An extreme example perhaps but it serves to illustrate another of the problems facing Higgins and his squadron - the problem of night-flying and of navigation which relied on visual contact with the ground.

Although 39 had been established as a day and night fighter unit most of its 'customers' (ie Zeppelins) preferred the nocturnal hours for their visits. Squadron pilots undertook a reasonable amount of night flying practice but nonetheless there were a few night flying accidents, including some fatalities. The airfield flares in common use at this time consisted of a bucket containing half a gallon of petrol, and were inefficient and wasteful, burning irregularly and lasting only thirty minutes. Higgins introduced a much more efficient flare - the 'Money' flare. This consisted of an asbestos wick in a wire container, fuelled with paraffin which caused it to burn steadily and for a reasonable length of time. They were normally arranged in an 'L' shape of six flares and pilots relied heavily on these to keep straight during take-off as well as to assist in finding their landing ground again at the end of the patrol.

By the summer of 1916, 39 Squadron was equipped with a mix of B.E.2cs, B.E.2ds, B.E.2es and B.E.12s. The B.E.2d and 2e were derivatives of the 2c but with slightly improved performance whereas the B.E.12 was a single-seater which, although more powerful than the B.E.2, was harder to fly and was consequently disliked by many Squadron pilots. Although the establishment was for pilots and observers on the B.E.2s, the majority of night sorties were flown without the observer and many machines were modified to have the observer's cockpit closed off and the Lewis gun mounted so that it could be operated by the pilot. A variety of armaments were available for use, ranging from machine guns (usually the .303 in Lewis but sometimes the Vickers), to a selection of rockets and incendiary devices. A weapon in use in France against balloons was the 'Le Prieur' rocket which was fitted into tubes attached to the outer pair of wing struts. These rockets were unreliable, with a tendency to explode in the tubes, and although used once or twice by 39, without success, were soon discarded. Similarly ineffective were 'Rankin' incendiary darts, designed to be dropped on the Zeppelins from above and they too were discarded. Individual modification of weaponry was the fashion on the Squadron and most pilots concentrated on the machine gun with a variety of mounting positions. Some went in for numbers and Captain Gran had three guns on his B.E.12 which was known on the flight as 'the fortified terror'.

The trend towards unofficial modification was led by 'B' Flight at Sutton's Farm, commanded by 2nd Lieutenant William Leefe Robinson. They were the first to discard the ineffective weapons in favour of just the machine gun, the reason being a desire to make their machines lighter to give them a better rate of climb, a bit more speed and a higher ceiling. Developments in the ammunition available for machine-guns had also influenced their decision.

Sutton's Farm 1917: standing (left to right) — Capt Stammers, Lt W.J.Tempest DSO, Lt W. Leefe Robinson VC, Lt Fred Sowrey DSO plus Capt Bowers. Seated (left to right) — Lt C.L.Brock, Lt C Duston and Lt Mallinson.

A new incendiary drum known as 'Brock and Pomeroy' had been introduced with the Pomeroy incendiary bullet being combined with a .303 explosive bullet designed by Squadron Commander F A Brock to blow large holes in Zeppelin fabric. The problem previously had been that no ignition had occurred even when the Zeppelin gas cells had been pierced, and it was hoped that the new rounds would be the answer - and so it was to prove. A German Airship commander later said, 'this pattern of incendiary ammunition was an invention of the devil.' A further problem during night engagements was that the gunsights available in early 1916 did not permit accurate fire, even against a 600 foot long Zeppelin! This was compounded by a natural desire of pilots to fire at too great a range, it being very difficult to judge range accurately when faced with such a large target. A precision gunsight was needed. Sergeant A E Hutton, an armourer of 39 Squadron, adapted the original bead foresight and vee backsight for night use by devising a systems of illumination. He bored out the base of the foresight for a small red electric bulb that sent its glow through a small hole bored in the bead; the backsight was illuminated with three pinpoint holes, one in each arm of the vee and one in the base.

Power for the lights was provided by a two-volt flashlight battery. This system worked well in the B.E.2s which had their exhaust guards extended back beyond the cockpit to eliminate glare which would otherwise have masked the dim light of the sight. Similar lighting was provided for the cockpit instruments, which also had their dials painted with luminous paint. The stage was set for the contest.

39 Squadron had had its first brush with Zeppelins as early as 25th April when *LZ 97* flew near Hainault Farm and was attacked by two B.E.2s, one of which was flown by 2nd Lieutenant William Leefe Robinson. He had reached 8,000 feet when he saw the Zeppelin some 2,000 feet above, he opened fire but his tracers fell short and the airship quickly climbed away leaving behind a very frustrated Robinson. The other pilot, Captain Harris, also got within 2,000 feet but his gun jammed.

For the remaining months of Summer 1916 the public continued to demand action against the German raiders who were still seemingly raiding with impunity. Meanwhile, the pilots of the Home Defence squadrons were continuing to gain experience in the hazardous occupation of night warfare and anti-Zeppelin operations. Certain Flight Commanders, including Leefe Robinson at Sutton's Farm, instituted studies of Zeppelins and their performance, and examined accounts of previous engagements to try to discover some means of defeating these giants. This led to the unofficial modifications of aircraft and armament mentioned previously. In July the Squadron had moved to new landing grounds with HQ at Woodford Green, 'A' Flight at North Weald Bassett and 'B' Flight remaining at Sutton's.

Saturday 2nd September 1916 was a dull, rainy day and no flying was scheduled at Sutton's Farm, the comment being made that 'it doesn't look like Zepp weather today', The opposite proved to be the case and a large raid of sixteen Army and Navy airships began crossing the East Coast of England at about 10 pm.

At 11.05 pm the telephone rang in the duty office at Sutton's Farm.

'Take air raid action!' shouted the ops officer. Robinson was duty pilot and he climbed into his B.E.2c, 2092, and checked his cockpit lighting. He then checked his single Lewis gun which had all ammunition drums full of the new Brock and Pomeroy bullets, plus tracer for sighting. Satisfied, he settled into his seat and gazed at the cloud-covered night sky.

'Petrol switches on'

'Suck in'

Thumbs up . . . . .'Contact'

The engine burst into life and the airfield flares were lit as Robinson yelled 'Chocks away!'

2092 bumped off down the field and, getting airborne soon climbed above the shallow ground fog into the clear September sky. Leefe Robinson's orders were to position himself on the patrol line between Sutton's Farm and Joyce Green. From this point on the words of his official report, still preserved in the Imperial War Museum, take up the story. . . .

'I went up at 1108 pm with instructions to patrol between Sutton's Farm and Joyce Green. I climbed to 10,000 feet in 53 minutes. I counted what I thought were sets of flares - there were a few clouds below me but on the whole it was a beautifully clear night.

'I saw nothing until 1.10 am when two searchlights picked out a Zeppelin about southwest of Woolwich. The clouds had collected in this quarter and the searchlights had some difficulty in keeping up with the aircraft. By this time I had managed to climb to 12,900 feet and I made in the direction of the Zeppelin, which was being fired on by a few anti-aircraft guns, hoping to cut it off on its way eastwards. I very slowly gained on it for about ten minutes - I judged it to be about 200 feet below me and I sacrificed my speed in order to keep my height. It went behind some clouds, avoided the searchlights and I lost sight of it. After about fifteen minutes of fruitless search I returned to my patrol. I managed to pick up and distinguish my flares again. At about 1.50 am I noticed a red glow in the North east of London. Taking it to be an outbreak of fire I went in that direction. At about 2.05 am a Zeppelin was picked up over NNE London (as far as I could judge).

'Remembering my last failure, I sacrificed height (I was still at 12,100 feet) for speed and made nose-down for the Zeppelin. I saw shells bursting and night-tracer shells flying around it. When I drew closer I noticed that the anti-aircraft fire was too high or too low, also a good many rose 800 feet behind. I could hear the bursts when about 3,000 feet from the Zeppelin.

'I flew to about 800 feet below it and fired one drum along it from bow to stern. It seemed to have no effect. I therefore moved to one side and gave it another drum along its side - without much apparent effect. I then got behind it (by this time I was very close - 500 feet or less below) and concentrated one whole drum on one part underneath. I was at a height of 11,500 feet when attacking the Zeppelin. I had hardly finished the drum when I saw the part fired at glow. In a few seconds the whole of the rear part was blazing. When the third drum was fired there were no searchlights on the Zeppelin and no AA was firing. I quickly got out of the way of the falling Zeppelin and, being very excited, fired off a few red verey lights and dropped a parachute flare.

'Having little oil or petrol left, I returned to Sutton's Farm landing at 2.45 am. On landing I found that I had shot away my machine-gun wire guard, the rear part of the centre section, and had pierced the main spar several times.'

The flaming wreck of the *SL 11* (Schutte-Lanz 11) landed at Cuffley. Leefe Robinson was exhausted, stiff and frozen when he landed - to receive a telephone message from headquarters congratulating him on his success and requesting his report! He collapsed on his camp bed and fell into a deep sleep only to be roused early on the Sunday morning by jubilant fellow officers wanting to drag him off to Cuffley to see 'his' Zeppelin. By the time they reached the site of the burnt-out wreck it was already crowded with sightseers as Leefe Robinson's combat and the flaming destruction of the *SL 11* had been witnessed by millions in and around London. The site was guarded by RFC and Army personnel in an effort to preserve as much of the wreck as possible for intelligence purposes. It took the party from Sutton's Farm some time to persuade the guards that they had some claim to a quick look. Within forty-eight hours over 10,000 spectators had been to the site and numerous pieces of the Zeppelin had been removed as souvenirs. Hauptmann Wilhelm Schramm and his fifteen crew members all perished in the crash and were later given a full military funeral - much to the annoyance of many Londoners who considered them no better than murderers. What Leefe Robinson thought is not recorded anywhere.

Any image of the lone fighter searching the night skies for the intruder would be mistaken as Robinson was only one of many airmen airborne that night, including others from 39 Squadron, 2nd Lieutenant C D Rose from North Weald Bassett patroling the line North Weald to Hainault and 2nd Lieutenant A de B Brandon from Hainault Farm patrolling the line Hainault to Sutton's Farm. These first patrols were sent up at about 11 pm while the second patrol, which got airborne about 1 am, consisted of: 2nd Lieutenant F Sowrey from Sutton's Farm to patrol Joyce Green to Farmingham; 2nd Lieutenant J I Mackay from North Weald Bassett for the North Weald to Joyce Green line; and 2nd Lieutenant B H Hunt from Hainault Farm to patrol the line Joyce Green to Farmingham. Ross stayed airborne for two hours and then crashed his machine on landing, a frequent occurrence in these early days of night flying. Sowrey came back with engine trouble after a quarter of an hour and Brandon after half an hour. However, Mackay reached his patrol height of 10,000 feet and, when near the Joyce Green end of his patrol line, he observed the *SL 11* held by a searchlight to the north of London. Giving

2nd Lt William Leefe Robinson VC. He became a national hero after shooting down *SL 11* over London in September 1916. A relieved British public shouted his praise and he was awarded the VC. (*Crown Copyright / RAF photograph*)

chase, he was within a mile of her when suddenly she burst into flames and tumbled earthwards - victim of Leefe-Robinson. Returning to Joyce Green he spotted another airship over towards Hainault and gave chase only to lose sight of her after about fifteen minutes. A similar situation confronted Hunt, he was just about to attack the *SL 11* when it burst into flames, in the sudden brilliant light Hunt spotted the *L 16* only a short distance away. He at once gave pursuit but dazzled by the glare he lost sight of the airship and so he resumed his patrol line - only to have a third frustrating chase about half an hour later. 39 Squadron were not the only people active and No 50 Squadron at Dover sent up three machines with other aircraft airborne from No 33 Squadron at Beverley and from various Naval air stations.

The initial newspaper reports made no mention of Leefe Robinson but everyone was united in the jubilation over this victory against the previously immune giant raiders. It was not until the 5th September that the papers announced the name of the pilot and then there was a public outcry that this 'hero' should be rewarded. This was soon followed by the official announcement of the award of the Victoria Cross to 2nd Lieutenant Leefe Robinson for his action. His photograph appeared everywhere and he became the darling of the nation, with particular affection being shown by the people of London. Money rewards of some £3,500 had been contributed by businessmen for the first airman to shoot down a Zeppelin over Britain and this now went to Leefe Robinson. There was some dispute as to if he, as a 'gentleman', should accept such a reward and the War Office soon solved the problem by passing a regulation to prevent any such public acknowledgement in the future.

William Leefe Robinson was the archtypal Royal Flying Corps officer - handsome, flamboyant and dashing. He was born on 14th July 1895 in Southern India, his father being in the Indian Service. He joined the army and ten days after the outbreak of war in 1914 was gazetted to the Worcester Regiment. However, he soon transferred to the RFC as an observer and over Lille was wounded in the arm. On convalescence he gained his pilot's wings and was sent to join the Home Defence units, eventually finding his way to 39 Squadron in April 1916. He was a popular figure both on the squadron and in the area around Sutton's Farm, although some of his airborne antics occasionally caused loss of temper amongst the local villagers. Farmer Tom Crawford, the owner of the field which became Sutton's Farm airfield, often had cause to complain about 'B' Flight scaring his cows and rattling the windows of his farm buildings.

Following this first kill, morale and confidence on the Squadron grew and Leefe Robinson began to influence the tactics of other pilots. He decided to save even more weight on their machines by only half loading the ammunition drums, with forty-seven rounds, arranged armour-piercing, Brock and tracer and each aircraft was to carry only three such drums. Intensive night flying practice was carried out as was live gun firing in the gravel pits near the airfield.

On the night of 16th September Leefe Robinson was on duty again when a raid warning was given. In the now famous B.E.2c 2092 he trundled off down the grass strip only to crash in flames, narrowly escaping injury as the aircraft became a burnt wreck. Towards the end of 1916 he was posted, as a newly promoted Captain, as Flight Commander to 48 Squadron.

On 8th April 1917 he took a flight of Bristol Fighters across the Front lines and met Richthofen's Circus. Four of the Bristols were shot down, including Leefe Robinson who was sent to Holzminden Prisoner of War Camp. He was released after the Armistice in a very poor state of health, caught influenza and died a few months later. The effect of his victory on the population of London was immense and the general public no longer feared the Zeppelins as they had done previously. As each day went by the defence forces became more experienced and the morale of the home defence Squadrons rocketed. The Naval Intelligence Division at Whitehall had by now perfected the interception of the radio messages passed by the Zeppelin crews as they were forming up for raids, and so were able to give the ground and air defences some forewarning. The warning system was to prove its worth against a raid on the night of 23rd September 1916. This raid by four of the new Super Zeppelins and eight older models included Kapitan-Lieutenant Alois Bocker in LZ 33 and Oberleutnant Werner Petersen in LZ 32, two experienced Zeppelin commanders. After crossing the East Coast Bocker steered a direct course for London and was soon engaged by the searchlights and guns surrounding the city which, for once, were proving to be very accurate. LZ 33 was bracketed by bursting shells and, near Bromley, one burst inside the airship's hull destroying one gas cell and riddling others with shrapnel. The hydrogen in the cells did not ignite but was rapidly escaping from the ruptured cells into the atmosphere. Bocker turned his ship towards the sea while his crew tried to repair the damage and reduce the rate of height loss which by now had reached some 800 feet a minute. By this time the aircraft defences were also alert and active, and a number of B.E.2s were airborne, including 2nd Lt Alfred de Bathe Brandon, an experienced anti-Zeppelin aviator who had joined 39 Squadron when it formed in April 1916. Brandon now sighted the crippled LZ 33 over Chelmsford and attacked her for some twenty minutes, firing 'Brock and Pomeroy', with no apparent result, but he was forced to abandon his pursuit after losing the airship in cloud. Meanwhile Bocker and his crew were desperately trying to maintain height by throwing overboard as much weight as they could. This availed them little and the stricken ship continued to sink earthwards, coming to rest in the marshland off Mersea Island. The crew jumped from the airship, and Bocker destroyed it with a few well placed signal flares. Shortly afterwards he and his crew were taken prisoner by the local policeman who arrived by bicycle, attracted by the blazing wreck of the Zeppelin.

There has always been some doubt as to what part Brandon's attack played in the destruction of *LZ 33*, and whether the ship would have been doomed without his intervention. It is inevitable that his attack must have further damaged the gas cells although members of the crew were later to state that they knew nothing of his attack. Rightly, he was officially credited with a hand in the destruction of the *LZ 33*.

Later the same night Brandon spotted another Zeppelin caught in the searchlights and headed towards it. This was Petersen's *LZ 32* and it had already been spotted by Lieutenant Fred Sowrey in B.E.2c No 4112.

Sowrey, another experienced campaigner on 39 Squadron, had like Brandon, been ordered up on the instruction to take air raid action. He had been patrolling for some two hours when at 00.45 he noticed an airship caught in the beams of the searchlights. In the words of his report:

'I at once made in this direction and manoeuvred into a position underneath (the Zeppelin). The airship was well lighted by searchlights but there was no sign of any gunfire. I could distinctly see the propellors revolving and the airship was manoeuvering to avoid the searchlight beams. I fired at it. The first two drums of

ammunition had apparently no effect, but the third one caused the envelope to catch fire in several places, in the centre and on the front. All fire was traversing fire along the envelope. The drums were loaded with a mixture of Brock, Pomeroy and tracer ammunition. I watched the burning airship strike the ground and then proceeded to find my (landing) flares. I landed at Sutton's Farm at 1.40 am on the 24th. My machine was B.E.2c 4112. After seeing the Zeppelin had caught fire, I fired a red verey light'.

Like all pilots who flew at 10,000 feet plus in an open cockpit, Sowrey was suffering from the effects of cold and lack of oxygen. Leefe Robinson was one of the first to congratulate him and concocted a warm drink to revive the exhausted pilot. As soon as Sowrey had scribbled his report he was bundled into Leefe Robinson's new Prince Henry Vauxhall car (part of the 'proceeds' from the *SL 11* reward) and was driven off to the scene of his success. *LZ 32's* destruction was witnessed by the population of London and as in the case of the *SL 11* the site was soon swarming with sightseers. The wreckage fell at Snail's Hill Farm, South Green, near Billericay, where it burned for some forty-five minutes. A *Times* correspondent reported:

'(The ship) lay with her nose crumpled and bent out of shape, but the framework of her girders was strong enough to hold together. As she lay it did not seem possible that the fabric was burnt off its gaunt ribs until one noticed pieces of molten aluminium and brass in the debris.

'One realised the cost of such a craft even looking at the wreck. Lying on the ground was a red leather cushion. This covered the seat of the engineman and the ghastly evidence still to be seen showed that he died at his post. One at least of the petrol tanks had burst in half, and

Lt Fred Sowrey, second from right, in front of his B.E.2c 4112 probably at Sutton's Farm. This B.E.2c went to Canada in 1919. (*P.H.T. Green collection*)

the heat of the burning spirit had melted the edges until they looked like some fine fretted lace. There were the remains of an air mattress and a blanket. Curious evidence of the crews' breakfast still remained. There were slices of bacon and hunks of brown, greasy 'Kriegsbrod' with delicately sliced potatoes.'

A grim picture of the reality of the total destruction of a Zeppelin. Naval Intelligence Officers also discovered a copy of the latest code book used by the German airship crews and were thus able to maintain their invaluable radio interception service.

For their actions on the night of 23rd September Brandon and Sowrey were both awarded the Distinguished Service Order (DSO). Brandon's name was never as well known with the general public, as his victory was not in the spectacular fashion of Robinson - or Sowrey. The score to 39 Squadron was now three Zeppelins in three weeks. Morale on the Squadron rose to an even greater height and the exploits of the Zeppelin destroyers became popular throughout Britain. The admiration for 39 Squadron by the 'man in the street' was immense and even the inhabitants of the villages around the airfields found a new level of tolerance to the antics of the pilots.

Morale amongst the German Airship Services was, however, not so high any more and the loss of these two naval airships in a single night was to have far reaching consequences. These victories had established the power of the aircraft in air defence - contrary to the opinion expressed by Mathy in 1915 in the heyday of Zeppelin supremacy. Even if in the future Zeppelins made successful raids on England, the great psychological war had been lost, as these raids would no longer effect the morale of the English Civilian population as deeply as they had in the dark days of 1915 and early 1916.

There was to be only one more large-scale determined raid on London. On the night of 1st October 1916 a force of Zeppelins crossed the east coast on course for London. LZ 31 on its way to the capital dropped three bombs of heavy calibre in a direct line for Sutton's Farm with one bomb falling near the airfield and another on it, making a crater some twenty-five feet in diameter and wounding a sentry. Intentional retribution or accident, it was not to pass unchallenged.

At midnight, Robert Kochin, Captain of LZ 24, reported seeing an airship blazing and tumbling to earth somewhere in the region north-east of the docks. He was witnessing the destruction of LZ 31, sister ship of LZ 32, at the hands of another pilot of 39 Squadron - 2nd Lieutenant Wulfstan Joseph Tempest. The commander of LZ 31 was one of the most famous of all airship commanders, Kapitan-Leutnant Heinrich Mathy. Tempest had been ordered up sometime earlier and, having one of the stripped down B.E.2s easily climbed through his designated patrol height of 8,000 feet until at 1145 pm he was at 14,500 feet over southwest London. Shortly afterwards he spotted LZ 31 caught by the searchlights and he turned towards her but when he was still some five miles from the airship his mechanical pressure fuel pump broke down which meant that he had to hand pump almost constantly to keep up the pressure in his petrol tank.

'As I drew up to the Zeppelin, to my relief I found that I was quite free of AA fire for the nearest shells were bursting quite three miles away. The Zeppelin was now nearly 12,700 feet high and climbing rapidly. I therefore started to dive at her, for, though I held a slight advantage in speed she was climbing like a rocket and leaving me standing. I accordingly gave a tremendous pump at my petrol tank and dived straight at her, firing a burst into her as I came. I let her have another burst as I passed under her and then, banking my machine over, sat under her tail, and flying along underneath her, pumped lead into her for all I was worth. I could see tracer bullets flying from her in all directions, but I was too close under her for them to concentrate on me. As I was firing I noticed her begin to go red inside like and enormous Chinese lantern and then a flame shot out of the front part of her and I realised she was on fire. She then shot up about 200 feet, paused, and came roaring straight down on me before I had time to get out of the way. I nosed-dived for all I was worth, with the Zepp tearing after me, and expected every minute to be engulfed in flames. I put my machine into a spin and just managed to corkscrew out of the way as she shot past me, roaring like a furnace. I righted my machine and watched her hit the ground with a shower of sparks. I then proceeded to fire off dozens of green verey lights in the exuberance of my feelings.

'I glanced at my watch and I saw it was about ten minutes past twelve, I then commenced to feel very sick, giddy and exhausted, and had considerable difficulty in finding my way to the ground through fog, and in landing I crashed and cut my head on my machine gun'.

LZ 31 crashed in a field just outside Potters' Bar killing all of her crew. 2nd Lieutenant Tempest joined the Squadron role of honour as a Zeppelin destroyer and for his exploit was awarded the DSO.

Thus in one month 39 Squadron had been responsible for the destruction of four of the 'invincible' monsters. Never again did the Zeppelins come to raid London, although isolated raids were made against other targets. During the

A satirical yet historical commemoration of the air war 1914-18. The caption in the top left-hand corner says 'presented to XXXIX Squadron, RAF, per diem per noctem'. The map shows North Weald, Suttons Farm, Hainault Farm plus flaming Zeppelin and B.E.2c. Origin unknown.

ensuing months other units were to score victories against the Zeppelins but although 39 were involved in a number of engagements no further success was forthcoming.

From the middle of February 1917 a new threat entered the skies over London...German long range bombing aircraft. The Gotha and Giant aircraft were in the long term to cause much greater destruction than the Zeppelin but never held the same terror for the civilian population. The initiative was now starting to slip away from the defence forces again as the Germans were making constant improvements in their airships and long range aircraft wheras the Home Defence Squadrons were still primarily equipped with the antiquated B.E.2s; this led to a number of frustrating engagements. [In his biography *Under British Flag*, Captain T Gran mentions that 39 Squadron was allocated six

S.E.5 aircraft at Sutton's Farm in the summer of 1917. By 8th July only three had arrived and they were sent to join 'C' Flight at Hainault Farm. However, this was to be a short-lived innovation as on 24th July the aircraft, and Captain Gran, were transferred to No 4 (MD) Squadron. This information is not recorded elsewhere and cannot be verified.] In October 1917 Captain Charles Chabot, a Flight Commander on 39, had an indecisive engagement with two Zeppelins and his report reflected his anger with the apparent lack of support from the higher authorities with respect to equipment. This report provoked a reply from the HQ of General Ashmore, Commander of London defence (aircraft, guns, searchlights and balloons). Chabot was asked to elaborate his comments and proceeded to make his views felt in no uncertain terms. The arguments proved convincing and General Ashmore duly authorised the Squadron to undertake trials with the Bristol Fighter. This two-seater biplane, with a top speed of 113 mph at 10,000 feet, a ceiling of 20,000 feet and a rate of climb of 838 ft/min (10-11 minutes to 10,000 feet), was vastly superior to the B.E.2s and 12s. It also carried a harder punch with a fixed front-firing Vickers gun and either single or twin Lewis guns mounted in the Observer's cockpit behind the pilot.

Despite an early flying accident with the new type (the first Bristol Fighter which 39 received was written-off only a few weeks after it had arrived), the balance was beginning to level again. The defenders were able once again to reach the attackers, although for many months the Squadron had a mixture of B.E.s and Bristol Fighters until all the B.E.s had been replaced by mid-1918. Although no spectacular successes were immediately forthcoming, the increased capability of the defenders drove the long range bombers to abandon daylight raids for a while. With the Zeppelins only attacking on certain favourable nights the by now fairly well organised Home Defence Squadrons saw little activity.

In September 1917 39 (HD) Squadron had concentrated at North Weald Bassett with three flights ('A', 'B' and 'C') and a total complement of between fifteen and eighteen aircraft - still a mix of B.E.s and Bristol Fighters. Now under the command of Major G Allen, crews carried out intensive flying training with particular emphasis being placed on the still hazardous job of night flying. Although Squadron personnel were kept reasonably busy not all their time was taken up with work, and being so close to London meant that entertainment was not difficult to find. Officers frequently visited the well-known London restaurants and nights spots or spent many an hour in the theatres of the West End. Among the avid theatre-goers was Lieutenant 'Tommy' Thompson who was courting the star of one of the shows and, when the show moved to the theatre at Hastings, he decided to go and see her there. On 8th December 1917 Tommy Thompson persuaded his observer, Lieutenant Stoneham, to accompany him on a 'flight test' of their Bristol Fighter. After getting airborne the observer asked his pilot where they were going...'To Hastings to see Ivy!' came the reply.

On arrival at Hastings Tommy decided to give the crowds along the sea front a free show and proceeded to execute a series of loops, rolls and Immelmann turns, at the end of which he turned to his observer... 'Right Gerry, find me a landing ground.'

Realising that they were short of petrol they put the aircraft down in the grounds of a nearby stately home. Arrangements were made for petrol to be brought to the aircraft the next morning from the nearest airfield and having secured the aircraft, and introduced themselves to the owner of their improvised landing ground, the two aviators departed to the Grand Hotel. The following morning mechanics from the nearby Naval air station arrived with fuel for the aircraft which was soon made ready for the return flight to North Weald. Despite the fact that it had been raining heavily all night the Bristol started on the first swing of the propeller. Leaving the sun of Hastings the crew soon discovered that the area around North Weald was obscured by thick low level cloud which caused them a few problems in finding the airfield. However, they eventually landed to face the 'welcoming' committee led by the Squadron Commander - the outcome of the debrief is not revealed by the author of the account!

It was not always possible to get away from the airfield to seek entertainment and so entertainment was brought to the airfield - sometimes with unexpected consequences. One night in March 1918 the officers decided to arrange a concert for the airmen with the performance to include a number of talented ladies from London - plus their chaperones. After giving an excellent concert the ladies were invited to dine in the officers mess and just as the port was on its second time around the Air Raid alarm sounded. The ordered scene changed rapidly to one of frenzied activity as orders came through for the first patrols to get airborne, and there were hasty attempts to get organised. It also meant that the ladies would be stuck at North Weald until the All Clear went as it was considered not safe for them to travel back to London. Amidst the normal activity of operational flying the Duty Officer was kept busy with frequent telephone calls from anxious mothers ringing up to discover the fate of their daughters. Regular entertainment and relaxation was provided by the numerous local public houses and, for the airmen, the Salvation Army Canteen on the airfield.

A detachment was forced to leave the by now comfortable surroundings of North Weald in order to set up 'D' Flight of 39 Squadron at the new airfield of Biggin Hill. On 1st December 1917 a party of groundcrew erected the tents that were to be the temporary accommodation of 'D' Flight. Shortly afterwards six B.E.2s and B.E.12s under the command of Captain Fanstone arrived to take up residence. This Flight of the Squadron proved to be very short-lived as by the end of the year the Flight had been transferred from 39 Squadron to 78 Squadron and in January 1918 it became the nucleus of 141 Squadron. It was business as usual for the other three flights. The standard operating procedure in early 1918 was for no daylight standing patrols as aircraft would be sent up as required. However, at night there were standing patrols along laid down patrol lines. When called out each flight sent up one aircraft to fly along the designated patrol line; of the three aircraft one would fly at the specified height eg 10,000 feet, one about 500 feet above and one 500 feet below. The logic went that if you met another aircraft at your height it must be an enemy!

This somewhat dubious system was supplemented by a code of air to air signals, but even so mistakes were still quite frequent, as on the occasion when two Squadron aircraft met over North Weald and in the words of the report 'had a spirited encounter' - fortunately without causing damage to either aircraft.

1918 continued reasonably quiet and although raids were made on London and the Eastern Counties, 39 Squadron met with no notable success until May. The final 'kill' by 39 Squadron was made on the night of 19th May 1918 when forty-one German bombers (thirty-eight Gothas, two recce-aircraft and one Giant) took part in the last great aeroplane raid on London. This final fling proved to be a disaster for the raiders. One of these was brought down over East Ham by a Bristol Fighter of 39 Squadron, flown by Lieutenant A J Arkell with Air Mechanic T C Stagg as gunner. Arkell closed with the formation of bombers at 10,000 feet over London and vigorously attacked one of the Gothas. The aircraft broke formation and

The Bristol Fighter replaced the B.E.2s in 1917 and enabled the Squadron to meet the German long-range bombers and improved Zeppelins on even terms. This is possibly not a 39 Squadron aircraft but shows well the mechanical starter.

tried to escape by diving down towards the city, hotly followed by Arkell. The pursuit continued until the aircraft were only 1.500 feet above London when at last the Gotha was hit again and again and, with her pilot either dead or wounded, crashed into the ground.

The battle for the skies over England was won and by the summer of 1918 it became clear that the Germans had been forced to abandon their bombing offensive. With the evacuation of the Belgian coast and the loss of airfields it was improbable that any further raids would be made; consequently, a number of the Home Defence squadrons were given warning orders to prepare to move to France. 39 was one of these.

In the Order of Battle for the Royal Air Force dated 11th November 1918, 39 Squadron is listed as being attached to the 65th Wing at Bavichove, France. On 8th November most of the ground personnel and equipment had embarked for France but the aircraft and aircrew never left North Weald. Like so many other squadrons in the now huge Royal Air Force, 39 was to feel the weight of the post-war reduction in strength and on 16th November was officially disbanded at North Weald. The first glorious chapter in the life of the Squadron was brought to a close.

2
Kings Lynn
to the Khyber Pass

The mad postwar rush to reduce the military establishment had slowed down by the summer of 1919, and, when the situation had stabilised, a review was undertaken to decide on the peacetime requirements of the Royal Air Force.

On 1st July 1919 a ceremony was held at Biggin Hill renumbering No 37 Squadron as No 39 Squadron. Command of the Squadron was given to Squadron Leader P Babbington with an initial establishment of seven D.H.9a day bombers to be based at Biggin Hill. There are few details of Squadron activities during this period but it seems that a continuation of role similar to that of 1916-18, but with more emphasis on day flying, was the plan. The following extract from *39 Squadron Standing Orders dated 1 July 1919* throws some light on the question:

39 SQUADRON STANDING ORDERS - 1 JULY 1919

1. During the day the Squadron Commander will always lead his squadron into the air but at night he should not fly but carry out organisation on the ground.
2. 1st Class Ops pilot/observer authorised for day and night Ops.
   2nd Class Ops pilot/observer authorised for day ops only.
3. Each 'Flying Officer' (ie aircrew) to be responsible for:
   a. Supervising all repairs, alterations and adjustments carried out to his machine.
   b. Reporting the fact to his Flight Commander, whenever his machine becomes unserviceable, and making every effort to ensure that his machine is kept serviceable.
   c. Seeing that his machine is fitted with the signal codes in use at the time.
   d. Seeing that his machine, when serviceable, has tanks full of petrol and oil, and radiator full of water. If in frosty weather there is a danger of the radiator water freezing owing to the sheds being unheated, officers will be responsible for seeing that arrangements are made for re-filling them. If possible with hot water, with the minimum delay.
   e. Ensuring that the guns and W/T apparatus on his machine are serviceable.
   f. Familiarising himself with the position of all aerodromes, landing grounds, light-houses etc within 50 miles of his own aerodrome.
   g. Keeping his machine fitted up for night flying in accordance with the prescribed pattern.
   h. Being acquainted with all Op orders and Instructions which may be from time to time issued. Knowing the areas over which the Squadron patrol lines pass.
4. In addition to the above, and in times of 'Special Vigilance' he is responsible for:
   a. Running up engines daily, at dawn.
   b. Ensuring all flying kit available for immediate use.
   c. Ensuring that full belts or drums are fitted to machine guns.

The revival in the fortunes of the Squadron was to be short-lived as on 20th December the decision was made to reduce 39 to the status of a cadre unit and move it to Uxbridge. In the postwar political and economic situation there was little money forthcoming for the RAF and the whole future of the Service began to look very uncertain. However, by reducing units to cadre strength a number of potential squadrons were kept in being requiring only the bare minimum of equipment. Information about the squadron is very limited for this period except to say that two moves were made: the first in March 1920 from Uxbridge to Kenley, and a year later to Spitalgate near Grantham in Lincolnshire.

On 1st April 1921 things began to improve with the decision to bring 39 Squadron up to full strength under the command of Squadron Leader T S Impey. By 15th May the Squadron was up to full establishment of personnel but only equipped with Avro 504 trainers which were used for pilot training and generally preparing the Squadron to receive its new operational aircraft. In February 1922 Squadron Leader A A B Thompson took command of the

Squadron, and during the early months of the year the unit gradually acquired its full complement of nine D.H.9a aircraft. The D.H.9a was a two-seat biplane day bomber, developed from the earlier D.H.9 which had seen operational service in the closing months of World War I. Powered by a single 400 hp Liberty engine, the D.H.9a (or 'Ninak') was capable of a maximum speed of 128 mph at sea level and had a service ceiling of 19,000 feet with an endurance of 5¾ hours. It had the standard RAF bomber crew of two - pilot and observer, with an armament of single .303 in Vickers gun on the port side of the cowling - synchronised by Constantinesco gear - plus either single or twin .303 in Lewis gun on a Scarff ring in the rear cockpit. The bomb load was a modest two 230 lb bombs under the wings.

Although very rugged, the 9a was heavy on the controls - one test pilot of the period commented that he never flew the 9a if he could avoid it on the grounds that he was not strong enough! This lack of responsiveness on the controls created problems when the aircraft was flown in close formation - a role in which 39 Squadron was to specialize in the seven years that they were

Although the D.H.9a instrumentation was regarded as somewhat basic, there does not appear to be room for much else! (*Sir Walter Dawson*)

equipped with this type. Landing caused problems for many a pilot due to the unusual undercarriage arrangement, which consisted of two 'vee' struts and a straight axle fixed to the strut with 5/8" elastic. This elastic was fitted by a team of seven men, three sat on the ground in line at each side of the axle and the seventh man stood by the axle end ready with a set of long handled tongs. One team of three hauled on the 5/8" elastic, in the manner of a tug of war team. It was then clamped by the tongs man and passed to the three-man team on the other side who repeated the process. This was quite a job as there were thirty-three turns of elastic at each end. The net result was a very good undercarriage for a smooth landing, but if the aircraft hit the ground roughly - or came to a ridge - then it would, in the words of one 39 Squadron pilot, 'behave like its close relative - the golf ball!' This produced some interesting but not always desirable results.

The Liberty engine was a 12-cylinder water cooled 'vee' engine and was generally reliable although the operations log of the Squadron contains a fair number of incidents of engine failure resulting in aircraft returning to base or diverting elsewhere. It was the water cooling system that caused most difficulties and pilots soon learnt the tell-tale signs that indicated land as quickly as possible. From a servicing point of

view the engine was easy to work on and spares could even be obtained from cars as the generator and battery ignition system had been adapted from that of the Model 'T' Ford. Engine controls consisted of three levers: throttle; extra air control (to give weaker mixture at altitude) and an advance and retard control.

For the remainder of 1922, the Squadron settled down into a peacetime training routine of formation bombing sorties, pilot training, navigation and gunnery. The emphasis changed in 1923 as 39 Squadron was selected to give the RAF formation flying display at the Hendon Pageant in June, and also to represent the RAF in bombing trials against the Navy in August.

Particular attention was paid to close formation flying - by flights and squadron - and, as mentioned above, this was not the easiest of activities in the 'Ninak'. Apart from being heavy on the controls, the difference between comfortable cruising speed and maximum speed was rather small. Moreover, the aircraft was sluggish at building up speed and if an aircraft got a few yards out of position in a formation turn, for example, the formation would have to cover quite a distance before regaining an even pattern. There was also the very real hazard of mid-air collision and once or twice after practice sorties squadron aircraft returned with bits of tailplane missing.

In preparation for the show all the aircraft were re-painted overall with silver dope and each was given a black code number painted on the nose. The squadron establishment was now twelve aircraft.

The display for Hendon was to comprise two synchronised formations, each of five aircraft, and to keep close to the aerodrome and to each other, the formation would do 'cross-over' turns. This meant that in a left hand turn the two aircraft on the left of the leader slid across above his tail and formed up on his right, while the two aircraft originally to the leader's right crossed below his tail and thus finished up on his left. It took some strong arm and leg work to persuade the 'Ninak' to comply with these directions! The Squadron deployed to Hendon in June and then on the 30th the two formations took off simultaneously - side by side - using up all the space at the small Hendon airfield and

Close formation flying, especially in such unresponsive aircraft as the D.H.9a, was a hazardous occupation and on a number of occasions aircraft returned with bits of the tailplane missing. This photograph was taken in early 1923 during rehearsals for the Hendon Pageant of that year and before the aircraft were repainted overall in silver dope. (*Sir Walter Dawson*)

39 Squadron displayed at most of the Hendon Pageants in the mid 1920s. Here, their D.H.9as are engaged in some pre-Pageant Flight formation rehearsal. *(P.H.T. Green collection)*

eliciting a few silent prayers that neither leader would swing inwards. Airborne, each formation turned outwards and manoeuvred to approach the aerodrome from opposite directions in 'V' formation, to cross each other as near to the centre of the airfield as possible. This was repeated in line abreast and then both elements of the formation went into simultaneous 'whirlygigs' with aircraft chasing each other's tails in a circle. To conclude the display the two formations returned to 'V' formation and landed one after the other. No problems had been encountered and by all accounts the event was a great success.

A number of the pilots taking part in the Pageant had originally been posted to the Squadron to act as bomb aimers for the Navy trials in August. It had been decided earlier in the year to use officer bomb-aimers for the trials and to this end a number of ex-Cranwell cadets were posted to 39 Squadron (they were Lacey, Mitchell, Brown, Coventry, Riccard, Pelly, Johnston and Dawson). All had left Cranwell with some twenty hours solo on Avro 504 trainers and had originally been 'farmed out' to

various units to qualify for their wings. On arrival at 39 Squadron four of the 'new boys' were lucky and dodged the bomb-aiming job (Lacey, Pelly, Coventry, Dawson) and were instead selected to fly as pilots in the squadron displays - including the Hendon Pageant. Sir Walter Dawson recalls part of the preparations:

'Preparation for the bombing trials was the second major pre-occupation of the Squadron in the first half of 1923. As part of the work up, all the aircraft had to be modified to take the new 'course-setting' bomb sight as a replacement for the old drift sight. This modification involved removing the internal cross bracing wires in the fuselage and replacing them with circular multiply bracings, thus creating a hollow fuselage, which was decked in to provide a space on which the bomb aimer would lie to operate the sight. The sight was fitted to the floor of the fuselage, at the forward end of the decked-in area. A semi-circular aluminium shield was fitted to the underside of the fuselage to give some protection to the sight and the bomb aimer.'

The modification was needed urgently to allow crews as much time as possible to train with the new sight. The fitters and riggers worked exceptionally long hours to complete the task as quickly as possible, and, in recognition of this effort, the officers of 'A' Flight invited the NCOs and airmen of the flight to supper at a

25

pub in Grantham. The officers agreed to provide transport, supper and unlimited beer - and also to ensure that every man got safely back to his billet after the party!

With the aircraft now ready, a programme of intensive training with the new sight was instigated and on 24th May the Squadron moved to Bircham Newton, Norfolk, where they had the aerodrome to themselves, for further training. A chalk target was constructed on the far side of the aerodrome - this target was the shape and size of HMS *Agamemnon,* which was to be the Navy target in the trials. For the next couple of months Squadron crews proceeded to 'plaster' this target with 8 lb practice bombs.

So far all training for the August trials had been conducted against static targets so on 2nd July another move, this time to Eastchurch, to practice bombing a moving target - at sea (this target consisted of floats towed at a safe distance behind an RAF launch). Whilst at Eastchurch a formation display was arranged on 6th July for visitors from the Swedish Navy - and 39 Squadron came close to losing a complete flight of aircraft! One side of Eastchurch aerodrome was not clearly marked and the surrounding area was very flat. After the display the 'A' Flight formation touched down outside the airfield perimeter - and on the wrong side of a deep ditch. The leader, Flight Lieutenant Smith, spotted the

ditch and proceeded to 'hop' over it - followed by the rest of the formation. All landed, eventually, on the aerodrome and taxied back to the parking area. It was decided not to include this manoeuvre in the Squadron routine display!

On the 27th of the month the final move was made to Gosport for the trials. Attacks were spread over several days and were at various heights up to 14,000 feet, and included individual and formation attacks using 8 lb practice bombs filled with Stanic Chloride. The results were never revealed to Squadron crews - who promptly took this to mean that they had offended the Navy by being too accurate! The move back to Spitalgate was made on 9th August and life settled back to a normal training routine after what had been a few very hectic months.

In March 1924 the Squadron officially became No 39 (Bombing) Squadron as part of a new scheme of classification of all RAF units.

39 Squadron Officers at Eastchurch, July 1923. Rear (left to right): Daly, Lacey, Beesley, Barlow, Page, Hadley, Mitchell, Lywood. Centre (left to right): Coventry, Riccard, Pelly, Groom, Burt, Dawson, Johnson, Brown, Ridgeway. Seated (left to right): Lucas, Barnett, Neale, S/Ldr Whittaker, Smith, Thomson, Moffat. On ground (left to right): Gauntlett and Coles.

39 Squadron D.H.9a aircraft in loose line-abreast. Note the Squadron number in the circle on the fin. This is a pre-1926 shot as the aircraft do not carry the crest on the nose which was introduced by the C.O. in that year.

A year later, on 6th March 1925, command of the Squadron passed to Squadron Leader Hugh Vivian Champion De Crespigny MC, DFC, who was to stay with 39 for the next five years and be associated with it for many years more. Life continued much as usual with routine training in bombing, mainly in formations of six to nine aircraft, gunnery, navigation and photo reconnaissance. Squadron strength was still twelve aircraft, split into three flights ('A', 'B', 'C') - a fairly typical structure. The annual Hendon Pageants were still one of the highlights of the year for 39 Squadron and prior to the 1926 display Squadron Leader De Crespigny introduced an unofficial Squadron motif which was painted on the noses of the aircraft - just behind the code number. The badge, shown opposite, comprised a pair of pilots wings supporting a bomb, the RAF initials and a crown above the bomb, and the Latin motto 'DIU NOCTUQUE' in a scroll below the bomb.

This was the first time that the 'DIU NOCTUQUE' motto, later to become the official Squadron motto, was put into a badge. The motto was intended to be translated as 'BY DAY AND BY NIGHT' and it remained as 'DIU NOCTUQUE' until some time in 1936 when it was changed to 'DIE NOCTUQUE' the reason for this may be that the original Latin motto could be translated as 'BY GOD BY NIGHT' - which, while it may have reflected the thought of the early night fliers, was not the intention.

A copy of the crest was forwarded to the Air Ministry and given official approval and was later given sanction by the Royal College of Heralds.

Although the bomb load was 230 lb bombs, it was more common to carry a single 230 lb bomb on a channel type carrier under the fuselage. A variety of alternative loads were available using combinations of 112 lb and 20 lb bombs on underwing and underfuselage stations. Very rarely did the '9s carry the full bomb load as in the words of one pilot, 'there was no airfield long enough for the beast to get off the ground fully loaded!'

A major change in the Squadron's future was foreshadowed in 1927 when it was given the designation 'mobile' - which meant that the unit had to be ready to deploy anywhere worldwide at just four days notice. All Squadron personnel had to be fit for overseas service which included the proviso that each man should have at least three years left to serve and on investigation it was found that some 25% of personnel were almost 'time expired' and so they were quickly replaced with men having the required number of years to do so. In January 1928 the Squadron was moved to Bircham Newton, near Kings Lynn in Norfolk, and, at the same time, De Crespigny was told of a proposed move to Risalpur (in the North West Frontier Province - NWFP), India at the end of the year.

While outline plans for the move were being made, 39 continued its normal routine of formation bombing training and the Operations Log for 1928 contains almost daily reports of nine aircraft formation bombing sorties, the following extract for 13th August being typical:

'Report of Raid Leader - S/Ldr H V de CRESPIGNY, MC DFC. Raid No 7:- I beg to report that nine aircraft left the ground at 1537 hours and flew on a direct course to FOULNESS. The Deputy Leader (F/Lt Payne) left the formation shortly after taking off and returned to BIRCHAM NEWTON with engine trouble.

'The formation crossed the CAMBRIDGE - ALDEBURGH line at 1635 hours and arrived at FOULNESS 1720 hrs; climbed over the sea opposite FOULNESS to 10,500 ft, and recrossed the land on course to target at 1806 hrs.

'A formation of nine fighters attacked 1½ miles north of SOUTHEND and continued to attack until the formation was at SOUTH OCKENDON. The attack commenced at 1825 hrs and finished at 1835 hrs.

'Two formations of fighters were seen on the outskirts of LONDON at a distance of approx five miles; they did not attack. They were seen at 1841 hrs.

'No 7 Target was bombed at 1855 hrs and the formation returned to BIRCHAM NEWTON on a direct course. Recrossed the CAMBRIDGE - ALDEBURGH line at 1924 hrs, and landed at BIRCHAM NEWTON at 2000 hrs.'

The Squadron practiced three basic types of formation bombing - coded 'A', 'B' and 'C'. They consisted of: 'A' - Arrival over coast at 18,000 ft, lose height to target, bomb and return to coast at low altitude; 'B' - Arrival over coast at 18,000 ft, maintain height to target, lose height to coast; 'C' - Arrival over coast at 18,000 ft, fly indirect course to target, maintaining height.

Bombing was normally done above 10,000 ft unless the formation was forced lower by the weather conditions, when it could be as low as 1,000 ft. Sortie lengths were on average four to five hours - a lengthy time in the not too comfortable 9a, particularly above 10,000 ft.

The raid report detailed above very much tells the story of Squadron operations throughout 1929, even to the extent of one aircraft having to return early with engine problems. It has been mentioned earlier that the D.H.9a suffered frequent engine problems, and, despite the fact that the Squadron had been operating the aircraft type for seven years, radiator leaks were still common - there being no apparent solution to the problem. Another feature of these formation raids was that one aircraft would carry a service Umpire and another would carry a member of the press, thus ensuring fair play and good publicity!

A further change in the pipeline was a re-equipment to come into effect prior to the move to India. The D.H.9a were to be replaced by the Westland Wapiti biplane day bomber, an aircraft of similar size but superior performance and reliability. The Westland Wapiti IIa was powered by a single 480 hp Bristol Jupiter VIIIf engine, giving a maximum speed of 140 mph at 5,000 feet. Generally, the performance of the Wapiti was not that much better that the '9a (the endurance was in fact an hour less), but engine reliability and bomb load were significantly better. As the Wapiti had an air-cooled engine it was hoped that the problem of the D.H.9a engine would not recur.

Towards the end of 1928 two modified Wapiti prototypes were delivered to Bircham Newton to give Squadron crews an opportunity for intensive flying practice on the new type before going to India. After an initial few sorties for conversion to type, crews flew with a full war load of dummy bombs (the bomb racks being wire locked to prevent accidental release).This combination meant that the two unfortunate aircraft took very heavy punishment, and by the end of the year were in no condition to go to India! The impending move to a part of the world infamous to British Military ventures brought the Squadron into national prominence and the newspapers spoke of the 'Flowers of England's Youth' being sent to 'the Grim North West'.

At last the fateful day arrived, and on 29th December 1928 Flight Lieutenant E A C Britton left Bircham Newton with a party of sixty-nine airmen, on the start of the journey to India, initially by rail to Southampton to board the MV *Nevasa,* a 7,000 ton troopship. At 1600 hours the *Nevasa* left Southampton on its twenty-one day journey to Karachi. Doubts as to the seaworthiness of their floating home soon passed around the Squadron - doubts which were not eased by a rough passage in bad weather across the Bay of Biscay.

A total of 1,400 airmen (11 and 39 Squadrons) and soldiers were packed into the three decks and, as some 90% of these were sick during the first part of the voyage, conditions soon became intolerable. The Squadron even lost a man, LAC 'Tubby' Hayman went missing for two days and even though a search was made he could not be found. However, just before a casualty message was sent to the Air Ministry he was discovered - wedged in a dark recess

Above: **Line-up of D.H.9as at Bircham Newton in early 1928, shortly after their arrival.**
Below: **J7818 and J7819 over Hendon during rehearsal for the 1926 Pageant.**

between the girders of a bulkhead and the sides of the ship - unconscious from sea-sickness. He recovered in the sick bay but had two red eyes until March. However, life soon settled down on board to the boring routine of card games but at least the weather was bright and sunny from Gibraltar onwards which allowed the troops to take to the deck. During a coaling stop at Port Said the they were disembarked for a route march through the desert - a little light relief from the confines of the troopship. The rest of the journey went according to schedule and Karachi was reached on 19th January 1929. This was but the first part of the journey and there then followed a three day train journey on the 1,200 miles from Karachi to Risalpur. The first train, carrying the CO and eleven officers, arrived at Risalpur on the 21st, the remainder of the Squadron followed in a trooptrain and arrived a day later. It was a widely held view that the train journey was even worse than the ship - as the train had wooden slats, there was no air conditioning and the men were only given one blanket each to lie on. Nevertheless, after an exhausting twenty-four day journey, the Squadron had arrived at its new home - tired, unhappy and a little dispirited.

39 SQDN. MAIN OPERATING AREA

CHITRAL

GILGIT

KHYBER PASS

AFGHANISTAN

Nanga Parbat 26660'

KABUL

RISALPUR

PESHAWAR

KOHAT

HIMALAYAS

LAHORE

QUETTA

MULTAN

DELHI

INDUS

INDIA

KARACHI
(R.A.F.
DRIGH RD)

BOMBAY

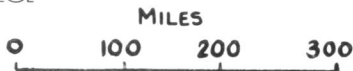

Map 2: India

MILES

0   100   200   300

— · — · —   INTERNATIONAL BORDER

LAND OVER 1000m

LAND OVER 3000m

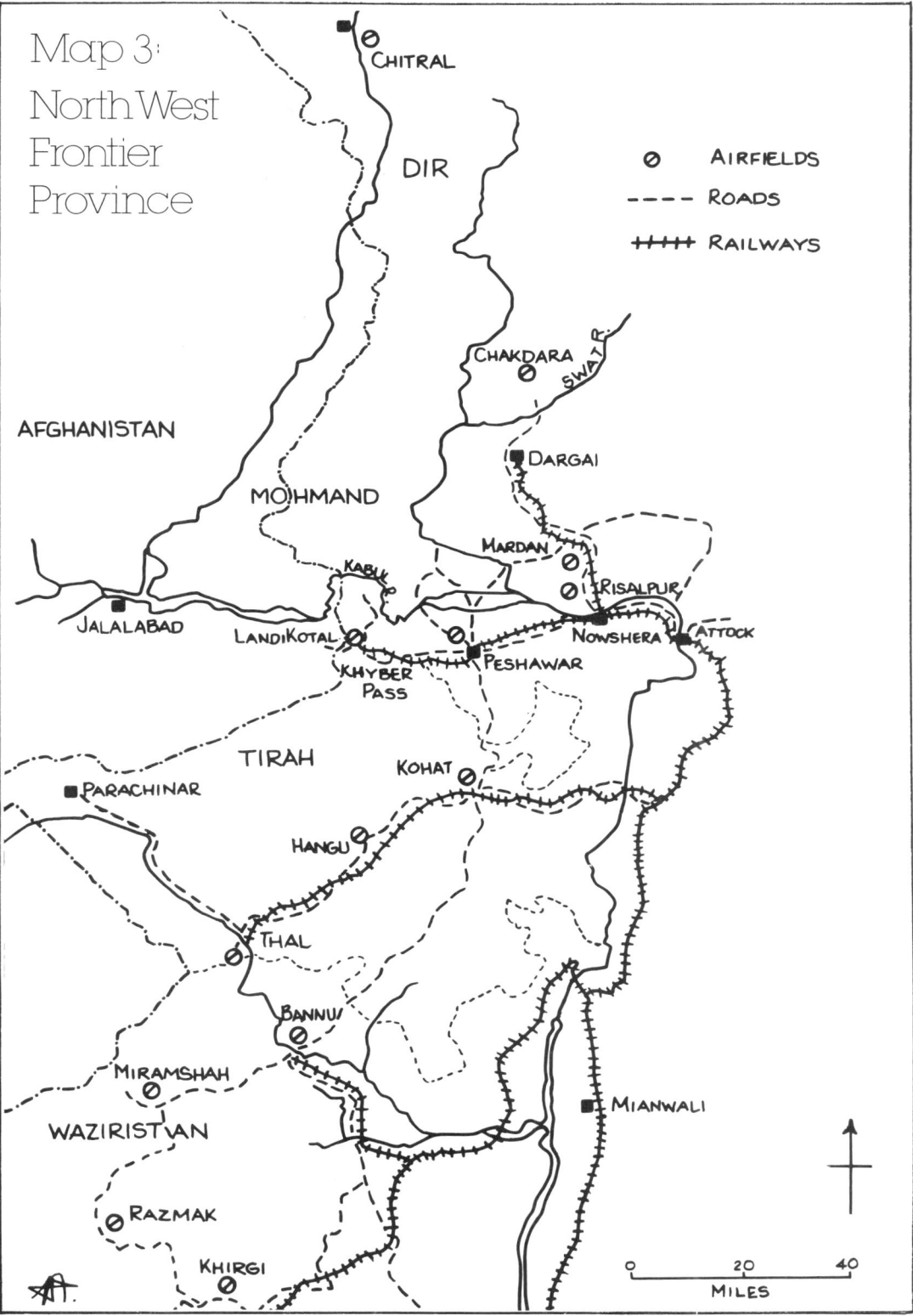

Map 3:
North West
Frontier
Province

AIRFIELDS
ROADS
RAILWAYS

CHITRAL

DIR

AFGHANISTAN

MOHMAND

CHAKDARA

SWAT

DARGAI

MARDAN

RISALPUR

KABUL

JALALABAD

LANDI KOTAL

NOWSHERA

ATTOCK

KHYBER
PASS

PESHAWAR

TIRAH

KOHAT

PARACHINAR

HANGU

THAL

BANNU

MIRAMSHAH

MIANWALI

WAZIRISTAN

RAZMAK

KHIRGI

0   20   40
MILES

31

3

Guardians of the Frontier

Risalpur Cantonment was some 25 miles east of Peshawar in the North West Frontier Province, modern Pakistan, a lush area in the winter months but a veritable desert in the summer. The Army were already present at Risalpur (literally 'Place of Cavalry') in the shape of the 15/19th Hussars, 21st Indian Lancers, 'E' Battery Royal Horse Artillery and various other units and during the ten years that 39 Squadron was to spend there, relations varied from - 'good old Air Force' to 'damn infernal machines, they frighten the horses'.

Accommodation for all was pre-Indian Mutiny bungalows equipped with antiquated electrically driven punkahs to provide some cooling in the hot dry summers. The punkahs were not needed in winter as the temperature dropped to around 45°F - and so in winter the RAF units wore blue, changing to Khaki drill in April with the arrival of warmer weather. The aerodrome itself suffered from the dry conditions as, being gravel, it became very dusty. To remedy this, a special grass was imported from Australia and planted on the aerodrome. However, a great deal of water was needed to keep the grass alive, and so a pumping system was built to draw water from the nearby Kabul river. To pro-

mote good RAF/Army relations, this water supply was diverted once a week to the polo pitch of the cavalry regiments.

Although most of the Squadron had arrived in January, the aircraft did not arrive until March 1929. The Wapitis had been crated in England and shipped to Karachi, RAF Drigh Road, where they duly arrived in February 1929. A party of fitters and riggers from Risalpur re-assembled the 'Wops', and, after air testing, the aircraft were flown to Risalpur via a refuelling stop at Multan. The first 39 Squadron aircraft arrived at Risalpur in early March, and the rest over the next six weeks.

The Squadron was part of No 2 (Indian) Wing, along with 11 (B) Squadron who were also stationed at Risalpur. When all the Wapitis had arrived, Squadron strength was twelve aircraft, split in the standard pattern of four aircraft in

RAF Station Risalpur, North West Frontier Province, India. The home of No.2 Wing, consisting of 39 and 11 Bomber Squadrons for ten years. Note hangars at top centre. (*Crown Copyright / RAF Photograph*)

each of three flights, 'A', 'B' and 'C'. Each flight was to a large extent self-contained with its own riggers, fitters, armourers etc and there was a certain amount of inter-flight rivalry as well as inter squadron (11 v 39).

Life at Risalpur soon settled down to a regular pattern of training. De Crespigny had commanded the Squadron during its days at the Hendon Pageants when 39 dominated the formation flying displays and on arrival in India he was determined that the Squadron should maintain its high level of proficiency in formation and to this end frequent practice sorties were flown. A separate aircraft flew above the formation and took a series of vertical photographs for use in the post-flight debrief. After landing, De Crespigny had copies of the photographs rushed to his office and proceeded to debrief the pilots. This detailed, and irrefutable, evidence ensured that everyone kept on their toes. The first working parade of the day was at 0700.

1930: nine Wapitis in close formation. The C.O., Sqn Ldr De Crespigny, was determined that 39 should be proficient in close formation flying so he had a spare aircraft fly around the formation taking photographs for use at debrief. (*M. Roe*)

This was followed by early flying for about one hour, breakfast at 0815, back to work at 0900 and all flying ceasing at 1200 in the hot season - except in times of active operations or when behind in the training programme. One reason for ceasing flying at midday was that it became turbulent in the afternoon, with temperatures shooting up to 120° in the shade - making accurate flying, gunnery and formation difficult. No such restrictions applied when operations were in progress.

Further problems during times of peace were caused by supply difficulties largely caused by the depression of the 1930s, and the financial constraints of that period. The Indian Government imposed strict limitations of fuel and spares. Spare parts and other equipment could only be obtained in small quantities and so each training sortie was designed to include as many different exercises as possible. Hence a typical sortie might comprise: a height test with full war load; mosaic photography (ie overlapping photographic cover of a small area); wireless training; navigational and meteorological flight. These varied sorties sometimes created unforeseen difficulties. Sergeant Pilot Whitwell and ACI Roe (Armourer/AG) were briefed for just such a varied sortie, commencing with a met

flight. On a met flight the Armourer/AG carried a large aneroid barometer on his knees and noted the pressure, in millibars, every 1,000 feet in the ascent and descent. He also took the ambient temperature using a thermometer strapped to one of the wing struts - a system of cords raised a sliding magnifying glass over the face of the thermometer to enable the gunner to read the temperature scale.

On this particular sortie, the crew had climbed to 15,000 feet on the met test, and then carried out a photographic task of a 10 x 5 mile area around the Khyber Pass. . .Pilot to Air Gunner,

'Pretty cold up here, how do you feel?'

'Pretty chilly'

'Right we'll get down quickly after this last photo run.'

The quickest way to get a Wapiti down was to spin, and so the pilot duly spun the aircraft. It was usual to do no more than three turns, so after five or six turns. . . Air Gunner to Pilot,

'How about pulling her out Jack.'

'What do you think I'm trying to do!' came the reply.

Both crewmen had forgotten that there was a 230 lb bomb under each wing - and the said bombs were having a somewhat adverse effect on the spin. Furthermore, the bombs were wired on to prevent accidental release. Fortunately the pilot recovered the aircraft at 1,000 feet and flew back to Risalpur - where, by agreement, the crew said nothing about the incident. The groundcrew were nevertheless somewhat suspicious as the whole aircraft had to be re-rigged following its exertions!

At times the Squadron was called on to perform unusual missions as on 24th July 1929 when Squadron Leader de Crespigny and Sergeant Lockhead left Risalpur on a mercy flight to Bangkok. They were carrying drugs which were needed to save the life of the heir to the Siamese throne, but, after a night stop at Ambala, a message was received saying that the drugs were no longer required. A more intensive mercy mission in 1929; which involved all the frontier squadrons, was supply dropping to villages in the Peshawar Basin which had been isolated by the flooding of the Kabul and Indus rivers. Hundreds of villages were isolated and the frontier squadrons flew at maximum effort dropping food, blankets, medical equipment and other essentials. Flight Lieutenant D F Anderson, the Station Parachute Officer at Risalpur, had devised a method of suspending sacks of corn from the bomb carriers. The sacks were stiffened with wooden battens and given a bomb lug attachment for suspension on the bomb carriers, a static-line-controlled parachute was attached to the sack and the crew could then drop this store like a bomb.

On 1st January 1930 Squadron Leader de Crespigny was promoted to Wing Commander and, on 25th January, was posted to command No 2 (Indian) Wing Station, Risalpur. Thus he continued his association with 39 Squadron. In the same month, the Squadron had its first fatal accident since 1924 when the outside aircraft of a formation was struck by a bird. Sergeant Wren tried to control the aircraft, but the bird, - a Rock Eagle with a nine foot wingspan - had smashed a number of wing struts which caused the upper wing to collapse. The aircraft crashed and both crew, Sergeant Pilot Wren and Corporal Jefferies, were killed.

The new Commanding Officer, Squadron Leader S B Harris DFC AFC, arrived on 4th April and it was under his leadership that the Squadron was to be transformed from the 'Flowers of England's Youth' to 'Veterans of the Frontier'. [This comment by the press created problems in India for 11 and 39 Squadrons who were called 'The Flowers' by men already there.]

On 1st January 1877 Queen Victoria was proclaimed 'Empress of India', thus all military establishments in India celebrated the Proclamation Day anniversary amidst much pageantry and ceremonial. At Risalpur on 1st January 1930, the army units, including the cavalry in their parade uniforms, assembled on the cavalry parade ground about half a mile North of Risalpur aerodrome. The RAF part of the celebration was to be a flypast by 39 Squardon. Prior to the display, Sergeant Nunneley took his Wapiti up for a post-engine-change air test. Unfortunately, the engine cut out shortly after take-off with the aircraft heading towards the shining ranks of soldiers on the parade ground. The only clear space was right in front of the parade and so Nunneley positioned his machine for a forced landing. All hell broke loose with terrified horses throwing their riders and bolting off into the surrounding countryside. The dignity of the cavalry was somewhat shaken and it took days to round-up all the horses.

The Squadron had been sent to India partly as a result of the successful use of aircraft against tribal insurgents in Mesopotamia in the 1920s. It had been realised then that air power could be used to dissolve potential tribal risings. There were many ways in which these aims could be achieved. Shows of strength could be made by flying over areas of potential trouble. If trouble did break out then aircraft could be used as an independent strike force of in co-operation with ground forces.

Bombing villages destroyed the livelihood of the insurgents and constant harrying attacks could disperse concentrations of tribesmen. The type of raid varied greatly from single aircraft, to flights of three, to squadron, wing and even group attacks - as will be seen in the following accounts of operations by 39 Squadron. Army co-operation could take the form of close-support against tribesmen, recce, message-dropping and even supply dropping.

In May 1930 operations began in the Mohmand District, north of the Khyber Pass. Punitive expeditions here had begun in 1847 when the British Army was first involved in counteracting attacks by tribesmen into the Peshawar Plain, which was considered by the tribes to be open ground for cattle stealing. These new air operations marked the Squadron's first action in India and early in May the following orders were promulgated:

OP ORDER NO.1 39 (B) SQUADRON

An attack on NWFP from MOHMAND COUNTRY is expected at dawn on 2 May. The RAF may be required to operate against the expected attack.

OC 'C' Flight is to detail 2 aircraft to be ready to leave the ground at 1500, equipped as follows:

16 x 20 lb bombs.

Front and rear guns with full ammunition (300 round front, 6 magazines of 97 round rear)

Full petrol and Oil tanks

Course setting Bomb sight

One aircraft to be equipped with T21 and TF W/R Sets

OP ORDER NO.2 39 (B) SQUADRON

The 2 aircraft now known as BATTLE FLIGHT will remain at readiness until 2000 hours. At 2000 'C' Flt will be relieved by 'A' Flt; at this time the following procedure to take place.

Below: **Line-up of Westland Wapitis in front of the hangars at Risalpur, in January 1930. The sturdy airframe of the Wapiti IIa coped with the rigours of operations in this part of the world, but the water-cooled engines proved troublesome at first.** *(M Roe)*

Above: **The 230 lb (RFC) and 20 lb (Cooper) anti-personnel bombs, attended here by LAC Roe, were the largest and smallest bombs used in the 1930 ops against the Haji of Turangzai. The tradition of writing messages on bombs was continued here with 'The Haji Special'.** *(M Roe)*

Map 4: Peshawar District

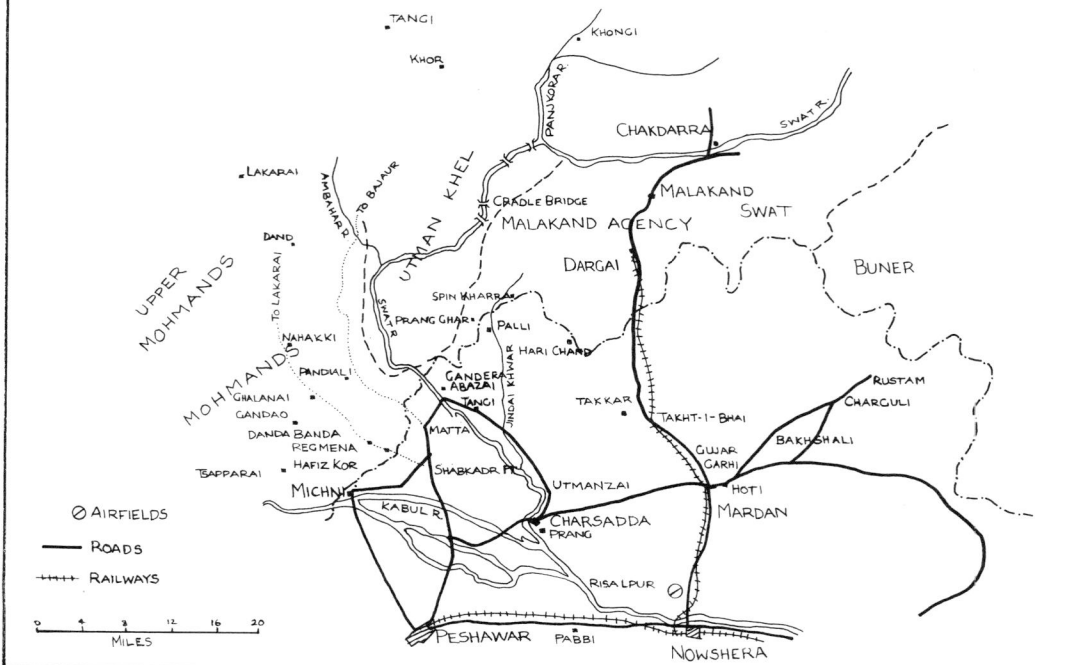

- TANGI
- KHONCI
- KHOR
- PANJKORA R.
- CHAKDARRA
- SWAT R.
- LAKARAI
- AMBAHAR
- TO BAJAUR
- CRADLE BRIDGE
- MALAKAND
- SWAT
- UTMAN KHEL
- MALAKAND AGENCY
- DAND
- TO LAKARAI
- UPPER MOHMANDS
- SWAT R.
- SPIN KHARBA
- PRANG GHAR
- PALLI
- HARI CHAND
- DARGAI
- BUNER
- NAHAKKI
- PANDIALI
- JINDAI KHWAR
- GANDERA
- ABAZAI
- TANGI
- TAKKAR
- RUSTAM
- CHARGULI
- MOHMANDS
- GHALANAI
- GANDAO
- DANDA BANDA
- REGMENA
- HAFIZ KOR
- MATTA
- TAKHT-I-BHAI
- BAKHSHALI
- TAPPARAI
- SHABKADR Ft.
- GUJAR GARHI
- MICHNI
- KABUL R.
- UTMANZAI
- HOTI
- MARDAN
- CHARSADDA
- PRANG
- Ø AIRFIELDS
- ——— ROADS
- ++++ RAILWAYS
- RISALPUR
- 0 4 8 12 16 20
- MILES
- PESHAWAR
- PABBI
- NOWSHERA

Map 5: Tirah

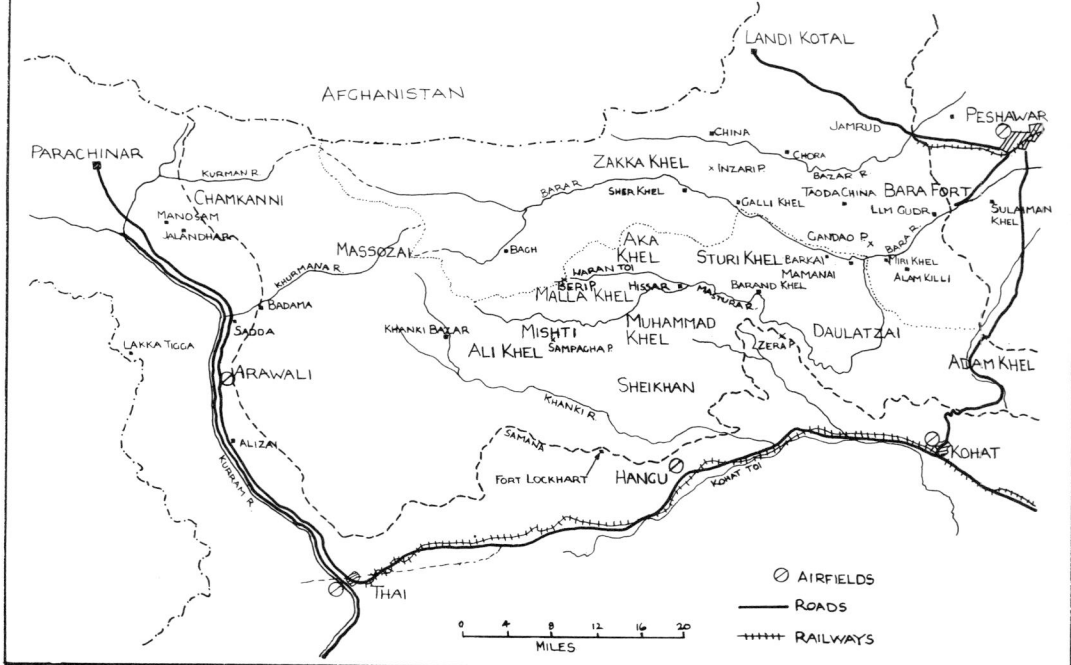

- LANDI KOTAL
- AFGHANISTAN
- JAMRUD
- PESHAWAR
- PARACHINAR
- KURMAN R.
- CHINA
- CHORA
- BAZAR R.
- BARA FORT
- ZAKKA KHEL
- × INZARI P.
- TAODACHINA
- CHAMKANNI
- MANOGAM
- JALANDHAR
- BARAR
- SHER KHEL
- GALLI KHEL
- LLM GUDR.
- SULAIMAN KHEL
- KHURMANA R.
- MASSOZAI
- BAGH
- AKA KHEL
- GANDAO P. ×
- BARA R.
- BADAMA
- WARAN TOI
- STURI KHEL
- BARKAI
- PIRI KHEL
- ALAM KILLI
- LAKKA TIGGA
- SADDA
- KHANKI BAZAR
- BERIP
- MALLA KHEL
- HISSAR
- MATURA R.
- MAMANAI
- BARAND KHEL
- MISHTI
- MUHAMMAD KHEL
- DAULATZAI
- ADAM KHEL
- ARAWALI
- ALI KHEL
- SAMPAGHA P.
- ZERA P.
- ALIZAI
- KHANKI R.
- SHEIKHAN
- SAMANA
- KURRAM R.
- FORT LOCKHART
- HANGU
- KOHAT TOI
- KOHAT
- THAL
- Ø AIRFIELDS
- ——— ROADS
- ++++ RAILWAYS
- 0 4 8 12 16 20
- MILES

Map 6: Waziristan

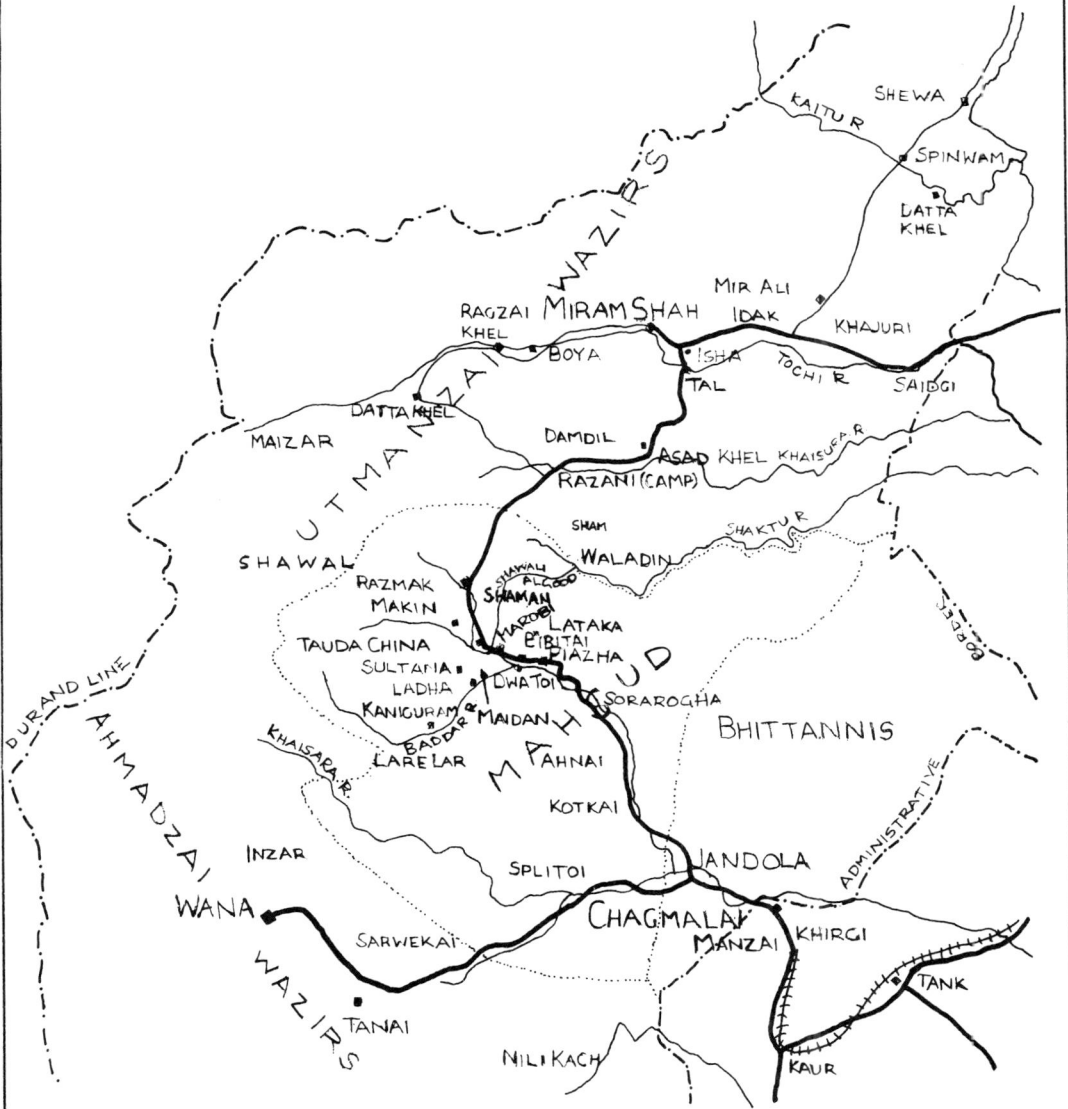

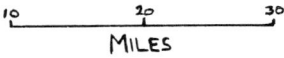

SHEWA

KAITUR

SPINWAM

DATTA
KHEL

RAGZAI MIRAMSHAH
KHEL

MIR ALI
IDAK

KHAJURI

BOYA

ISHA

TAL

TOCHI R

SAIDGI

DATTAKHEL

MAIZAR

DAMDIL

ASAD KHEL KHAISURA R

RAZANI (CAMP)

SHAM

SHAKTUR

WALADIN

SHAWAL

RAZMAK
MAKIN

SHAWAL
ALGOD

SHAMAN

MARGE

LATAKA

TAUDA CHINA

SULTANA
LADHA

KANIGURAM

BADDAR

BIBITAI
PIAZHA

DWATOI

MAIDAN

SORAROGHA

AHNAI

BHITTANNIS

KHAISARA R

LARE LAR

KOTKAI

DURAND LINE

AHMADZAI

INZAR

SPLITOI

JANDOLA

ADMINISTRATIVE

WANA

SARWEKAI

CHAGMALAI
MANZAI

KHIRGI

WAZIRS

TANAI

NILI KACH

KAUR

TANK

WAZIRS

UTMANZAI

JD

MAH

———— ROADS

++++++ RAILWAYS

10   20   30
    MILES

1. All bombs at present on 'C' Flt aircraft will have their detonators removed and will be transferred to aircraft of 'A' Flt.
2. The locks of all Vickers Guns and Bolts of Lewis Guns will be removed and taken to the Sqn armoury for safe custody.
3. A warning notice calling attention to the fact that aircraft are armed is to be hung in a conspicuous place on each aircraft carrying bombs.
4. At 0500 the next day, all locks and bolts to be returned to aircraft and Battle Flight wheeled out on to the aerodrome, with bombs re-detonated, and ready to leave the ground.
5. 'B' Flt to take over at 2000.

This system was modified so that although the bombs were without detonators, and lock, bolts and ammo for the guns were kept in the armoury, the whole Squadron was 'at readiness'. Each flight in turn was nominated as Battle Flight and, although at no higher state of readiness than the rest of the squadron, the Flight Commander had to know the whereabouts of his pilots and crews and ensure that the flight was always ready for action.

On 10th May, the following instruction was issued giving details of the first raid in the Mohmand campaign, and so ordering 39 Squadron's first raid.

No 2 (I) Wing Station Operation Order No.2
SECRET
1. INFORMATION
   Letters of warning should reach the HAJI of TURANGZAI and BADSHAH GUL by midday today 10th May. They are being told that if they have not removed themselves meanwhile the Government will take such action as it sees fit at any time after daybreak on 11th. Air reconnaissance (1630 10th May) reports that a body of the followers of the above men are in the area R.2468 to R.0993 to R.3788.
2. INTENTION
   To carry out bomb attacks on the followers of the HAJI of TURANGZAI and BADSHAH GUL in the event of the ultimatum referred to above not being complied with.
3. EXECUTION
   (a) One Aeroplane from No 11 (Bomber) Squadron is to take off at 0600 hours on 11.5.30 and proceed to area R.2468 - R.0993 - R.3788 to find WS & D. This aeroplane is to fly at 6,400 ft above sea level and is to carry 2 way W/T. The result of WS & D finding is to be transmitted to this Wing Station as soon as found.
   (b) All serviceable aircraft are to be at 15 minutes notice to leave the ground from 0630 hours 11.5.30 onwards. All aeroplanes are to be loaded with full complement of 20lb bombs except the parachute Test Section aeroplane which will carry 112 lb bombs. No guns or ammunition are to be carried.
   (c) On receipt of orders to take off the Wing will proceed in formation of Squadrons line astern and will rendezvous over PABBI with No 1 (I) Wing at 6,400 ft ASL. Both Wings will fly in right hand circuits until rendezvous is complete.
   (d) No 1 (I) Wing will lead and will fly at 6,800 ft ASL to the target which will be detailed later. No 2 (I) Wing will fly at 6,400 ft ASL.
   (e) Bombing will be carried out in Wing Formations of squadrons and Flights in line astern. Both wings will carry out four runs over the target during which all bombs are to be released. There are to be intervals of five minutes between Wings 500 yards between Squadrons and 200 yards between Flights. Squadrons will be stepped down 200 ft and Flights sufficiently to avoid slip streams.
   (l) On completion of the bombing attack the wing is to reform into Squadrons line astern and is to return to the aerodrome.
   (m) Immediately after arrival all aircraft are to be rearmed and re-fuelled.

Operations, as per this Order, commenced on 11th May 1930 and were to continue with hardly a break until 15th August 1930 - although the area of operations shifted from Mohmand County (11th May - 11th June) to Utman Khel (30th May - 17th July) to Waziristan (7th July - 22nd July) and finally Tirah (6th August - 15th August). The 11th May raid was a Group raid, that is No 1 and No 2 Indian Wings combined, against the Hadj of Turangzai and Badshah Gul.

The tribesmen had been given forty-eight hours warning that if they did not remove themselves they would be bombed. The aircraft dropped 20 lb bombs so that the maximum number of bombs could be dropped in a short time to impress the tribesmen with the power of the Government. Tribal casualties were thought to be three dead and five wounded; this kind of information was usually obtained by the local Political Agent. The Squadron was active again the next day but this time only as a flight of three, led by the CO, Squadron Leader Harris. The following passage is the official squadron report on this action, taken from the Operation Log.

'On arrival over the area at 0700 hrs I immediately sighted a party of six men dressed in white running in the direction of Sadar Garhi. This party had obviously come down the Loe Khwar, but when I sighted them I estimated that they

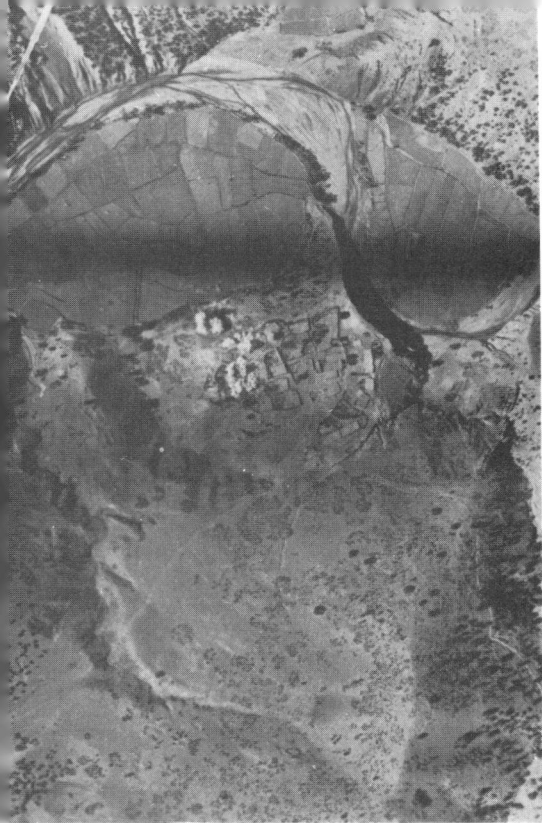

Left: **Bombs bursting in Marga Marsanzai village during the 1930 ops. Medium level bombing by the Wapiti was normally done in Flight or even Squadron formation.** *(M Roe)*

Right: **39 Squadron Wapitis passing over Kohat in Flight formation whilst returning from a raid in 1930.** *(M Roe)*

were approx 200 yards east of the Administrative border and was thus unable to take action against them. Between 0700 hrs and 0915 hrs the whole area was completely and carefully searched and although the aircraft were fired at, no movement of any kind was observed. At 0915 hours I saw a party of approximately 20 men in a Nullah Bed near some caves. A red blanket was hanging on the side of the Nullah overhanging the caves. A bomb attack was immediately carried out and altogether 56 x 20 lb bombs were dropped. Of these, four in one salvo secured a direct hit in the Nullah bed in front of the caves and the average error of the remainder was approximately 100 yards in different directions.'

This 12th May engagement was a typical action with small parties of tribesmen being attacked in an attempt to prevent larger gatherings and to show the natives that they were never safe from the forces of the Government. For the Squadron, the scale of operations varied from day to day; from single aircraft, to flights, and, at times such as 15th June, the requirement was for four full squadron strength raids. The 16th June was similar and Squadron aircraft dropped 979 x 20 lb bombs, 183 x 112 lb bombs, 24 x 230 lb bombs and twenty containers of BIBs (Baby Incendiary Bombs). A justified comment could be 'using a sledgehammer to crack a walnut', as was later said of American saturation bombing in Vietnam, especially on days such as 21st May 1930 when three aircraft sighted three or four isolated tribesmen and so dropped 28 x 20 lb and 8 x 112 lb bombs and fired 336 rounds of .303 ammunition - without any apparent result. On many sorties no movement was seen, and 'likely' targets were bombed. Generally, the amount of damage inflicted was small but the psychological effect was much greater. On sorties which were not tasked against definite targets, aircraft were allocated areas to patrol for possible targets and stayed on patrol until all bombs were used or low fuel dictated a return to base.

During 1930 operations the airfields at Peshawar and Miramshar were used as staging grounds. The tabular summary below shows the extent of Squadron operations in the summer of 1930. Substantial effort was being expended against small targets, but the success of each campaign was notable, although short lived.

BOMBS DROPPED

Date	Area	H.E. (Tons)	B.I.B.	Hrs flown Hrs min
11.5.30 - 11.6.30	Mohmand	27	1,188	244-40
30.5.30 - 17.7.30	Utman Khel	37	12,276	287-45
7.7.30 - 22.7.30	Waziristan	15.5	11,484	297-40
6.8.30 - 15.8.30	Tirah	27.5	3,564	262-30
Totals		107	28,512	1092-35

Of the weapons used, the heavier bombs were mainly 1914-1918 vintage and inevitably there were a fair proportion of duds. The BIB (Baby Incendiary Bomb) deserves a mention as little appears to have been published about it. The Wapiti carried 792 BIBs in four boat-shaped boxes (198 in each box) attached to the bomb carriers. Each bomb was a 5" x 1" tin case around an aluminium cartridge containing cendite which was set-off by a 28-bore cartridge head. When dropped, the bombs were kept nose down by a steel plug in the nose of the container and this, on impact with the ground, acted as a firing pin for the 28-bore cartridge, which in turn ignited the incendiary mixture, which burned fiercly at 3000°C for three to five minutes. The ballistics of these weapons was erratic and so they were dropped from 1,000 feet to ensure the correct distribution of bombs over a reasonable area. Dropping these by the hundred looked impressive and was effective against the inflammable structures of native villages, and when used against isolated tribesmen hiding in rock-strewn valleys.

Aircraft serviceability was excellent and after an initial problem with the early Jupiter engines had been rectified at Squadron level, the Wapiti gave very few problems. With a little dexterity, the Wapiti could be flown from the rear cockpit, but to do this the gunner had to remove his lap-type parachute and put it on his seat; by so doing he was raised high enough to see over the engine cylinders and could also glimpse the Air Speed Indicator in the front cockpit. A spare control column was stowed on the left-hand side of his cockpit and this was fitted into a floor socket to operate the ailerons and elevators. Rudder pedals were permanently fitted as was a throttle control.

On one occasion, Sergeant Whitwell and AC Roe were on air-to-ground firing practice when the ammunition belt of the front gun broke. Whitwell was determined not to abort the sortie and ordered the gunner to fly the aircraft in an orbit while he attempted to mend the broken belt. The repair required gymnastic skill as the ammunition box was behind and below the pilot's rudder bar. Whitwell unstrapped and climbed down, his feet sticking out above the cockpit. The repair took some twenty minutes but was a success, the crew completed their 200-round firing and returned to Risalpur. 1930 was a busy year for 39 Squadron and within weeks of the summer campaign coming to a close, the Squadron was ordered to co-operate with ground forces on the biennial relief of the Chitral garrison.

Chitral, the capital of the princely state of Chitral, was approximately 130 miles north of Peshawar, and not far from Soviet Badaksham. The garrison of this, the most northerly outpost, was 1,000 Indian troops who served a tour of duty of two years and were then relieved. Chitral was isolated from the rest of India by the mountain ranges of the Hindu Kush and the main relief route through British territory was by way of the 11,000 foot Lawarai Pass some thirty miles south of Chitral. It was also possible to reach Chitral via Rawalpindi, but this route took many weeks through difficult terrain via Kashmir and Gilghit.

So every two years a relieving battalion would assemble at the rail-head at Dargai to start the three week journey to Chitral. The following account is by Matt Roe, an Armourer/AG on 39 Squadron, who took part in the 1930 Chitral Relief. The story starts at Dargai:

'At this stage of the journey a baggage train of mule carts was the main means of transportation, and the final order to commence the long and arduous - not to mention dangerous - march, would be given. This after the usual military ceremony - bands playing, bugles sounding, much shouting and all the excitement of a military expedition breaking camp at dawn, with the tropical sun rising with all its glare and beauty over the glistening icy peaks of the far Himalayas. Mules would perform with all the stubborness of their kind - runaways and screaming sepoys getting them into line until the companies finally set off with a jingling of chains and the bedlam of noise appropriate to the occasion. The first objective was Chackdara Fort in the Swat valley via the Malakand Pass along a good military road that for much of its

Wapiti armament at Miranshah, 1930: 230 lb, 112 lb and 20 lb bombs, B.I.B.s (baby incendiary bombs — an early type of cluster bomb), Mk.3 Lewis guns and ammunition drums plus belted ammo (.303) for the front Vickers guns. *(M Roe)*

way runs parallel to the remains of that historic route immortalised many centuries before by Alexander the Great. A few miles beyond Chackdara the road comes to an abrupt end at the foothills of the Hindu Kush. As the mountain track winds upwards through gorges and over precipitous paths the going grows worse with every mile and the column becomes a long snakelike line winding slowly forward.

'The wheeled vehicles were left behind at Chackdara and it is here that the mules come into their own as pack animals. All the stores and equipment are transferred to mule pack and the extended column proceeds in single file along the narrow mountain track, not without danger as even the sure footed mule sometimes falters and the remains of the fallen can still be seen on the hard rocks a thousand feet below. The long jezail of the Pathan, or perhaps a stolen .303 Lee Enfield, always took its toll - perhaps only for the fun of having a crack at something moving but more often than not as part of a well organised sniping venture.

'Prior to 1930 the relief had never been accomplished without some action, with a quota of the relieving force struck down by tribal bullets - it was a case of outlying pickets, scouts, rearguards and all the tactics of a military column on the march in Tribal Territory. When the column stretched at some points in single file for as much as ten miles it is easy to imagine the vulnerability to ambush of such an expedition.

'Seen from the air it was a most impressive and picturesque sight, and 39 Squadron had ample opportunity to take a grandstand view. From dawn till dusk constant armed patrols were the order of the day. Each patrol saw this thin Khaki and brown line winding along and frequently doubling back on itself - with all too often a little stationary knot of mules and men to mark the scene of a traffic jam with perhaps an animal lying kicking on its side with a sepoy sitting on its head while his comrades undid the heavy pack.

'In order to assist and speed up the Chitral Relief the Army was persuaded to accept air escort and reconnaissance; it was also planned to feed the column by supply dropping. This would save much in the way of transport and increase the mobility of the Force.

'Nine aircraft were loaded and took off in Squadron formation, each one looking like something pre-historic with its odd assortment of goods suspended so awkwardly and in some cases swaying dangerously. Fortunately, the first drop was only a few miles beyond Chackdara, but even so many of the packages sagged clear of their steadying crutches and were 'swinging free'.

'Two aircraft had to jettison to avoid mishap when the static cords came loose and threatened to release the parachutes. This actually happened to an aircraft of another squadron; and the release gear failed to operate. The fully opened parachute exerted a terrific drag on the port wing and the Wapiti went into a steep diving turn; as luck would have it Shakot landing ground was nearby and the pilot Sgt Clark - made an excellent job of putting the machine down.

'The Squadron reached the dropping zone - a small piece of level ground not far from Chackdara Fort and the drop was made; there were a few 'hang ups' due to some of the loads sagging on their cables and twisting. Fortunately the soldiers assumed that this was normal! The second effort was more successful. The bundles were attached to the bomb carriers overnight; the tension in the cables was adjusted before take-off next morning and the static lines were secured more effectively. The remainder of this supply dropping operation was normal routine; there were no more difficulties and the army were most grateful for the help.'

In addition to food supplies, the Squadron also experimented with aluminium cylindrical containers with impact-taking crushable heads. These had parachutes housed in the rear end. They were highly successful, but only special stores were permitted, normally beer, cigarettes, mail and newspapers. The three weeks of this operation saw the relieving force climb over the Lowarai Pass, descend 11,000 feet into the wonderful valley of Chitral, and complete the remaining thirty miles to their new home amidst the beautiful scenery of that fertile valley.

Message dropping also had its lighter side. Sergeant Pilot Nunneley had a 'close friend' who was a schoolteacher at Kohat and, as the Squadron used the air-to-ground firing range at Kohat, he would often land there to visit the lady. On the return flight to Risalpur he would get his air gunner to drop a message in her garden. Unfortunately, message dropping was a delicate art. On this occasion, Nunneley was too high for accuracy and the message bag, with a three foot long multi-coloured silken streamer, overshot its target by fifty yards and landed in the rose garden of the General Officer Commanding Kohat District. This message, full of terms of endearment, was duly delivered to the GOC by his native gardener. About half-an-hour later Nunneley landed at Risalpur to be met by the Orderly Officer and Orderly Sergeant with orders to escort him to the CO. The GOC was not impressed with the message and had 'phoned Risalpur while the Wapiti was still in the air. Sergeant Nunneley was duly 'de-briefed'!

Social life on the Squadron was well organised and sport was a popular pastime with all ranks. Cricket, rugby, football and hockey were regular inter-squadron sports between 11 Squadron and 39 (B) Squadron. The station also had a fine set of tennis courts. The officers paid for, and built, a swimming pool near the Officers' Mess and the airmen, ever keen to keep in step, used the Reserve Water Supply as a pool! Officers had to serve five years in India before they were eligible for posting elsewhere, and so great attention was paid to making life as comfortable as possible. All ranks had Indian bearers to do chores, which included being brought tea in bed. The Squadron even formed its own dance band which performed at functions in the Messes, and also achieved distinction by frequent appearances in the glittering ballroom of Government House at Peshawar.

In January and February 1931 an enquiry was held by the Frontier Defence Committee to review the effects of air power on the problem of frontier defence and to consider proposals put forward by the Air Staff in a memorandum entitled 'What air control means in war and peace and what it has achieved.' Although this history concerns only 39 Squadron, the enquiry is worth looking at as it provides a useful insight into how the Air Staff, the Army, the Political Agents and the Government of India viewed the campaigns of 1930 and how they saw the future of RAF India. As a preliminary to the enquiry a lengthy questionnaire was sent to all interested parties as a basis for discussion.

Extracts of the questionnaire from the section on the Royal Air Force are included below:
80. Do you consider that the advent of air power has altered the tribal problem in a very marked degree?
82. What in your opinion are the advantages and disadvantages of the air weapon in comparison with troops.
    a) for the defence of the district border; and
    b) for offensive operations in tribal territory?
83. Do you consider that the use of the air weapon arouses more resentment than the use of force in other ways?
84. Are you in favour of the continued use of the air weapon?
86. Do you consider that the air arm without the use of troops for offensive purposes could force the submission of recalcitrant tribes?
88. Assume a position in which a hostile lashkar has managed to reach the district border. Do you think that without the use of troops to invade tribal territory or for purposes of offence the air weapon alone employed against the lashkar against its bases and the villages from which it comes would suffice to break it up and remove the menace?
89. Do you consider that in view of the delay usually attendant upon the concerting of a tribal rising on a large scale the immediate application of the air weapon under the direction of the Political authorities can prevent the necessary unanimity amongst the tribes from being achieved?
93. Are you of opinion that an adequately defended Scout Post provided with water supply and rations should be able to hold out successfully against tribal attack if the Royal Air Force has a free hand to take

Wapiti J9381 and J9493 on the chocks at Risal-pur, being serviced. Note the bomb carriers and bombs under the wings of J9493.

offensive action against the attacking lash-kars, their bases and the villages from which they are drawn?

94. Would the Scouts themselves be satisfied in the event of their posts being beseiged in relying on air action only without the co-operation of ground Forces?

Now before going on to consider the enquiry, let us look at the Air Staff proposals. Air Marshal W G Salmond, Air Officer Commanding RAF India, expounded the basis of the proposal of the Enquiry. The Air Staff were of the opinion that on the Frontier and in Indian Defence generally, too little account was taken of the advent of air power, and too little use made of it to save money and lives. They considered that 'air power immensely strengthens the police functions of the armed civil forces, and given certain provisions regarding its employment, can prevent tribal trouble developing into a serious menace and consequently will render the employment of mobile columns on punitive expeditions into tribal territory unnecessary.'

This was the 'save money' argument; the 'save lives' came with argument that ground troops were under increased danger from tribesmen using rifles in place of flintlocks whereas aircraft were not under threat from rifle fire.

Therefore, the Air Staff proposed that the Government of India 'should recognise that the RAF is the primary striking force to be employed

at the outset in all punitive tribal operations, under the general direction of the chief political authority concerned.' To this end, the Air Staff proposed an increase in the establishment of the RAF Frontier Force (Northern Command) of two heavy Transport Squadrons and one single-engine bomber squadron. A financial statement was included showing the cost of these proposals; however, to offset the increase the Air Staff proposed a substantial reduction in the Army element of Frontier defence enu-merated unit by unit.

A wide ranging summary of evidence was taken by the Committee, based on the question-naire plus submissions by the Air Staff and General Staff. The Air Staff quoted at length from the previous experience of similar opera-tions in Iraq on which the general conclusion had been that the chief value of the RAF from the point of view of internal security was the 'deterrent effect which their presence had exerted on the natural turbulency and lawless-ness of the population.' From this starting point a detailed analysis of all frontier campaigns since the turn of the century was made - to highlight where air-power could have made the campaign shorter and less costly in men and money. Inevitably, the enquiry degenerated into a slanging match between the RAF and the Army. Part of the Army reply to the Air Staff memorandum is reproduced below to show the 'flavour' of the proceedings! -

Mohmands 1927

35. The attempt by the Air Staff to magnify the very minor and half-hearted threat which the Faqir of Alingar offered in 1927 is ludicrous. The situation in 1927 caused so little appre-hension that it was not thought necessary even to recall General Cassels, the District Commander,

from a few days' leave, although he was within easy reach. The Faqir had no support from the Lower Mohmands, the hostilities consisting only of the Faqir's personal following of the Upper Mohmands. The lashkar was disheartened by lack of support and had no determination to fight. The R.A.F. do themselves scant justice when they say it took them 40 hours to disperse the lashkar - it bolted at the first bomb, as both the military and political intelligence had anticipated it would.

A slightly stiffer Mohmand lashkar, in 1930, proved, in the same area, that air attacks on lashkars cannot always expect this success. It is worth noting, too, that the Faqir of Alingar and other leaders of the 1927 Lashkar were amongst the first in the field against us in 1930. The effects of the 1927 air operations do not seem, therefore, to have been very durable.

Conclusion.

37. A consideration of the Air Staff Memorandum leads us to the following conclusions, confirmed by recent experience of air operations:

  (i) That so-called 'air control' would be ineffective against anything but minor and localized opposition.
 (ii) That aircraft alone are unable to guarantee the effective support to civil armed forces in tribal territory that military forces can do.
(iii) That air action by itself is of necessity purely punitive, and is, in fact, a reversion to the discredited 'burn and scuttle' policy, with the added disadvantage that it frequently inflicts casualties on women and children.

The enquiry also spent much time taking evidence from a wide range of 'interested' parties; including Political Agents, regional army commanders of regulars and irregulars and Government Officials. The general consensus was support for the Air Staff proposals and the draft report of the committee accepted this and recommended that the proposals be adopted, with a gradual increase in RAF establishment. Of more direct interest in this history is the detailed consideration of procedures for the employment of air power - such as the use of warning notices before the bombing of native villages and the psychological effect of the bombing. The Political Agents thought highly of the influence of the RAF on tribal attitudes and in their opinion the natives respected the strength exhibited by aerial bombardment. However, they supported the use of warning notices - the so-called 'Warning Ultimatum of Air Attack' which stated when bombing would commence and explained that after that date villages would be liable to attack without further warning. The villages were not

to be entered again until the tribesmen concerned had submitted, and permission was given by the Government. The notices also stated that aeroplanes must not be fired on and would retaliate at once with bombs and machine-guns. In 'normal' times (ie the months between revolts) it was the task of the Political Agents to explain the system of warning notices to the tribes.

It was very fortunate for 39 Squadron that the enquiry was so favourable to the RAF, otherwise after only one year on the Frontier the future for the Squadron could have become a little bleak!

In February 1931 the Squadron deployed to New Delhi to take part in the celebrations at the inauguration of New Delhi, the opening of the Imperial Secretariat, the Council House and other public buildings. This was the last time that the Wapiti was flown in Squadron formation for display purposes. The display area was the civil aerodrome at Safdar Jang close to the tomb of the Moghul warrior, the Nawab of Ouhd. The display started with a mock battle, which took the form of close support to a beleaguered garrison. Plenty of noise and action was provided by the use of blank ammunition, ground explosives to coincide with dummy bombs, a burning fort, supply dropping and even dummy parachutists. This, followed by an exhibition of formation flying, secured the admiration of the crowds and it was after this event that the papers spoke of 39 Squadron as 'Veterans of the Frontier'. The 'Flower of England's Youth' had become an experienced frontier squadron. On 23rd April 1931, the aircraft were given identification markings in accordance with an instruction issued by HQ RAF (India): 'Two black bands one foot wide around fuselage one immediately to the rear of the identification circle, the other immediately in front of the leading edge of the tail plane'.

All gunners of whatever basic trade were expected to achieve fourteen words per minute Morse Code but most were able to do at least twenty. This wireless recce was an important element in ground co-operation operations such as the Chitral Relief, when a ground party from the Squadron would accompany the Army units with a WT Set. It was not unknown for gunners

Opposite: **The landing ground at Gilghit, one of many remote little airfields around northern India. The photograph gives an excellent impression of how inaccessible such places were, and crews would brave appalling weather, flying up the valleys with cloud on the surrounding hills, to bring in supplies. Photograph taken in 1935.**

to send fictitious messages when on training flights as on one occasion over the Khyber Pass when the message sent was: '20 000 Russians advancing down the Khyber Pass. Request instructions.' The laconic reply came back, 'Surround them'.

Throughout 1931 the Squadron was involved with recce of various tribal areas, particularly Mohmand territory, 'In order to gain and maintain acquiescence of tribes in the passage of aircraft over their territory, and to acquire useful information of the lives of the tribesmen.' Special attention was to paid to: gatherings and movements of personnel and animals; state of crops and fields; presence of water; presence of snow during winter; weather and visibility. Such information then became the basis for planning ground and air operations, as well as being useful to the local Political Agents in their dealings with the tribes.

A major change took place on the Squadron at the end of 1931 with the Wapitis being replaced by Hawker Harts. The replacement aircraft were tropicalised versions of the Hart, designated Hart II (India), and featured low pressure tyres,

tropical radiators and desert equipment. The Hart was smaller than the Wapiti but its single 525 hp Rolls-Royce Kestrel 1b engine gave it a superior performance with a maximum speed of 148 mph at 5,000 feet and a range of 430 miles. However, normal cruising speed was 120 mph, quite a change from the 90 mph of the Wapiti. Matt Roe recalls the initial problems:- 'The extra speed meant that goggles had to be tighter; maps, log-books, and other paraphanalia had to be carefully stowed and tied. Another immediate result of the extra speed was that bombing results worsened for a while.' While most aircraft were Hart II (India), two aircraft, K3131 and K3132, were Hart Specials based on the Audax airframe. There was one Audax, K4862, on Squadron strength. Armament was the same as the Wapiti with a fixed synchronized .303 Vickers gun on the port side of the engine cowling and a .303 Lewis gun on a modified Scarff ring in the rear cockpit. The Hart carried similar bomb loads to the Wapiti with the same type of manual release. The Hart was to stay in Squadron service until the eve of World War Two. Most of the other frontier squadrons re-equipped with the Hart at about the same time and this aircraft was to prove highly suitable for the type of operations demanded of it - it was easy to handle, reliable and maintained good serviceability. The engineering requirements were daily inspections, 20-hour and 40-hour inspections, and periodic overhaul.

A handling party was sent from Risalpur to RAF Station Drigh Road to assemble the Harts which had been shipped out to India in crates. The Hart was fitted with much more effective wheel-brakes than those on the Wapiti and the first two aircraft to land at Multan, en route to Risalpur, nosed over and finished upside down; the pilots had used a Wapiti-style application of brake with unfortunate results! The crews were only slightly injured but the aircraft were badly damaged and were sent back to Karachi by rail for repair. During the years that 39 were equipped with Harts it was common for aircraft to be inter-changed between the Hart units of the NWFP, particularly between 39 and 11 Squadrons at Risalpur.

The re-equipment programme took place in November and December 1931 and the Hart was soon in action with operations against the 'Red

Front cockpit of Hawker Hart K2895, Risalpur, 1932. No.39 re-equipped with the Hart in late 1931 and this excellent, robust aircraft served the frontier squadrons well until the eve of the Second World War. Note how many of the instruments are identical to those of the D.H.9a.

Shirts' from December 1931 to February 1932. Serious trouble had broken out in the Mardan, Swabi and Nowsherra districts and the Squadron undertook reconnaissance sorties in co-operation with an Army ground force. Aircraft were also used for 'propaganda dropping', which took the form of leaflets and on one occasion, small dolls that were dressed in Red Shirt uniforms and labelled 'Red Shirt', which was the generic term given to the rebellious tribesmen. There is no record of the effect of this propaganda on the tribesmen, but as with most of these tribal disturbances, the campaign was short-lived. All

aircrew carried 'Protection Certificates', better known as 'Goolie chits', in case they were forced down in hostile territory. Safe return of the airmen ensured a reward from the Government and 'foul play' brought retribution.

When this campaign was concluded the Squadron returned to its normal training routine and the remainder of 1932 was fairly quiet. During these quiet periods, the Squadron performed the important task of obtaining high quality vertical photo cover of the border areas and large parts of the North West Frontier Province. Although 39 Squadron, along with the other bomber squadrons, spent most of its time on anti-tribal operations, it must be remembered that RAF India also existed to protect the frontiers from invasion. Both Afghanistan and Russia posed threats to the North West Frontier, and contingency plans ('Blue Plan') had been

Not a very successful landing for Hart K2122 — though this does demonstrate the robust nature of this type, as it has suffered very little damage.

drawn up for the squadrons to bomb targets in Afghanistan should such an attack materialise. The Mohmand territory was a frequent trouble-spot and operations were mounted against the area in March and September 1932. Although campaigns were usually short, their effect was often short-lived in that the tribesmen felt able to create further trouble within a matter of months. Success lay not in ending tribal disturb-ance, which were a way of life on the Frontier, but in preventing large-scale groupings of tribes-men which might present a more serious danger.

The main operation of 1932 was the biennial relief of the Chitral garrison which took place in September and October. In addition, special flights were called for as on 16th April 1932 when 39 Squadron acted as escort for the Viceroy and Vicerine of Peshawar from Rawalpindi to Peshawar: 'On 16th April three aircraft of 'A' Flt, led by the Commanding Officer, met the Avro X over Rawalpindi and escorted it to Attock, where they were joined by the remaining flights (of the squadron). The whole squadron then escorted their Excellencies to Peshawar, flying in squadron formation above and behind the Avro X. The squadron dived in salute as their Excellencies were de-planing at Peshawar.' A similar escort was provided on 21st April from Peshawar to Kohat.

From April to October each year the Squad-ron was at reduced strength as each flight took turn to spend eight weeks at the hill depot of Lower Topa in the Murree Hills. This was done mainly to allow personnel to get away from the often unbearable conditions at Risalpur in the hot season. Lower Topa was 6,000 feet up in wooded country, some twenty-five miles from Kashmir, and therefore was much cooler than the Peshawar basin. On these detachments, the mornings were devoted to lectures, drill parades, kit inspections and courses, and the afternoons to a wide variety of sport. RAF families from all over the North West Frontier went to the depot, officers by their own arrangements and airmen on training courses. This applied to 11 (B) Squad-ron as well, so each Squadron was reduced to only two flights during the summer.

Lower Topa was only one of many such depots, but was entirely RAF, the hill country within a twenty mile radius of the town of Murree being dotted with such camps used as hill stations by the Army, during the hot season. In the cool season, the depots were held in care

The hill depot at Lower Topa, Murree Hills, the summer camp of RAF India. The Squadron sent one its flights in rotation to the depot between April and September each year.

Hawker Hart, Risalpur 1934. The spinner and wheel hubs were painted different colours for the three flights and the engine cowlings were highly burnished. Note the tail trolley.

and maintenance but, before the weather warmed up in April, working parties were sent to prepare for six months of intensive use. The camp buildings were neat stone bungalows roofed with corrugated iron, with all the normal facilities of an RAF Station - except of course, aircraft. All pilots and air gunners had to complete an intensive ground training course in such topics as airmanship, navigation, theory of bombing, gunnery, aerial photography and wireless. Lectures were only a part of the course and a great deal of time and effort was put into drill and ceremonial, with a full ceremonial parade and kit inspection on Saturday mornings. All the inspections were carried out as a competition for the Bailey Cup which had been provided by a previous C-in-C RAF India. The breakdown for the station detachments was: No 1 detachment April - May, No 2 detachment June - July and No 3 detachment August - September. However, if a frontier war broke out or appeared to be imminent there would be no Summer camp, as was the case in 1930 with the Mohmand operations.

When at the depot, all work ceased at 1230 and the rest of the day was devoted to entertainment and relaxation. For the adventurous, there were ponies for hire and for two rupees a good pony could be hired for a day and a pleasant time spent riding through the beautiful forests which covered the Murree foothills. The town of Murree itself held many attractions but the RAF came under Indian Army Orders and personnel had to wear uniform with belt and side-arms when 'walking-out'. This caused problems to some as white European girls would not be seen with anyone below the rank of Sergeant. It was possible to find the company of attractive Eurasians although this was not encouraged. Some airmen solved the problem by wearing civilian clothes although this was strictly against regulations. There were a number of good restaurants but discrimination was common - for example there were signs such as 'Sergeants and Europeans only - dogs and troops not admitted' displayed outside a restaurant. For the officers there was a very active social life with a large selection of Officers Clubs, many of them Army, within a few miles of Lower Topa. Many officers went hunting for bear or panther in the local hills. All in all, the camps were considered to be light relief in the dusty existence of RAF India.

September - October 1934 saw the Squadron involved yet again with the Chitral Relief. The operation commenced on the 15th September and from then until the 10th October, the

Squadron flew regular mail-dropping sorties to the column as it wound its was slowly along the route to Chitral. However, on the 11th October the column ran into armed tribesmen on the west bank of the Pnajkora River, south of the Jandol Khwar and requested continuous air reconnaissance. Aircraft of 39 Squadron were on station from 0830 to 1730, under the control of the Column Commander. Two bombing raids were mounted in the afternoon against tribesmen in sangars on the hillsides and the column reported 'good shooting, definite results'. It was a similar story on the 12th with a recce aircraft calling up a morning raid on enemy sangars which were holding up the column. Following this action, the column continued on its march unmolested. Tribal casualties over the two days were estimated by the local Political Agent as eighty killed and wounded. This was a classic example of air-to-ground co-operation and set the scene for all the army co-operation exercises with which the Squadron was involved on the North West Frontier.

On Sunday 31st May 1935 breakfast at Risalpur was violently disrupted. Everything began to shake, cups, saucers and plates went flying in all directions. Men jumped through open windows and ran out of the doors because they recognised the signs for what they were - an earthquake. At Risalpur the effects of the quake were very minor, small earthquakes being a fairly common occurrence in this region of India. However, over at Quetta (some 300 miles south-west of Risalpur) the earthquake was far more serious and practically wiped out the personnel of No 5 (AC) Squadron and No 31 (B) Squadron who were stationed there. Hangars and barrack blocks collapsed burying airmen and married personnel. Rescue operations were soon mounted and 39 and 11 Squadrons from Risalpur, 17 and 60 Squadrons from Kohat, 20 Squadron from

Peshawar and 28 Squadron from Ambala were all involved on rescue flights. On 1st June six aircraft of 39 Squadron flew medical officers to Quetta to assist in the relief, and flew evacuee passengers back to Risalpur. The remnants of the two Quetta squadrons moved to other stations to reform - 5 Squadron moving to Risalpur and 31 Squadron to Karachi.

The favourite trouble-spot on the Frontier, the Mohmand Territory, flared up again in August 1935. This campaign, from 16th August 1935 to 23rd September, proved to be a micro-cosm of the ten years 39 Squadron spent in India, with small-scale bombing of tribesmen, leaflet dropping and demonstration flights, destruction of villages and restriction of tribal movement. Like many of the tribal disturbances, it started with a small gathering of tribesmen cutting down telegraph wires and firing on pro-Government tribesmen, this time along the Gandab road near Abazaind around Dand. Certain tribal leaders then decided to destroy the Gandab road and its Frontier Police posts and a lashkar of some 2,000 men, mainly from Burham Khel, Isa Khel Safit and Mohmands, gathered near Dand. Air operations commenced on the 16th with armed patrols flying over the insurgent area with orders to bomb any concentrations of tribesmen. When it became obvious that the area of unrest was spreading, No 1 (India) Group ordered a demonstration flight by thirty-eight aircraft over the area, and the dropping of warning notices to the effect that the Burham and Isa Khel areas 'would be bombed com-

All twelve Squadron Harts on parade for the visit of Sir Philip Sassoon, Under Secretary of State for Air, Risalpur 1934. Aircraft nearest the camera is K2120.

K2088 and other squadron aircraft at 12,000 ft above the Laworie Pass, taking vital supplies — in this case beer (!) to Gilghit. The black bands around the fuselage were identification marks carried by all aircraft following an HQ RAF India order of 1931.

mencing on the 19th and continuing until further notice with the object of forming an economic blockade of their country and forcing them to submit to the Governments' will.'

To prepare for these operations, 39 Squadron was withdrawn from the road patrols, being replaced by 20 (AC) Squadron, and on the 18th Group Captain N H Bottomley, the Group Commander, briefed crews at Risalpur on the proposed operations. Operations were divided into three phases although No 2 Wing were only involved in the first two. The object of *Phase I* was to force the inhabitants to evacuate their villages and *Phase II* to prevent them moving in the open, tending their cattle or ploughing their fields - the economic blockade. All *Phase I* bombing took place on the 19th with aircraft dropping 8½ lb practice bombs as sighters followed by 20 lb and 112 lb bombs on the villages of Kuni, Burham Khel, Lagham, Halkai Pindiala, Mazak, Maban, Charpo, Sara Shah, Kuhai, Tangi, Dajlung and Ahmadi Khor. *Phase II*, the 'blockade' commenced on the 20th with continuous armed patrols being maintained over the troublespots and crews instructed to bomb and strafe any tribesmen. Formation bombing of villages was also carried out; the 29th August being a typical day: 'Six patrols were carried out, two of which dropped pamphlets. One flight attack was made on Mulla Kallai and two aircraft commenced a photographic survey of the Black Mountain area in conjunction with political disturbances in that district.'

Operations settled into a regular routine of five or six armed patrols per day (112 lb bombs plus Lewis gun) with most aircraft dropping bombs on opportunity targets or on selected villages and water holes. In mid-September a ground force of four Brigades assembled in the Gandab valley for an advance on Nahakki pass and village to quell the revolt. At certain times during the advance of this force, the Squadron was called on to maintain an 'Offensive Flight' at forty-five minutes readiness for close support operations. However, this was never called to action and on 23rd September the Squadron was stood down when news was received that the rebel tribes had agreed to the Government terms.

1936 opened for the Squadron with a detachment, from the 1st to the 9th of January, to Singapore on the 'training and reinforcement programme.' Regular, usually once a year, squadron deployments to Singapore gave practice in long distance flying and operating aircraft away from base. At Singapore the Squadron used the range at Seletar for dive-bombing practice, using an armoured motor boat as a target, and level bombing in flight formation.

Although the foothills of the Himalayas were beautiful to fly around they also presented many dangers. Crews were often operating in excess of 15,000 feet, through mountain passes, in aircraft with only one engine - and in open cockpits. Cold was a major problem, especially when flying from the heat of the river basins into the cold mountain air and then back again to the hot areas. It is surprising, therefore, that the sickness level amongst Squadron aircrew was not very high. Not only was the cold a problem but also the frequent snow storms. On 16th March 1936 three aircraft went to Drosh (Chitral) to carry out the quarterly inspection of the landing ground and to carry stores to the garrison. All three suffered from icing-up of the air intakes and the consequent difficulty of maintaining engine power. One aircraft, K1417, crewed by Flight Lieutenant G H Shaw and LAC C Germain, was forced down and crash-landed at Krappa on the Bin river. Shaw ordered his gunner to jump when the engine failed and thick cloud obscured the ground. Unfortunately, Germain's parachute released before he could leave the aircraft and he became entangled; he resumed his seat to await the now inevitable

51

crash. The Hart was wrecked by the crash but the crew suffered only slight injuries and were rescued and helped by the local Political Agent. The next day, the Risalpur medical officer collected the crew by car and took them back to Risalpur. Later, the aircraft was dismantled and moved to Dir, 18 miles away by native labourers.

Part of the training routine included 'Group Collective Training Exercises', designed to 'gauge' the efficiency of Bomber Flights and Squadrons in their ability to fulfil the roles allotted to them in peace and war, and particularly to test:
1) The ability of Squadron and Flight Commanders to navigate accurately under difficult conditions and time attacks accurately.
2) Accuracy of bombing after long flights.
3) The effectiveness of refuelling and re-arming arrangements at Arawali.
4) The ability of Squadron and Flight Commanders to interpret instructions rapidly and issue effective oral and written orders.

A typical exercise would include level and dive bombing by single aircraft, plus flight and squadron formation bombing. Like the Singapore deployments, these exercises were held once a year on average and kept the Squadron on its toes. Throughout the year crews, especially new crews, trained in the 'Arawali procedure' - ie, refuelling and re-arming at Arawali. After refuelling, aircraft usually flew on to the Kohat bombing range, to drop a few practice bombs.

The summer of 1936 saw 39 Squadron in action with a demonstration flight on 20th June over the Jalkoti area. The political authorities had ordered the Jalkoti to report on the 7th July and it was thought that they might not turn up. However, the demonstration flight had the desired effect and no trouble developed. A similar small scale operation took place in October when three aircraft (8th October) flew a recce and demonstration over Asil country because of a deterioration in political relations with the Asils.

Another of the regular elements of training was Squadron deployments to RAF Drigh Road (Karachi) on Armament Training Camp (ATC). From 23rd January to 4th February 1937 the Squadron was at Karachi, flying training sorties: level bombing against moving targets, and air-to-air gunnery. Over this period nine crews completed the course in air gunnery and individual bombing, and six crews in flight bombing.

In March 1937 the Government decided to punish the Macha Khel, for causing disturbances and unrest, by destroying the village of Raghazi Khel - on the left bank of the Tochi River, about eight miles from Miramshah. The destruction of the village took two days, during which six raids were flown and over 9,000lb of bombs dropped.

However, the disturbances continued to spread in Waziristan and Mahsud country. The Squadron took part in a demonstration flight over Razmak area on the 8th April, but the Government decided that action was necessary and ordered the destruction of the village of Dalta Khel; bombing by 'A' and 'B' Flights on the 19th April began the destruction. Aircraft refuelled and re-armed at Arawali and each Flight flew two more raids, some aircraft taking vertical photographs. Further raids on the following two days completed the destruction, some aircraft dropping incendiary and petrol bombs to set fire to the tinder-dry houses.

The remainder of 1937 was reasonably uneventful although on the 9th September Squadron aircraft were tasked to bomb Laswandi village.

The 1938 Combined Operation Exercise took place in early February with the exercise briefing taking place on the 1st February at Tengah (39 had been in Singapore since mid-January and moved to Tengah on the 27th

Airfields quickly become lakes when subjected to heavy rain. Note the cockpit covers.

A classic picture: the lone flyer against the back-drop of the wild but beautiful scenery of the Himalayas. The extreme cold was a major problem in the open cockpits of the Harts.

January). During the two days of the exercise, the Squadron flew a number of fighter patrols plus bombing attacks on Naval vessels, the principal target being HMS *Dorsetshire*. Dive-bombing attacks were delivered in formation, with up to nine Harts diving at the target!

In April 1938, 39 Squadron deployed to Miramshah to counter disturbances in the Badar Algad and Maintoi Valley areas. On the 18th three aircraft flew a reconnaissance of the villages to be destroyed: Ghundakai Giga Khel; Pondia Khel; Sperewani Giga Khel; Torzhawar and the villages at 646088. Intensive bombing began the next day with 'A' Flight bombing the first two villages, 'B' Flight the third, and 'C' Flight the last two. This campaign of bombing continued up to the 24th April, with aircraft also flying 'blocking' missions within the prescribed area. Following the normal practice of issuing the tribes with a warning order that operations were to begin, a prescribed area was defined and anything within that area after the date set by the Government was considered hostile. Thus aircraft were free to open fire at anything within the area or block; these missions became known as 'blocking'. Operations in this area continued until 18th May. In the meantime the Government had decided to punish the Madda Khel

tribes for not controlling the Faqir of Ipi who was a notorious inciter of rebellion against the Government, and was living in their territory. 39, 11, 27 and 60 Squadrons were tasked with bombing villages while 5 Squadron from Arawali flew blocking sorties. 39 Squadron ceased operations on the 22nd and returned to Risalpur the next day. However, after two quiet months, the Squadron was back in action again from the 2nd to the 26th August bombing targets in the Ahmedzai Country, west of the Kurran River. In September the Squadron was again at Miramshah, this time operating in the Mami Rhoga area (12th-15th September). The final operations of the year took place from Miramshah against the Madda Khel for continuing to give sanctuary to the Faqir of Ipi but as usual, this was only a short campaign (4th-8th December).

Although in early 1939 the Squadron was again involved against tribal disturbances, by early summer it was apparent that war against a major power was becoming a distinct possibility. At the same time, news arrived that 39 Squadron was to convert to the Bristol Blenheim in May/June and would then probably move to Singapore.

The Squadron had been a frontier defence squadron for ten years and during that time had taken part in innumerable anti-tribal operations. The effect of the air control policy may be debatable but bearing in mind the almost continuous history of tribal disturbances in the region since the late 19th Century, it is fair to suggest that the use of air power in place of and in support of ground forces helped to contain tribal revolts. For ten years 39 Squadron played a major part in this policy.

4

Welcome to the Desert

By June 1939 the Squadron had received its full complement of nine Blenheim Mk.1 aircraft, along with a substantial change-over of personnel, although very few of the newcomers were experienced on the new type. The short-nosed Blenheim Mk.1 was the first monoplane operated by 39 Squadron and was a major advance on the old Hart which was some 100 mph slower. The Blenheim was powered by two 840 hp Bristol Mercury VIII engines giving a maximum speed of 260 mph, although normal cruising speed was only 200 mph. Armament consisted of a single .303 Vickers in a dorsal turret with a fixed .303 firing forward; and the standard bomb load was 1,000 lbs. The aircraft allocated to 39 Squadron were finished in standard brown/green camouflage and were given the squadron identification code letter 'XZ'.

Very little time was available for crews to work up on the aircraft at Risalpur as Warning orders were received for a move to Singapore, to strengthen the defences of that vital port. Thus, on the morning of 6th August, nine Blenheims left on the first leg of the journey to Singapore. This was to prove a disastrous flight, the story of which is told below in the words of Squadron Leader Sid Sills DFM (then, LAC Sills WOP/AG):

'The monsoons threatened but so far there had been nothing more than a slight build-up of cloud over the mountains to the North. Risalpur looked green and pleasant as the first vic, led by Wing Commander Ankers, rumbled off, each aircraft well loaded down with its normal crew of three, plus two extra groundcrew to assist on the trip, and a whole heap of spares and personnel luggage. The second vic soon followed, led by the Squadron Commander and then ours, led by the O/C 'A' Flight.

'This first leg to Ambala took only two hours and was covered without incident. Until we landed that is, when Number two on our left wanted to be different: he pulled the wrong toggle and one Blenheim finished up on its belly. A local reserve aircraft was readied and everything was switched from one to the other.

'So, three hours later, nine aircraft took off, bound for Allahabad, a three hour trip across the centre of India. The Blenheim was a fast aircraft but the monsoons were faster. By the time we reached the airfield at Allahabad it was flooded, only a series of tall pylons marking the one firm runway on which it was safe to land. The first eight landed safely and taxied off to a hard standing. Number nine landed safely but somehow got a swing on, went off the runway and over on to its back. No one was injured, fortunately, but a lot of spares and luggage got very wet. This time there was no replacement aircraft. Because of the weather conditions we stayed there for three days until a break presented itself and on August 9th off we went, eight aircraft, still Singapore bound, headed for Calcutta.

'This leg was worse than that previously experienced. The cloud was dangerously low and the rain heavy as only Indian monsoon weather could give. The Blenheim has a warning horn that sounds when a pilot forgets to lower his undercarriage and on this trip a new use was found for it. With the aircraft flying at ground level it was used to warn crossing keepers to open their gates to let us through as we followed the railway lines! We had been airborne for less than two hours when disaster struck. Lightning struck at least three aircraft. That of the Wing Commander caught fire, and although two of the passengers were able to parachute to safety, the other three died with the aircraft. A second aircraft was forced into a spin from which it recovered in such a condition that it had to be left on the ground in Calcutta in an unflyable condition. In the third, the radio caught fire, this being put out by the only extinguisher and the assistance of nature - those four cups of coffee for breakfast weren't wasted after all. And so six aircraft only were considered serviceable enough to continue and since this wasn't enough for the job in hand, a few days were spent awaiting the arrival of replacements, and patching up the rest.

'Rangoon was the next port of call, across the Bay of Bengal and down the Siamese coast.

The monsoon wreaked havoc again and once more two aircraft were lost. One, unsure of its position and running low on fuel landed in what the pilot thought was a lush green field. It turned out to be a disused tin mine twenty feet deep and all aboard had to swim for their lives. The second, quite sure of its position but less sure of its fuel landed on a beach, again with no one injured. The rest arrived safely at Mingaladon, the Rangoon airport, but all had a tale to tell of heavy rain, strong winds and a far from pleasant trip. But a week's rest - among Rangoon's night life! - and off we went, via Mergui Island to Alor Star, our first airfield in Malaya. Apart from a refuelling delay in Mergui due to a shortage of Chamois leathers with which to filter the petrol, these two legs proved uneventful, but the next morning the jinx struck again and all aircraft were forced to return after less than an hour's flying because of the phenomenally bad weather. A couple of hours wait and the clouds lifted sufficiently for the mass take-off on the last leg to Tengah - where all aircraft arrived without further incident, and not without a great feeling of relief, on August 19th. It had taken 13 days to cover less than 20 hours of actual flying time - with the loss of six aircraft and three crew'.

After this inauspicious start, the Squadron had arrived at Tengah, although within a matter of days a move was made to the civil airport at Kallang. This short move was made in formation and each vic of three aircraft did a roller at Kallang, flew out to sea to reform, circled the island and then landed. It was rumoured that this was done to encourage the locals to believe that twice as many aircraft were reinforcing the defences!

The stay at Kallang proved reasonably pleasant, the airfield being located on the edge of the town - and immediately adjacent to the 'Happy World Cabaret'. The wooden huts with banana-leaf roofing made good accommodation, although the interiors were a little spartan. So, life was comfortable and in the latter part of 1939 the war seemed a long way away. Those crews who later served in the Western Desert were to remember these months with longing.

From April to October the Squadron underwent a work-up period with the new aircraft; a programme of navigation, high- and low-level bombing, and photography. All dive bombing was done on the range at Seletar. During this time a 'show the flag' trip was made to Kuching in Borneo, a touch of light relief from the humdrum of training. Worse was to come from late October onwards when training flying was cutback to save fuel, to enable stockpiles to be built-up for operational flying. The net result of this was that crews were averaging only two trips a month, a grand total of four or five hours! To fill in time there was an extensive series of inter-service visits and ground training. Much of the latter was devoted to recognition especially of Japanese shipping, as 39's role included anti-shipping strikes. Exchange visits with the Navy had their problems, such as the time when the submarine became stuck on the sea-bed or when the minesweeper was caught in a tremendous storm! However, on the occasions when the Navy flew in the Blenheims, scores were evened! Social visits also took place, to such renowned places as the Tiger Balm factory and the Tiger Beer brewery, the latter being distinct favourite with Squadron personnel. As a sideline, the Squadron was involved in the construction of a holiday camp about 100 miles north of Singapore where crews went to relax between periods of 'intense' flying. In April 1940, the Squadron was ordered to move back to India, to Lahore. Six aircraft left Kallang on the 16th April and were established at Lahore by the 25th, where they stayed for six weeks. Whilst at Lahore, a 60-hour inspection was carried out on all aircraft by the aircrew, the groundcrew still being in transit on the high seas. The CO, Squadron Leader 'Al' McD Bowman, personally washed down all the

Blenheim I L8387 (XZ-F) at Singapore, 1939.

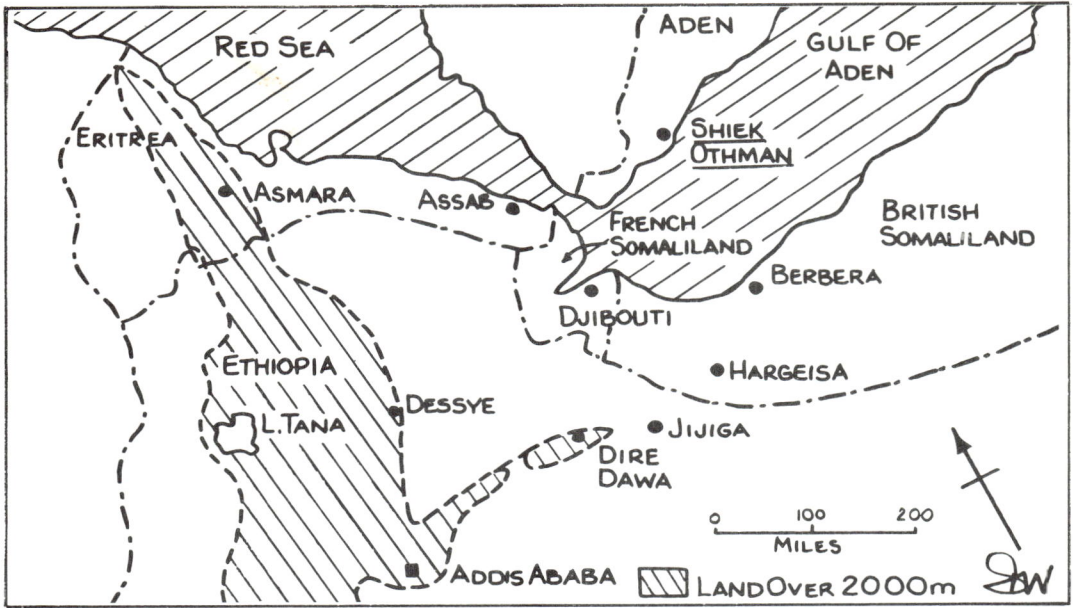

Map 7: East Africa 1940

aircraft with petrol/oil and water as he claimed to have insufficient technical knowledge to help with the servicing!

On 5th May, another move, this time to Karachi where orders were received for a further move westwards, the eventual destination to be Sheikh Othman in Aden; 39 Squadron was to be part of an air reinforcement of Middle East Command (MEC) along with 11 Squadron who had moved from Risalpur to Singapore with 39: together they were identified as No 2 Indian Wing. During the stay at Karachi, three more aircraft were added to the Squadron inventory to bring it up to the full establishment of nine. On 6th May all nine left on the first leg of the long haul to Aden. Refuelling stops were made at Jiwani and Sharjah before six aircraft night-stopped at Shaibah and three at Bahrein. They joined up the next day at Shaibah and flew on via Habbiniya, Lydda (six aircraft), Ismailia (three aircraft), and finally to a night-stop at Heliopolis in Egypt. Here the aircraft stayed for a few days for cleaning and servicing prior to the final few legs flying. All departed on the 12th to Wadi Halfa and Port Sudan; finally reaching Sheik Othman the following day after refuelling at Kamaran Island.

When 39 Squadron arrived in Aden, the Italians were still not at war so the Squadron settled down into a training routine of navigation, bombing and gunnery, as well as taking part in exercises with the Navy and the French Army and Air Force. Servicing was done by the air-crew and groundcrew borrowed from other units until, at last, the Squadron groundcrew arrived in the SS *Khandallia* after their long journey across the Indian Ocean. It was June 10th and a great party was arranged to celebrate the reuniting of the Squadron. However, the party had only just started when the CO was called away; he returned a few minutes later with the news that the Italians had that day entered the war. Thus, with everyone in reflective mood, the party came to a halt as duty rosters were organised and final preparations made for the coming hostilities.

At this time the Italians had 200,000 troops in Eritrea and Abyssinia as against 9,000 British and allied troops in the Sudan and 9,000 in Kenya. However, the Italians were heavily committed in trying to hold down Abyssinia. Nevertheless, in July the Italians occupied Kassala (twelve miles inside the Sudan) and in August they moved into British Somaliland, the defenders of which were eventually evacuated from Berbera. Meanwhile, British forces had been built up to 75,000 men in Kenya and 28,000 in the Sudan and Churchill ordered attacks to be launched from Kenya at the earliest opportunity.

As part of both defensive and offensive operations, 39 Squadron, along with the other allied squadrons, provided vital air support. Thus, for

39 Squadron, Singapore 1939. A pleasant social environment with crews flying only four or five hours per month because of fuel conservation measures.

39 Squadron re-equipped with the Blenheim I in 1939 and later in the year had a disastrous flight from Risalpur to Singapore, losing six of its nine aircraft en-route. The sojourn in Singapore to 'strengthen the defences' did not last long and the Squadron moved to the Middle East. Note cockpit covers and Squadron code letters 'XZ'. (Tom Perkins)

most of the latter part of 1940 the Squadron was involved with raids in indirect support of land forces and on reconnaissance missions against enemy airfields and ports. The majority of these raids were by single aircraft or flights of three and it was very rare for the whole Squadron to take part in one operation, although in the early phase of operations a number of Squadron raids did take place.

39 Squadron's first operational sortie of the war took place on the 12th June when seven aircraft attacked the airfield at Diredawa in Abyssinia. Three of the Blenheims made dive-bombing attacks on the hangars and munitions dumps whilst the other four made high-level bombing runs. The results were not spectacular

but a number of hits were made on the munitions dump and the railway station adjacent to the airfield. The only response from the Italian defences was desultory light AA fire which caused no inconvenience and no casualties. The Squadron's first raid had been a success although the damage caused had been light. The above details are paraphrased from the raid report submitted by the Squadron Commander; fortunately however, Sergeant Sid Sills (who was later to be awarded the DFM after more than fifty sorties with 39 Squadron) remembers the occasion clearly... 'It was the 12th June that 39 became fully operational. The first briefing took place the same evening and crews were told of their first target, Diredawa, one of the largest airfields in Abyssinia. The CO told everyone of their expected roles and then all aircrew went to their aircraft to load the bombs. Most aircraft were loaded with four 250 lb and four 25 lb (anti-personnel) in the bomb bay and on the external fuselage bomb racks; a full complement of ammo was placed in the aircraft for the WOP/AG, while the single Browning in the wing received similar treatment. Then all went to bed to await the 6 am call.

'My aircraft, Blenheim 1, L8384, piloted by P/O White and A/C Wright as WOP/AG, had been detailed to carry out a low-level dive-bombing attack on the Diredawa petrol dump, so we took off in the second vic of aircraft, joined in open formation at 14,000 ft and set a direct course to the target. This took us across the Gulf of Aden, crossing the Somaliland coast a mile or so South of Djibouti, and then across the wild territory of Abyssinia. It was not a long flight, only about 1 hr 50 mins, so that we arrived over Diredawa at breakfast time - in the hope that the station would be unprepared and have no aircraft airborne.

'And so it was. There was no sign of life as the first vic dropped its bombs from 14,000 ft, and as the smoke and dust rose from their strike our vic made its shallow dive, aiming at the clearly marked petrol dumps. On the pilot's 'now' we released the bombs in a short stick at about 2,000 ft - the front gun could be heard chattering away. The aircraft began to lift because of its reduced weight, and as we flew low across the airfield, we could see people running hither and thither, confused. Turning through 180 degrees we flew back across the main buildings with front and rear guns firing until we passed the airfield boundary. Then we climbed to about 10,000 ft to rejoin the formation for the return to Aden where we landed some 3 hrs 50 mins after take-off.

'The whole episode had been no more testing than a practice bombing sortie because there had been no enemy intereference; no aircraft attacked or came to meet us. Nevertheless, it had been an interesting experience and we considered ourselves lucky that surprise had been achieved.'

During the night Italian aircraft made three raids on Aden, including Sheikh Othman, but caused very little damage. Italian bombing raids on Sheikh Othman became fairly common in the next few months and usually took place at 11 pm, with effects that were often spectacular but ineffective. A number of air raid shelters were built, consisting of a six foot deep trench with a corrugated cover raised six inches above the lip of the trench, wich a single layer of sandbags on top of the cover. Tom Perkins recalls these shelters: 'There were a great many Arab labourers at Sheikh Othman and it was their habit to leap into the shelters - with their dogs - as soon as the air raid siren sounded, and hence the shelters became very crowded and uncomfortable. Thus it became squadron practice to stock up with beer and sandwiches when the canteen closed at 1030 pm and then sit on top of the shelter, in comfort, watching the raid take place.'

A single aircraft raid was made on the 13th June against the airfield at Assab; two 250 lb bombs were dropped on a group of aircraft destroying one and damaging four others. By now the Italian defences had improved and a raid on Diredawa a few days later met a hot reception from heavy but inaccurate flak. The formation made a dive-bomb attack from 10,000 to 6,000 feet but results were not observed. As Diredawa was one of the main Italian airfields it received a great deal of attention from 39 and other squadrons. So far very little had been seen of Italian fighters but another Diredawa raid, on the 24th, was intercepted by Fiat CR.42 fighters which attacked the formation vigorously. Blenheim L4920 dropped out of the formation and was last seen heading east on one engine. The aircraft eventually crash-landed in Somalia; two of the crew were rescued by the Somali Field Force and returned to Shiekh Othman, but the third crewman was killed. The standard evasion tactic for a single Blenheim against a fighter or fighters was for the Blenheim to open up to full throttle and dive down to sea/ground level and this manoeuvre proved remarkably effective.

Operations were continued day and night over Abyssinia and Somalia and on 15th June LAC Ford shot down a CR.42 which attacked his aircraft, one of the first victories claimed by the Squadron. More often than not the Italian fighters were reluctant to attack more than a lone Blenheim and if the Blenheim ran for it the fighters did not pursue.

The Blenheims maintained a high serviceability record, to the credit of the groundcrew, despite

By mid 1940 the Squadron had moved to Sheikh Othman, Aden to take part in the war against the Italians. Here, 39s Blenheim IVs sit in the background whilst centre-stage is a Gladiator of 94 Squadron. *(George Beckett)*

atrocious operating conditions. Sheikh Othman had very little rain but frequent dust and sand storms which created soft patches of shifting sand with the result that aircraft which had been parked on firm sand would suddenly become bogged down and neat stacks of bombs left on dispersals would vanish! No doubt these bombs are still coming to light today as the sands continue to shift!

Loading bombs under these conditions could be hazardous but as a general rule Arab labour was used for manhandling bombs. Using a piece of eight feet long timber with a hook in the middle to locate in the lug of the bomb, six labourers could easily lift a 250 lb bomb and with some difficulty could manage a 500 lb bomb. Sometimes a bystander would shout 'Agreb!' (Arabic for scorpion), at which the bomb-carriers would leap in all directions and the bomb thud into the ground next to the toes of the last man to release the timber! This led to a delay in moving the bomb as it would be some while before the labourers could be persuaded to approach the area again.

Aircraft losses were difficult to replace as the number of Blenheim squadrons wanting replacements far exceeded the number of available aircraft. However, on the 16th June, five aircraft of 11 Squadron arrived at Sheikh Othman and were attached to 39 Squadron for operational duties. This was not the first, or last time that the two squadrons worked and lived together and it was a reunion of old comrades from Risalpur. Sometime during the summer of 1940, 39 Squadron acquired a number of Blenheim IV aircraft but the Operational Record Books for this period are missing and details are not therefore available. A number of raid reports survive and these state that Mk.IVs were being used although no serial numbers are given.

On 15th July, six aircraft, four from 39 and two from 11 Squadron, attacked a hotel in Diredawa which was being used by high-ranking Italian officers. The first flight of aircraft ran in and straddled the hotel nicely with their bombs, but unfortunately the second formation released early and their bombs dropped near a hospital - luckily causing no damage. Diredawa was the target again on the 22nd with three aircraft attacking the airfield area. On the return trip one aircraft developed engine trouble. The pilot decided that he would not make it back across the Red Sea and decided to land in French-held Djibouti. By common consent, all three aircraft landed, to be met by the French garrison who then supplied the crews with a hearty breakfast and assistance to repair the faulty engine. Regretfully time came to leave; after take-off the aircraft formed up in vic and proceeded to give the 'airfield' a farewell 'beat-up'. In the middle of this, they noticed a large military convoy approaching the airfield, which, much to the consternation of the crews, fired on the Blenheims! Suitably chastened, they flew back to Sheikh Othman to report the incident. It was later learnt that the convoy had been Vichy French on its way to take control of the airfield at Djibouti. A few minutes longer over breakfast and the three crews and their aircraft would have been captured.

The operations log for 22nd July contains a very serious note: 'Beer ran out today in the Airmens canteen, as it has already done in the Officers and Sergeants Mess. The Command reserve of beer is now exhausted and it is reported that we shall have to wait some time for a new shipment!' In the dusty, dry conditions of Aden, beer was a vital commodity and far superior to the local water - hence the very sincere note of woe on the demise of supplies.

In July the Squadron flew 136 hours on forty-seven operational sorties which included shipping reconnaissance plus a number of attacks on troop concentrations and convoys; the latter operations often flown in company with Gloster Gladiators of 94 Squadron from Sheikh Othman.

Co-operation with the Gladiators was not always good, as on the 8th when a lone Blenheim was set upon by two Gladiators but fortunately no damage was caused. By the 7th August, 39 Squadron was reduced to seven aircraft but two of these, plus crews, were transferred to 11 Squadron to give both squadrons a strength of five aircraft. Therefore, 'A' and 'B' flights were combined into a single flight of five aircraft, which also had a 'part-share' of three aircraft of 8 Squadron which were used as a training flight for new pilots and air-gunners.

The following report illustrates the period: 'Flight Sergeant Thomas was pilot of the third Blenheim of a flight detailed to carry out a dive bombing attack on a gun position which was giving a lot of trouble to our troops holding Tughargan Gap. During his dive, Flight Sergeant Thomas saw an enemy fighter attack his leader. He released his bombs and pursued the fighter, which quickly manoeuvred and delivered a frontal attack. During this swift attack by the fighter, Flight Sergeant Thomas's Air Observer, Sgt 'Tubby' Hogen, was killed and he himself received a 12.5 mm explosive bullet in his right shoulder, rendering his arm useless. He managed to avoid further attacks from fighters and, using his handkerchief to stem the flow of blood, he set course for Berbera 40 miles away. Having his right arm useless he was unable to operate the undercarriage and flap control levers. He attempted to make a landing with the undercarriage retracted. The landing was successful, doing very little damage to the aircraft, It is estimated that he had been flying in this condition for 20 minutes and when he landed his body was cold from loss of blood. His Air Gunner, who had remained at his post to beat off further fighter attacks was unaware that his pilot and air observer had become casualties, until they landed. By this superhuman effort, Flight Sergeant Thomas saved the lives of his air gunner and himself, thereby setting a high example of courage and determination to all.' Thomas was subsequently awarded the DFM.

At the end of August, intelligence reports were received that Arab dhows were massing in Assab harbour, and it was feared that they might be used to ferry a large armed force across the Red Sea to attack Aden. To prevent too large a concentration of dhows, and to impress the natives with the might and power of the British, it was decided to use the squadrons in Aden to conduct a one day intensive bombing campaign of Assab and its environs. Thus, from one hour after dawn to one hour after dusk on the 1st September, twenty-four raids were flown by the Aden squadrons, including six by 39 Squadron. As attacks were made from high level results were difficult to observe; however, reports were later received that a great many of the natives had left with their dhows rather than risk a repeat bombing.

Throughout September and October the Squadron continued day and night operations against Italian positions across the Red Sea, as well as anti-submarine and shipping patrols along the Red Sea. The 200 mile stretch of water between Sheikh Othman and the Italian-held areas, claimed many a Blenheim which was trying to limp back to base on one engine; however, the Blenheim proved very reluctant to sink. On one occasion in August 1939 an aircraft was forced to ditch after shrapnel had severed a fuel line. The pilot was able to put the aircraft down alongside HMS *Ceres* and the crew were picked up before they had a chance to get their feet wet! The aircraft then floated for over thirty minutes and a great deal of equipment was salvaged from it; meanwhile, the crew were well entertained by the Navy.

A major change in the fortunes of the Squadron came on 23rd October when 39 was given a Mobile War Establishment of two Flights, sixteen aircraft, thirty officers and 374 airmen! However, the reality was somewhat different to the theory and aircraft strength remained at three or four operational airframes. The designation 'Mobile' meant that the Squadron could expect and must be prepared for, short notice moves.

In October the CO, Squadron Leader Al McD Bowman, was awarded the DFC: 'This officer had led 11 most successful raids into enemy territory. Once, when one of his bombers was crippled and being attacked by fighters, he succeeded in beating off the attack, thereby allowing the crippled bomber to reach British territory. He successfully organised and carried out an attack in conjunction with fighter aircraft which destroyed 3 petrol dumps and a large ammunition dump in Macaaca...

'This officer has shown great determination and zeal in leading his Squadron, by day or night on bombing raids, thereby installing confidence and setting a courageous example of leadership. By his untiring efforts and example his Squadron has upheld the lead set by him and have gained many successes against the enemy.'

In November, 39 Squadron was ordered to proceed to Egypt, re-equip with new aircraft and transport and become fully mobile by the end of January 1941. This notification arrived on the Squadron on the 24th and on the 26th the CO issued a Movement Order for the Squadron to move to Egypt 'at an early date.' There were only four aircraft fit to fly in the air echelon (L8385, L1498, L8612, L8384) and the remainder of the Squadron air and groundcrew were to be transported by sea. Three aircraft left Sheikh Othman early on the morning of the 29th November for Port Sudan, via Kamar, an island staging post. The fourth aircraft had been delayed by engine trouble but joined the formation later the same day at Port Sudan. The following day all four continued the journey, night stopping at Wadi Halfa then flying on to Helwan on the 1st December. The original intention was for 39 Squadron to stay at Helwan while it built up to full establishment of aircraft, personnel and equipment. However, on the 2nd December orders were received from HQ RAF Middle East that three aircraft and crews were to be detached for an indefinite period to 45 Squadron and proceed with that unit to the Western Desert for operations against the Italians in Libya. The solitary Blenheim left in Helwan was joined by the rest of the Squadron when the sea party arrived on 9th December at Port Suez.

Meanwhile, the three aircraft detached to 45 Squadron had left on the 8th for the airfield at Quattaf. On the following day two of these aircraft flew 39's first operation in its new theatre - a high altitude bombing raid on the airfield at Sollum.

On the 12th December a lone Blenheim on a decoy raid at El Gubbi was intercepted by twelve CR.42 fighters. The pilot adopted the standard evasion technique by putting the nose of the aircraft down into a steep dive and going flat out for low level. The guns on the Blenheim jammed soon after the encounter began but nevertheless the aircraft reached low level and sped off across the desert jinking violently. The fighters soon gave-up the chase, having caused no damage whatever to the Blenheim in spite of the odds.

At this time the Western Desert was littered with airfields and Landing Grounds (often just a patch of sand with one or two tents) but there was always a requirement for more, a situation which became even more pressing with a front-line that was very rarely static. Thus, one day in December a Blenheim of 39 Squadron was sent to the LG at Mersa Matruh in Egypt to investigate to feasibility of establishing a forward base there. The crew were a little suspicious when they arrived as the field was deserted, and the many bomb craters along the runway made landing difficult and the pilot had to keep swerving the aircraft to avoid these obstacles. Unfortunately, at the end of the landing run the port wheel slid into a crater and it took thirty minutes of heaving and shoving to get it out again. Having formed an adverse opinion of the place, the crew wasted no time in getting airborne again - although finding a clear path through the craters did prove difficult. Their report on their experience caused great consternation at Head-

quarters, as officially, Mersa Matruh had been abandoned and mined!

Meanwhile, the detachment at Quattaf was still conducting operations against the Italians. Principally this took the form of hit-and-run attacks on airfields to keep the enemy fighters occupied chasing elusive Blenheims rather than ground-strafing Allied troops. This policy proved very effective and losses were kept down as the Blenheims were ordered to turn and run as soon as they were interecepted and only to drop their bombs if a favourable target was found.

However, on the 9th January 1941 the detachment was recalled to Helwan and preparations were made to hand over all the remaining aircraft and equipment to 11 Squadron. On the 17th of the month a farewell party was held for 11 Squadron and the Blenheims - a sad moment as the two squadrons had been together for twelve years. Shortly afterwards, 11 Squadron moved to Crete where they were involved in the debacle that befell that island in May 1941.

39 Squadron then moved to Heliopolis to re-organise prior to receiving new aircraft and equipment. The advance party left Helwan on the 22nd and for the next few days a number of road convoys moved the rest of the Squadron. On arrival at Heliopolis the Squadron was without aircraft for a short while and was affectionately known as the '39th Regiment of Foot' while it lolled in the fleshpots of nearby Cairo. This situation did not last long because the first of the new aircraft was collected from Takoradi, Gold Coast, on the 26th - a Martin 1174 Maryland I, serial AX689. The ferry crews flew a somewhat daunting route - Takoradi, Accra, Ikeja, Kano, Maiduguri, Fort Lamy, El Fasher, Wadi Seidna, Wadi Halfa, Cairo. When France left the war rather sooner than anyone had anticipated, quite a store of Marylands, crated and uncrated, en route from America to the French forces had accumulated at Takoradi and it was some of these aircraft that were the first to be sent to the Middle East. Later, the same route continued to be used with new aircraft arriving by sea in crates or flown across the Atlantic from the eastern seaboard of South America (via Ascension Island). From Takoradi the aircraft formed into air convoys formating on a Navigation Leader - usually a Blenheim or a Bisley - for the trip to the Air Park in Egypt.

The first aircraft acquired by 39 Squadron was finished overall in blue and was quickly nicknamed *Blue Pencil* by Squadron crews. For the next few weeks this was the only Maryland on the Squadron and it was used intensively for pilot conversion. At this time, Squadron aircraft strength included a Miles Magister, P2401, used for light communications duties, and a Hawker Hind, K6826, for light communications duties and flying training. In early February all crews flew the Hind for front and rear gunnery practice and as part of a general flying refresher. During the same period all the pilots went solo in *Blue Pencil* in preparation for collecting more aircraft from Takoradi. A party left Heliopolis for Takoradi on the 15th February; the same day that the Magister crashed in bad visibility near Cairo during a cross country navigation exercise. The aircraft was a write-off but the crew escaped without injury.

Before their new aircraft arrived, the Squadron groundcrew were given the job of overhauling twelve Blenheim IVs of 55 Squadron whilst the latter were on mass leave. By the 24th, the Squadron had received four Marylands. These aircraft were originally destined for the French Air Force and thus all the instruments were all calibrated and labelled in French. This caused one or two problems initially -especially amongst the Navigators who apart from contending with fairly basic equipment also had the problem of converting the metric units to the familiar imperial. To this end conversion charts were provided alongside the equipment! Although the Maryland was basically a bomber it was primarily used as a long range high-level reconnaissance aircraft during the months its was flown by 39 Squadron. For this job a 14" focal length Williamson Camera was fitted in a vertical mounting.

The Maryland was powered by two 1,200 hp Pratt and Whitney Twin Wasp S3C4-G engines. It was capable of a modest 278 mph at 11,800 feet, but had a range in excess of 1,200 miles. For normal operations it carried a crew of four - pilot, navigator/photo, WOP/AG and lower turret gunner. Those WOP/AGs who converted from the Blenheim soon found one major difference between the two aircraft - namely, 'the superior quality of the Bendix radio installation in the Maryland compared to the British RX 1082/TX 1083 in the Blenheim. The Bendix R/T capability was outstanding even at ranges of 200 miles plus; it also had an improved D/F facility and, as many of the valves were encased in metal envelopes, it was far more rugged. The groundcrew also liked the new aircraft as it was easier to service than the Blenheim and had outstanding reliability.'

During March the Squadron continued its build-up of equipment and conversion of crews and towards the end of the month was ordered to move to Shandur in the Canal Zone. 39 Squadron was the first RAF unit to use this base and on arrival the runway was still being built although Shandur later became one of the major RAF bases of the Desert theatre. By the 28th of March the entire Squadron had arrived at Shandur.

The next two weeks were taken up with training and familiarisation which included naval co-operation exercises with units from Alexandria harbour. During this period the Squadron was built up to full strength of aircraft and crews. A number of Australian and New Zealand crews arrived to add to the truly international flavour of 39 which now included British, Australians, New Zealanders, Tasmanians, South Africans, an American and a Fiji Islander. For a time the majority of the Squadron was in fact Australian. Sadly the original Maryland, *Blue Pencil,* crashed at Heliopolis on a training sortie from Shandur killing all four crew, the first casualties with the new type.

In February, German troops had begun to arrive in the Desert theatre to bolster the Italian forces. On the 12th February an obscure German officer arrived to command these troops - Lieutenant-General Erwin Rommel. Moreover, with the German army came the Luftwaffe in considerable numbers. From mid-February onwards the *Afrika Korps* built up its strength rapidly and on 31st March Rommel attacked the Allied Forces on Cyrenaica, the latter having been weakened by troop movements to Greece. The Allies fell back and Rommel pursued; by the 9th April he had re-taken Cyrenaica and by the 12th the vital port of Tobruk was under seige. However, this particular nut would not crack so Rommel bypassed it and pressed on.

This was the situation when, in early April, a warning order was issued to 39 Squadron for the 'formation of a flight, to move into the Western Desert in the near future for reconnaissance duties.' On the 15th April 1941 four aircraft, crews and ground support party moved to Maaten Bagush satellite, which was also occupied by 55 Squadron. Operations began the following day with a high level reconnaissance of the whole of Tripolitania and Cyrenaica.

With the fall of Greece on the 24th of April the Squadron's area of operations was extended to Malta and the Aegean Islands. Sorties were usually some 5½ to 6½ hours long, which was physically tiring as there were no facilities in the aircraft for the 'necessities' of life, and with no heating it was very cold at 20,000 feet plus, furthermore, as the crew were separated from one another the only contact was by intercom.

Despite the failure of a minor British offensive in May, the situation remained fairly fluid. During this time, the Squadron was making daily reconnaissance flights over the battle area and the Mediterranean and was earning great praise from the Air-Officer-Commanding, Air Commodore Collishaw. However, the price was high: one Maryland failed to return from a reconnaissance over Derna on the 5th May and two more were lost on the 8th May.

Above: **Maryland AH284 undergoing a service at a landing ground somewhere in the Western Desert in 1941, while another of 39 Squadron's Maryland strategic reconnaissance aircraft comes into land.** *(Imperial War Museum, CM 1102)*

Below: **A Blenheim IV of 39 Squadron en route to Alexandria by road, 1941.** *(W.G. Laxton)*

Again we call on Sid Sills, to give us an insight into a typical Maryland sortie, or, as it was to turn out, not so typical ... 'On 11th May 1941 we took off from Fuka Satellite in AH298 (pilot - F/Off Sid Ault, WOP/AG - Sgt Taff Williams, A/G - Sgt Ginger Pulling, and myself as Nav) after the normal breakfast in the mobile kitchen - tinned sausages and tomatoes, thick bread and even thicker tea. We climbed steadily to our 25,000 feet operating height for the day and headed more or less due West. A different operating height was chosen each day just to confuse any possible enemy aircraft of AA. There were no nav aids in the Western Desert of over Libya so we used a mixture of known landmarks and DR navigation, checking course by a wrecked aircraft here, an unusual wadi there, and best of all the huge barbed wire fence and forts constructed by Mussolini. We aimed for the large port of Benghazi and the local airfields of Berca and Benina. It was, to quote a cliche, a normal milkrun.

'It was about 380/400 miles to Benghazi, nearly three hours flying on the chosen route, to pass Benghazi to the South and then approach from the sea and be heading for home when taking the photographs. En route, movement on the ground was being recorded, and there was plenty, mostly vehicle convoys and an occasional camel train, easily visible in the clear air. The horizon was some 140 miles ahead, making navigation easy. Everything was normal as we approached Benghazi and there was only desultory AA fire from below which appeared to have our rough direction but not our height. So I took photos of the port and recorded shipping positions. On this course we passed over the airfield of Benina and again took photos and noted that there seemed to be more aircraft on the ground than normal.

'To reach Benina we had to change course slightly but maintained height, indicated speed being 140 miles per hour. As we neared Benina it was obvious that something was happening there. We had been over the day before and there was very little activity, whereas today there must have been more than 100 aircraft on the ground, mostly Ju 52s. Over the airfield we flew, taking photos the whole time and deciding this was most important, flew back again and took more. After discussion among ourselves it was decided that something must be done, and our pilot being the only Officer aboard and therefore 'in charge' decided on attack. We flew into the desert to the East of the airfield and then descending to a height of about 2,000 feet where we felt we were hidden from the airfield defences, we circled and then with the throttle wide open we dived on Benina, choosing a line where the Ju 52s seemed to be thickest, all front guns hose-piping. For myself I could only sit and watch and I know many aircraft were hit although we saw no fires. Keeping at ground level we continued for some twenty minutes before climbing away and returned to base five hours thirty minutes after take-off.

'Subsequent events showed the Ju 52s to be part of the Crete invasion force and we were therefore, the first to see it and to bring the news back to base.'

On 12th May 'B' Flight 24 Squadron was attached from Shandur to 39 Squadron in the Desert for operational duties, thus boosting the strength of the detachment.

The military situation deteriorated on the 20th of the month when German glider-borne troops began the assault on Crete. A period of intensive reconnaissance operations followed over the new battle area as the Squadron continued its role as the 'eyes' of the AOC. The Squadron Commander, Wing Commander Bowman, shot down a Ju 52 transport early in the campaign and similar victories were claimed by other pilots during the course of the campaign. The battle of Crete was, however, a very one-sided affair and the evacuation of Allied troops to Egypt commenced on the night of 28th May and continued until 1st June. During the evacuation, 39 Squadron flew 'Fleet escort' missions an untypical role but suitable aircraft were in short supply.

At the same time the Squadron was on the move again; this time to Wadi Natrun, on the Cairo - Alexandria road, with Fuka Satellite being used as an Advanced Landing Ground (ALG). The operational side of the Squadron was based at Fuka whilst the workshops and clerical support were at Wadi Natrun.

Fuka Satellite was typical of these desert bases, with no 'hard' permanent runways, no hangars or control tower - just stacks of petrol and oil cans and tents scattered all over the place amidst the barren desert landscape. The desert wind, the 'Khamsin', made life even worse as the sand got into everything, food drink and clothing. There were also clouds of vicious flies that descended on any exposed food, making an already unpalatable diet even worse. Newcomers to the desert took quite a while to get used to conditions. Also, it was prudent to check beds and cloths for scorpions and other desert nasties.

Two more aircraft were lost on consecutive days in mid-June. However, it was not only the enemy that were proving a threat to Squadron aircraft. Due to the inability of allied fighter pilots to recognise the Maryland, a tour was made of fighter bases to give the fighter pilot an opportunity of having a close look at a Maryland - and then, hopefully, not repeating their mistakes! This tour took place on the 7th June when Flying Officer Ault took a Maryland to the Hurricane bases at Sidi Haneish, Quasaba and Gerawla. It appeared that the Maryland was being mistaken for the Ju 88, a not unnatural error when you consider the similar silhouette of the Maryland, especially from below.

The aircraft behaved well in the sandy conditions and, despite the fairly heavy losses of May/June, morale on the Squadron was high. Living conditions were reasonable with comfortable messes at the main airfields, and the bonus of relaxation on the beach of the lagoon at Maaten Bagush - each aircrew member was, in theory, meant to 'relax' there at least every third day. It goes almost without saying that this admirable arrangement very rarely worked in practice! Life was not always this comfortable, however, since the Squadron frequently found itself living in tents. This is particularly true of the period late 1941 to 1943 when the Squadron moved from place to place at frequent intervals, often operating from semi-prepared stretches of desert - and most LGs were just that, there being a great profusion of these Landing Grounds throughout the desert. The basic tent could be improved by digging out the internal area of the tent for both extra space and temperature comfort and with up to six people in a ridge tent it was important to make the living area as comfortable as possible. It was quite amazing what some people were able to achieve with the meagre resources available. Alternately scorching hot by day and cold by night, the desert was an undeniably hostile environment. George Beckett comments: 'Life in camp centred on boredom, lack of palatable drinking water (it was invariably highly chlorinated, very salty and dispensed from a bowser), monotonous rations and very basic hygiene and sanitation - especially when assailed by a bout of dysentery. Plumbing was non-existent; holes in the ground sheltered by sacking being the norm - although on occasions a rough wooden seat was provided.'

Such facilities were not to the liking of 39 Squadron and so six Yorkshire lads were provided with a 3-tonner lorry and verbal instructions to scour the desert and 'obtain' any items of furniture and such like that could be of use to the Squadron. They had been away for a week with no word and were just about given up for lost when, on the eighth day, they returned - with a lorry laden with 'obtained' items including sides of beef, live chickens, tables, chairs, crockery and cutlery; and furthermore, towed behind the lorry was the piece de resistance - a six-seater wooden lavatory (bearing the insignia of a famous Guards regiment). These items of desert flotsam and jetsam were quickly divided up in democratic fashion (and no questions asked) - two seats to the officers, two to the NCOs and two to the airmen - shortly afterwards, a number of signals flashed around the Western Desert concerning a series of 'nocturnal raids by persons not thought to be German or Italian'. Sadly, the magnificent throne later became the victim of a German bombing raid; fortunately it was not occupied at the time!

In July a detachment of three aircraft commenced operations from Burg el Arab with reconnaissance flights over southern Greece, Crete and the eastern Mediterranean. The remainder of the Squadron continued to operate from Fuka Satellite and was brought up to strength by the attachment to it of No 2 Free French Flight, commanded by Lieutenant-Colonel Du Marnier. The co-operation between the two units was outstanding and a great feeling of comradeship was built up during the months spent together. Close co-operation and camaraderie existed between 39 Squadron and 16 Squadron, South African Air Force, who also flew Marylands. At this time the Squadron was under the command of No 201 Group and was heavily tasked with a wide range of reconnaissance missions in various parts of the theatre. It was not uncommon for a single aircraft to be attached to a particular HQ for a specific operation, for instance an aircraft was once detached to Palestine to provide reconnaissance cover for operations in Syria.

During August a rest camp was established at Ras el Kancry where Squadron personnel were able to 'enjoy short periods of rest in pleasant surroundings' to lighten the burden of desert living. The idea was good but in practice the Squadron was so heavily committed on operations that personnel could only take limited advantage of the facility. However, towards the end of the month a rumour was rife that the Squadron would shortly be having a period of rest followed by re-equipment.

The rumour turned out to be partly true when, on 26th August, a number of Bristol Beauforts, plus crews, arrived from England, to also commence operations from Fuka Satellite. In the meantime the detached flights of Marylands re-united at Edku - although three more aircraft were lost in the period 23rd July to 31st August, one of which had been intercepted and shot down by eleven Me 110s. On 9th September 1941 the Squadron moved back to Wadi Natrun for the promised rest and re-equipment. The Marylands, except for a detached flight of 39 Squadron which continued to operate from Edku until January 1942, were handed over to 12 Squadron, SAAF, and 39 formally took over its new role as a Beaufort bomber Squadron.

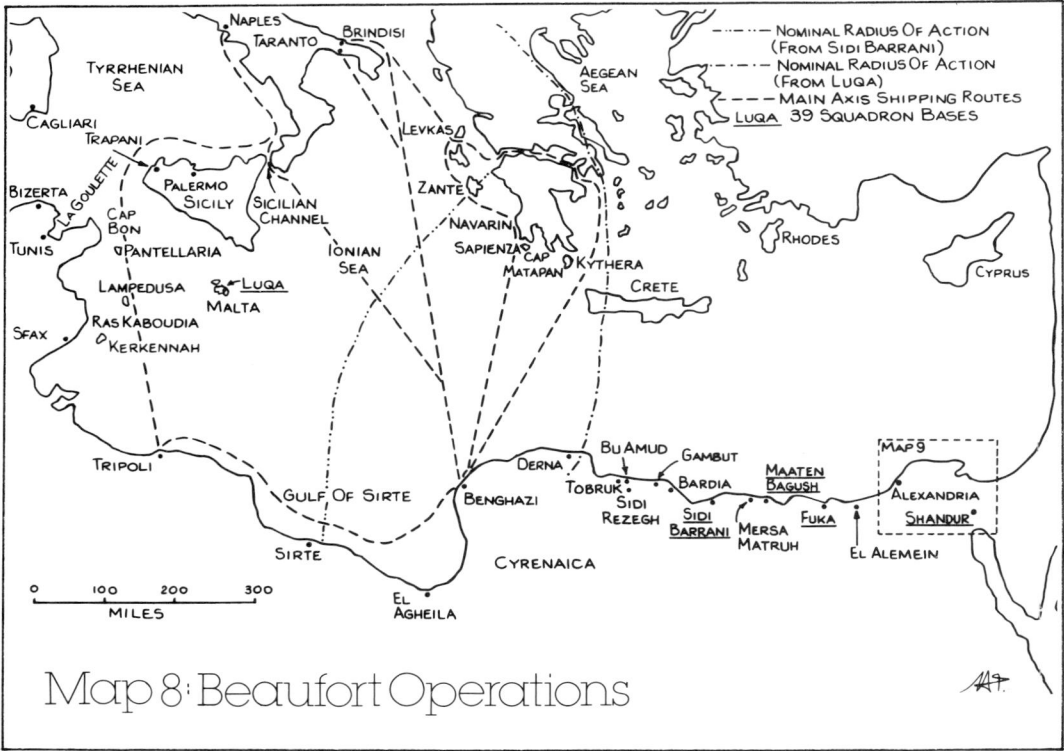

Map 8: Beaufort Operations

Legend:
- —‥—‥— Nominal Radius Of Action (From Sidi Barrani)
- —‥— Nominal Radius Of Action (From Luqa)
- ——— Main Axis Shipping Routes
- LUQA 39 Squadron Bases

Tyrrhenian Sea

Naples · Taranto · Brindisi

Aegean Sea

Cagliari · Trapani · Levkas · Zante · Rhodes · Cyprus

Bizerta · La Goulette · Palermo · Sicily · Sicilian Channel · Navarin · Sapienza · Cap Matapan · Kythera

Cap Bon · Pantellaria · Ionian Sea · Crete

Tunis · Lampedusa · LUQA · Malta

Sfax · Ras Kaboudia · Kerkennah

Tripoli · Gulf Of Sirte · Benghazi · Derna · Bu Amud · Gambut · Maaten Bagush · Map 9 · Alexandria · Shandur

Sirte · Tobruk · Bardia · Sidi Rezegh · Sidi Barrani · Mersa Matruh · Fuka · El Alemein

El Agheila · Cyrenaica

Scale: 0 — 100 — 200 — 300 MILES

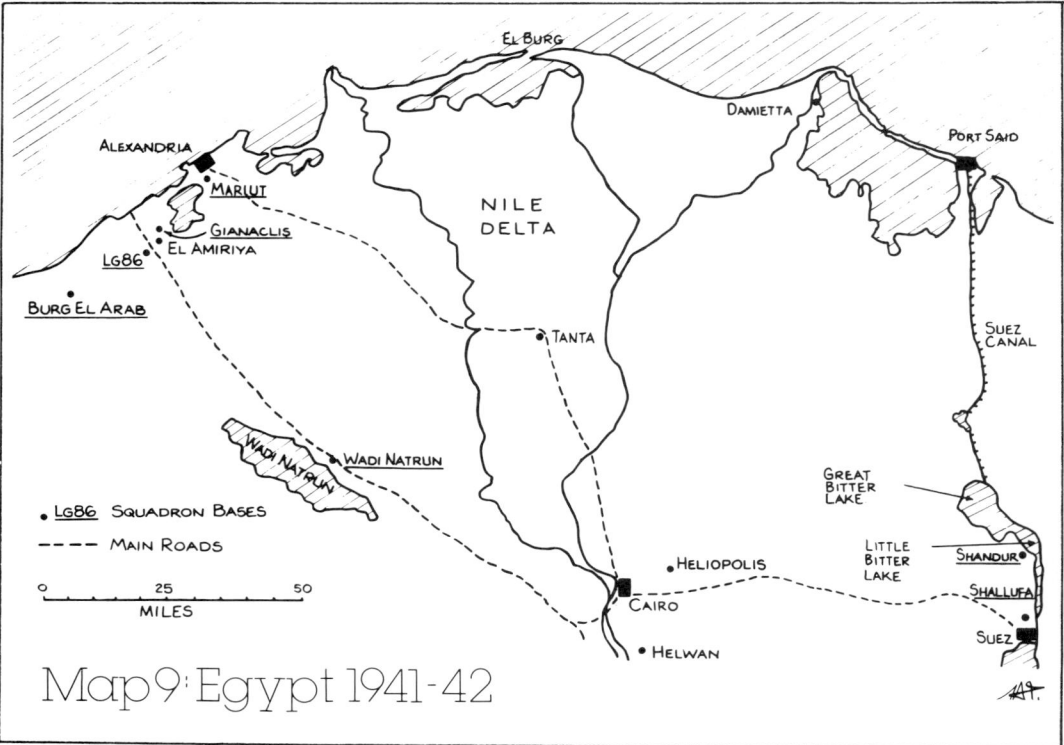

Map 9: Egypt 1941-42

El Burg · Damietta · Port Said

Alexandria · Mariut · Gianaclis · El Amiriya · LG86 · Burg El Arab

Nile Delta · Tanta · Suez Canal

Wadi Natrun

Great Bitter Lake · Little Bitter Lake · Shandur · Shallufa

Cairo · Heliopolis · Suez

Helwan

Legend:
- • LG86 Squadron Bases
- – – – Main Roads

Scale: 0 — 25 — 50 MILES

5

Beaufort Weather

The Bristol 152 Beaufort 1, powered by two 1,130 hp Bristol Taurus VI engines, was capable of a maximum speed of 265 mph at 6,000 feet and had a normal range of 1,035 miles. The range could be increased to 1,600 miles by fitting an auxiliary tank in the bomb bay, and 39 Squadron used this modification to operate at extreme range on many occasions.

During the two year period that the Squadron flew the Beaufort it was to become famous for its exploits as a Torpedo Squadron but when the Squadron was first equipped with the Beaufort they used it as a bomber, with a maximum load of 1,500 lbs, normally two 500 lb and two 250 lbs. The aircraft carried a crew of four - pilot, navigator, wireless operator (WOP) and Air Gunner (AG). Self defence armament consisted of two .303 Vickers 'K' guns in gimbals in the nose, one .303 Browning in a cupola under the nose and fixed to fire rearwards, one or two Vickers guns in a dorsal turret and two .303 waist guns. However, the armament varied from aircraft to aircraft as not all had the fixed cupola gun and some had a single gun in the dorsal turret.

Although the majority of aircrew were new to the Squadron and arrived with the aircraft during the re-equipment phase, one or two ex-Maryland crew (usually Navs or WOP/AGs) did convert to the Beaufort and most of them were not impressed. The crew accommodation was better in that there was an access corridor between all four crew members and, luxury of luxuries, an Elsan. However, the single engine performance of the Beaufort Mk.1 was a problem.

Comments from pilots vary from 'unable to maintain height on one engine' to 'we experienced trouble from the Taurus engines and performance on one engine was poor, partly due to the high air temperatures during the day.' Fortunately, the serviceability and reliability of the aircraft was good and, even more fortunate, they were capable of taking a tremendous amount of punishment and remain flying. This factor will be well illustrated in the accounts of Squadron operations in this chapter.

As many tasks involved sea navigation and shipping reconnaissance, a naval officer, 2nd Lieutenant R A R Wilson, was attached to the Squadron as a navigator/observer, but with special responsibility to teach sea navigation and shipping reconnaissance. His impression of the Beaufort: 'I flew in the Beauforts on practice torpedo attacks and considered it more dangerous than the Albacores and Swordfishes of 826 Squadron, which I had just left. The Maryland also had its moments, such as the time the pilot nose-dived to escape an Me 109 and we reached 420 mph plus!'

In early September, 39 Squadron was quickly brought up to strength and intensive training was the order of the day at Wadi Natrun. This included conversion to type, navigation and ship reconnaissance. Many of the aircrew were already experienced on the Beaufort having come from 22 Squadron and 86 Squadron, both of which had successfully operated from the UK in 1940/41 against German naval units. These operations from the UK had shown just how vulnerable the Beaufort was, and had led to a concept of operations which involved the aircraft seeking cloud cover. Over and around the UK, cloud cover could be almost guaranteed and therefore losses would be kept down to an

Crews at Mariut, 1941. Left to right: Sub/Lt Cunningham, Doc Matheson, Ken Grant, Derek Bee, Ray Matthews, Sub/Lt Wilson, Basil Bone. *(Stan Gooch)*

39 Squadron re-equipped with Bristol Beaufort I in 1941 and began a glorious but costly era of anti-shipping torpedo operations. W6519 at Fuka 1941. *(George Beckett)*

acceptable level. However, this concept of operations was not so reliable when it was transferred to the almost invariably clear skies of the Mediterranean. The irony of this situation led to the clear blue conditions of the Mediterranean being referred to as 'Beaufort weather.' What then was to be the future of the Squadron?

After the frustrations of the minor British offensives of mid-1941 in North Africa, Churchill was more determined than ever to build up the strength of allied forces there in preparation for a major offensive to drive the enemy from North Africa. This was to be General Auchinleck's *Crusader* offensive, which eventually got under way on 17th November with the intention of drawing out and destroying Rommel's armoured forces. Since June, Rommel had been suffering from, and was to continue to suffer from, a shortage of reinforcements and supplies. This was largely due to the efforts of the aircraft strike forces operating from Malta, with contributions from Egypt. Between July and November 1941, some fifty Axis ships (carrying 200,000 tons of supplies) had been sunk, causing Rommel's Chief of Staff, General Fritz Bayerlein, to comment, 'by the end of September only a third of the troops and a seventh of the supplies which we needed had arrived. This was a terrible handicap in our race for time with the British.'

The British *Crusader* plan failed and Rommel counter-attacked. However, his tank strength was low and he had no reserves whereas Auchinleck was able to feed fresh armoured forces into the battle to stabilise the situation and slowly regain the initiative. Eventually, lack of supplies and reinforcements forced Rommel to retreat and by 12th December he was back at the Gazala Line. To preserve the bulk of his forces he continued to retreat so that by January 1942 he was established at Agheila. The *Crusader* offen-

sive petered out as the Allied forces were not strong enough to continue and on 5th January an Italian convoy entered Tripoli bringing Rommel the first substantial re-supply he had received for months.

However, to return to September at Wadi Natrun. 39 Squadron, now under the command of Wing Commander R B Cox, commenced operation *Plug*. This was the code-name given to sea reconnaissance sorties carried out in search of enemy supply ships and was carried out twice a day by two aircraft flying on parallel courses. Such sorties were needed because Axis shipping was suspected of trying to avoid the aircraft based in Malta by sailing towards south-west Greece and then turning south for a dash for Benghazi. Although tasked with compiling and passing sighting reports for use in planning larger attacks, Squadron aircraft also carried out bomb and machine-gun attacks on enemy merchant vessels (MVs).

To reduce the effort involved in long transits to the reconnaissance areas a policy was implemented at the end of September of sending detachments of aircraft to operate from Advanced Landing Grounds (ALGs) in the Western Desert. As a result, for the next two years the Squadron was frequently scattered between several desert bases, and later between the Desert and Malta. On 15th October, the Squadron HQ and main base was established at Mariut and here the Beaufort element was joined by the Maryland Flight which was still heavily committed on high-level strategic reconnaissance tasks. The official reason for the move was 'to facilitate

Above: **Who says it never rains in the desert?. Pilot Officer Stan Gooch surveys the remains of his tent area, Mariut, December 1941.** *(Stan Gooch)*

Below: **A waterlogged Mariut, December 1941 and the Squadron Engineering Officer makes plans to move the Beauforts to another Landing Ground.** *(Stan Gooch)*

and increase operational efficiency by closer and more direct liaison with No 201 Group.'

Mariut thus became the Base Landing Ground (BLG) for the Squadron and from there aircraft moved to the ALGs in preparation for specific operations. During the last few months of 1941 the Squadron was using ALGs at Maaten Bagush, Sidi Barrani (LG05), Fuka Satellite and El Gubbi (Tobruk) and during November, 201 Group HQ moved to Fuka for the purpose of 'directing and controlling the operations of sea reconnaissance units.' However, in mid-December unusually heavy rains completely waterlogged Mariut and the Squadron was forced to use Aboukir as its BLG. Fortunately, all except one of the Beauforts were away at the time at various ALGs. By the end of the month, Mariut was so waterlogged that immediate evacuation was ordered as there was a danger that the dykes holding back the waters of Lake Mariut would burst and flood the airfield. The move started on the 27th December and was completed in two days - soggy equipment and tents being packed up and the unserviceable Beaufort stripped down and sent by road. The Ju 87 and the Magister managed to get airborne off the somewhat wet airfield and flew to one of the ALGs. The former had been allocated to the Squadron at the end of 1941 (November or December), being one of eleven aircraft which ran out of fuel behind Allied lines. It was allocated the serial HK 827, repainted in RAF colours, serial and roundels and flown by 39 Squadron pilots on exercises to give gunlaying practice to the naval units in Alexandria harbour. Those crews who flew the aircraft prior to it being taken off Squadron strength sometime in mid-1942, recall it as a 'basic, uncomfortable, utilitarian aircraft.'

In mid-December, Wing Commander A Mason took command of the Squadron. The strikes

from Malta, Blenheims by day, Swordfish and Albacores by night had been so effective that it became essential for the Axis forces to neutralise Malta's striking power. Thus, in December 1941, an air armada of some 600 aircraft was assembled in Sicily under the command of Kesselring with orders to destroy Malta to safeguard Axis shipping. In early 1942 Malta was pounded heavily and enemy fighter patrols around the island made anti-shipping strikes virtually impossible. Thus, in late February the Wellingtons and Blenheims were moved to the Middle East and the stage was set for 39 Squadron to join the onslaught from North Africa..

January 1942 saw the departure of the last Maryland, to 203 Squadron, and the introduction of a new role for 39 Squadron with the start of torpedo training. At the beginning of the month, 'B' Flight went to Shandur for a torpedo familiarisation course while 'A' Flight continued the task of sea reconnaissance until their turn came for conversion. The torpedo used, and which was to be the main weapon of the Squadron of the next two years with Beauforts and Beaufighters, was the British Mk.12 torpedo which weighed a basic 1,505 lb plus 445 lb of TNT in the warhead. Designed as a naval weapon, it was not intended for air-dropping, but nevertheless proved effective in this mode of delivery. The normal setting of the torpedo was forty knots for ranges up to 1,500 yards, or twenty-seven knots up to 3,500 yards - although these latter parameters were seldom used. Running depth was preset and detonation was either magnetic or contact. The usual height for a drop was 75 feet ($\pm$15 feet) at a speed of 140 knots (-10 or +20 knots) and in level flight

En route by road to Aboukir. Note the Stuka in the background. (W.J.Laxton)

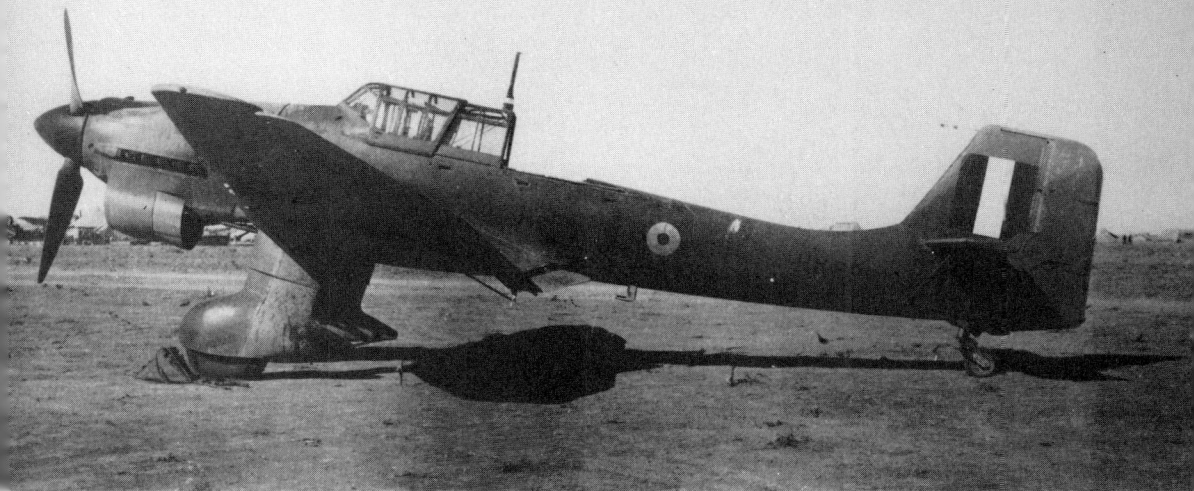

Airworthy captured Ju87 (Stuka) in livery of the RAF. This aircraft became the 'property' of 39 Squadron RAF and was frequently flown by pilots of 39 Squadron, whilst stationed at Lake Mariut LG for gun laying practice by Units of the Royal Navy in Alexandria Harbour, Eygpt, 1941. *(G.W.Beckett)*

$\pm 2\frac{1}{2}^{o}$ - rigorous requirements - but the torpedo was a temperamental weapon and required accurate delivery. Such accuracy had to be achieved while considerable judgement of target range, heading and evading action was also required and so it was generally considered that eight or nine simultaneous drops were needed to ensure a single hit.

On 29th January, 'A' Flight had commenced its programme of torpedo training at Shallufa. This took the form of low flying practice over and around LG86, a favourite area for off-duty Squadron personnel to go snake hunting, followed by dummy torpedo attacks against Nelson Island in Aboukir Bay and against RN destroyers and minesweepers. Hand-in-hand with the flying side of the course went a series of lectures on tactics and ship reconnaissance. Having concluded that one could not rely on 'the inevitable cloud', some discussion on tactics was necessary. Approaches to targets were to be made at ultra low level since flying at wave-top level had its own dangers - especially with a flat sea surface giving a poor horizon. On the final run-in, the aircraft was to be climbed to the minimum acceptable torpedo release height (60 feet and the drop made at 1,500 yards) The aircraft was then to be held down as the ship loomed larger and larger until, at the last moment, execute a quick hop over the superstructure and

flash away down on the wave tops at the far side - at the same time hoping to see a tell-tale smoke and water column from the victim, scanning the sky for other members of the formation - and any sign of the inevitable opposition in the shape of Me 110s and Ju 88s. A great many of the pre-planned strikes were intended to have an anti-flak and anti-air escort of Beaufighters but in practice this frequently failed to materialise for one reason or another. On the occasions that the Beaufighters were present, the anti-flak aircraft flew in before the torpedo Beauforts and beat hell out of the escort vessels in an effort to reduce the barrage facing the Beauforts during the vulnerable dropping phase.

This then was the tool with which the Squadron, in co-operation with the other anti-shipping squadrons of Middle East Command, approached the task of denying supplies to the *Afrika Korps.* The first opportunity soon came. On the morning of 23rd January, a Blenheim of 203 Squadron sighted a large convoy making a dash for Tripoli and passed the details to the force which had been assembled at Berca Satellite, Benghazi, to attack such convoys when they came within range. The strike force consisted of Blenheims of 5, 11 and 14 Squadrons, Albacores of 826 Squadron and three torpedo-carrying Beauforts of 39 Squadron. The force was scrambled and, on locating the convoy, the Beauforts (piloted by F/Lt Taylor, P/O Grant and P/O Jepson) led an attack on a large MV - the 14,000 ton liner *Victoria,* described by Count Ciano 'as the pearl of the Italian merchant fleet.' The convoy was made up of MVs strongly escorted by battleships, cruisers and destroyers making some twenty-thirty ships in all. Although an intensive flak barrage was thrown up on all sides, the Beauforts held their course and dropped their torpedoes from 1,500 yards. All were seen to be making good tracks and a dense column of smoke was seen to come from the liner, indicating at least one hit. Thus crippled, the liner was attacked again later on the day by the Albacores of 826 Squadron and a number of Wellingtons. A reconnaissance of the convoy the following day showed the liner to be missing - presumed sunk, for which 39 took some of the credit.

During February, both Flights continued their work-up in the torpedo role with particular emphasis being placed on formation attacks. On the 13th, seven aircraft were sent to the ALG at Bu Amud, just behind the front line, in preparation for a strike on an escorted tanker. On the 16th a search was made for the vessel but it was not sighted and the Beauforts returned to base the following day. Between 20th January and 9th March Squadron strength had been supplemented by the attachment of a number of crews from 47 Squadron. The following extract from the log book of Sergeant A J Coles typifies a 'training' month:

EXTRACT FROM THE FLYING LOG BOOK OF SGT A.J.COLES

Date	Hour	A/c type & No.	Pilot	Duty	Remarks (including results of bombing, gunnery etc)	Flying times Day	Night
1.2.42	1205	Anson AX270	P/O Papas	Pass	Base - A/S Patrol - M. Bagush - Base	5.20	
2.2.42	0800	Beaufort W1094	P/O Sanderson	W/Op	Dummy torpedo attacks	0.55	
4.2.42	0815	N1165	P/O Sanderson	W/Op	Formation Torp attacks - Nelson Island	1.30	
5.2.42	1625	N1035	P/O Sanderson	A/G	(Local) Formation attacks - port engine u/s	0.15	
6.2.42	1030	W1165	P/O Sanderson	A/G	(Local) Formation attacks, with F/O Gooch	1.00	
6.2.42	1535	N1035	Sgt Harvey	Pass	(Local) Formation attacks, with F/Lt Beveridge and Sgt Elliot	1.00	
9.2.42	0845	N1035	P/O Sanderson	Obs	Dummy torpedo attacks - Nelson Island	0.45	
9.2.42	1055	W1094	P/O Sanderson	W/Op	(Local) Formation attacks with F/Lt Beveridge	1.20	
9.2.42	1525	W1094	P/O Sanderson	A/G	(Local) Formation attacks with P/O Warton	0.35	
10.2.42	1400	W1094	P/O Sanderson	W/Op	(Local) Formation attacks with 'A'+'B' Flights	1.15	
13.2.42	1410	W1094	F/O Gooch	A/G	Air Test	0.25	
16.2.42	1125	W6519	P/O Way	W/Op	Local flying in Delta area	1.05	
21.2.42	1510	W6495	P/O Sanderson	W/Op	Base to Sidi Barrani (with torpedo)	1.55	
23.2.42	1450	W6495	P/O Sanderson	W/Op	Sidi Barrani to base (with torpedo)	1.30	
24.2.42	1240	W6495	Sgt Harvey	A/G	Practise torp attacks on 3 cruisers, 6 destroyers	1.50	
26.2.42	1000	W6495	P/O Sanderson	W/Op	Base to Dekheila	0.30	
26.2.42	1500	W6495	P/O Sanderson	W/Op	Dekheila to base	0.20	
26.2.42	2125	W6495	P/O Sanderson	W/Op	Night flying - low flying over sea		1.15
27.2.42	1100	N1035	P/O Sanderson	W/Op	Observer photographing camp with F.24	1.00	
						22.30	1.15

W/Cdr Mason   O.C. 39 Squadron

F/Lt Beveridge   'A' Flight Commander

Above: **Beauforts in their habitat — low over the sea en route to a strike. Aircraft approached the target at very low level and then climbed to 60 feet to release the torpedo. Note ASV aerial under port wing of DD906/C.** *(W.H.Armstrong)*

To make up for the inactivity during February, March was to see the first classic torpedo strike by 39 Squadron in the Mediterranean. Eight Beauforts led by Flight Lieutenant A M Taylor took off in the afternoon of 9th March to search for a convoy reported to be heading for Tripoli. At 1640 the formation located the convoy of four MVs, three cruisers and six or seven destroyers at position 3325N 01746E (approx 170 miles NE of Tripoli), steering a course of 045 degrees at some ten to twelve knots. The convoy had an air escort of three Ju 88s plus at least one Me 110. The Beauforts should have had an escort of Beaufighters but this had failed to turn up at the rendezvous and Taylor had elected to press on without it. Approaching the convoy he called the formation into line astern and commenced his attack run. He elected to make his main attack against the cruiser force which was considerably in front and to port of the main body of the convoy and therefore more vulnerable. All eight aircraft made successful drops, with one torpedo aimed at the largest MV and the other seven at the cruisers. Forcing a way through the barrage of flak, the formation emerged on the far side of the convoy - to be met by the escorting Ju 88s

and Me 110s. This time however it was to be the Beauforts' day; one Ju 88 was shot down by Flying Officer Bee's aircraft and, not to be outdone, Flying Officer Leaning's gunner damaged an Me 110. All eight Beauforts broke through the defences and flew back to North Africa, four making night landings at Bu Amud and four at Sidi Barrani. The outcome of the strike was one MV hit, one cruiser hit, one destroyer hit and possibly sunk, one Ju 88 destroyed and one Me 110 damaged - all for the cost of one Beaufort slightly damaged. The Squadron received a signal of congratulations from the C-in-C Mediterranean and Alistair Taylor was granted the immediate award of the DFC. It was very successful strike, although unusual in the small degree of damage suffered by the Beauforts.

A number of strikes were made in April and a total of 132 operational hours were flown, there was also yet another change in operational policy. Since the Squadron's Beauforts were being used for long range strikes and the range of the aircraft was insufficient for it to return to base following a strike, it was decided that in future the aircraft would fly on to Malta after a strike for refuelling and replenishment. One such strike took place on the 14th April.

Twelve Beauforts, including four of 22 Squadron, deployed to the ALG at Bu Amud on the 13th April on standby for a strike on a large convoy approaching Tripoli from the north. The following morning one of the 22 Squadron aircraft took-off to locate the convoy, shadow it and pass a position report back to Bu Amud. At noon the strike force of eight aircraft took-off and headed north in three formations, Flight Lieutenant Beveridge and Flying Officer Leaning leading sections of three and a third flight consisting of Flight Lieutenant Lander and Pilot Officer Belfield of 22 Squadron. They were

Beaufort I N1170 crash-landed at Sidi Barrani 27 March 1942. Good view of flaps. (*P. Green*)

joined by an escort of four Beaufighters, a valuable asset during the transit past the German fighter bases on the North African coast. The strike force flew on to a position south-east of Malta and then began a creeping line ahead search for the convoy, based on the information from the reconnaissance aircraft. Unfortunately, the Beaufighters had to leave the force and return to base as they were getting perilously low on fuel. Keeping low over the water, the Beauforts continued their search and sighted the convoy at 1645. The four MVs, two of 12,000 tons and two of 10,000 tons, were escorted by six destroyers on the flanks and by no less than ninety-six aircraft (Me 109s, Me 110s and Ju 88s). The Beauforts moved into attack formation, hugging the waves, hoping that they would not be seen until the last moment. Their luck was out, for as they neared the release point they were spotted by the circling fighters and waves of fighters peeled off to attack the forlorn striking force. It was a race for time and although all eight Beauforts managed to drop their torps, almost immediately three aircraft were shot down as they were swamped by fighters. Shortly afterwards, Pilot Officer Belfield's aircraft was hit and damaged; he cleared the convoy and ditched safely, all the crew took to the dinghy and were later picked up. A fifth aircraft, that of Pilot Officer Seddon, was so badly damaged that it was forced to ditch six miles from Malta. Their dinghy was useless so two of the crew tried to swim to Malta; Pilot Offficer McGregor reached a rock ledge, collapsed exhausted after his five hour swim, and was rescued the following morning. The rest of the crew were never seen again. Of the three aircraft to reach Malta, that of Flight Lieutenant Lander was badly shot up, most of the tail had been shot away and the hydraulics wrecked;

cannon shells had damaged the starboard aileron, smashed the windscreen and covered everything inside the aircraft with oil. Flying Officer Leaning and Flying Officer Gooch flew in tight formation to Malta, F/O Gooch's aircraft having sustained hits on the fuel tanks and hydraulics made the job of staying with his leader very difficult. F/O Leaning's aircraft was totally undamaged - not even a single bullet hole! This aircraft was the only one in fit condition to fly back to base.

Five aircraft lost and two badly damaged; a black day for the Squadron. Such losses in crews and aircraft could not be sustained; fortunately it was not repeated although losses throughout the Beaufort period were heavy. Shortage of crews and aircraft was a constant problem for 39 Squadron.

As mentioned above, aircraft and crews of 22 Squadron had operated with 39 Squadron during April but 22 left at the end of the month for the Far East with five of their own aircraft plus three handed over by 39. This left 39 Squadron very short of serviceable aircraft and crews and although no replacement aircraft were immediately forthcoming, among the new crew arrivals at the end of the month was an experienced Beaufort pilot who was to become a legend in the Mediterranean - Squadron Leader R P M (Pat) Gibbs.

However, since no new aircraft arrived, May was a quiet month for the Squadron and between 20th - 30th May there was an intensive refresher programme at Shallufa. Gradually new aircraft arrived from the MU until by early June the Squadron was almost back up to strength.

For a while we must move back to April to consider another change in the fortunes of the Squadron - the arrival of the Beaufort Mk.II. This was notable for two main reasons: firstly, the superior performance of the two 1,200 hp Pratt and Whitney Twin Wasp S3C4-G engines, namely the ability to stay airborne on one engine; and secondly, the more extensive use of ASV (Air to Surface Vessel) Mk.2 radar, which was eventually fitted to all the Beaufort Mk.IIs. Using yagi aerials in the wings, the ASV was quite efficient, but, as the majority of operations were flown below 150 feet above sea level, full use of ASV could not be made. Furthermore, jamming from land stations in Sicily and other Axis territory became very intense and frequently made the sets almost unusable. Overall, the Beaufort Mk.II was a great improvement over the Mk.I and proved to be a reliable aircraft with few handling difficulties.

By the end of the year the Beaufort Is (and modified IAs) had been replaced by IIs for operations and the two or three Mk.IAs on Squadron strength tended to be used only for

Beaufort DD906 with Flying Officer I McIntyre, RCAF, at the controls. (*W.H. Armstrong*)

training, communication duties and ASR. Throughout 1942 and early 1943, Squadron aircraft strength was nominally some twenty-four to twenty-six aircraft, although it was unusual to have more than twelve available at any one time. The Squadron kept itself informed of the whereabouts of Beauforts in transit through the Middle East and those at repair bases in Palestine and Egypt and thus was able to 'obtain' by various methods any 'spare' aircraft in an effort to keep up front line strength.

It was to be a feature of Beaufort operations in the Mediterranean the 39 Squadron would acquire crews and aircraft from any source at any opportunity to make good the losses on operations. Hence, a crew transiting Egypt on their way to the Far East might well find themselves co-opted into 39 Squadron and sent off into the Western Desert.

Another important role performed by the Squadron was anti-submarine patrols, the majority of which were notable only for their monotony. Some years ago an article was published claiming that no Beaufort had ever sunk a submarine whereas a submarine had sunk a number of Beauforts - the submarine having sunk a MV which was carrying crated Beauforts. However, on 14th January 1943 a Beaufort of 39 Squadron whilst on convoy protection 136 miles south-east of Malta attacked an Italian supply submarine. 'The submarine was attacked with depth charges - the Beaufort carried four for this

task - which blew its bows into the air and brought it to a halt with a list to starboard. The aircraft then carried out machine-gun attacks on those of the crew who were on deck, and when a second Beaufort arrived over the submarine to relieve the first, the crew of the submarine appeared on deck waving white garments indicating surrender. One of the convoy escort destroyers soon arrived on the scene to pick up survivors and as the submarine sank stern first, the destroyer signalled 'well done RAF.'

The importance to Rommel of each convoy can be assessed from his action following the arrival in Tripoli on 5th January of a convoy carrying fifty-five tanks, twenty armoured cars, anti-tank guns and various supplies. Not much, but enough for Rommel to think of taking offensive action. On 20th January he issued this order of the day to his troops: 'You have survived severe fighting against a greatly superior enemy, but your fighting spirit is unbroken. At this time we are numerically stronger than the enemy before us. To destroy them the Army will start to attack, today...'

He struck, and the Allied forces were caught off-guard and were forced to withdraw. By the 29th Rommel arrived in Benghazi, but since he was short of fuel and supplies, he was forced to halt and consolidate. Both sides prepared for an offensive but it was Rommel who struck first, swinging round south of the Gazala line in an offensive launched on 26th May. By 13th June, Rommel was in control of the tactical situation, and General Richie decided to withdraw his battered army to El Alamein defences on the frontier of Egypt. At the end of the month, Tobruk surrendered and Rommel stood at his high point in the desert war - on the threshold of Egypt.

When the 8th Army retreated, the RAF units also had to move back towards Egypt and by early June, 39 Squadron was back at its former base of Shandur. In their absence, much had happened to the small desert strip. The old part of the airfield had changed little but alongside was a new airfield consisting of a large conglomeration of hangars and buildings. While based at Shandur, the Squadron used the airfield at Gianaclis (LG226), on the coast near Alexandria, as an ALG. Aircraft were kept at the ALG for immediate readiness operations and were reinforced when necessary for larger pre-planned strikes.

At the end of May, the crew of a Beaufort which had been shot down near Crete in November 1941 returned to the Squadron. The three who returned were F/Lt Lenton, Sgt Cereley and Sgt Macconnici; the fourth member of the

crew, Sgt Langley, having been taken prisoner in Crete. The re-united three had joined up with the partisans in Crete and worked with them for the seven months that they stayed on the island. Lenton was awarded the Military Cross and Cereley the Military Medal for their work on the island with the partisans. Unfortunately, no further details of what they did has emerged as the information is still classified.

Meanwhile, the situation in Malta was becoming critical with severe shortages of fuel and other supplies, and it was essential that a relief convoy should break the seige. To improve the chances of success, one convoy was to be despatched from Alexandria and a second convoy from the UK via Gibraltar, with both convoys timed to arrive at Malta within twenty-four hours of each other. Fortunately, the air assault on Malta had reduced in intensity because Rommel needed the offensive aircraft from Sicily to build up his strength for the final push on Cairo. As a consequence, the main danger to the convoys came from the Italian Battle Fleet based at Taranto, which had the capability of putting massive striking power to sea. To counter this threat, two squadrons of torpedo-armed Beauforts and six torpedo Wellingtons were put on standby. No.217 Squadron flew their Beauforts from England to Malta while 39 Squadron moved a force to the ALG at Sidi Barrani.

The smaller UK convoy does not concern this history, but two of its six MVs did eventually reach Malta with much-needed supplies. The fate of the larger convoy of seven MVs, plus naval escort, which sailed from Alexandria on 12th June concerns us closely. On the evening of the 14th June, reconnaissance aircraft spotted the main Italian Battle Fleet seventy miles south of Taranto and heading south. Immediately, four Wellingtons from Malta were ordered to attack the fleet, but only one aircraft was able to drop its two torpedoes and the result was not observed. 217 Squadron was tasked with a dawn attack but of the nine aircraft which took-off from Malta, only one scored a hit, disabling a cruiser which was left for a nearby British cruiser to sink. Nevertheless, the Italian fleet held its course and the Alexandria convoy 'marked time' to await the outcome of further strikes. During the night, the Italian fleet had come within range of Beauforts based in Egypt, provided that after the attack the aircraft flew on to Malta. The official account given in the operations log is sparse and Ralph Barker's account of the strike provides a more graphic view of this operation. As well as giving a first class account of the strike, reconstructed from the memories of crews that took part, it gives an excellent insight into Beaufort operations generally.

'Mason and Gibbs handled the briefing between them. 'You'll see cruisers and destroyers on the way in,' Gibbs told them. 'Ignore them. Go for the battlewagons. Follow me.' Gibbs was back in the scrap again, and his manner was gay. Mason set course as far out to sea as he dared, but for the next two hours they flew in a fever of apprehension, knowing that aircraft from the landing grounds just out of sight on the port side had been attacking the British convoy, and it was too much to hope that twelve Beauforts would pass by unnoticed.

They flew at fifty feet along the coastline past Gambut, past Tobruk, past Gazala. At last they were off Derna, near the northernmost promontory of Cyrenaica. From this point they would be flying directly away from the mainland. The danger of fighters would be behind them.

It was here that they met their first mischance. Some miles behind the formation, one of the tail gunners saw splashes in the water. He took them to be falling bombs. There was no shipping in sight, he could see no aircraft, and he was puzzled. He called his skipper.

'I can see what look like bombs falling in the water about five miles behind us. Can't see anything else.'

'Keep your eyes peeled.'

The splashes had not been caused by bombs. A formation of Me 109s had been on the way from an airfield near Derna to give protection to German bombers attacking the British west-bound convoy. They had been carrying long-range tanks. When they saw the Beauforts, they jettisoned their auxiliary tanks and gave chase. The German fighters attacked from the southeast, diagonally behind the Beauforts. Many of the crews saw nothing until the Beaufort on the extreme left of the formation suddenly broke in half at the turret, the two parts crashing into the sea independently, the front half in flames. Mason rammed the throttles of his Mk.I Beaufort hard forward but several of the faster Mk.IIs shot past him, leaving their leader behind.

All the Beauforts weaved frantically, very close together, the tail gunners firing at the fighters whenever they came within range. Several of the guns in the new Mk.IIs jammed. Nevertheless, the German pilots showed great caution, picking out only the most rearward of the weaving Beauforts and diving down from the beam to a position astern. In this way the corresponding Beaufort of the extreme right was shot down. The pilot, formerly on Sunderlands, had asked for a posting which would give him more action. It was his first torpedo operation.

Mason found himself last but one in the shattered formation. The distinction of being last now fell to a sergeant-pilot named Daffurn.

His gunner called up to tell him that three fighters were on his tail. He was a long way behind the leader. His gunners opened up at the 109s, but the guns jammed almost at once. The wireless op fired a long burst from the side guns, and was immediately silenced himself by return fire, pieces of shrapnel piercing his hand, arm and legs. The three fighters were now attacking together, one from the port quarter, one from the starboard quarter, one from dead astern. They kept 800 to 100 yards distant, out-gunning the few Beauforts still able to fire. They changed their tactics now, pointing their noses at the target, pressing the trigger continuously, watching the fall of the tracer, and then pulling the nose gently up until the tracer could be seen falling on the target.

Daffurn's tail gunner gave him the position of the fighters and a running commentary on the fall of the tracer. All Daffurn could do was to weave continually. Suddenly his feet shot off the rudder bars as the rudder received a direct hit. The tail gunner watched the rudder jerking brokenly from side to side. Daffurn's feet were thrust back and forth and the aircraft swung from left to right, out of control. With a tremendous effort he forced his feet down on the rudder bars and at last held them steady. He found that the control wires had also been damaged, the rudder only operating when the pedals were completely depressed.

All this time, as the aircraft weaved involuntarily and even more violently, the cone of fire of the fighters had been searching for them. Bursts of fire struck them from time to time, the radio was shot clean out of its housing, tracer disappeared into the engine nacelles, and the aircraft, now a flying collander, whistled shrilly as it went along. But miraculously the engines still responded and Daffurn flew on.

The hosepipe firing of the German fighters, effective as it might be, was wasteful of ammunition; and at last they turned away. One other Beaufort pilot had been forced to turn into the coast and crash-landed his damaged aircraft behind the German lines, and one or two others had jettisoned their torpedoes under pressure. Daffurn, with a badly damaged aircraft, no guns, no radio, and an injured gunner, decided it was hopeless to continue and turned back for Sidi Barrani. Some of the others found their petrol consumption so increased during the running fight that they now had no hope at all of striking and reaching Malta, and they too turned back. When Mason finally took stock, he found that he had only five of his twelve aircraft left.

Such a start to an operation might have persuaded many men to turn back. All the remainder had aggravated their fuel consumption worries; and Gibbs' turret was unserviceable. But the thought of giving up did not occur to them. They closed their ranks, got into rough formation again, and pressed on.

A Maryland had gone on ahead to reconnoitre and to home the Beauforts on to the target by radar. Mason's wireless operator identified the transmission at fifty miles range. Their track was good. Visibility was unlimited and they were some ten miles distant when they caught their first glimpse of the battle fleet. In the same moment, the Maryland appeared and fired off a star cartridge in the direction of the target. The calm sea now erupted into great gouts of water as the 15-inch guns of the battleships put down a splash barrage in front of them. It was their first experience of this form of defence, but they kept low down on the water. The Italian ships were almost dead ahead, slightly to port. There were four destroyers out in front, in line abreast and equidistant, like the prongs of a rake; and a mile behind the destroyers they could see the two battleships, very close together, one perhaps a quarter mile behind and slightly to starboard of the other.

The sparkling sea beneath them was pock-marked with splashes, and the pale clear sky filled abruptly with dark blobs of cloud. Most of the flak was bursting above them at 200 feet. The Beauforts started taking evasive action, gently at first and then increasingly as they closed the range. Mason's original plan of attack had been to lead six aircraft himself round to the starboard side of the battleships while Gibbs took his six straight in on the port side. Mason now had two other aircraft with him, and Gibbs one. Mason intended to stick to the same plan.

At five miles range there was a tremendous bang underneath Gibbs' aircraft, and it floundered for a moment, but Gibbs soon brought it under control. The undercarriage had been damaged and the hydraulics punctured, but the torpedo was still there. Creswell, Gibbs' navigator, had survived an earlier crash in the desert in which his pilot had been killed at his side and in which Creswell had grabbed the controls, eased himself into the pilot's seat, and landed the plane safely behind enemy lines, where he was eventually retaken during the *Crusader* advance. Creswell now stood next to Gibbs, prepared for the worst, protecting with a tin hat that part of his anatomy which he judged most vulnerable.

Mason had just begun to swing away to port to skirt the leading destroyers, so as to develop his attack from starboard of the battleships, and Gibbs was just turning to starboard, when the leading battleship itself began to turn. Since the battleship was bows on to them, and any turn it made must present them with a beam shot, Mason and Gibbs arrested their turns and came back on to their original course. The leading battleship was clearly turning to starboard. Soon they would be able to see the whole length of it.

Whatever the Italian plan may have been, it had evidently become confused under the threat of attack. The two battleships were less than 400 yards apart; and the second battleship, after beginning a turn to starboard, altered helm and turned sharply to port. For one incredible moment it seemed that the two great ships would collide.

Meanwhile, Mason and Gibbs were leading their formations through the combing destroyers into the attack. There was no question now of either pilot manoeuvring. The leading Italian battleship had turned broad-on to the Beauforts and all they had to do was to run in straight and drop.

Mason and Gibbs both took the chance offered them and went for the leading battleship. But as Gibbs lined up on the target, his aircraft and that of the aircraft formating on him, flown by Dick Marshall, an Australian, were hit by flak from the destroyers. Oil seeped all over the floor of Gibbs' aircraft, and Marshall had his rudder control shot away, his elevator-trimmer control cut and his hydraulics punctured. Both pilots were thus forced to drop their torpedoes prematurely at some 2,000 yards distance. Mason saw the two aircraft break away across him just before he dropped.

Once again, when faced with a mammoth target, Beauforts had dropped at too great a range. Partly because of the intensity of the flak, partly because of lack of experience in judging distance against capital ships, none of the torpedoes was dropped closer than a mile. The battleships steamed on.

All five Beauforts survived the attack and reached Malta. Gibbs belly-landed his damaged Beaufort while Marshall swung as he landed and hit a damaged Beaufort of 217 Squadron on the edge of the runway. Both aircraft burst into flames and were destroyed. Marshall and his crew escaped.

Had their numbers not been reduced by more than half off Derna, no doubt 39 Squadron would have registered a hit. As it was, they claimed several; but the smoke they saw rising from the *Littorio* was the result of a direct hit from a 500 lb bomb dropped by the Liberators just before the torpedo attack.

After debriefing, the five crews to get through to Malta went to their respective Messes. They had fought their way through a protracted fighter attack, seen their comrades shot out of the sky, and come through some of the thickest flak they would ever see. Gibbs, normally a non-smoker, accepted cigarette after cigarette from his gunners. Now the tension was over, they all talked at once in a flood of excited chatter, and the line-shooting began. Suddenly they found they were ravenously hungry; and what they needed above everything was a drink. But now the importance of the convoys whose free passage they had been trying to ensure was brought home to them with a depressing force. The food they sat down to was bully beef and hard biscuits; and there wasn't a drink to be had.'

Despite the fact that this strike had caused no damage to the Italian fleet, it was discovered, later in the day, that the Italians had turned around and were heading back to Taranto. It was too late to stop the Alexandrian convoy returning to port, but the strike had distracted the enemy battle fleet and given it cause to reflect on the dangers from Allied aircraft.

While in Malta, Gibbs proposed that a small detachment of 39 Squadron should operate from Malta, as the bases in Egypt were proving to be at such extreme ranges from most targets. Back in Egypt a few days later, he continued to press his views and eventually secured agreement for a detachment of five aircraft to operate, under his command, from Malta. The first of these experimental detachments of five aircraft arrived at Luqa, Malta, on 22nd June and for the next few weeks, operated with the twelve Beauforts of Wing Commander Davies' 217 Squadron, which also included some aircraft of 86 Squadron. Pat Gibbs' arguments were to prove valid over the next three months as the Malta-based aircraft saw most of the action; in fact, they had arrived just in time to take part in a second strike on a convoy destined for Tripoli and Benghazi and routed via the Greek coast. The first strike, by 217 Squadron, had sunk the 7,600 ton German MV *Reichenfels* but four Beauforts had been lost.

This was the first chance that Gibbs had had to apply some of the hard-learned lessons of torpedo operations which he had gleaned over the North Sea. He was a firm believer in strikes by formations of nine to twelve aircraft, attacking from both sides to split the defensive fire. He also believed that the air escort, usually Beaufighters, should be used for flak suppresion as well as anti-air.

Thus, on the 23rd June, twelve Beauforts of 217 and 39 Squadrons, led by W/Cdr Davies and S/Ldr Gibbs, left Luqa to attack the convoy in the Ionian Sea. The aircraft, in four sub-flights of three aircraft, positioned to approach the convoy of two heavily laden MVs and four destroyers, and then turn in to attack both MVs from both sides simultaneously. In the attack, two Beauforts were shot down and one so badly damaged that it crash-landed back at Malta, however, one MV was hit and was seen

stern down and stationary. A reconnaissance sortie later in the day relocated the convoy in Taranto harbour and discovered that one MV was so badly damaged that its cargo was being transferred. Five days later the convoy left Taranto again, but following an attack by torpedo Wellingtons it returned to port once more. An enlarged convoy of three MVs and eight destroyers sailed on the 3rd July. This unusually large number of escorts reflected the importance of these supplies to Rommel.

Early on the 4th, a Beaufort strike force set off to search around the Greek coast for the convoy but didn't make contact and returned to Malta. Later in the day, a reconnaissance aircraft located the convoy fifteen miles south of Zante, and it was decided to mount a dusk strike. Gibbs planned the attack for eight Beauforts plus Beaufighter escort, but in the event only six Beauforts got airborne, and during the outbound flight, two of these had to return to base, as did a number of Beaufighters. This left Gibbs with only four Beauforts and five Beaufighters, to attack a heavily defended target at maximum range from Malta. All four dropped their torpedoes, while the Beaufighters did their best to distract the gunners on the destroyers. The largest MV was hit and forced to put into a Greek harbour for repairs. The two surviving MVs reached Benghazi on the 5th. The nominal forty-eight hour journey had taken three attempts and sixteen days, and the delay provided much-needed breathing space for the 8th Army to strengthen its positions at El Alamein. Gibbs and Stevens got back to Malta but the other two Beauforts failed to return.

In July Wing Commander Davies was posted back to the UK, and Gibbs was promoted to Wing Commander and given command of all the Beauforts in Malta. His command consisted of aircraft and crews from 39, 217 and 86 Squadrons, and it was not until 15th August that the majority of his command consisted of 39 Squadron aircraft - with the transfer of the main body of the Squadron's aircraft from Egypt to Malta. Nevertheless, the unit was known as 39 Squadron Detachment in Malta.

Before we look at the operations of this joint unit, it is worth recalling then occasion when a 39 Squadron Beaufort crew hijacked an Italian aircraft!

During July, Gibbs led his diverse command on a number of strikes, including a strike on the 28th July against a large MV near Sapienza in southern Greece. Nine Beauforts took-off from Luqa early on the 28th and located the convoy just before midday. As the Beauforts ran in one of their number fell victim to the intensive flak and crashed into the sea. Another aircraft was hit in the port engine as it cleared away from its attack on the MV, and the pilot, Flight Lieutenant Strever - a South African, realised he would have to ditch as he had insufficient height to reach the coast. For two of his crew, the two New Zealand WOP/AGs - Sgts Wilkinson and Brown, this was the second time they had been shot down within a fortnight. The only Englishman on the crew, was the navigator, Pilot Officer Dunsmere. Strever ditched the Beaufort and Wilkinson released the dinghy from its stowage in the port wing. Soon, all four were safely in the dinghy and bobbing around some five miles off the coast of Sapienza. Some time later they were spotted by an Italian Macchi C.202, which circled the dinghy and then departed. Shortly afterwards a Cant seaplane arrived overhead and landed nearby to pick them up - and take them into captivity. After a two-hour flight the Cant landed and they were taken for a very mild interrogation, followed by a change of clothes and a good meal - and the news that they were to be taken to Taranto the next day. At breakfast the next day the crew had a chance to discuss their future...

'I've worked out where we are, 'said Wilkinson. 'Either Levkas or Corfu. Taranto can't be more than 200 miles. If we don't do something quickly we'll be prisoners by lunchtime.'

'Not a hope here,' said Dunsmere. 'We've about as much chance of eluding them here as a bunch of film stars at a world premiere. Better wait until we get to Taranto.'

'You know what they say,' said Strever, 'the best chances come immediately after capture. Once they get us to Taranto there will be no more of this being feted like transatlantic flyers. Life will start to get tough then.'

'Has anyone thought of trying to capture the aircraft and fly it to Malta? Malta's about 350 miles I reckon.'

'I've thought of it, Wilkie,' said Strever. 'I thought of it yesterday. We probably had a better chance then than we'll get today. They're bound to mount a guard on us now. Still, we'll keep our eyes open.'

At that moment they were taken to the seaplane and were airborne and on course for Taranto at 0940. The interior of the aircraft was crowded with four Italian crew, the four prisoners and an Italian guard. At the half-way point the prisoners decided it was now or never and Wilkinson leapt into action, knocking out the wireless operator and seizing the gun from the lax guard. Strever took the gun and secured the 'co-operation' of the pilot. Soon all the Italians were overpowered and while Strever took the controls and turned the aircraft towards Malta, Dunsmere and Brown tied up the new prisoners. Dunsmere tried to work out a course for Malta but had no maps and no definite idea

of their position, so he drew a rough sketch map of the Central Mediterranean and showed it to the Italian navigator who made a few corrections. With this information, they decided to make straight for Malta, but with the proviso that if they had no visual contact within thirty minutes they would turn due west and make landfall on the toe of Italy to obtain an accurate position. This they had to do, and as they neared the toe of Italy, at 1130, the Italian engineer changed to the secondary petrol tanks and indicated that there was only enough fuel for another hour. They turned again for Malta and flew on, not wanting to consider what would happen if they missed Malta. With the fuel gauges on empty they spotted the island of Gozo and, a few minutes later, the coast of Malta. As they neared the coast of Malta, they were intercepted by ten Spitfires, the first of which sprayed the wing of the Cant to 'persuade' it to land. They landed on the water and climbed out onto the wing waving white garments to show the Spitfires that they were non-hostile. The Spitfires circled for a while and then departed. An Air Sea Rescue launch from Malta picked them up one and a half hours later. They were given a jubilant welcome when they arrived back at the Squadron, just in time to recover their personal kit which had been divided up amongst other members of the Squadron. For their exploits, Strever and Dunsmere were awarded the DFC and Wilkinson and Brown the DFM.

From mid-July 1942 to June 1943, when the Squadron ceased operations with the Beaufort the operations of the Squadron can be split up into five phases, which depended largely on the shipping routes being used by the Axis convoys the availability of supplies in Malta and the position of the front line in North Africa. The following information is extracted from a report written in 1943 by the Squadron Commander:

PHASE 1 (Malta) August - October 1942.
During this period the types of attacks carried out were:-
1. Daylight torpedo strikes of nine Beauforts escorted by up to sixteen Beaufighters, against enemy shipping off the Greek coast. Shipping in passage from Brindisi to Benghazi or Tobruk sailed in convoy approx every 14 days.
2. Moonlight strikes by one or two aircraft generally operating at extreme range against the above shipping. All this occurred during the period when the enemy was preparing for the El Alamein offensive.

PHASE 2 (N.Africa)
This phase occupied the few weeks prior to the El Alamein offensive and the two weeks of the

Nice shot of 39 Squadron aircraft which shows aerials and guns very well, and the open hatch in front of the turret to help keep the interior of the aircraft cool. (*Ralph Barker*)

offensive. The Squadron was located about 30 miles behind the front (Gianaclis) and could just reach the enemy shipping lanes Crete to Tobruk, about 350 miles distant. Daylight torpedo strikes were carried out using six to eight Beauforts with an escort of six Beaufighters. Dawn attacks using two or three single Beauforts were carried out against shipping off the Tobruk coast. This type of operation had to be adopted owing to the enemy sailing times and the lack of suitable Beaufighter escort during the offensive.

The success of the Beaufort and Wellington torpedo strikes in the period preceding and during the El Alamein offensive not only prevented supplies entering Tobruk, but forced other shipping to use Benghazi, with a consequently longer land route.

PHASE 3 (Malta)
When the 8th Army approached the Egyptian - Cyrenaica frontier, the port of Tobruk became unusable, and Benghazi almost useless. Enemy shipping commenced using the Sicily - Tunis -

Tripoli route. The Squadron therefore ferried to Malta for:-
1. Stand-by to attack the Italian battle fleet when relief convoys were run from Egypt to Malta.
2. Stand-by to attack the enemy battle fleet during the North West Africa campaign.
3. Anti-shipping offensive on the Tripoli - Tunis - Sicily sea lane.

A torpedo force of twenty-two Beauforts with two squadrons of Beaufighters was mustered during this phase, but in spite of a few alarms was not required to attack the enemy fleet. Torpedo rovers by day and moonlight were commenced as soon as the Middle East convoy replenished the petrol supply. Mining of ports from Tripoli-Tunis-Bizerta-Palermo carried out.

PHASE 4 (N. Africa and Malta)
December 1942 - January 23rd 1943
This occurred about the time of the Tripolitania offensive. In Malta a flight of six Beauforts remained for anti-sub patrols, mining and torpedo rovers, while the other flight, of twelve aircraft, returned to the Middle East for operations and training.
1. Torpedo and mining ops were carried out from forward landing grounds (ALGs) against shipping off the coast of Tripolitania.

Beaufort I, L9875 at Luqa, Malta. This aircraft was lost on 3 September 1942 when it crashed into the sea. (P.H.T.Green)

2. Training consisted of normal Squadron training for a number of new crews, and dark night torpedo attacks, using flares (see page 85/6) by twelve experienced crews.

PHASE 5 (Malta) January - June 1943
The Squadron was reunited at Malta when Tripoli was captured. The only shipping lane open to attack was in the Sicilian narrows, or from Sicily to Naples. Shipping strikes were made day and night, either with the moonlight or using the dark night techniques. Rovers were carried out in search of shipping, and there were day strikes off the Calabrian Coastline. Mining of Sicilian and Tunisian ports continued. When the Tunisian campaign finished in mid-May, the only shipping to be attacked was found near the the Straits of Messina.

'The 'score' during this ten-month period was 103,600 tons of shipping hit, sunk or severely damaged, for an expenditure of seventy-eight torpedoes and sixteen bombs (250 lb) on fifty-one operational sorties. Furthermore, one submarine was sunk with four depth charges. sixty mines were laid outside Axis ports and sixty 250 lb bombs dropped on harbour installations. This was achieved at a cost of eighteen crews lost on operations and two on training; seven crews, or part crews, became POWs.'

Let us now look at these operational phases in more detail. During August 1942, the entire operational effort of the Squadron was from Malta as little other than admin and support facilities were left in Egypt. Thus, two 39 Squadrons existed; the operational side under W/Cdr Gibbs at Luqa, and the HQ, admin and support set up at Shandur under W/Cdr Mason. This situation was regularised at the beginning of September when W/Cdr Mason was posted and F/Lt 'Pop' Bruce, the Squadron adjutant, assumed command of what was now called '39 Squadron in Egypt'. All aircraft, equipment and aircrew still in Egypt were posted to 47 Squadron. The detachment under 'Pop' Bruce was moved to a transit camp and spent its time playing sport and undergoing refresher training in rifle drill, bayonet practice, gas drill - and PT. However, this situation did not last long and both elements of the Squadron were soon reunited.

Meanwhile, things in Malta were desperate, with shortages of fuel, spare-parts and munitions. Torpedoes were always in short supply as they had to be brought to Malta by submarine and crews were instructed to bring their torpedoes back if the first three aircraft scored hits on the target ship. Furthermore, an aircraft on a rover patrol for opportunity was only to drop if a suitable large target presented itself. The situation improved greatly following the success of the El Alamein offensive and the increase in the quantity of supplies reaching Malta.

The lack of supplies also affected living conditions, and during the worst stages of the siege of Malta life was grim and uncomfortable. Accommodation was in single-storey stone buildings, often damaged, and somewhat cell-like with their spartan furniture. Likewise, meals were frugal and uninviting - no wonder Strever and his crew appreciated the excellent meals given them by the Italians! Maltese wine was fairly plentiful but not really popular and the local brewery was out of action. Social life was very limited as the nearby town of Valetta offered very few attractions. Although the fighter squadrons had a club on the sea front and sea bathing could have been exploited, the Squadron was very much base-bound. Add to this the constant threat of air attack, and the 'outdoor' life of the desert of a few months previous began to appear attractive. However, when the Squadron returned to Malta in November, after its sojourn at Shallufa, the situation was very different. Conditions, both operational and social, had greatly improved, to such an extent that this period has been recalled by many as the most comfortable of the whole Beaufort era.

For the Squadron in Malta, August 1942 was a month of high readiness but little action. 39 Squadron was held in readiness for a similar operation to that of July in support of a relief convoy to Malta from the UK, and the threat to be guarded against was the still intact Italian battle fleet at Taranto. Gibbs had some fifteen Beauforts under readiness but was never called on to use them, the existence of a strike force and the memory of the harassing attacks of July being sufficient to keep the Italian fleet in port.

On 1st July, Rommel had launched his assault on the El Alamein positions, but the defence was stronger than he anticipated and by the 4th, his depleted forces at the end of overstretched lines of communications, were forced to go onto the defensive. It was now the turn of the Allies

Eric Harvey runs up the port engine at LG 86, just before a test flight.

to exert pressure, but both sides were too weak to force a decision. Auchinleck reported that he would need time to build up his army, and that he would be unable to launch a major offensive before mid-September. Rommel realised that the initiative had slipped and that unless he received reinforcements and supplies before the end of August he would be unable to launch an offensive to seize Cairo and that his position would become desperate. Therefore, he insisted that his Italian allies should send him the necessary material - at all costs. Reluctantly they agreed and August was to be a do-or-die month in the shipping lanes of the Mediterranean.

In late August, Gibbs' outfit consisted of aircraft from 39 and 86 Squadrons (217 having left for the Far East) and he was able to muster some twenty Mk.I Beauforts. None of the Mk.II Beauforts were available as the station personnel at Luqa, responsible for servicing the Squadron aircraft, were not qualified to service the American engines! It was not until the Squadron returned to Egypt in October that it again acquired a majority of Mk.IIs.

The first of Rommel's promised supply ships left Naples on 16th August. Escorted by destroyers and six aircraft, the *Rosalina Pilo,* an 8,300 ton MV carrying a mixed load of fuel, ammunition and general cargo, elected to use the shorter route round North Sicily and thence to the North African ports. The convoy was sighted by a PR Spitfire - the usual means of locating such movements - and a Beaufort

strike was ordered. Six Beauforts, nine Beaufighters for anti-flak and dive bombing, plus the unusual luxury of eight Spitfires, made up the attacking force. Locating the convoy some thirty-five miles west of Lampedusa, the strike leader led his six Beauforts into the attack, while the Spitfires engaged the convoy air escort and the Beaufighter anti-flak and dive bombers went to work distracting the enemy gunners from the six torpedo aircraft. One of the Beaufighters dropped its bomb load on the stern of the MV just as the torpedoes began their runs. As the Beauforts cleared the far side of the convoy they witnessed two devastating explosions on the MV. Post-strike reconnaissance revealed the MV abandoned and later sunk. Furthermore, one Ju 88 and one Me 109 were shot down all for no loss to the strike force.

At this time, 39 were coupled with 235 Beaufighter Squadron to work with them. As a result, an excellent working relationship built up in which all elements of a strike were familiar with each other's methods.

A typical daylight torpedo strike would commence with receipt of the sighting report of the reconnaissance Spitfire or Baltimore, whose pilot normally returned to base to make his report in person rather than break RT silence. The strike leader would then assess his resources and plan his attack - relying heavily on his navigator to get him into the right position not only to locate the enemy but also to preserve the element of surprise until the last possible moment. After take-off, the Beauforts would rendezvous with their escort using a number of pre-arranged verey-light signals, to pass instructions - such as set course, take over lead, enemy fighter seen, prepare to attack, and top cover rise. Having formed up, the force set course and the Beauforts proceeded in arrow-head formation of vics of three at sea level, with the close-cover Beaufighters, ideally four aircraft, weaving on the wings, and the two anti-flak Beaufighters and top cover Beaufighters - ideally four - about two miles astern. About ten miles from the convoy, the top cover climbed to 2,000 feet, and at four miles close cover climbed to 500 feet.

The Beauforts would then split to attack the convoy from both sides. On many occasions the Italians, sailing close to the coast, neglected to place escort ships between the MVs and the coast mistakenly trusting shallow water to protect them from torpedo attack. This allowed the Beauforts the advantage of attacking from landward thus reducing the amount of defensive fire the convoy could bring to bear during the attack run. During the torpedo drop, the Beaufighters would go to work hitting the escorts and trying to keep the convoy air cover away from the Beauforts. The type and amount of convoy air cover depended very much on where the convoy was, the following being the norm:

1. Greek Coast (Autumn 1942) Ju 88, Macchi 200, Macchi 202, Cant 1007, Me 109: average total 25 aircraft.
2. Tobruk Coast (October offensive) Ju 88, Cant 1007, Me 109: average total 12-15 aircraft.
3. Tunisian Coast (Spring 1943) Ju 88, Cant 1007, Me 109: average total 5.
4. Italian Coast (Spring 1943) Ju 88, Me 110, Me 210: average total 15.

The single-engined enemy fighters generally flew circuits around the convoy at 3,000 feet with the multi-engine types down at 1,000 - 2,000 feet. The fighters tended to keep close to the convoy and not attack the Beauforts until after torpedoes had been dropped and then the fighters would set up quarter or stern attacks on any stragglers. For protection, the Beauforts would join up as quickly as possible after the strike and take evasive action at 30-50 feet above the sea. The Beauforts would try to stay in line abreast, slipping, turning and weaving to avoid the fighters. Generally, the fighters would give up the chase after three or four minutes and return to the convoy. On any strike, the more Beauforts there were the better, as it divided the enemy fire and gave a better chance of success and survival to all involved. Pat Gibbs in particular was determined that any of his aircraft would abort a mission only as a final resort and what might elsewhere appear a valid reason for aborting would not be accepted.

Meanwhile, the Italians, true to their word, were mounting another convoy to relieve Rommel. This was the 7,800 ton tanker *Pozarica* escorted by destroyers, a flak ship and seven aircraft. On 19th August Wing Commander Gibbs led a twelve Beaufort strike against the tanker. Unfortunately, the tanker was not as low in the water as was anticipated and so the depth setting on the torpedoes was too great, and all torpedoes ran under the ship.

The attackers lost a Beaufighter and two Beauforts although both Beaufort crews were picked up by the destroyer escort. Back at Malta thoughts were turned to a second strike, and plans were laid for a sortie the next day when up to date reconnaissance information would be available. This second strike consisted of nine Beauforts and eight anti-flak Beaufighters plus five dive-bomber Beaufighters. By this time, the convoy was nearing the Greek coast and it was here that the strike aircraft caught up with it. Gibbs scored a good hit as did one, possibly two other aircraft. One aircraft of the last sub flight was shot down, the crew being picked up by an escort destroyer. Post-strike PR showed the tanker stationary and leaking oil; later she was seen again, beached and abandoned.

However, the pace did not slacken as on the 24th yet another convoy was seen. This was the 1,500 ton tanker *Dielpi*. A nine-aircraft strike was mounted by 39 Squadron with the usual escort, although one Beaufort was late off and did not catch up with the rest until just before the attack. In fact, as he approached the formation, he was being chased by a Ju 88, but his problem was solved by one of the Beaufighters which shot the pursuer down. The attack went in and although an explosion was seen, no-one claimed a hit. In fact, the tanker had been damaged and had to put in to a Greek port for repairs. A few days later, she sailed again only to be met by 39 Squadron with nine Beauforts in a dusk attack. This time there was no escape and she received at least two direct hits and was soon ablaze and sinking. A fourth tanker, the 5,400 ton *Istria*, sailed by night to avoid the Beauforts and fell victim to a Wellington torpedo strike.

Despite persistent efforts by the Italians Rommel had still received nothing, and he was furious. The Italians tried again and sent the 5,000 ton tanker *San Andrea* at the end of August. The tanker had only one destroyer as escort and so hugged close to the Italian coast. Pat Gibbs led nine Beauforts and nine Beaufighters on the strike and elected to attack from landward and drop at close range to reduce the likelihood of the torpedoes fouling in shallow water. Gibbs' vic of three dropped at only 500 yards and as the second vic ran in, the tanker vanished in a spectacular sheet of flame and smoke. The tally for the 'campaign' was five sailed and five sunk - four of them falling to 39 Squadron - the *Rosalina Pilo* on 16th August, the *Pozarica* on the 19th, the *Dielpi* on the 24th and the *San Andrea* on the 30th - an outstanding achievement by any standards, and echoed in the words of Ralph Barker:

'Rommel's absolute dependence upon the petrol carried by the *San Andrea* made its destruction the plum of the whole Mediterranean campaign.'

The part played by the anti-shipping squadrons and 39 in particular, has been too often ignored in histories of the North Africa campaign. If Rommel had received the supplies he requested the course of the campaign in North Africa, and possibly the war, could have been very different.

Rommel launched his offensive on the El Alamein defences (the battle of Alam Halfa), on the 30th August - relying on the Italians for the promised supplies, which if they did not arrive within days, would mean the end of any attempt on Cairo and an inevitable retreat. By the middle of the second week in September, Rommel's offensive had petered out and he reverted to the defensive. Montgomery, who had replaced Auchinleck, in what many now consider an unjust dismissal by Churchill, prepared to launch his own offensive - operation *Lightfoot*, on 24th October.

In September, Pat Gibbs was posted back to the UK - an exhausted man after many hectic months. On the 11th, command of the Squadron passed to Wing Commander M L ('Larry') Gaine AFC. Shortly afterwards, the decision was taken to move 39 Squadron back to Shallufa in Egypt - five miles or so north of Suez. The first eight aircraft arrived at Shallufa from Malta on the 1st and a further seven the next day. At last, the aircrew from Malta and the support personnel who had been 'festering' in the Transit camp were re-united, a cause for rejoicing. A second cause for celebration was the introduction of a rest and recreation period, with the crews being sent on leave to Alexandria, Cairo and Palestine. However, the joy was short-lived as on the 7th orders were received to be ready to return to Malta on the 12th. The Squadron worked hard and managed to get fourteen aircraft serviceable and ready to go, only to have the order cancelled and instead seven aircraft were sent to Gianaclis with the combined 42/47 Beaufort Squadron, as part of a composite strike force under No.247 Wing.

On 26th August a mixed force, not including 39 Squadron, attacked a convoy at the very mouth of Tobruk harbour - a 6,000 ton tanker, 6,000 ton MV and 900 ton freighter. The tanker was sunk and later in the day the 6,000 ton MV went the same way. Three days later another tanker fell victim to a force of Wellingtons and on 2nd November, 39 Squadron put paid to yet another just off Tobruk.

In the first week of November, the Squadron sent nine aircraft back to Malta as the Axis convoys were now using the Western shipping lane to Tripoli, since the ports of Tobruk and Benghazi were unusable due to the Allied offensive. Furthermore, there was a danger of the Italian fleet attempting to interfere with operation *Torch* - the Allied landings in North Africa planned for 8th November.

Although the Beauforts had made dawn and dusk strikes in the previous months, it now became the practice to fly regularly at night both on 'moonlight rovers' and on 'dark night attacks' if a suitable target presented itself. The operational concept of these two methods of attack is outlined below in an extract of a report on operational procedures:

1. DARK NIGHT FLARE ATTACKS
This type of attack has been carried out on only two occasions in action but has been practiced frequently.

A sighting is made by an ASV Wellington, who after confirming the sighting, sends a sighting report on W/T to base. He then shadows the convoy, and lays down four flame floats 60 degrees on the starboard or seaward side of the convoy at a distance of ten miles. The aircraft (Search 1) switches on his S.I. rooster and replenishes the flame floats as necessary.

A number of Wellingtons and Beauforts are then scrambled and proceed to the scene of the strike, homing in on the S.I. or W/T. The Beauforts after locating the flame floats, circuit left hand on the far side of the floats. They then fly at different height bands in layers of 500 feet. As soon as an aircraft is near the convoy, a signal 491 and aircraft call sign is sent. When 60% of the 491 has been received (the search aircraft is notified of the number of aircraft setting off, the search aircraft will send a preparatory verey signal indicating that flares will be released. A single flare is released from 4,000 feet over the convoy and the S.I. rooster is switched off. The strike aircraft then head towards this single flare, decreasing the distance between themselves and the convoy. The search aircraft then lays down a curtain of twelve flares from stem to stern about two miles from the convoy, allowing for wind, etc. When the quarter of the ship has been reached, the aircraft turns aft of the ship and releases another eight to twelve flares.

When the target is illuminated, and silhouetted against the flares, the aircraft attack in the correct sector. To indicate to all the aircraft how the attack is progressing, each aircraft when it is making the final stage of the approach, will send a series of I's (with aircraft call sign), and a series of O's during the run out.

A dummy rendezvous may be laid down by the search aircraft to distract enemy attention. Additional Wellingtons are available to take over search or flare dropping if required.

2. MOONLIGHT ATTACKS

To search a coastal area of approximately 200 miles, three Beauforts are invariably briefed to patrol 4, 7 and 10 miles from the coast. The patrol is timed, so that the altitude of the moon is between 20 degrees and 40 degrees. The azimuth of the moon is also considered, since if flying down moon, or nearly down moon, the observer and W/T A/G must be detailed to search the moonpath.

The aircraft fly at approximately 100 to 200 feet into the moon, or 300 to 400 feet down moon, although if night fighters are observed, these heights may be decreased. It is only seldom that an aircraft can attack a ship directly on sighting, since night visibility rarely exceeds 2½ miles for visual ship location. The tactics adopted

have been to continue course for one minute and turn approximately on to reciprocal so the final approximate will bring the aircraft into the torpedo sector without having to perform a large turn close to the target.

The clear weather, clear sky, and moderate winds of the Mediterranean have aided this type of anti-shipping strike.

3. CONVOY FIGHTER COVER

Night fighters always have a red light (or two) in the nose and are thus readily detected visually, and also by S.I. No case is yet known where night fighters have actually been employed in protecting the convoy. This does not mean that night fighters are not encountered near a convoy or coast.

Sightings of night fighters average one to two aircraft per night. Chases by night fighters average one to two aircraft per week. Cases of night fighters firing - two cases in six months (night sorties per month - 70).

From the aspect of torpedo operations this period November - December 1942, was a quiet one for 39 Squadron in Malta. A number of day offensive sweeps around Malta were carried out as well as the moonlight rovers. However, the Squadron flew a number of bombing sorties - using 250 lb bombs; for example three Beauforts and three Beaufighters bombed Lampedusa on 23rd November. Further bombing sorties were flown at infrequent intervals throughout the remainder of the Squadron's Beaufort era. The main 'diversion' for the Squadron in the latter part of the month was an intensive phase of mining operations (referred to as 'gardening') against a number of Axis ports. The Beaufort was capable of carrying one 1,500 lb mine.

The end of November was a particularly intensive time for 'gardening', and in a four day period the Squadron planted thirty mines in the ports of Bizerta, Tunis and Palermo. All sorties were carried out in the late evening or early night to give aircraft some protection, but losses were suffered; one aircraft being lost on the 29th and two on the 30th. It is impossible to tell what fate befell these aircraft, a prowling night fighter or a simple accident.

Likewise, the moonlight rovers with their low level approaches over the sea at night had their natural hazards - well illustrated by John Coles (Sgt A J Coles WOP/AG) in this account of his last flight, on the evening of 25th February 1943: 'We took-off from Malta after midnight on a moonlight night, 25th February 1943, in our Beaufort (Crew: P/O Hewetson - Pilot; F/Sgt Bryce - Observer; Sgt Coles - ASV/ Wireless Operator; Sgt Bradford - Air Gunner) to attack a convoy of two Italian MVs escorted by two destroyers. They were heading North towards Naples from a Tunisian port (Tunis or Bizerta). I picked up the convoy on my ASV (Radar) screen at a position 95 miles 020 degrees from Marettimo island (off the West coast of Sicily).

'Jimmy Hewetson flew parallel with the convoy and about a mile away from it, keeping in the dark part of the sky. He turned in to attack, getting the convoy silhouetted in the moon's path - we were attacking one of the two merchantmen.

'Normally we kept right down on the deck and climbed up to sixty feet to release the torpedo. Suddenly something fundamental went wrong. There was an almighty bang, a flash immediately in front of me (inside the wireless cabin) - we had flown straight into the Tyrrhenian Sea, with our torpedo still in the bomb bay (I probably owed my life to being strapped in my seat and, as was my practice during night attacks, having placed my head against my parachute which in turn I held pressed up against the Bendix Radio Set).

'I quickly released the seat straps as water lapped round my feet - mercifully I was uninjured (save for a black eye where I made contact with the metal parachute release ring), swiftly moved to the rear hatch just behind the port wing, and pulled the dinghy release catch.

'Jimmy Bryce and Joe Bradford had appeared in the water nearby and were frantically urging me to launch the dinghy - I assured them I had just pulled the release catch. The aircraft sank very rapidly - it stayed afloat for perhaps 45/60 seconds but not before the dinghy had inflated.

'There was no sign of poor Jimmy Hewetson who must have gone down with the plane. The three of us who survived tried to get into the dinghy but found it to be upside down. After a tremendous struggle we managed to right it and struggled into it only to find shortly afterwards, to our horror, that it was leaking quite badly!

'Soon afterwards we spotted one of the Italian destroyers nearby, moving slowly and silently in the water and clearly searching for survivors (from one of the MVs which had been sunk by one of the other 39 Squadron aircraft of the sortie - I believe by F/O Cartwright who took off from Luqa at about the same time as ourselves to attack the convoy).

'I had a quick flash of inspiration and persuaded the other two to join with me in blowing SOS on our aircrew whistles (which we always carried fastened to the top of our battledress blouses).

'We were extremely lucky that the destroyer was gliding about on low engine power, with its crew apparently listening for cries of help from survivors, and that they heard our joint SOS

whistling. By this time we were having a job to keep still in our dinghy which by now was badly deflated. The destroyer came right up close to us - only a few yards away, albeit not close enough to rescue us - when to my dismay it started reversing! However it only went back far enough to enable it to alter course a few degrees to port to come up right alongside us.

'The first voice I heard from above us called: 'Combien êtes vous?' - to which I hastily replied 'Trois'. We soon struggled aboard the destroyer, with assistance, being exhorted to hurry up by the Italians (due to the presence of British submarines in the area).

'The Italians looked after us quite well - their first words after we set foot on deck were the traditional 'For you the war is over!' and on our way to Naples the Captain sent for Jimmy Bryce - the Senior NCO - and after unsuccessfully interrogating him on our aircraft, Squadron and airfield later explained why he had risked his crew and his ship to rescue us. It was a remarkable story! His brother who had been the Captain of an Italian submarine earlier in the war had been rescued by the Royal Navy after being depthcharged and obliged to surface and surrender. His brother, the destroyer captain, felt he had, in honour, a debt to repay.'

In mid-November 1942 the Squadron had no less than seventeen aircraft at Luqa but this was reduced to six in early December, the others returning to Shallufa as part of a decision to re-form 39 in Egypt with a full complement of crews, aircraft, ground personnel and equipment. The Malta Detachment continued to operate on anti-shipping strikes from Luqa, under the command of Squadron Leader Worsdell.

The re-organisation was not as straight-forward as planned as within days of the Squadron arriving at Shallufa an operational detachment was sent to Gambut on strike standby. Thus, the Squadron was split into three elements - two operational (Malta and Gambut) and one training (Shallufa). At Shallufa the training programme concentrated on moonlight and night flare attacks and formation attacks, as per the tactical appraisal above.

The reorganisation went ahead and by the middle of January some 300 personnel had been posted in. Just as the Squadron was beginning to feel organised everything changed again! On the 21st January all crews and aircraft were sent to Malta to join the survivors of the Luqa detachment. Those aircrew for whom there were no serviceable aircraft were put at the disposal of 201 Group and were 'loaned' to other squadrons and training units. The remainder of the Squadron personnel at Shallufa were amalgamated with the Station and, like the aircrew,

were loaned out - whilst at the same time maintaining a 39 Squadron name-tag against the day when the day when the Squadron would re-unite. By early February the hoped for re-uniting of the Squadron looked even further away when the aircrew at Shallufa were posted to 47 Squadron and 5 METS. Meanwhile the ground staff were sent to Gianaclis to assist the understaffed 75 OTU. It was not until March that the groundcrew again saw an aircraft from their own Squadron, when at the end of the month three Beauforts arrived at Heliopolis for major inspection and overhaul, and fitters and riggers were sent from Gianaclis to do the work.

While the ground element of the Squadron was moving around unsure of its future, the operational side at Malta was very busy. From January to March 1943 the Squadron was involved in three main types of operations: firstly, 'gardening' of such places as La Goulette, Kerkenneh, Scusse, Trapani, Sfax harbour, and Ras Kabondia; secondly, anti-submarine patrols in conjunction with Allied shipping movements - with one submarine being sunk on the 14th January; and lastly, moonlight rovers - usually by two or three aircraft but sometimes as many as five. The majority of rovers were notable for their lack of activity however, on the 17th January two aircraft attacked shipping in the Sicilian Channel. One dropped its torpedo and missed; the other ran in and then the pilot noticed he was attacking a destroyer and not the MV. He therefore decided to pull in and run in again. Unfortunately,

as he pulled away the aircraft was hit by flak - which shot the torpedo away!

In February the anti-shipping patrols were mainly in three areas: Sicilian Channel, Cape Bone - Keliba, and Cape Gallo-Marsalo. It was not until the 21st February that the Malta-based Squadron had the first major success. A six aircraft strike force took-off from Luqa at 1745 and located a tanker (7-10,000 tons) disguised as an MV. The formation approached unseen and found the target ideally placed for a torpedo attack - there was no close escort vessel and the tanker was almost stationary! Captain Don Tilley was the first to attack and his torpedo ran true, striking the tanker amidships with a flash and the traditional column of water. This attack was quickly followed by that of Flight Sergeant Gillies who planned his torpedo just astern of amidships with the same results. The third aircraft ran in, Flight Sergeant Deacon, his torpedo struck the same place as Tilley's and there was a tremendous explosion and flash which enveloped the whole ship. The shock wave had hardly died down when Pilot Officer Feast put a fourth

Above and below: **The end of the Beaufort era as Mk.IIs wait at Protville, Tunisia in June 1943 to be replaced by Bristol Beaufighters. It was** self-help at Protville and crews slept in or under their aircraft. The nose art on the left side of 'H' is unusual on the Squadron. *(W.H. Armstrong)*

Engine change desert style as a 39 Squadron Beaufort has its port engine replaced at Wadi Natrun.

torpedo into the stricken vessel - again, nicely amidships; another explosion and flash and wreathed in flames and smoke, the ship sank low in the water. There was no need for the other two aircraft to drop so they took their torpedoes back to Luqa. Later observation showed that the tanker had broken up - the target area was a mass of floating debris and burning oil. Following this strike the Squadron received a signal of congratulations from the AOC.

This success was followed up four days later when Flying-Officer Muller-Rowlands sank an 8,000 ton MV which had been hit and damaged earlier by Flying Officer Cartwright. March was another 'good' month with day and night strikes claiming two tankers (each of 10,000 tons), and two MVs (each of 5,000 tons). In the words of the pilot who sank one of the 5,000 ton MVs on the night of the 23rd: 'I hit the MV amidships on the port side, there was a large vivid flash with showers of sparks and debris followed by clouds of steam and smoke.'

Only one success in April - a large MV, on the 23rd. Two aircraft on a night rover located and attacked the vessel but only one torpedo dropped successfully. This ran true and damaged the vessel but did not sink it; the Beauforts

circled the crippled ship and called up a reserve strike of two aircraft to finish the job. Both dropped successfully at the now stationary vessel which erupted in flames and sank within five minutes. Generally, April was a quiet month and the Squadron spent much time on a training programme of lectures, gun practice on a sea drogue and formation attacks on naval units using a forward facing camera to film the attacks.

May saw a similar routine of anti-sub, anti-ship and 'gardening' operations plus a continuation of the training programme. On the 28th, however, it was rumoured that 39 Squadron would be on the move again. The rumour solidified the next day when the Squadron was taken off operations pending a move and re-equipment. A movement order was issued for all aircraft, aircrew and twenty-five key ground personnel to move to Protville, Tunisia. However, Larry Gaine had to bid farewell to his Squadron as he was to stay in Malta awaiting posting.

On the 1st June the Beauforts left Luqa for Protville, accompanied by the groundcrew in a Wellington. Unfortunately, no-one at Protville was expecting 39! When the Beauforts landed all they found was 100 or so unattended Spitfires and no accommodation or food. So life at Protville started with everyone sleeping in, under and around the aircraft.

This improvision only lasted one day for the aircrew as on the 2nd the crews were ordered to take the aircraft to Cairo, which they duly did the next day (via Castel Benito, El Adem and LG224). By the 5th the Beauforts were at 135 MU and the crews at Almaza transit camp (Cairo). Two days 'rest' and more news...orders for the crews to return to Protville and, as there was a shortage of air transport, they were to take the Beauforts! Arriving at Protville on the 10th, the weary crews found that the groundcrew had established some sort of Squadron camp by 'obtaining' a few tents. No rest for the aircrew though, as the aircraft had to go back to 135 MU! Within days of the Beauforts leaving the new aircraft arrived - Bristol Beaufighter Mk.X torpedo aircraft. 39 Squadron entered its next phase.

6

Torbeaus to Trains

On 1st June 1943, 39 Squadron moved to Protville near Tunis to convert onto the Bristol Beaufighter. The Beauforts were duly handed over and there followed a period of 'rest' until the 18th June, when the first six Beaufighters arrived. In the meantime, Wing Commander N B Harvey had arrived to take command of the Squadron. The Bristol Beaufighter had been produced in many versions to fulfil a wide variety of roles; the version allocated to 39 was the Mk.X, the intention being to continue the torpedo role but with a higher performance aircraft than the Beaufort.

The Bristol 156 Beaufighter X was powered by two 1,770 hp Bristol Hercules XVII engines, giving a top speed of 303 mph at 1,300 feet and a rate of climb from sea level equivalent to 5,000 feet in 3.5 minutes. The Hercules XVII was not supercharged and rapidly lost performance above 10,000 feet; the aircraft being rated at sea level. Armament consisted of four 20 mm Hispano cannon in the nose, two .303s in the port wing and four in the starboard, one .303 Browning in the dorsal cupola and a single Mk.XIV torpedo as the main weapon system.

Conversion started on the 19th with 'dual' instruction being given by the pilots of 144 Squadron. This consisted of being shown what to do and then doing it yourself while the 'instructor' stood beside the seat watching every move and trying not to intervene. It was not until the 25th that 39's own groundcrew arrived after a long, hard journey from Gianaclis. Pat Biegel, a Sergeant armourer posted from 108 Squadron, recalls his introduction to 39 Squadron at Protville:

'The Beaus and the Malta half of the Squadron were already there, tents had been erected and a hot meal awaited us. This was served by the officers, the first in line being the CO, Wing Commander Harvey, whom none of us had ever met. As we filed past he gave us a bowl of stew in return for which we shook his hand and introduced ourselves. Our first invitation to the Officers Mess came shortly after and we decided we would try and make an impression by donning our best tailor-made KD and even wearing ties! We need hardly have bothered, however, as ducking to enter the Mess tent placed us each in turn in the perfect position for a large Canadian Flight Lieutenant to cut off our ties just below the knot with an enormous pair of scissors.'

Dual and solo conversion flying proceeded at a fair pace and soon included formation flying, gunnery and practice torpedo attacks. By 1st July the Squadron was able to declare itself operational with twelve aircraft and sixteen crews. Acquired along with the Beaufighters were a number of experienced Beau crews who had no torpedo training; it was decided to use these crews to fly the flak suppression aircraft during strikes rather than retrain them to the torpedo role. On 10th July the Squadron was placed on standby along with 47 and 144 Squadrons for operations against the Italian fleet. This meant daily standby from 0600 to 1930 but did not prevent the Squadron from taking part in other worthwhile strikes when targets presented themselves.

39's Beaufighter account opened on the 11th July with a torpedo strike on a 4,000 ton MV which, escorted by two destroyers and a flak ship, was heading south down the coast of Italy

Some parts of Protville airfield contained remainders of its recent occupation, in this case a Focke Wulf Fw 190. (*W.H.Armstrong*)

to Naples. A strike force of four torpedo-armed Beaus and two anti-flak Beaus took-off from Protville led by Squadron Leader Muller-Rowland, an experienced Beaufort torpedo man. They located the convoy and while the anti-flak aircraft swooped down on the destroyers with cannon and gun the torpedo aircraft ran in on the MV. At least one torpedo ran true and the MV was hit in the bows, the metal crumpling under the impact of the explosion leaving the vessel crippled. A second torpedo had struck and damaged one of the destroyers. On the return flight to Protville the formation were attacked by Me 109s which shot down one Beau and caused severe damage to another which subsequently crash-landed at base. It was, nevertheless, a successful start for 39 Torbeau Squadron.

It was followed the next day by an eight aircraft (four torpedo, four anti-flak) strike on two troopships, 8,000 and 12,000 tons, in the Bonifacio Staights. The strike was led by Wing Commander Harvey. On the outbound leg, a number of aircraft peeled-off to strafe a train ferry and then rejoined the formation. The convoy was located and at least one hit was scored on the largest MV and one on the escorts, which was left burning fiercely. Flying Officer Curlee opened the Torbeau 'aircraft score' by shooting down an SM.79. However, the flak barrage put up by the convoy had damaged several of the Beaus, one of which had to ditch when its port engine burst into flames.

On the 13th, 39 Squadron was back in action with a strike on a 15,000 ton troopship, but the climax of this first hectic week came on the 14th when seven aircraft attacked a convoy of two tankers - 5,000 and 1,500 tons - escorted by two flak ships and with air cover of six Macchi 202s. Despite the tremendous barrage put up by the flak ships, the Beaus released their torpedoes accurately, with the result that the larger tanker blew up in a sheet of flame and the smaller one was left burning. The Macchis did not even attempt to intervene but one Beau was brought down by flak, and crashed into the sea and exploded on impact.

Thus, over a four day period, 39 had seriously damaged four MVs and two destroyers, shot down an SM.79, and destroyed a number of ferries - for the loss of three Beaufighters. This hectic activity could not be maintained, and in the remainder of July very few suitable targets presented themselves. The Squadron flew a number of eight aircraft patrols of rovers through 'likely areas' but with no notable success. As a tactical arrangement, 39 tended to operate a 1:1 ratio of torpedo to anti-flak aircraft and this seemed to work reasonably well. This tactical combination was the norm throughout the Beau period although by early 1944 the anti-flak escort was usually provided by another squadron, thus allowing 39 to concentrate on the offensive strike. On occasions, 39 Squadron flew anti-flak for others.

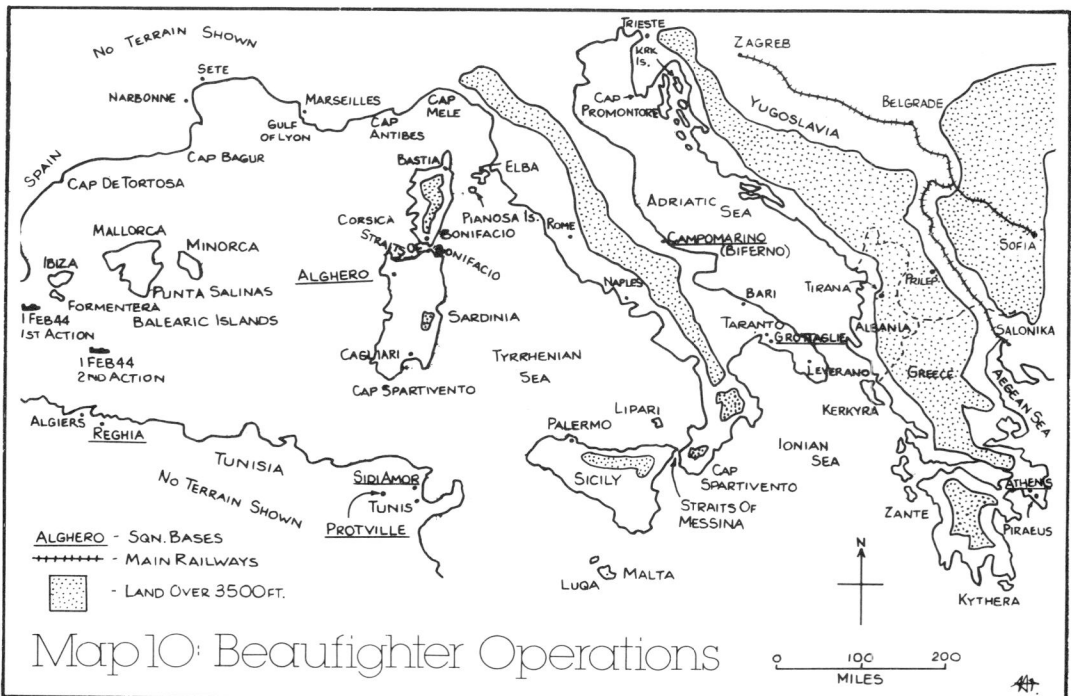

Map 10: Beaufighter Operations

The sequence of photographs on this page shows a typical Beaufighter torpedo attack on a convoy. As the Beaufighters weave in at low level at least one MV is in its death throes, wreathed in smoke. The date is 14th July 1943. *(W.H. Armstrong)*

The wastes of Tunisia would often resound with the strains of the Squadron song:

When you hear the news that a ship has been sunk,

that another Jerry cruiser is just a heap of junk,

then you know that the boys are going to get drunk

- That's good old 39.

Torping shipping

Everybody thinks it's awfully ripping.

Look out for that mast

Or it may be your last.

August was another quiet month with only one shipping strike, on the 16th, which scored hits on two MVs. This was but small reward for the numerous rover patrols flown along the Corsican and Italian coasts. If the area was short of shipping it was not short of enemy aircraft and many of the rovers were intercepted by Me 109s and Fw 190s. Generally speaking the Beaus were able to look after themselves with their excellent performance at sea level and the powerful armament of four cannon and six machine guns. This armament was put to good use at the end of August when the Squadron was tasked with offensive fighter patrols in the area north-east of Bastia, Corsica, to 'attack enemy transport aircraft reported to be evacuating essential equipment from Corsica.' The first patrol was flown by four aircraft early on the 23rd and three SM.82 transports, with German markings, were intercepted and shot down. Later the same day a larger patrol attacked thirteen Ju 52s and two SM.82s north-east of Corsica shooting down one Ju 52 and one SM.82 and damaging two other Ju 52s. A third patrol was sent up in the early evening and the two Beaus attacked a formation of five Ju 52s near Bastia, shooting down two. However, one of the Beaus was damaged and crash-landed at base.

The same routine was followed on the 24th with a total of four patrols during the day and a total of eight Ju 52s shot down and a further five damaged, In these actions two Beaus were shot down, one was damaged and crash-landed at base and another ditched for unknown reasons. The latter aircraft was that of Squadron Leader Petch, the formation leader of the first patrol, who ditched near Pianosa Island. The rest of the formation broke-off the attack on the Ju 52s and carried out 'ditching procedure', circling the downed aircraft looking for survivors and reporting the position of the aircraft for ASR. As they were circling they saw a launch set out from the island and pick up both crew members; satisfied that the crew was safe the formation returned to Protville and made its report. The following day, two aircraft flew to Pianosa Island to drop a container of food and money to Squadron Leader Petch and his Nav; one of

the aircraft was bounced by an Me 109 and was shot down. Over the ensuing days, Squadron aircraft regularly flew over the island looking for signs of the crew but no word was heard and it was therefore assumed that both crewmen were POWs.

The overall tally for the offensive patrols was eleven Ju 52s and four SM.82s shot down and seven Ju 52s damaged - for the loss of three Beaus shot down, two crash-landed and one ditched. The tally would probably have been better but the belt feed to the Hispano cannon was giving problems causing jams which could not be cleared in the air.

As October opened quietly, six aircraft were detached to No.5 METS at Shallufa for a two week torpedo training and refresher course. Each aircraft carried three extra personnel, aircrew and groundcrew, and with five people in the small cockpit area of the Beau it was not a particularly comfortable trip. Crews stranded away from base with unserviceable aircraft were usually picked up by Squadron aircraft and 'packed in the Beau like sardines.' For instance, on 8th October a signal arrived at Protville from the French authorities in Corsica:

'Flight Officers Heide and Deacon who in the sea on 24th are safe in Ajaccio'.

The crew, one of those shot down on the 24th, had spent four days in their dinghy before reaching Elba where they hid until they were able to escape in a small boat. They were picked up from Ajaccio by a Squadron aircraft on the 10th.

From the 11th to the 16th October the Squadron was back on standby for anti-shipping strikes but was also preparing to move to Sidi Amor, near Tunis. The aircraft moved to Protville I from Protville II on the 17th/18th as Sidi Amor was not ready. By the 21st the move to Sidi Amor was complete; two of the last aircraft to move were the Hurricane and the Beaufort which were used for pilot training and communications. The Beaufort was one which had been kept when the Squadron changed types but there seems to be no details of where or when the Hurricane came from, nor any reference as to its eventual fate, except that Squadron members are sure that it left the Squadron before the move to Sardinia in February 1944.

Standby was resumed with eight aircraft on the 22nd and 39 began to acquire ASV-equipped aircraft from 47 Squadron. As with the Beauforts, operational use of ASV was restricted because of ultra low flying heights and jamming from ground stations. From 1st November onwards the Squadron sent regular detachments to Grottaglie, near Taranto in southern Italy, to 'stand-by to attack shipping in the Adriatic and on the shipping lanes as far south as Crete.'

Above: **Protville, June 43 and No.39 Squadron acquired the Beaufighter Mk.X to continue the torpedo anti-shipping ops in the Med.** *(W.H. Armstrong)*

Centre: **July 1943 at Protville and crews indicate their plans for the future.;**

Below: **'B' Flight detachment at Grottaglie, June 1944.**

These detachments operated under the control of 286 Wing, part of 242 Group North-West African Coastal Air Force, and were rotated every five days or so between 'A' and 'B' Flight. The first strike was mounted on the 5th November when six aircraft attacked and damaged a 4,500 ton MV.

Sidi Amor did not remain the Squadron base for long; on the 19th there was a move to Reghaia although the detachment at Grottaglie was maintained until the Squadron was fully established at its new base. Pat Biegel recalls the move to Reghaia and conditions at the base:

'This move included the two pigs we had been fattening in preparation for Christmas. Trussed securely they were loaded into the bomb bay of the Squadron Beaufort, the closing of the bomb doors and start-up drowned their terrified squeals. On arrival we set up camp in the sand dunes near a little coastal village a few miles north of the airfield.

'At each of our camps I imagine that someone, probably the Adjutant, must have allocated the area to be occupied by the three messes, but there was never any of the regimentation of a tented Army camp and homeliness came before bull...t. The messes consisted of the larger EPIP (European Personnel, Indian Pattern) tents which could be joined in tandem to give any required floor space. One end, with adjacent kitchen tent(s) was for dining and the other, which contained a bar and easy chairs was for relaxation. Lightning was usually by Tilley pressure lamps although I think we were sometimes hooked onto a diesel generator. Around these messes we pitched our smaller individual tents known by their weight as '180 pounders' and sleeping anything from one to four. Headroom in these could be considerably increased by digging out the floor area by a few feet so that one entered by descending a couple of steps. 'Desert Lilies' provided the only organised sanitary arrangements and we bathed, washed and shaved outside our tents in bowls of cold water filled from the jerrycans on which they were stood.

'If our domestic sites tended to be primitive, our working conditions were even more so, one or two tents providing the only airfield accommodation and nearly all servicing, even to major tasks like engine changes, being done in the open. We armourers actually had two tents, one for servicing the somewhat temperamental belt feed mechanisms of the 20 mm Hispanos and another as office and arms store. I do not recall our ever having an official scale of small arms, but over the years we managed by fair means or foul to collect a motley but impressive array of light machine guns and rifles, with German Mausers in preponderance.'

The Grottaglie detachment flew regular anti-shipping and anti-submarine rovers while the HQ element and other flight settled in at Reghaia and also picked up new ASV-equipped aircraft from the depot at Setif. The new aircraft had another feature which was to affect the future of the Squadron - rocket projectile fittings. In place of the wing guns these aircraft were fitted with four launching rails on either side. The rails had three different elevation adjustments and for anti-shipping attacks were set to produce a spread pattern which was aimed to enter the water just short of the target so that the rockets hit below the water line. Sergeant Armourer Pat Biegel:

'The advent of rockets gave us armourers a greatly increased workload and the rocket prep. team was hard at it all day fitting fins, launching saddles and heads. The latter were tightened by hand until we had a few cases of heads vibrating loose in flight and subsequently falling off when the rocket fired. This left the pilot with the alarming sight of a rocket which remained on the rail with a jet of flame pouring from each end. The addition of a strap wrench to our tool kits soon cured this problem.'

Conversion to the use of RPs started in early December, with crews flying training sorties on the RP range. This course was completed by the end of the month except for one or two pilots who had been in hospital for most of the month. The conversion to RPs brought to an end the torpedo operations which 39 Squadron had been very successfully carrying out for over two years. However, the ship-busting role was to continue, using 25 lb head RPs. The designation 39 Torpedo Squadron did not change until the 31st March 1944 when the Squadron officially became 39 (Day Fighter) Squadron.

Meanwhile, from late November, the Squadron was flying standing patrols on 'offensive stopper patrols' to intercept German reconnaissance aircraft flying along the North African coast and in the area between the Balearic Islands and the Spanish mainland. The first success came on 2nd December when a Ju 88 was shot down near Ibiza. However, it was impractical to maintain standing patrols, and so the Squadron reverted to maintaining a standby of six aircraft which could be scrambled when required.

The following signal was received by 328 Wing during December from General Spaatz, Commanding General, Northwest African Air Forces:

'Your work in the protection of convoys against enemy reconnaissance aircraft reflects great credit upon your organisation and upon the operating efficiency of you and your command. I know that you will meet the greater

Aircrew relax in the Officers Mess at Reghaia, near Algiers. The Squadron was soon to leave North Africa for Sardinia. An assortment of clothing and footwear. (*W.H.Armstrong*)

A reproduction of the original 'Torbeau Menu'.

demands which are being made upon you daily with the same high standard of performance. Your record to date has been most gratifying.'

Another signal, from the Air Officer Commanding, Northwest African Coastal Air Force, ran:

'Please convey my congratulations to 328 Wing for their superb contribution to the present battle by sinking enemy supply ships.'

On 31st December 1943, Wing Commander Harvey took a detachment to Marrakesh in French Morocco for 'unspecified duties'. On arrival, the crews were accommodated by the Americans in a variety of buildings on the station. The aircraft were brought to the 'highest state of readiness' and crews put on standby for operations, but the nature of such operations was still not specified. The mystery was solved on 2nd January when the Squadron received instructions 'maintain dawn to dusk patrols over the town of Marrakesh'. This was to protect the meeting of Roosevelt and Churchill at the Casablanca Conference to discuss the future of the war in North Africa and Southern Europe. In co-operation with the AA defences, 39 Squadron was to protect the town from aerial attack, and standing patrols were flown from 3rd January in the area over and around Marrakesh. The

Squadron was still using a Beaufort for communications and training duties, and this arrived at Marrakesh on the 4th bringing spares. It then went unserviceable itself and stayed so for a couple of weeks.

This detachment was short-lived as an advance party of 32 Squadron arrived on the 7th. The plan was for 39 to hand over the defence commitment as soon as 32 were operational, and on the 10th responsibility was duly transferred. The detachment returned to Reghaia the next day, without the Beaufort and one Beau which were unserviceable.

Back at Reghaia in the period 1st-10th January no operational flying was done, although one aircraft was held on standby. Dawn to dusk patrols were flown on the 10th in the standard operational area, Ibiza - Spanish Mainland - Balearic Islands. These were limited to one aircraft at a time as, with the detachment not yet returned from Morocco, serviceable aircraft were few and far between.

A great deal of the Squadron task at this time concerned offensive fighter patrols, also referred to as long range stopper patrols under the code-name *Hamper*, in the area mentioned above. *Hamper* meant 'ops against enemy aircraft intending to attack, or make recce of, Allied convoys off the N African coast'. More often than not they were carried out in the area of the Balearic Islands. These operations took two basic forms; standing patrols of one or two aircraft were mounted to look for reconnaissance aircraft or larger formations, usually six aircraft, were scrambled to intercept known enemy strike forces or to cover specific Allied movements. A typical stopper action occurred on the 1st February when a flight of six aircraft, led by Flying Officer Cox, was scrambled from Reghaia at 1615.

The aircraft and crews were:

'B' - LX789 F/O N D Cox
             F/Sgt N C Baker
'I' - LZ484 P/O Pitman
             F/Sgt N Mitchell
'N' - LZ154 P/O J Finn
             F/Sgt J Garnett
'C' - NE371 F/Sgt J Cuthbertson
             F/Sgt H Nuttall
'A' - NE466 F/Sgt W Pryce
             F/Sgt P Farndon
'F' - NE412 F/Sgt F Cooper
             Sgt A Bridle

'The Patrol made for Formentara Island to interecept an enemy strike force thought to be in the region, but nothing was sighted in the patrol area and so the aircraft set course for base. In position 38°20'N 00°15'E, a large formation of aircraft was sighted flying at low-level over the water. The formation consisted of some twenty-five aircraft with what seemed to be stragglers in the rear. F/O Cox positioned the patrol to attack these aircraft, which turned out to be Ju 88s acting as a flight escort. As our aircraft came in to attack from starboard, the enemy turned and climbed steeply to meet them in a head-on attack. Aircraft 'J' exchanged fire with one aircraft and strikes were observed on the enemy mainplane. On breaking away to starboard, 'J' was attacked from the rear but managed to shake off the attackers with evasive action. Aircraft 'I' turned in to make a head-on attack, but was unsuccessful as the enemy aircraft turned away. 'N', which also made a head-on attack, observed strikes on an enemy aircraft. 'C' endeavoured to attack out of the sun and while maneouvering was himself attacked by a Ju 88.

'Aircraft 'A' attacked an enemy aircraft before he was in turn himself attacked by two enemy aircraft simultaneously. The aircraft he attacked was hit in the port engine which caught fire; this enemy aircraft was seen to crash into the sea.

'Throughout the combat all our aircraft were attacked continuously and aircraft 'F' (F/Sgt

Cooper and Sgt Bridle) was badly shot up after four engagements. During the first two attacks the port outer tank was holed and the aircraft began to burn. A further attack had enabled F/Sgt Cooper to get many strikes on one enemy aircraft which also commenced to burn. With both starboard and port tanks now leaking, the pilot successfully ditched 'F' while attacks were still being made on the aircraft. After ditching he saw another Ju 88 also in the water, presumably the one he had damaged during the head-on attack. Meanwhile, F/O Cox reformed the other aircraft and set course to attack another formation consisting of fourteen enemy aircraft in position 37°56'N 02°25'E. Aircraft 'A', being damaged set course for base. The other four attacked from the rear. The formation of enemy aircraft did not split up but turned onto a NW course and returned fire. Aircraft 'C' was again attacked by a Ju 88. F/O Cox damaged one of the aircraft in the formation which were believed to be the actual strike force. Our formation reformed and seeing no more aircraft in sight, set course for base.

'Aircraft 'C' was damaged and crash-landed at Reghaia. Two enemy aircraft were shot down and three damaged.'

F/Sgt Cooper and his Nav were picked up by an Air Sea Rescue patrol the next day; the patrol also picked up the pilot of the Ju 88 which F/Sgt Cooper had shot down.

Rumour was rife of another move, and on the 29th a party was sent to Alghero, in north-west Sardinia, to assess the suitability of the airfield as a Squadron operating base. The rumour was confirmed on the evening of the 3rd February when orders were received to break camp at Reghaia the next day. This was duly done, and a road convoy of Squadron personnel and equipment departed for Algiers, to board ship for the voyage to Sardinia. The ground personnel moved to No.1 Base Personnel Depot (BPD) to await sailing; meanwhile, the CO, with the air party and rear party of ground staff, stayed at Reghaia - under the control of 338 Wing - awaiting news of the safe arrival of the main Ground party in Sardinia. The sea party eventually left Algiers aboard the SS *Daniel H Lownsdale* on the 9th and, after braving the worst storm in the area for forty years, arrived at Cagliari on the 16th. After a two-day train journey, the shattered ground party reached Alghero and the airmen were put into temporary accommodation at Fertilla and the officers in 328 Wing Mess. Before long, lengthy and heated discussions between the Squadron and the Area Requisitioning Officer led to the take-over, on the 21st, of a pre-war lido situated on the coast between the airfield and the town. All personnel were then accommodated in permanent buildings.

February 1944 and a rough journey by sea to Sardinia to catch up with the rest of the Squadron at Alghero. The ground party unloads its goodies from the SS *Daniel H Lownsdale* at Cagliari. (*D. Jones*)

Although feelings were mixed, the general opinion was that conditions were not too bad.

'The layout of the Lido camp roughly resembled the capital letter E, but with the vertical side elongated to allow for about twice as many horizontal arms. The side and arms consisted of individual concrete beach huts sleeping one or two and a villa at one end and another near the centre were the Sergeants' and Officers' messes respectively. A road ran alongside the vertical side which contained only one entrance and the sea was only a few yards from the end of the horizontal arms. By erecting a barbed wire fence at either end we were thus able to completely seal ourselves in and keep the scavengers out. In addition to permanent accommodation, the Lido also offered us the unheard of luxury of running water in place of the jerry cans we had become accustomed to.

'At the Lido we revelled in the joys of a warm sea and a beautiful sandy beach and it was not long before boats of ingenious design began to appear. All these were, however, surpassed by the brilliant creation of Tom Bridges, the M.T. Sergeant, who produced a magnificent speed-boat out of a float from a CANT seaplane fitted with a Bedford truck engine. This boat was moored off the Mess and was reached by his smaller masterpiece comprising a pair of Airacobra overload tanks joined together side by side and powered by a battery charging engine attached to the rear boom.'

In the meantime, the air party had arrived from Reghaia, except one Beau and the Beaufort which were unserviceable. The first operational sorties from the new base were carried out on the 23rd February when the three aircraft flew search patterns for two missing Beaus of 272 Squadron, unfortunately without success. At Alghero, the Squadron came under the operational control of 328 Wing, and the stated operational policy was 'to carry out attacks on enemy shipping off the coast of South France'. Standby for this role was to commence on the 1st March and in the meantime crews undertook RP exercises in conjunction with Beaus of 272 Squadron as the latter would fly anti-flak escort on anti-shipping operations. Although 39 was still officially a 'Torbeau' squadron, torpedoes were no longer carried. The transition to RPs and cannon was recognised at the end of March when the Squadron was re-designated 39 (Day Fighter) Squadron. This event passed unnoticed by all except the armourers who had a change in establishment to reflect the change in weapons.

Pat Biegel again: 'We armourers were extended to the limit, but this became a cheerfully accepted way of life. It is pleasing to reflect that mistakes were few, but I recall with shame the episode of the anti-flak pilot diving through an inferno of defensive fire and pressing his gun button to hear nothing more than a metallic clang as four breech blocks slammed home on four empty chambers.

'At Alghero the rocket conversion training continued in earnest and Big Jack Harvey hit upon an effective way of involving us all in the progress of the crews. A small rock outcrop stood in the middle of Alghero bay a short distance offshore from the Lido. This was selected as the target for the final passing-out test of each crew, who made their attack run at dusk. When the whole squadron were comfortably seated along the shoreline with their bottles of vino Big Jack would start the proceedings by firing a green Verey light from the roof of the Officers' Mess. At this signal a Beau would 'swish' in at ground level from the landward side (their name of 'whispering death' was well chosen), climb on reaching the coast and then dive on the rock firing a salvo of eight rockets with a noise like tearing canvas. Cheers or groans greeted this performance while Jack stood like Nero holding up raised or lowered thumbs.

'As the rock carried a flashing navigational warning light this practice was eventually discouraged by the authorities and we built a ship silhouette target with 50-gallon oil drums in the hills near the airfield.'

RP training was affected by a period of bad weather and by a shortage of aircraft. The Squadron, however, did commence standby for operation *Hamper* on the 1st of March, while crews continued to practice formation RP attacks using sea-drogue targets. Operational standby did not commence until the 6th and was followed by three days of inactivity as no targets presented themselves!

The 10th started routinely enough with practice attacks on a towed target, but in the afternoon an anti-shipping strike by four aircraft (plus four anti-flak aircraft of 272 Squadron) was called for against a 3,000 ton MV sighted some twenty miles west of Marseilles. Squadron Leader Butler led the attack. Many hits with RP and cannon were observed and the vessel was last observed listing to starboard. An excellent

start to the RP era - and all aircraft returned undamaged.

Similar strikes were mounted throughout March. Two MVs were attacked on the 12th and one was left burning; the other turned out to be Spanish. This unfortunate incident provided much useful information of the effect of RPs - as shown by the following extracts from HQ letters dated 30th March 1944:

'Vessel *Cabo San Sebastian* attacked by Beaufighters, 18th March, has been towed to Barcelona after temporary repairs at Valicara. Surveyor who estimated damage gives following information: three impacts each about 15 centimeteres in diameter entered vessel on port side and in two cases went clean through the vessel, coming out on starboard side. Third entered well below water line in upward direction. No outlet found for this and no explosion damage is evident. Extraordinary damage caused by fire resulting from bomb impact which entered from top of vessel between bridge and funnel slightly to right, perforating bridge deck and upper deck to bunkers where was fired, and as result cargo in number two hold and lower deck also fired. No damage by explosion. Surveyor remarks perforating power considerable. One deck support cut clean through. Slight damage by machine gun fire in flooding hold made by two impacts. Reports confirm vessel would not have made port if attacked away from shore. Any further details will follow.'

The vessel set on fire was the 3,725 ton MV *Killisi* and to quote an Italian broadcast: 'the ship was set on fire and can be considered lost. Ten members of the crew were killed and fifteen injured.'

Similar success came on the 16th when two more MVs (5,000 and 3,000 tons) were left burning in the Gulf of Fos. Both were later seen by a PR aircraft at the entrance to the St Louis canal - one stationary and the other capsized on its starboard side. Even with these successes, it was the opinion of many authorities that the 25 lb RPs lacked hitting power and that better results would be obtained using a more powerful RP. These attacks provided a very sound start to the RP role and the 'Operational Comment' in the Squadron Ops Log reflects feelings on 39 at the time: 'This month's operations have proved the value of Rocket Projectiles as an anti-shipping weapon. Evidence shows that well trained crews can definitely sink vessels of a medium size, or cause enough damage to put them out of action for some time.'

In the early days of RP conversion, crews did have some doubt as to the hitting power and accuracy of RPs. Reports from squadrons operating from the UK had indicated that the RP was being used with some success, but that it was

The Beaufighter X in its RP (Rocket Projectile) fit which the Squadron turned to in place of the Torpedo. Each aircraft had 4 launch rails under each wing for 25lb or 60lb RPs, plus the four x 20mm cannon in the nose. The wing machine guns were unusable with RP rails fitted.

not causing sufficient damage to sink vessels much larger than the escort type. It appeared that the trend was to retain torpedoes for the attack on the actual target ship, and to use RP, AP and explosive heads, against the escort vessels and other small ships in the convoy. However, despite the not too encouraging reports, crews showed great interest in the device and constant practice on a land target proved that the RP could be fired with a reasonable degree of accuracy.

On arrival at Alghero, only attacks by single aircraft and pairs had been carried out on any scale. At once, practice formation attacks began in company with aircraft of No.272 Squadron taking the role of anti-flak. It had been realised that attacks by single aircraft demanded a high standard of flying for correct aiming of the rockets but to obtain the same results with a formation of aircraft, a fine degree of timing would have to be practised. Discussions after each exercise, and analysis of the cine films taken by each aircraft during the attacks, resulted in the adoption of a tactical drill for a standard formation of eight aircraft. Four would be armed with RPs and four to carry out anti-flak attacks with cannon. The tactics thus developed were employed on the first anti-shipping strikes from Alghero.

It was normal practice for Squadron aircrew to hold a conference every two weeks or so to discuss recent operations and tactics, as well as general aspects of flying. During one such discussion, it was suggested that double rockets should be used (25 lb AP heads) to increase the hitting power. This new device consisted of one rocket fixed to the launch rail with a second underneath it, and held to the first with steel brackets. The idea was implemented at Squadron level and experimental projectiles were made up and test fired on the RP range to study the capability and behaviour of the weapon. These tests continued throughout early April and were generally considered successful, although the oil-drum targets of the RP range were a 'soft' target.

Meanwhile, the social life at the 39 Squadron lido was rapidly developing: football, boxing and swimming activities were arranged. There was also a cinema show three times a week using films borrowed from the American film library. The highlight of the month was a visit by an ENSA party which included Florence Desmond, Kay Cavendish and Johnny Lockwood. The football team quickly established its superiority by winning the RAF Sardinia League (Played 6, Won 5; Goals: for 23, against 5).

The first half of April was quiet with no shipping strikes called for. The absence of shipping movements in daylight indicated that the Axis considered it too dangerous to move convoys by day and limited their movements to the hours of darkness. Having said that, however, a strike was mounted on the 6th against a 1,200 MV. During the attack, the strike leader noticed that the ship had International markings and the attack was discontinued. Partly due to the lack of shipping, and partly due to suspicions of the validity of International markings, a 'sink at sight' area was established. This assumed that any vessels entering the area without prior notification to the Allied Authorities were either enemy vessels, possibly with false markings or neutral vessels 'controlled' by the enemy. The new policy led to an attack on a MV with International markings which sailed into the 'sink at sight' area on the 19th April. Nevertheless, the main effort in April was devoted to intensive training, especially in the use of 60 lb RP heads on the range, and maintaining standby for *Hamper* sorties.

Towards the end of April, experiments were undertaken to examine the feasibility of making RP attacks at night. The Squadron anticipated that night rovers would be called for during the full-moon period and the general opinion amongst the crews was that such attacks were possible but with degraded accuracy. The other change concerned operational emphasis with first priority being transferred from anti-shipping strikes to 'stopper' patrols. The Squadron was tasked with protecting Allied shipping moving along the North African coast. Two types of patrol were instigated to achieve this task - *Dolphin* (off Cape Bagur) and *Trapper One* (20-60 miles west of Minorca). As with previous fighter patrols, the vast majority were notable for their boredom, although a Ju 188 on a reconnaissance mission was shot down on 1st May by a *Dolphin* patrol flown by Flying Officer 'Den' Derby and Flying Officer John Manners on their first operational flight. Although Flying Officer Derby was wounded in the side and right arm, he flew his aircraft back to base

safely and with photo proof of his kill. In this instance the pilot had he known, would have had a very personal reason for ensuring the safety of the convoy in question - he later learnt that his brother was on one of the Allied convoys in this area.

John Manners vividly remembers the incident: 'My pilot, Flying Officer 'Den' Derby, and I had been briefed to patrol in Beau 'N for Nuts' up and down an area of sea some distance from the Mediterranean coast of Spain and to keep our eyes peeled for enemy reconnaissance aircraft believed to use that route back to their bases after spying on our Middle East convoys. This was our first such sortie but I cannot remember any great feeling of excitement that at last this was the real thing. I was more concerned about arriving on patrol at exactly the right spot, keeping station during a long period of stooging up and down and eventually getting back to base with a minimum of error. Any idea of actually meeting the enemy seemed very remote.

'Once airborne and over the coast we dropped right down to zero feet and set off on the 300 mile flight to the patrol area. The Squadron took great pride in flying lower than anyone else, not only to avoid radar detection but also to more easily spot enemy aircraft silhouetted against the sky line. Shipping was also easier to spot in this way, although on moonlight nights we flew a little higher and searched the moonpath.

Navigator's Cockpit in a Beaufighter Mk. 10 looking to the rear. *(Ron Mettam)*

Navigator's Cockpit in a Beaufighter Mk. 10 looking forward. *(Ron Mettam)*

'We had not been on patrol long when we spotted an aircraft about a mile away, silhouetted just above the horizon. Aircraft recognition was not our strong point but we assumed it was an enemy aircraft as, to our knowledge, no other allied aircraft were in the area. Keeping as low as we could, we set off in pursuit. We were closing rapidly when some sudden deviations from the straight and narrow on the part of our quarry showed that we had been spotted and the distance between us was increasing again. Den opened up the taps to absolute maximum and the Beau roared away at top speed, gaining again but only very slowly as the Ju 88, as we now thought it to be, neared the coast. (We later decided that it had been a Ju 188) So began a straight race with no avoiding action on the part of the enemy. I reminded Den that 'the book' said it was unsafe to drive the Beau at full bore for more than ten minutes. This useless bit of information was completely ignored! Shortly after this, Den opened fire with the 20 mm cannon at what must have been extreme range, at the same time as we crossed the coast. Suddenly it occurred to me that the Ju 188 had rear-facing guns - and we were pounding along dead astern. Just then, bits of the enemy aircraft started breaking away and coming straight towards us so we pulled out of the way. With one engine smoking, the Junkers flew into the ground and disintegrated. We did a quick circuit to take photographs and then nipped back to the coast again. Den asked me for a course for base and mentioned that I had better come up front as he had been injured. I gave him the course and then scrambled over the cannon mags and main spar to stand behind him, on the pilot's escape hatch.

'Now the excitement was over, he looked pretty sick and seemed to think he might pass out at any moment. This was a bit worrying as the only way a Navigator could fly a Beau was by reaching over the pilot and flying on stick and throttle only. A few playful attempts at this in the past and 4½ hours in Link trainers suddenly appeared grossly inadequate. I cut through the right sleeve of Den's battledress and placed a field dressing on his wound. He was spattered on the face and arms with perspex chips from the shattered window. Another bullet had gone through the rudder cable and also through Den's flying boot causing another flesh wound. A further bullet went through an engine cowling, also missing everything vital.

Den didn't pass out - and bit by bit things 'up front' returned to almost normal so I nipped back to my seat for a while to check my course. I couldn't find any sound reason to change it by even one degree. I also tried to get a message out on the radio and got no answer.

'As we were otherwise blind behind I stayed where I was, but ready to dash 'up front' again if the need arose. In due course we made our landfall off the headland near Alghero - spot on, after four hours away.

'The traditional way to come home from an operation was to fly low over the bay and straight at the Officers Mess on the beach, pulling up at the last moment over the heads of fellow Officers waiting anxiously to check that all aircraft had returned safely. On this occasion Den seemed to thoroughly enjoy this manoeuvre though I confess I was a trifle anxious - hoping it all held together and the undercart was still intact and would lock down.

'All went well, the landing was normal and Den was whipped away in an ambulance while I went in to debriefing and then back to the Mess for the unofficial debriefing in the bar. Den was in hospital for several days and it was over three weeks before we flew together again.'

Flying Officer Derby was awarded the DFC for this mission.

Following the success against the Ju 188, the month continued with a strike against a 1,500 ton MV plus two escorts at the entrance to Sete harbour on the 6th when six RP Beaus of 39 Squadron plus six anti-flak of 272 Squadron pressed home an accurate attack despite intense flak from the ships and shore installations. However, this was to be the only ship strike of the month and for a week in late May the Squadron turned its attention to land targets - in the shape of radar stations. The first attack, and the first operational use of the double-headed RPs, took place on the 18th when four aircraft, each carrying eight of the new double-headed RPs, attacked the radar station at Cap Camarat. Many direct hits were scored with RP and with cannon fire. The target was left wreathed in smoke, extensive damage having been caused to the buildings and RDF towers. The double-headed RPs were most effective and as one crew commented, 'bashing radars is fun'. Following the success of this attack, two more were planned for the 20th, one against Cap Mele and one against Cap Antibes, but they were called off as the crews were walking to the aircraft because of extensive low cloud in the target area. Cap Mele was however, 'visited' on the 25th and Cap Antibes on the 27th - with equal success. A second visit was paid to Cap Camarat on the 26th and was notable for the damage caused to the 'Coast-watcher' and 'Freya' radar installations.

The combination of stopper patrols and anti-ship patrols made June a hectic month for 39 Squadron with over 121 operational sorties (460 hours) firing 240 x 25 lb RPs, - including some doubles - plus a good deal of 20 mm ammunition.

290·39·27 5 44/ 8˚ R.D.F STⁿ ANTIBES · 500′ A. T 39

Smoke engulfs the radar station at Cap Antibes following RP and cannon strikes on 27 May 1944. *(W.H.Armstrong)*

Continuing on the theme of changes in policy and role, June saw the start of night intruder sorties over the Italian coastline. Any aircraft which completed its designated sea patrol uneventually was given free rein to seek-out good targets inland, such as bridges, rail facilities and radars. However, the experience level of the Squadron took a plunge during the month when tour lengths were reduced from fifteen to twelve months. This made a fair proportion of 39's aircrew tour-expired overnight.

The moonlight rovers went both ways - a good start was made on the 1st when Flying Officer Cox planted his RPs into a 2,000 ton MV off Marseilles, causing the vessel to explode in a 'most impressive manner'. However, on the night of 8/9th two Beaus were lost, although the crew of one of them was picked up later off

Capris Island. The aircraft had been hit by ship and shore flak when attacking a small MV and one engine was put out of action. The pilot, Squadron Leader Curlee, then performed the remarkable feat of a successful single-engined ditching at night! He and Warrant Officer Adam then spent 2½ days in their dinghy before they were spotted by an ASR Warwick - which was not in fact looking for them but for another crew!

On the 10th, the Squadron was ordered to prepare for a detachment to Grottaglie near Taranto, and two days later nine aircraft plus support personnel left Alghero for southern Italy. The detachment was to 'carry out daylight shipping strikes on the North Adriatic and undertake consumption and performance tests with a view to crossing the mountainous regions of Albania and Greece to carry out shipping strikes in the Aegean Sea.' This policy was thrashed out at a council of war on the 13th June presided over by the AOC, Air Commodore Harcourt-Smith, and rovers began from Grottaglie the next day. The majority of the North Adriatic rovers were notable for their lack of suitable targets, and the Aegean Sea rovers, which started on the 17th performance tests having proved satisfactory, suffered from a similar lack of shipping targets. However, aircraft on the Aegean Sea rovers soon began to make their mark on the railway system in the Salonika region. Of two aircraft which flew the first rover, both ended up attacking rail targets near Salonika; unfortunately, one Beau flew into high ground and exploded. The other aircraft then encountered a Fieseler Storch light communications aircraft and, as the Beau was out of ammo, the pilot called on some patrolling Spitfires to exact retribution for the loss of 'L'. By the end of the month, train-busting in the Salonika region had become a Squadron speciality and on the 27th Wing Commander Innis busted six and Flight Lieutenant Charles a further five - as well as damaging bridges, track and buildings. A repeat performance was carried out the following day with a goods-yard full of locomotives and box cars vanishing in a hail of RPs and 20 mm cannon fire.

A new tactical approach to shipping was adopted in the last week of June when two Beaus flew in company with a 14 Squadron Marauder. The Marauder would cruise some five miles offshore using binoculars to pick up any coastal shipping. As soon as a target was located the Beaus were given details over the VHF radio and sped off at low level in the direction indicated. One of the earliest examples was also one of the most spectacular, when, on the 22nd, a force of fifteen small MVs under the wing of an 800 ton flak-ship was picked up off Maestra Point. The Beaus sped into the attack hugging the waves and loosing their RPs at the last minute whilst at the same time spraying their targets with cannon fire. Flight Lieutenant Marshall summed up the episode, 'we were fortunate enough to surprise

a large concentration of small vessels and were able to inflict considerable damage before what could have been serious opposition from the flak-ship developed.'

The effect of RP, and cannon fire, on small vessels could be very spectacular as often the ship would disintegrate into a mass of debris.

Similar Marauder/Beau sorties were flown throughout July and with notable success as an ever growing list of small and medium MVs fell victim to 39 Squadron. The majority of rovers consisted of a two hour search possibly enlivened by a thirty second attack. The theory ran that anything moving, by land or sea, under petrol power was fair game as only the 'bad Guys' had access to petrol supplies.

Back at Alghero, meanwhile, no operational sorties were flown between 12th - 19th June, the moon having lost its usefulness at the end of the first week. Flying was restricted to RP training and air tests, with routine servicing and compass swings filling in the time. The lido became even more like a holiday camp as many of the aircrew were tour-expired and without a care in the world'. New arrivals, a frequent occurrence as Squadron losses were heavy in the period May to July 1943, often thought they had gone to the wrong place as all they saw were people in swimming trunks, sunbathing

On course from Alghero, an excellent view of the plan form of the Beaufighter, note RP rails and ASV aerial. Anti-shipping ops gave way to attacks on land targets and train-busting became a favoured occupation when the Squadron moved to Biferno in Italy. (W.H.Armstrong)

and sailing the Mess boat *Saucy Sue.* Things livened up, socially not operationally, on the 16th with the start of what turned out to be a 48-hour party to say farewell to Wing Commander 'Jock' Harvey, who was leaving the Squadron on posting to Middle East Staff College. The party was enhanced by the timely landing of a Beau which arrived via Malta, with a supply of beer (it is said that this aircraft broke all previous beer-carrying records by a Beau). After this mammoth 'binge', personnel had twelve hours to recover before the arrival of the new CO. Wing Commander A R De Innis DFC arrived on the 19th, from 242 Group, to take command of 39 and was to stay with the Squadron through the rest of the Beaufighter period and into the early months of the Marauder.

Alghero remained quiet in early July with efforts being made to get all the aircraft serviceable for a move to join the detachment at Grottaglie. On the 6th July, the road party left for Cagliari followed by the rail party the next day. Both groups joined the same convoy for Naples but on different ships, one of which was the *John W Brown.* After a pleasant voyage the convoy arrived in the Bay of Naples on the 9th with 'Vesuvius looking most impressive in the evening sunlight.' However, the next day, an officer from the advance party visited the two Squadron groups and informed them of a change of destination, instead of Grottaglie it was to be Campomarino, near Termoli, on the Adriatic Coast. The news was greeted with enthusiasm, as the Squadron detachment at Grottaglie had not sent very encouraging reports of the base and its surrounding area. The equipment and personnel from the convoy spent a few days at Naples and eventually arrived at Campomarino on the 15th. Meanwhile, the Grottaglie detachment continued operations until the 11th and then prepared the remaining eight aircraft for the move to Campomarino whence they arrived on the 13th. 39 Squadron had joined the Balkan Air Force (BAF).

Campomarino airfield consisted of a number of nissen huts and an ever increasing amount of Pierced Steel Planking (PSP) for runways, taxiways and dispersals. The Squadron share was a number of nissen huts used as messes and airmens quarters, plus a mass of assorted tenting dumped beside the road. From this mass the officers and SNCOs selected what they needed and soon an 'impressive' canvas camp srang up. Life under canvas was tolerable during the Adriatic summer but when winter came the road became a river of mud and the tented area was either a sea of mud or the ground was rock-hard with frost.

Except for detachments, Campomarino was to be the home of the Squadron for the rest of the war. The official name was Campomarino but it was more often recorded as, and known

by crews as, Biferno. The confusion arises from the fact that there were two distinct parts to the 'airfield'. On the coast was the single runway plus dispersals, control tower and engineering support; inland was the HQ of BAF plus Messes, living accommodation and admin facilities. Close to the airfield was the mouth of the Biferno river and it is this that led to the airfield being referred to as Biferno by crews. The other area was known as Campomarino, after the local village. In the ensuing pages of this and the next chapter the two names are used to refer to both places; by making the names interchangeable it reflects the 'confusion' of the period!

Operations commenced immediately with a four aircraft intruder patrol on the 14th July along a stretch of railway WNW of Belgrade; seven trains were attacked, but one Beau was shot down and one badly damaged. From late July onwards, the Squadron's area of operations tended to shift further into Albania and Yugoslavia, and eventually the latter was receiving most attention - often in direct support of Tito's partisans.

The train-busting rovers gave crews mixed feelings. There was the exhilaration of flying at high speed and low-level along the valleys of Greece, Albania and Yugoslavia often below layers of cloud that covered the surrounding hills. Pilot and Nav would wave to the peasants who were tilling the fields on the sides of the valley and the peasants would wave back and smile. Then, within moments, the peaceful scene would change if a train was sighted further up the valley. Peaceful thoughts would fade as the crew set up their aircraft for its attack on the target. As the aircraft sped towards the train, the pilot would fire a series of bursts of cannon fire and, possibly, a number of RPs, aiming to destroy the loco and as many trucks and wagons as possible. At the same time, the crew would hope to see the driver leap from his cab and make for safety beside the track - since most of the drivers were native Slavs and Greeks. Within seconds, the attack would be over and the aircraft would fly on looking for fresh prey, leaving a smoking, steaming wreck behind. On a 'good' day one aircraft could account for five or six trains and maybe a bridge or two as well. Nevertheless, they were high risk sorties for apart from the natural hazards of low flying in confined spaces, and often poor weather, a well-sited rapid-firing flak position - on a bridge for instance - could find the Beau a fairly easy target once the element of surprise had been lost. On many of these intruder sorties, aircraft used the ALG at Leverano in southern Italy as a refuelling stop.

For a variety of reasons, by the 16th the Squadron had only one aircraft serviceable so a

48-hour stand-down was ordered to enable the groundcrew to get more aircraft on line. Aircraft availability was very variable as losses were high; six aircraft were lost in July, four of which crashed (or in one case crash-landed) in enemy territory, and combined with the extensive damage suffered by aircraft which got back, meant that a serviceability rate of six out of a nominal twenty to twenty-five aircraft was good going! So that the hard-working groundcrew could keep in touch with operations...

'the CO hit upon the idea of preceding our weekly film shows with a short talk followed by a selection of the best camera gun films from the recent operations. I recall gripping my seat at one of these films which showed a narrow valley with near vertical sides rushing past at arm's length on either side. Just as the sheer wall of rock at the end seemed to be entering the camera lens it suddenly fell away below and a hilltop radar station appeared in sight with the smoke plumes from a salvo of rockets streaking towards it. A voice alongside me gasped 'Christ, that was hairy' and recognising it as belonging to the navigator of the attacking aircraft I whispered 'you should know, you were there'. The reply to this was 'Yes, but this is the first time I've ever seen it because I had my head well down in the back when all that was going on!''

An opportunity soon arose to test the social facilities of the Biferno area when, on the 15th, a number of officers were promoted. A party was held in the Termoli Officers Club and its environs, the general verdict, of those who could remember much about it, was 'not bad wine and nice views.' One of the officers in question had celebrated his promotion that morning by busting a number of trains in Yugoslavia.

By the 19th, the groundcrew had managed to get four aircraft serviceable and advantage was taken to mount yet another new type of operation - a strike against a pre-arranged land target. The strike was carried out, by four Beaus with four Mustangs as escort, on the chrome mine at Dhomokos. The mine was hard to find as the local topography played a dirty trick on the Navs - a nearby lake was dried up and only found with difficulty. However, when located, the target was suitably treated to RP and cannon fire and left covered in smoke and with extensive damage to the storage sheds. The main aim of the strike was to support the local partisans since the mine was being used as a strong point for operations against them. As such it marked the beginning of closer co-operation between the strike aircraft of Balkan Air Force and the partisans.

The Squadron became heavily involved with local construction work, a change from explosive demolition, in the last week of July and first week of August. An RP target was built out of empty petrol drums on the beach at the mouth of the Biferno river, and was in use by August 5th. The range was to see extensive use for training new crews and for demonstrating to visiting 'Air Officers' the value of the RPs. The second project was the construction of a concrete patio outside the Officers Mess -an idea instigated by the Doctor as good for the body and soul. While recovering in the bar from an exhausting session of concrete mixing one of the Squadron pilots overhead a Spitfire pilot shooting a line about low flying. 'I say old chap, have you ever been fired down at from hills.' To which the 39 Squadron pilot interjected, 'fired down at from hills.' Listen chum, I've been fired down at from ships!' The unofficial Squadron motto was 'none flew lower'!

Five aircraft were sent to Reghaia on the 25th and stayed there five days with no operational flying and no idea of what they were there for. Some of those left at Biferno thought it was a sneaky way to get out of mixing concrete.

An important visitor arrived at Biferno on the 8th August - AOC Balkan Air Force, AVM W Elliott CB, CBE, FCC. On his visit to 39, he spoke to all the aircrew at a gathering on the grass by the peri-track. His message was that, in view of the heavy losses suffered by the Squadron in the past month, he proposed to replace most of the intruder patrols with strikes against pre-arranged targets. However, he asked the Squadron to bear in mind that the underlying principal was still the total disruption of the enemy communications network.

Accordingly, the first three weeks of the month were taken up by almost daily strikes against a wide variety of land targets. For example: fuel and ammunition stores (Jablanca and Prilep); oil refineries (Sisak and Zamcanje); barracks (Paracin and Elbar); harbours (Zaganthos); observation posts (Uljan Island) and power stations (Krka). The number of Beau squadrons at Biferno was increased by the arrival of 16 SAAF and 19 SAAF and mixed squadron strikes now took place with 39 sometimes acting as anti-flak and not carrying RFs.

Good news was received on the 25th August when it was learnt that the crew of an aircraft shot down over Albania on 21st July were safe and on their way back, having stayed for a while with the partisans. Flying Officer 'Pip' Williams and Flying Officer Clifford arrived back on the 26th and were taken on a tour of the camp to recount their escapades. Pip Williams commented: 'I shot such a solid line of British propaganda that the Partisans are now practically anti-communist!'

From:- **Flying Officer S Williams. 138052.**
No.39 Squadron, RAF CMF.
Date:- 14th September 1944

Sir,

I have the honour to report that on July 21st, we (F/O Clifford, Pilot, myself Navigator (W), took off from Leverano on an intruder patrol in the area South of Salonika.

At 0835 hours together with aircraft 'T' we attacked a locomotive drawing ten box cars and trucks in position 4030N 2233E. Hits were scored with cannons and the locomotive was left steaming.

We then proceeded along the railway line and at 0840 hours a train was sighted on a bridge in position 4039N 2232E.

We then attacked with cannons scoring hits on the locomotive and were followed by aircraft 'T' who attacked with four RPs. During the attack accurate 20 m.m. flak was experienced from both ends of the bridge and it is thought that we were hit on the starboard side of the fuselage although no damage was seen. Aircraft 'T' reported on V.H.F. that he was damaged so it was decided to set course for base.

A few minutes later the pilot F/O WP Clifford informed me that his instruments were showing a failure of the port engine, so I put on my parachute pack, refastened the armour plate doors at the rear of the cockpit and sent a message to base on HF/IF. The other aircraft was called up on V.H.F. and informed of our situation.

As it was more than likely that we would have to continue on one engine we altered course to avoid the mountains and asked aircraft 'T' to inform Base that we were in trouble. He answered that we were heading for KORITSA and that there was flak around our aircraft. Neither the pilot nor I saw this flak and at the time we were over 12 miles South of KORITSA, and not heading towards it as aircraft 'T' said. My pilot then informed aircraft 'T' that we would try to make Base on one engine, and he replied by giving us a Q.D.M. which we ignored as it would have taken us over one of the highest mountains.

At 0925 approximately the port engine began to vibrate violently and I was told to bale out by my pilot. Unfortunately the wireless transmitter fell off its brackets and I was unable to open the escape door more than half way. At the same time the A1134 intercom went u/s and as the aircraft was losing height rapidly, I signalled O.K. to the pilot on the warning buzzer. I then jettisoned the cupola and tried to lift the transmitter off the escape hatch although this was very difficult as the armoured doors opened and the aircraft was vibrating violently. The aircraft then spiralled to port, causing the

water tank and the camera to fall on the door. The aircraft turned over twice, the port engine being on fire and on the third turn I was thrown through the cupola. I pulled the rip cord immediately and the next I recall was being on the ground. I released my harness etc and hid everything under a bush as I could hear voices nearby and the language sounded most unfamiliar. From behind a bush I saw two boys of twelve years armed to the teeth with rifles and hand grenades, and as they were both wearing red stars on their hats I went up to them and told them that I was 'Inglese'. They immediately started hugging me and shouting 'Partisani'. Within a few minutes a crowd of Partisans had gathered and after they had collected my kit I was taken to a Partisan Command Post, where I had to shake hands with thirty or forty of them. I spoke in Italian to them and they informed me that the aircraft had crashed nearby and that they hadn't seen another parachute. I then asked if they would take me to the crash but they told me that I would have to wait there until their 'Commandanti' arrived. They offered me a drink of wine but as it was ten times stronger than Gin and nearly choked me I asked them for some water. They returned with a glass of sour goats milk although this only made the wine burn in my throat.

A few minutes later another partisan came in and informed me that my pilot was in a nearby monastery suffering from burns, and that I would be able to go there once I had been seen by the Commandant.

The Commandant dressed in British battle-dress eventually came and began speaking German to me. I told him, in Italian, that I was English, but this only made matters worse as he wanted to know why I understood a Terdeschi (enemy) language. He asked me for an identity card and could not understand when I told him that we do not carry them in the air. Identity discs were of no use whatever and it was not until I was taken to an English 'speaking' woman that he decided that I was English.

After a meal consisting of maize bread and goats' milk I was taken with an armed escort to the monastery where I met my pilot for the first time. As he was badly burnt I asked the Commandant if there was a doctor about, but although he kept saying 'Si, Si', he was very reluctant to do anything and was more interested in my Mae West and dinghy.

We stayed the night at the monastery and the next morning set out for a partisan hospital which was supposed to be one hour's walking away. After four and a half hours walking we eventually arrived at the hospital at Krakes where we were given a grand welcome by an Italian Dr Bruschi, who treated my pilot's burns. The

Partisans and the Partisan girls were very good to us and gave us everything that they had although their supplies were rather small.

After six days we were visited by an English captain and an A.C.2 parachutist. They stayed with us for a day and gave us escape instructions and told us that they would notify headquarters that we were safe.

On the 21st August, we left the hospital with the usual armed escort, for the Headquarters of the British mission. We arrived there after two and a half hours walking up and down mountains and for the first time in a month we had a decent meal. Almost immediately we left for a hide out near the coast, arriving there just before dark. The path down to the coast was very difficult and we were very disappointed that night as we waited for four hours and no boat turned up, so we had to return to the hide out again. The next night a boat was heard although it did not come close in so we had to return again up the cliff side. We learnt that the signalling had been bad and the boat would not take the risk as the Germans who were only two and a half miles away were also signalling. On the fourth night we again went down to the coast, I being given the work of signalling and much to our relief the boat came in and after unloading supplies we were taken out in a rowing boat to a M.T.B.

The voyage over was most unpleasant and we reached Brindisi at 0730 the following morning looking like a couple of shipwrecked mariners.

During our stay in Albania the Partisans and the British Mission were very kind to us'.

The briefing given by AVM Elliott was reinforced at the end of the month at another briefing given by an Army Intelligence Officer who stated that 'a heavy air offensive was planned for the next seven days. This would seek to totally disrupt enemy lines of communication, and the task of the Beaufighter Wing was to bring all rail movements in Albania and Greece to a standstill.'

The offensive began, but for 39 Squadron it was to be overshadowed by news that hit Biferno early on 8th September 1944. The giant Italian liner *Rex*, 51,000 tons and holder of the pre-war Blue Riband Atlantic speed record, was at sea off the coast of Trieste, and the Germans planned to use her as a blocking ship at Trieste. Other squadrons made up a number of RP strikes in the morning and by early afternoon the news that the *Rex* had been hit by at least fifty RPs and was sitting damaged in an inlet near Capodistra. At the strike briefing the CO said he expected up to 50% casualties! In the afternoon, 39 generated six aircraft and with two aircraft of 19 Squadron, a strike force, led by Flight Lieutenant Bob Pitman, set course from Biferno at 1700. The weather was appalling, with low cloud and poor visibility. but the position given and the route navigation defeated the elements. As the strike force shot across the top of a range of hills, there was the *Rex*, beached, listing to port and on fire at one end. Without delay, all aircraft pressed home the attack scoring direct hits with their RPs and leaving the vessel burning from stem to stern. The first two aircraft had an unopposed attack, but the rest were met by a barrage of flak put up by the positions around Trieste. However, the element of surprise had been achieved and all aircraft got away undamaged and flew back to Biferno with crews in a jubilant mood. The *Rex* was finished. The Beaufighter Squadrons of the Mediterranean and BAF had placed over 100 RPs in the liner. The death of the *Rex* was recorded by a Movietone camera and later in the month a cameraman arrived at Biferno to film the crews who had taken part in the attack at a simulated briefing and at their aircraft. The aircrew became filmstars for a day!

Following the excitement of the *Rex*, it was back to overland work, with a slight change of role in the disrupting lines of communication. First-light patrols were carried out, and sightings of enemy MT concentrations reported to base by VHF. The Beaus then had to avoid the temptation of attacking MT targets and instead block the roads in front of and behind the targets thus penning up the enemy convoy so that a strike force of Spitfires could finish the job. Since rail travel by daylight was extremely hazardous, trains were fewer in number, and so a policy was adopted of cutting stretches of railway line and collapsing bridges.

In the latter part of September, a tremendous storm tore the tented camp at Biferno to pieces and even de-roofed some of the Nissen huts. Thus, a six day non-flying period ensued to repair the damage, let the airfield dry out, re-site the tents, build drainage ditches and so-on. Some of the more enterprising tied their tents between trees and then pegged down the trees! With the rapid onset of winter, conditions at Biferno were to get much worse.

In mid-October, a very 'nasty' rumour circulated in the 39 tented empire. The story was that the Squadron would soon convert to the Martin Marauder medium bomber, and crews would be given the option of staying with 39 and converting to the Marauder, or staying with the Beaus and moving to other squadrons. However, the rumour was soon forgotten and life settled back to its regular routine of intruder patrols and sea rovers.

November was notable for two events: the advent of strikes by large groups of aircraft,

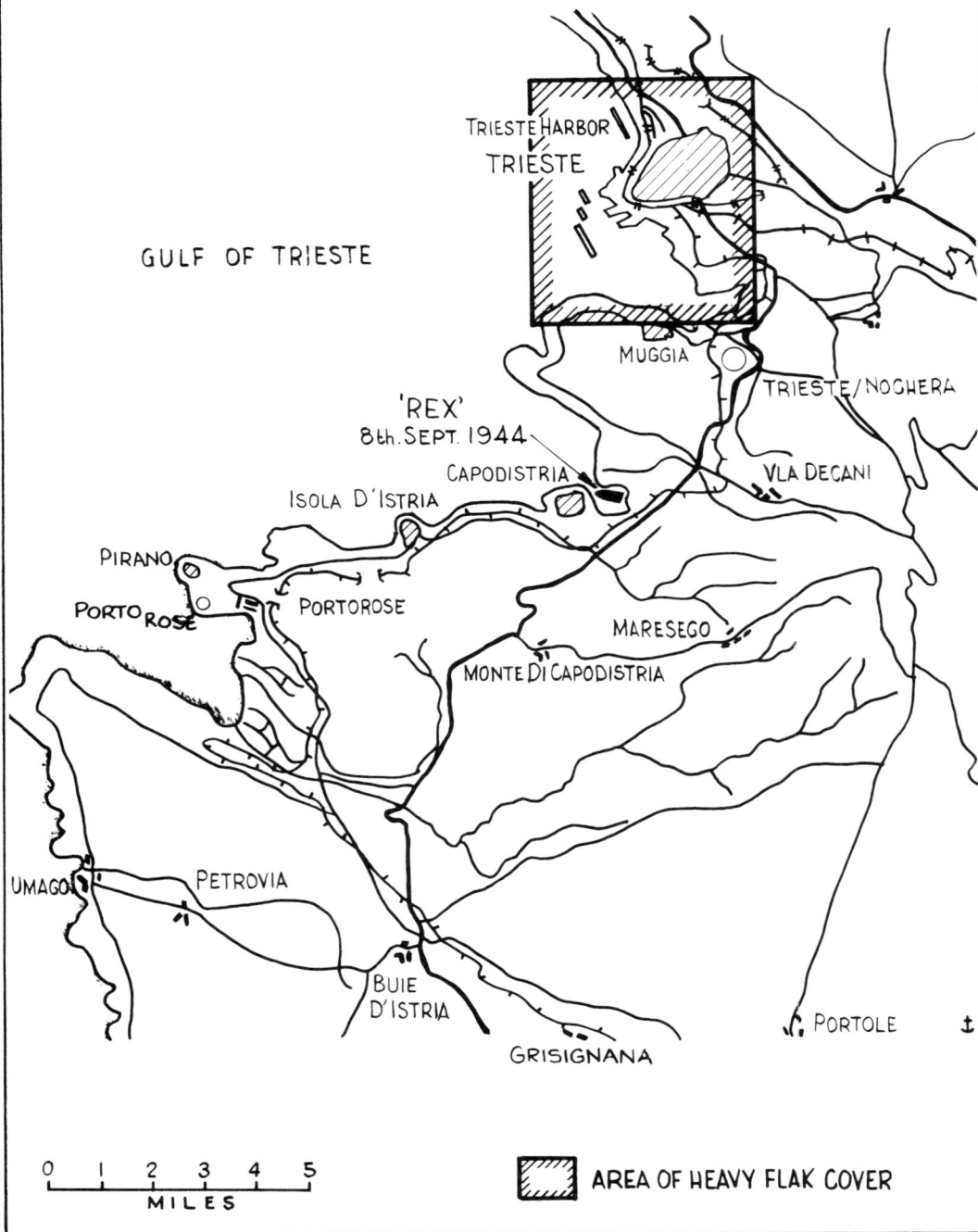

Map 11: The Sinking of the 'Rex' 8th. Sept. 1944.

TRIESTE HARBOR

TRIESTE

GULF OF TRIESTE

MUGGIA

TRIESTE / NOGHERA

'REX'
8th. SEPT. 1944

CAPODISTRIA

VLA DECANI

ISOLA D'ISTRIA

PIRANO

PORTO ROSE

PORTOROSE

MARESEGO

MONTE DI CAPODISTRIA

PETROVIA

UMAGO

BUIE
D'ISTRIA

PORTOLE

GRISIGNANA

0 1 2 3 4 5
MILES

AREA OF HEAVY FLAK COVER

Wing Strikes, and confirmation of the Marauder rumour. The poet of the Squadron Line-Book recorded the events of the 7th November thus: 39 and BAF spoke of many things. Of smoke and flames and rocket strikes, of palaces and Kings.' Seven aircraft had attacked the Albanian royal palace at Tirana, formerly the palace of King Zog but used as a German barracks. This was part of a mass strike by twenty-six aircraft (39 Squadron, 16 Squadron SAAF and 19 Squadron SAAF - plus escort) on targets in the same area. The benefits of a large strike in splitting the defences were partially offset by the risk of

RPs streak away from the aircraft towards the Lussin Picolo power house.

collision in the target zone with Beaus 'whizzing in all directions attacking different targets, very off-putting and disconcerting.' Furthermore, everyone arrived back at base at roughly the same time and had to jockey for position in the landing queue. A repeat performance at King Zog's palace was played by eleven aircraft of 39 Squadron on the 1st with the result that, 'furniture and curtains were seen leaving the palace by windows on one side as RPs entered the building on the other.'

A reminder of the proposed demise of the Beaus arrived on the 22nd in the form of thirty-four 'assorted aircrew' who turned up at the Squadron to await conversion courses on the Marauder. Many still thought and hoped it was all a bad dream until the final shattering blow fell on the 25th. In the line book, it is recorded (heavily outlined in black) thus:-

1369 39/1 17·12·44 F8" //F.F.O. 500' 0815 M.K. POWER HOUSE AT THE LUSSIN PICOLO

'From behind sombre curtains come muffled sounds of weeping and gnashing of
teeth.
For the days of the Beaufighter Boys of
39 Squadron draw close.
The old order changeth and giveth place
to the new.
They whose voices were once great in the
land, fold their tents and creep silently
away. And they who remain, lament
bitterly.
For today four crews were shattered in
our midst and sent away, the pilots on
the right hand and the navigators to
the left. The blow fell, and lo!
it was a Postings Form, reading thus:

TO CONVERT TO MARAUDERS IN THE MIDDLE EAST (pilots) ————	TO JOIN 272 Squadron
S/LDR PAYNE	F/SGT POTTS
F/LT SETTLE	F/LT WEBB
F/O WREN	F/SGT ROE
W/O McMURCHY	F/SGT ROBSON
F/SGT MULLENS	

IT IS THE END

WOE IS US --- OH, LACK-A-DAY!

The break-up of crews commenced on the 2nd
December when the first of the pilots went to
the Marauder 70 OTU at Shandur, Egypt, while
their Navigators went to 272 Beau Squadron.

As light relief in the period of sorrow, the
Squadron acquired eight new turkeys for the
farm yard; they proved to be a war-like breed
and as soon as they were in the pen with the
birds of other squadrons, they were seen in
tight 'vic' formation attacking a greater number
of 213 Squadron birds. However, despite their
numbers, the latter appeared to be ill-disciplined
and the 39 Squadron force, egged on by most
of the Officers Mess, had the better of the fray.
Throughout December, while the Marauder
element of the Squadron carried out conversion
sorties, the operational side continued intruder
and rover missions. On the 16th the Squadron
sent a detachment of six aircraft to Athens with
Flight Lieutenant Bob Pitman as detachment
commander. The Athens detachment were met
on their arrival by crews of 108 Beau Squadron,
and their first impression was that everyone was
carrying a gun. They were just about to enquire
why when a burst of machine-gun fire from 'just
up the road' brought home the fact that they
were rather close to the front line of a local war.

Ron Mettam recalls one aspect of this war: 'My
pilot, Benny Harris RCAF, myself and two others
slept at one end of the Mess in a room with
french windows on three sides. We slept with
loaded revolvers under our pillows and arranged
metal trays against the windows to give us a few
seconds alarm should anyone enter.'
The war was between the Allied-supported
Government forces and the forces of KKE (the
Communist Party of Greece) and ELAS (Ellinikos
Laikos Apeleftherotikos Stratos); civil war had
broken out on 4th December when the German
forces fled. The six Beaus were tasked to pinpoint and attack individual houses and other
buildings being used as strong points, ammo
dumps and Headquarters by the rebels. The
unusual nature of these tasks meant that crews
were using city street maps to locate and attack
targets. The Beaus had arrived at Hassani airport
just after midday on the 16th and two of the
aircraft were airborne again at 1605 for the first
strike, the target being the Athens radio station.
A few minutes after 4 o'clock the station ceased
to operate as it was devastated by cannon and
RP fire. The longest operational sortie flown by
the detachment was forty-five minutes, the
shortest fourteen minutes (including three
separate runs at the target!). The average was
twenty to twenty-five minutes. Crews recall the
strange sensation of taking-off and almost
immediately diving down at a target. As much
of the job was battering strong points that were
causing problems to ground forces, the detachment sometimes operated an airborne 'on-call'
(cab-rank) system whereby aircraft would be
called in by a ground controller, 'Sunshine', to
hit specific targets. A modification was made to
allow the RPs to be fired in pairs and so enable
four separate runs to be made and thus obtain
greater accuracy, and economy of RPs as the
60 lb heads were in short supply. This proved
useful on the 21st when five aircraft attacked
Averof prison which was being used as an ELAS
HQ. Each aircraft aimed at a different section
of the U-shaped building and, as a result, it was
methodically battered. Although Ron Mettam
was not on this strike, he went into the ruins
with ground forces to survey the damage: 'Not
only had all the concrete been blown out from
between the first floor joists, but many of these
had been bent and twisted, although at least nine
inches thick. We 'liberated' the prison bell and a
statue from the courtyard which had been turned
into a 'shinless wonder' by a 20 mm cannon shell.'
A graphic description of an RP attack was
given by an employee of a local silk factory:
'Zee airplanes come, zey go 'whoosh, whoosh,
Bang' and zee walls she fall down.'
German-officered rebel forces captured AFHQ
at Kifisia and turned it into a strongpoint. 39

Squadron was called on to destroy *one* room containing secret interrogation equipment - but to leave the rest of the building intact. Benny Harris and Ron Mettam took-off, escorted by a Spitfire to mark the target with tracer. Ron Mettam: 'We took-off at dusk and at the target I nearly shot down the Spitfire which was tracer-marking the target. He was making a second run as we fired our first pair of rockets and I was using my Browning on a pair of Bofors guns I had spotted in the grounds of the building, just in case. We broke the 39 dictum of one run and clear-off and made four separate runs.' Later photographs showed that the room had disappeared while the rest of the building was untouched. Sometimes aircraft operated as spotters for naval bombardment, watching in awe as six-inch shells crashed into buildings before going in with RPs to 'tidy-up.'

Such accounts are typical of the work carried out by the detachment at Athens. Air Marshal Sir John Slessor viewed the results of some of the RP strikes and commented, 'the 39 Squadron detachment were more effective than all the other squadrons at Kalamaki together, and their rockets had more effect upon the ELAS forces than any other single factor in the whole campaign.' By the end of the year the ELAS position in Athens was untenable, particularly after 39 had wiped-out a large proportion of the ELAS leadership in one strike on a HQ building where a conference was being held. The rebels tried to escape to the surrounding hills to continue the fight but 350 of their commandeered vehicles were destroyed in a spectacular RP and cannon strike. A cease-fire agreement was signed on 12th January 1945 and 39 Squadron flew its last operational sortie from Athens on the 14th - a reconnaissance flight to Evvoia Gulf. The day before, the Athens detachment had been told that they were to join 108 Squadron and that the Beau crews at Biferno were to be divided between 108 and 272. However, this was changed and the detachment returned to Biferno on the 18th, handing over their aircraft to 110 MU at Brindisi. At Biferno crews were split up, some to join 272 Squadron and others to convert to the Marauder. Some crews stayed together and moved to 272 at Foggia on the 25th. Many looked on it not so much joining a new unit as creating another detachment of 39 Squadron.

Throughout January, the Marauder strength was increased as new aircraft were collected from Catania and more pilots arrived back from Shandur suitably 'converted'. The last operational Beau sortie from Biferno was the 4th January when two aircraft flew a weather reconnaissance between Zagreb and Fiume. It was farewell to the Beau after eighteen months of varied and hectic operations.

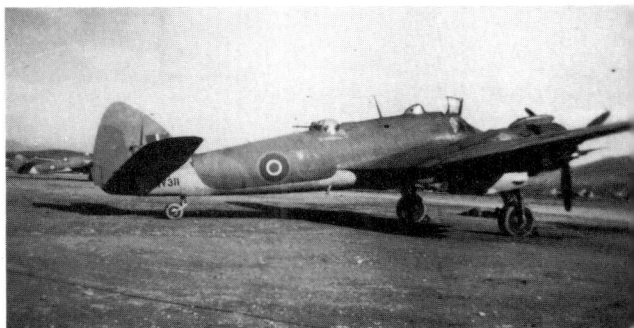

Above: **NV311/G on the dispersal at Athens in December 1944, part of the 39 Squadron detachment which operated against the Greek Communist forces in the city.** (*F.Barton*)

Below: **Christmas Menu 1944 — Marauders arrive left, Beaufighters depart right.**

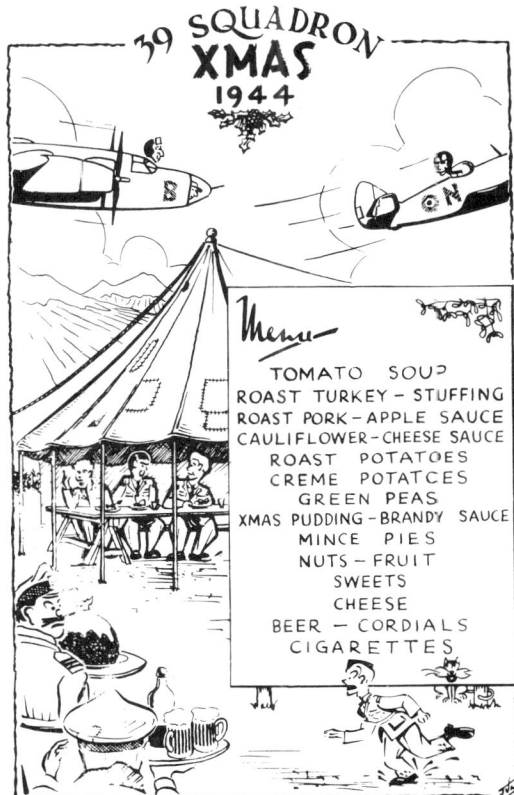

7

On, On to Novska

Christmas 1944 brought the normal festivities of fancy-dress football matches, and the officers serving Christmas dinner to the airmen. Shortly afterwards, thoughts at Biferno turned to the New Year and the advent of operations with the Marauder.

The Martin 179 had gone into production without a prototype and was the fastest bomber flying. It first flew on 25th November 1940, and quickly acquired a notorious reputation which led to the nicknames of 'Martin Murderer' and 'widow maker', although on closer examination it becomes evident that to the large extent the aircraft was given an undeserved bad press.

Its introduction to the European theatre was far from auspicious; when the 319th Bombardment Group moved from the USA to North Africa they left the USA with forty-seven aircraft and arrived in North Africa with only seventeen! However, it must be borne in mind that the aircraft were flown overweight and at extremes of range. Thus, it is hardly surprising if pilots at Biferno in late 1941 felt some trepidation at the reputation of their aircraft. The Marauder OTU at Shandur (No.70 OTU) did little to improve the reputation of the aircraft. However, it was generally liked by the instructors although there were incidences of aircraft bursting into flames in the air for no apparent reason and crashing in the desert. Nevertheless, the general impression was that once the aircraft was understood by both aircrew and ground crew it was an excellent machine in every way.

In fact, the B-26Gs and Fs, Marauder IIIs, flown by 39 Squadron proved to be reliable and safe if flown with care. Powered by two 2,000 hp Pratt and Whitney Double Wasp R-2800-43 engines, the Marauder was rated at 305 mph at 15,000 feet, with a service ceiling of 28,000 feet. On 39 Squadron, B-26Gs operated with crews of six: Pilot; second Pilot/bomb aimer; Navigator; WOP/AG; mid-upper gunner and rear gunner. The aircraft flown at the OTU at Shandur had four forward-firing .5 inch Brownings attached to the fuselage which the pilot was meant to use for ground strafing. However, the Squadron aircraft did not have these guns fitted and the pilot just 'drove the aeroplane'. If confronted with this simplified statement of their role, the pilots could always produce this quote from *Picture Post:*

'Much has been said of the spirit of fighter pilots, and much has been said of the tremendous responsibilities that make the heavy-bomber pilots wise beyond their years. The Marauder pilot is a combination of both. He has much of the flair of the fighter pilot, which comes from flying an aeroplane that takes-off and lands at more than 100mph, but he also has more than his share of the seriousness that comes to boys in their 20s who fly in combat with a great deal of money and a great many lives held firmly in their grip on the control wheel.'

The points which pilots recall are the high approach speed of 140-160 mph, the long take-off run required when fully laden, and, worst of all, the habit of the electro-hydraulic propeller to go fully fine and run away on take-off, with potentially disastrous consequences. Overall, however, the aircraft were remembered for their reliability and the fact that they were exhilarating to fly - if the requirement for attention to detail and firm handling were born in mind. Many of the pilots arriving on 39 Squadron late in 1944 were straight from training schools, having flown Oxfords, but took to their aircraft as if they had years of experience.

The self-defence armament consisted of two .5 inch waist guns in the rear fuselage, operated by the WOP, a mid-upper turret with two .5 inch guns, and two further .5 inch guns in the tail fairing which were semi-remote controlled. Offensive armament was a bomb load of up to 4,000 lbs - usually in the form of 250 lb and 500 lb bombs. Although 4,000 lbs was the normal operational bomb load, 'beginners' (crews new to the Squadron) flew their first few operational sorties with a 3,000 lb load.

As usual with American-built aircraft, the crew compartment was very comfortable, with cushions, padded arm-rests and ash trays; helmets were not worn, just ear-phones and throat mikes. Another feature the pilots liked was the armour plated protection of the cockpit area. The large armour-plated slabs on the port side of the fuselage not only gave a feeling of security, but provided a suitable area for Squadron artists to paint bomb symbols to indicate the number of raids the aircraft had made. Furthermore, the back of the pilots seat was also armoured. Each aircraft was identified by a single white letter on the nose section and a two-letter three-number serial number in black on the lower part of the fin. Decoration was completed by standard RAF roundels and the Squadron emblem, a 'winged bomb', on the nose. Also, in the early days at Biferno, the aircraft sported 'nose-art' such as 'Supermouse' and 'Gloomy Sunday' but all were removed when Wing Commander Griffiths took command of the Squadron.

Marauder 'W' in flight, the Squadron 'winged bomb' emblem is painted on one of the cockpit armour plates. Despite having a bad reputation from its early use in the United States, the Marauder proved to be a rugged, reliable aircraft if handled with care.

The plan for January 1945 was intensive training involving crew conversion, formation flying, individual and formation bombing. Unfortunately the weather intervened and the first week of the New Year saw alternate blizzards and rainstorms sweeping the airfield and turning the camp, and especially the tented living accommodation, into a quagmire. To counter the boredom the main distraction was 'vine and vermouth' stakes in the bar. During December 1944 and early January 1945 some Marauder crew members accepted offers from the Beaufighter guys to fly as observers on strikes over Yugoslavia - just to 'get the feel of things.'

On the 5th January, two crews did manage to get airborne for a sortie around the local area, but in the following three weeks, flying was limited by the continuing atrocious weather. In the meantime, the Athens detachment returned and departed to pastures new as more Marauders continued to arrive.

On the few occasions that crews did get airborne, they paid visits to the bombing range of Jabouka Island - said by some to be the safest place to be when 39 Squadron was on bombing training. Early in the training period, the first official photo taken by a Squadron Marauder was of this Island and the bombs of the attacking aircraft bursting some distance away. This photo was put on display to Squadron crews with a

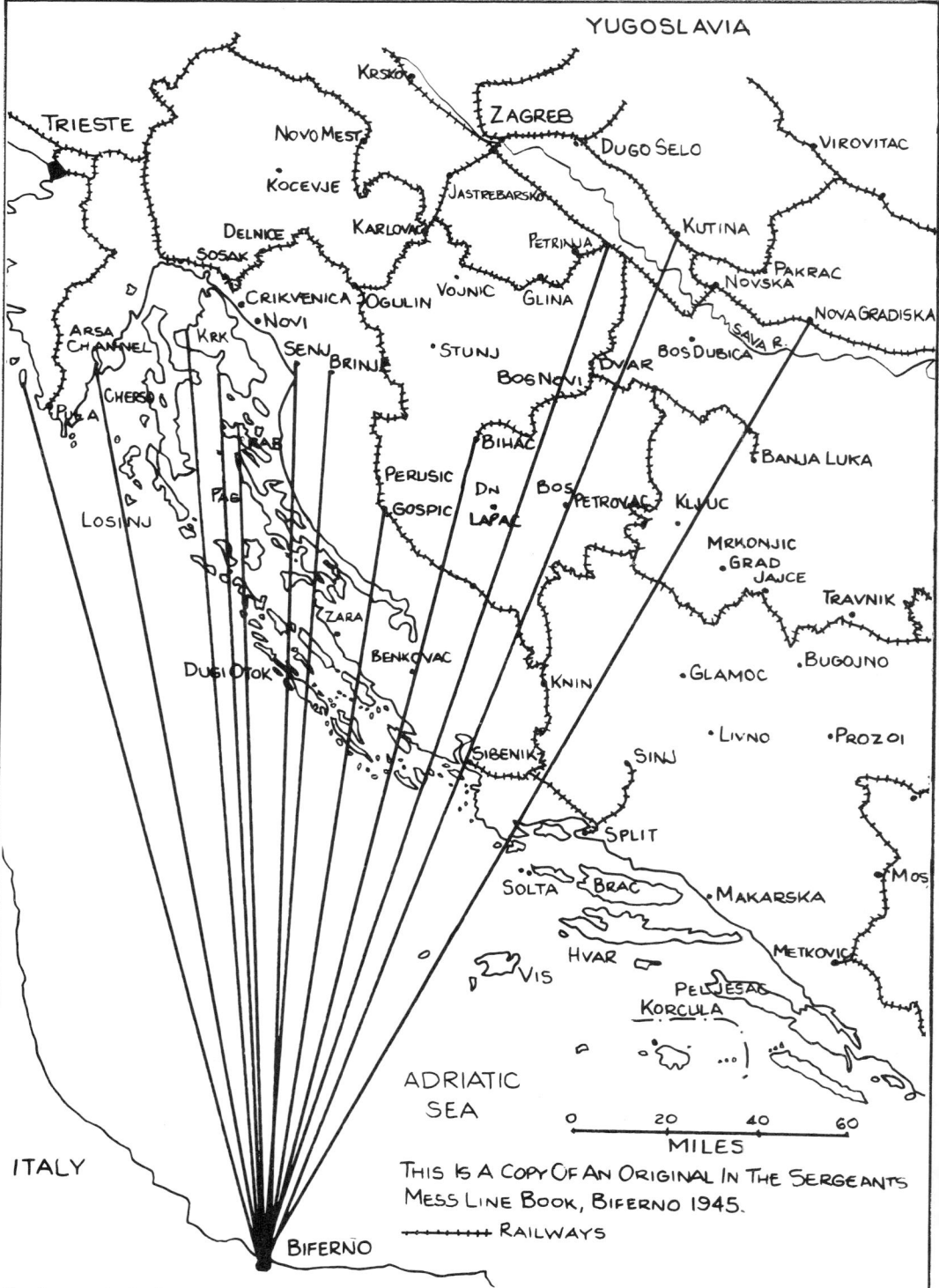

Map 12: Marauder Operations 1945

This is a copy of an original in the Sergeants
Mess Line Book, Biferno 1945.

⊢—┼—┼—┼—┼—┼— RAILWAYS

The 'drivers' seat of a 39 Squadron Marauder. Pilots found the cockpit layout more luxurious than British aircraft with comfortable seats, arm rests and ashtrays. (*Jack Callum*)

reminder that this was in fact the target and the idea was to hit it and not just to frighten it with near, and not so near, misses!

The last day of January brought an improvement in the weather and on that day two 'miracles' happened: firstly, the Squadron got five aircraft airborne to attack Jabouka Island; and secondly, they actually succeeded in hitting the Island no doubt due to the excellent advice of the bomb-aimers ... a typical conversation between pilot and bomb-aimer being recorded thus:

'Left, left, left, ... right, right, right ...steady, steady ...left, left ...' 'quiet man the bombs have gone!!' silence.

By the 1st February, the Squadron had fourteen aircraft and a full complement of crews, and the training programme intensified in the first week of the month to bring the Squadron to operational readiness. Rumour claimed that 39 was due to go into action on the 7th. For once, rumour was true, and Peter Kennedy recalls 39's inaugral Marauder action:

'Today was of course a big day for the Squadron. The operations room was something to be

seen - Woolworths on a bargain day would best describe the scene, but nevertheless a very punctual start was made at 1315 hours when twelve two fan bombardment bedsteads took to the air and headed North to 'hammer the hun'. Unfortunately, the hun suffered little and the fields of Yugoslavia greatly - but we all knew that the spirit was there!'

The target was the railway station and marshalling yards at Senje; three boxes, each of four aircraft, bombed from 6,500 feet and a number of hits were observed in the target area, confirmed by the bombing photograph, damaging the railway line.

As with the vast majority of raids in the remaining months of the war, the Marauders went unescorted as the Luftwaffe appeared to have deserted the skies over Yugoslavia. Enemy aircraft were occasionally seen but always at a distance and expressing no interest in the formations of Marauders. However, 'Wing raids' were escorted by Mustangs, usually 213 Squadron, or Spitfires.

The Squadron was airborne again the following day with twelve aircraft tasked to attack the garrison area and the HQ of 21/22 Mountain Corps at Brinj. Unfortunately, four aircraft, including Squadron Leader Payne, the raid leader, had to return to Biferno with engine trouble leaving boxes of two, three and three. The target area was covered in snow and some crew members recall being fascinated by the strangeness of the dark bomb bursts in the white blanket of snow.

Above: **39 Squadron was a very young Squadron as can be seen from this group — typical crew, left to right: Rex Waller (Nav), Bill Madeley (W/OP), Jimmy Spence (A/G), Tom Grossett (Pilot). Maurice Webster (Bomb aimer), Len Wilson (A/G).**

Opposite: **A pensive-looking CO, W/Cdr De Inniss, with harness and life-jacket. The Squadron engineering officer, F/Lt 'Plumber' Flowerdew confers with F/Sgt James. Good view of the PSP dispersals and taxiways that made up Biferno.**

Much of the tasking given to the 'Biferno Bomber Wing' - 39 Squadron and 25 Squadron SAAF Marauders and two Italian Baltimore Squadrons - followed the broad policy of 39 Beaufighter Squadron - ie disrupting communications. There were frequent raids on targets on the Brod to Novska railway line, and the Novska to Zagreb railway lines, mainly marshalling yards and stations. Bombing was normally done from medium level (6,000 - 10,000 feet), but poor weather sometimes resulted in runs being made at lower altitudes, just above the mountain tops. Comments from crew members included: 'We were so low over Konjic that we had to fly into a valley to open our bomb doors!' On February 9th the prime target of Sisak was unsuitable

because of bad weather, and the Squadron diverted to the secondary target at Konjic. Engine trouble plagued the Marauders including 'Z for Zebra' which, to quote the record, was 'suffering from an overdose of gremlinitis, with lights flashing on and off, and dials and rev-counters registering nothing but the makers name.' 'Z-Zebra' was eventually air-tested and declared flyable although the odd gremlin continued to put in an appearance.

After four operations in four days, a two-day stand-down was declared. The time was utilised for the serious business of the Officers v Sergeants football match, with the Sergeants continuing their winning streak with a 3-2 victory.

Generally, life at Biferno was simple if a bit rough, but morale was good. This has been ascribed amongst the aircrew to the fact that everyone was fairly young - mostly 20 to 25 - and that for many it was their first taste of operational flying in a foreign country. The basic four-man tent could also, with a little improvision and initiative, be turned into a reasonably comfortable lodging. A wooden frame for a bed could be obtained from a local Italian carpenter for the price of a few packets of cigarettes, and when the frame was strung with rope a serviceable end product resulted. Certainly this was far

Biferno, New Years Day 1945. The winter of 44/45 was very severe and the tented camp became a nightmare at times. However, morale on the Squadron was high, this photograph is either just before or just after one of the numerous snow fights.

superior to the alternative of a groundsheet on the floor. Many residents elected to dig out the interior of the tent so as to allow room to stand upright. Initially, lighting was by hurricane lamps but later on electric lights were installed. Heating was the big problem and a variety of 'Heath Robinson' stoves were constructed for burning oil.

Conditions were made worse in the winter of 1944/45 by severity of the weather, some of the worst recorded in South Italy. Blizzards were frequent, and when the snow thawed the whole camp became a sea of mud. Severe storms tore away tents and blew in the roofs of huts used for briefing rooms and messes. Toilet facilities were the usual primitive 'plank and pit' variety although no roof was provided for the surrounding screen!

Social life was limited but varied. It was limited because of the almost daily requirement of full Squadron raids, and varied between visits to the WVS canteen, the messes, and trips to the aircrew leave centres at Sorrento and Rome. However, visits to Rome were infrequent until after VE Day in May. Alternatives were: swimming in the Adriatic, sporting events, picture shows in the Station cinema and in the messes and the opportunity to visit local Italian families. Such visits were not encouraged; the locals tended to be very reserved, and trade was the main point of contact to barter cigarettes and chocolates for eggs and dairy products.

Peter Hatcher recalls the normal menu: 'The staple diet consisted of 'oleo' margarine which was better suited for use on undercarriage oleos, soya links (sausages made from soya beans) and McConachie's stew (canned in WW1) - with luxuries such as eggs, usually acquired by forbidden barter with Italian farmers.'

When the war ended, the opportunity for travel increased and visits to Sorrento (Naples), Rome and Riva (on Lake Garda) became more common.

The most successful of the February raids took place on the 13th against the marshalling yards at Bihac; twelve aircraft, less one that failed to get airborne, undertook the unusual procedure of flying over the target twice - once to admire the peaceful scene and then to disturb the peace! Intelligence reports showed that all four major lines were cut, two badly damaged, and the yards were put out of action for a considerable time.

When an early morning raid was planned, crews were gathered from their various resting places for an overnight briefing. This was often followed by news that the plans had changed and that the Squadron would be stood down until the afternoon! However, when the time to go finally came, everyone climbed into transport for what some considered the most dangerous part of the whole mission - the drive from the camp to the airfield.

The airfield consisted of a single North-South runway, plus taxiways and dispersals, made up of PSP laid on hard sand, in the low lying land next to the sea at the South end of the Bay of Termoli. However, the base camp containing the living accommodation and administrative headquarters was a mile or so inland and some 300 feet or so higher up. Transport between the two was in 3-ton trucks on a road that descended along the side of an almost vertical escarpment, but with a 90-degree bend about halfway down. Negotiating this 'road' was often made more hazardous by meeting the American Engineer Unit - on their way to effect runway repairs - coming the other way!

In the first three weeks of February, the Squadron had flown nine missions all of which had been 'easy' in the respect that flak had been light 'and ineffectual'. The 21st February was to be different.

The target was the harbour installations at Arsa Channel, a coaling jetty on the eastern coast of the Istrian Peninsula which the Squadron had attacked earlier in the month when no serious opposition was evident. However, as the three box formations approached the target, line-astern of 25 Squadron SAAF (Marauder), all were surprised to see the latter disappear from view in thick clouds of flak from 120 mm and 88 mm guns. As 25 Squadron cleared the target, 39 ran in, by which time the AA gunners had their guns properly layed. The formation bombed from 10,000 feet and each box in turn was bracketed with black/grey puffs of flak. The crews were able to hear rather too clearly the thump of exploding shells and the occasional whistle of shrapnel. The number three box led by Archie Ross suffered the worst, and as the tail gunners of the first two boxes watched they saw three Marauders emerge from the flak and dive away in the direction of Biferno. Then they spotted the fourth aircraft flown by Sgt 'Red' Redman, making a solo run on the oil storage tanks at Pola a little way from the main target. He had become separated from his box during the tight-turning evasive action of the leader, and he decided to go for the oil tanks. This may well have saved his life as the tail of the No.1 aircraft (Archie Ross) had been peppered with shrapnel, and this area would equate with the front half of a Marauder in the No.4 position, where Red Redman should have been. All aircraft got back to Biferno - all except one had been hit - and one aircraft, that of 'B' Flight commander, Squadron Leader Settle, had over sixty holes in it of various sizes. Archie Ross's tail gunner, Les Charteris recalls the raid: 'Before we arrived at the target area, with light puff-ball flak everywhere, we knew we were in for it. We climbed above this, only to run into heavy black flak. This seemed to increase all the time and you could hear the thump-thump of the bursts. In spite of this, all aircraft kept good formation, and we started the run in with the calls 'bomb doors open' and, 'steady, hold it' from the bomb aimer. Suddenly a red flash of light seemed to play all around the tail position and I was hit with shrapnel in both legs. A little later, after the bombing run, I was hit again in my right arm and back. Later, I managed to crawl out of the gunners tunnel and (I don't know how) crawl over the cat-walk to the front cock-pit were my wounds were dressed by the Navigator, Ken West. He was really good. The pilot, Archie Ross high-tailed it back to base in record time.

'I was told afterwards by my crew, that the tail position was a shambles, with the rear fuselage full of holes. In fact, most of the aircraft was peppered, including the port engine which was leaking badly. If there had not been the very heavy armoured plating at my back and sides that would have been my lot.

'I was taken to the field hospital at Termoli and thence to the base hospital at Foggia. After about 20 operational flights my short stay with 39 Squadron was over, and I was in Hospital until November 1945, Italy and the U.K.'

The battle-scarred aircraft came as a shock to the groundcrew, but plans were soon in hand to patch them up, Sergeant Davey requested 'three sticks of solder and a dozen spam tins.'

Peter Hatcher also recalls the raid: 'A succession of easy strikes against lightly defended targets, had led the *Trente Nova*[1] crews to

(1) For obvious linguistic reasons, the Squadron was frequently referred to as *Trente Nova (39)*.

adopt a somewhat blase attitude towards operations. Therefore, when during the evening of Tuesday 20th February, twelve crews were called for briefing, they felt more concern over their interrupted entertainment, than for what lay before them.

'Reporting to the briefing tent, they settled down to the usual animated chatter while waiting for the briefing to start. The arrival of the Senior Flight Commander together with the I.O. brought something of a hush, and the business of the evening began.

'The crew's usual high spirits were soon restored, when the target for the a.m. sortie was announced. It was to be Arsa Channel. Most of the crews had been there before, and it was known as very lightly defended.

'The general briefing, in the shape of the German Command in Northern Italy, was to take a hand in providing the happy warriors with a salutary lesson before February 21st was over.

'Wednesday morning dawned bright and cold. The crews were called early and breakfasted on the customary 'operational' eggs and bacon. Breakfast over, they assembled for pick-up and transportation to the airstrip some three miles away. Many were of the opinion that this journey by 'gharry' (3-ton lorry), through the village and down the side of the steep escarpment to the strip, was by far more dangerous than any operational sortie.

'On arrival at their Squadron dispersal, 'Met' briefing was accomplished and individual crews commenced their own specialist tasks, bomb loads and guns were checked and flight plans completed.

'By this time it was obvious that this was not to be the usual two or three box attack. All over Campo, the bomber dispersals were humming with activity, with 25 SAAF and the two Italian Stormo squadrons also readying themselves for flight. This meant some thirty-six aircraft would soon be heading north for this seemingly insignificant target.

Marauder 'I' on one of the PSP dispersals at Biferno, engines running.

'With some fifteen minutes to our own start up, 25 SAAF were already taxying out and heading for the runway and soon a further twenty-four Double Wasp engines spluttered into life as 39 got down to business.

'The stream of Marauders ahead began to take-off one by one, as our own twelve aircraft taxied slowly towards the take-off point, while astern the Italian Balts' were beginning to start up.

'Then it was our turn, and engine run-ups completed, the 39 stream roared off down the strip, lifted off, wheels up and climbing away into the crisp, blue Adriatic morning, seeking out the formation leaders and forming up for the flight northwards.

'Formations complete, courses set, guns tested, the crews relaxed and looked around, to see ahead and astern, the closely formating Marauders and Baltimores of the other Squadrons, cockpit cover and gun turrets glinting in the early morning sun.

'An hour later, with the target ETA approaching, the crews began to ready themselves for the actual attack. Bombardiers struggling forward into the nose compartment and settling over their bombsights, navigators gathering up maps and logs and moving into the seat alongside the pilots, and gunners carrying out final checks on guns and turrets. Preparations complete, attention was focused on the formation ahead as they began their target runs.

'As the first South African box of four went in, we were astonished to see them enveloped in a tremendous box barrage of flak, repeated as the second and third boxes made their runs. More than a few sighs of relief were breathed as all three formations were seen to emerge apparently unscathed, and begin the turn and run for home. Now it was out turn.

'39s three boxes of four aircraft began the gently diving turn onto the bombing run, 'bomb doors open.' Outside, the sky was suddenly darker and the noise was intense as the black flak bursts began to come closer and closer; the aircraft filled with the acrid smell of burnt cordite. The rattle of shell splinters along the fuselage could be heard as the aircraft were shaken and rocked from side to side, the pilots fighting to maintain the tight formation necessary for a good bomb pattern. Last second corrections were made as the box leaders lined up on the target, 'bombs gone', and we were through. The lead pilot's aircraft in a steep, tight turn diving to escape the pounding 88 mm barrage; the pilots in the No.3 aircraft fighting hard to maintain their position on the inside of the turn as they pulled the power off, while those of the No.2 aircraft were pouring on the power to keep position on the outside of the turn.

'At last all our formations were through, and the crews were able to look around and take stock of themselves and the damage to their machines. None of the aircraft appeared to be unscathed, and ragged holes could be seen on wings and fuselages.

'The run back to base was uneventful and soon the Squadron was going into echelon starboard and line astern for landing. One by one the battered B-26s dropped onto the PSP strip, trundled to the end and turned off, taxying around to the Squadron dispersals. At the crew debrief, the full story of the raid began to unfold with all squadrons reporting badly damaged aircraft, including some write-offs, and the Italian formation having lost their formation leader to a direct hit.

'39 had learnt a lesson ... Never take your enemy lightly, or you may not live to regret it.'

For 39 Squadron, the result was two aircraft declared total losses (X—X-Ray, P—Peter) and the 23rd February was declared a stand-down while the remaining aircraft were patched up. The Squadron 'Mayfly' (operational availability) on the evening of the raid (22nd) looked like this:

No.39 Squadron RAF	Mayfly
Aircrew Available	W/Cdr Innis
	S/Ldr Payne + crew
	P/O Thompson + crew
	W/O Meikle + crew
Aircraft Available	'A' 'T' 'W'
Aircrew Not Available	
Detached	F/O Horbury
	Lt Marshall
	Lt Pole
Sick	W/O Goodwin
	Sgt Brown
	Sgt Tinker
	Sgt Charteris
Released	F/O Wren + crew
	F/O Ross + crew
	Lt Collins + crew
	F/Sgt Mullens + crew
	Sgt Redman + crew
	W/O Moss + crew
	Sgt Owen + crew
	W/O Dingwall + crew
	Sgt Fisher + crew
	Lt Denny + crew
	Lt Wright + crew
	F/Sgt Willis + crew
Aircraft Not Available	
Inspection	'J' 'S'
U/S Hydraulics	'B'
U/S Enemy Action	'F' 'G' 'I' 'K' 'N'
	'O' 'P' 'R' 'X' 'Z'

Attack on a coastal battery in Yugoslavia.

Arsa Channel was the target again on the 25th and the Squadron once more followed 25 Squadron in. As before, the first formation vanished in heavy flak, but before reaching the target 39 were diverted to the secondary target of the harbours at Jablanac. Daily raids, by nine or twelve aircraft, continued throughout February with occasionally two raids being made on the same day. A Squadron-formation bombing run, a box of twelve, was made on the marshalling yards at Sisak. The airfield was fog-bound on the last day of February, and gave the Squadron a chance to thrash 19 Squadron SAAF at football; there was plenty of 'blood' on the pitch following the massacre of 14-0 of the Officers Mess by the Sergeants Mess. 2nd March saw a change of CO with Wing Commander De Innis handing over to Wing Commander Griffiths, who arrived from 334 Wing at Brindisi.

On the 4th March the Biferno Marauder Wing was withdrawn from operations for two weeks of intensive formation bombing training. Instead of 'On On to Novska' it was 'Back Back to Jabouka' and that innocent little island became once again the focus of attention. Morning and afternoon sorties were mounted daily with boxes of three and four; by 9th March the pattern of bombing had improved greatly, and the Squadron was declared partially operational again the following day. The first operation was on the 11th, against the gun emplacements on Rab Island. Both boxes (one of six, and one of four) dropped good patterns over the target area, and went away pleased with their efforts - only to learn later from intelligence that the guns escaped unscathed. It was the same target next day for eight crews, with photo evidence that at least four emplacements were hit. Rab Island received its third consecutive visit on the 13th.

Training, and targets such as Rab Island and the road bridges at Gospic, continued to be the order of the day until the 19th, which was the official end of the two-week training period, when the Squadron was declared fully operational. To celebrate the return to normality, twelve crews attacked troop concentrations at Bihac on the 13th, although patchy cloud cover meant that results were hard to observe.

The Operations Log contains the following 'operational comment' for March: 'Following a 10 day period of training, it was the Squadron's job to hamper the enemy's communications in Yugoslavia in an effort to prevent the movement of reinforcements from the North to South Partisan Front, which has been the scene of a recent partisan thrust.'

The third week of March saw daily raids on a variety of targets, ranging from: 'the NAAFI run; - base - Rab Island - base' to targets on the Brod-Novska railway line. Furthermore, the 20th saw the first leaflet dropping by 39's Marauders. On the return from a raid on the marshalling yards at Nova Gradiska, aircraft dropped leaflets in German over the garrison town of Karlbag in an effort to persuade the German soldiers to give up their 'lost causes'. Unfortunately, most leaflets fell in the water and crews were not convinced that the local fish could read German!

Good grouping on the marshalling yards at N. Sisak, 27 February 1945. Attacks on rail communications in Yugoslavia were one of the main Squadron tasks. Most sorties were formation bombing from boxes of four aircraft.
(R.J. Tennant)

The propaganda exercise of leaflet dropping became a frequent occurrence in the remaining months of the war with leaflets in German giving details of Allied victories and Axis defeats and exhorting the soldiers to surrender. Leaflets were also dropped for the benefit of the partisans and other Yugoslav people with details of the war and messages from their leaders overseas. Exactly what effect these leaflets had on their recipients was never discovered, but on one occasion they had a very adverse effect on the formation that dropped them. The leaflets were taken on board the aircraft in 20 lb bundles wrapped in brown paper and tied with string. Over the drop area the string was removed and the bundles dropped out of the forward bomb bay; the theory being that the tightly packed bundles of leaflets would break open in the slipstream of the drop aircraft and float gently

Close formation shot of Marauder 'O', astrodome retracted. Note 'bomb' markings denoting missions flown. (*K.J.Salter*)

earthwards. However, on 9th April the No.6 aircraft, piloted by Dennis Bowyer, became the unwilling recipient of unopened bundles dropped by the aircraft above and in front. The mid-upper gunner cried out a warning as the bundles struck the rear part of the aircraft giving the tail gunner quite a fright. The tail was damaged so the aircraft left the formation and returned to base. However, it was diverted elsewhere as the runway was blocked. Inspecting the damage later, the general view was that the aircraft was lucky to have escaped so lightly. It seems that the string had not been removed from the bundles.

The last five days of the month were notable for five stand-downs and an all time classic football match, recorded, thus in the line book:

'A day of victories - *Monty drives on, Russians advance towards Austria,* and *39 Squadron beats 213 Squadron,* in the finest game ever played at Car ,omarino. Aircrew representatives were: F/ɔgt Bill Flanagan (Goal), F/Lt Dave Nixon (Right Back), Sgt Bill Roberts (Inside Right) and Sgt Alex Naper (Left Half). A late kick-off enabled the majority of the Squadron to see the game, and the total attendance must have been between 350-400!

'After about twenty minutes play, '39' went ahead with a well-taken goal by Roberts and due to some sterling work by the defence half-time was reached with '39' still in the lead.

'Early in the second half '213' equalised, but almost at once '39' put on the pressure and the lead was regained with a gem of a goal by Asher (Inside Left). A Beautiful cross from the right flank, and a beautifully taken header, left the goalkeeper with no chance. The '39' team retained their ascendancy until the final whistle, but '213' never gave up and at least two hundred spectators breathed a sigh of relief when it was all over.

'Final score: 39 Squadron 2, 213 Squadron 1. A match we shall all remember in the years to come.'

'And so, back to war again, with the Squadron being stood down!

'April 1st, and a return to operations with 39 bombing a ploughed field instead of the nearby rail yards at Popovaca. April Fool!'

The title of this chapter comes from the unofficial Squadron motto 'On On to Novska' which was the battle cry of the Squadron football team supporters, as well as being an important rail junction in Yugoslavia.

The rail yard at Madari was attacked the following day, and this is how the raid was recorded by a Squadron poet:

Again today the lads went out,
from good old Thirty-Nine,
There was no more ploughing to be done,
so they hit the railway line.

Efforts in April varied between hitting targets and ploughing fields, although by now there was little of the latter as the Squadron was becoming more accurate with each raid. However, on the 10th a formation of ten aircraft ended up some 70 miles off track as the formation leader was trying to do his own map-reading, with a map draped over the control wheel. The formation circled Zagreb, one of the most heavily defended targets in Yugoslavia, while the leader tried to discover his position - a piece of information that any other member of the formation could have told him! Defended by over 300 heavy and medium guns, Zagreb was strictly a night target and here were ten forlorn Marauders cruising over the city at 8,000 ft in broad daylight. Fortunately no flak was forthcoming and the fighters basking in sunshine on the airfield stayed put — no doubt the defences were as amazed as the members of the formation.

It was unusual for small-scale bombing to produce direct victories. A box of five aircraft attacked the coastal guns on Krk Island on the 16th April and results were assessed as 'fair'. It was later learnt that the garrison surrendered to local partisans the day after the raid, having had two guns destroyed in the raid and having no wish for a repeat performance!

Throughout April, 39 Squadron flew daily or twice daily ops, with coastal guns being frequent targets. From mid-April onwards no opposition (flak) was experienced and crews were at times almost reluctant to disturb the peace of the countryside. April 3rd to 13th was such a period of intensive ops - with double ops on most days - resulting in an average of twenty-four sorties a day and a total of 310 hours in just seven days. The Squadron dropped approx 300,000 lbs of bombs, 200 packets of leaflets, and took 630 photographs.

After its early days of difficulty, 39 Squadron had now acquired a reputation for consistent accuracy in formation bombing. However, this peak of efficiency had been reached in the closing months of the war and by early May the signs that victory was imminent were obvious to all. Many of the crews greeted this with a tinge of sadness for they considered that their contribution was just beginning. 39 Squadron made its last operational raid of the war on 4th May, when two boxes each of six aircraft attacked Popovaca.

On May 7th the entire bomb wing at Biferno was stood down while everyone huddled around radio sets waiting eagerly for the announcement of the final surrender of the Axis forces in Europe. The good news was heard the next day, 8th May, 'Peace in Europe, VE Day'. A programme of special events was arranged in celebration:

1000 - ½-hourly lorry transport to the beach.
1500 - Squadron cinema:
    Prime Minister's speech.
1600 - England v Scotland soccer match.
1800 - Open-air party at the cinema, NCOs and airmen guests of the Officers; bars open until midnight.

The rejoicing was tempered a little, but only a little, by the rumour that the Squadron was soon to move to the Pacific theatre to take part in the final stages of the war against Japan. Quite a number of crews volunteered to go to the Pacific, as they were convinced that they still had an important contribution to make. May 9th was another day of celebration:

0800 - Breakfast, until 0900.
1115 - Thanksgiving service at the cinema.
1415 - Transport for swimming.
1800 - Officers & NCOs v Airmen soccer.
2045 - Film show at cinema.

The following day was a 'rest day' for recovery from the previous two days! However, on the 11th it was back to work and the Squadron put up two waves each of six aircraft on cross-country navigation exercises. The routine of peacetime flying came to an abrupt end on the 15th May amidst growing tension over the Trieste affair.

'N' for Nuts, Wing Commander Griffith's aircraft high over the Appenines in May 1945.

Although Trieste was an Italian city, it had been occupied by Communist troops in the closing months of the war and Tito wanted to retain it. Eventually, there was confrontation between Allied troops and the Communists, and although the Yugoslav claim was recognised, it led to bitter resentment against the Allies. 39 Squadron assumed the role of mercy fliers for the evacuation of Allied personnel from bases in Yugoslavia. Eight aircraft were sent to Zara to evacuate personnel of 213 Squadron as anxiety was expressed over the safety of RAF personnel due to the changed attitudes of the Communist partisans to the Allies. On the 16th, it was the turn of 6 Squadron to be evacuated.

This brief spell of activity over, it was back to training again with formation flying, gunnery and bombing. On the 27th, the Squadron received the first of its post-war shake-ups, with a re-shuffle of crew lists and a reduction in Squadron strength to twenty-one crews; the remaining 44 aircrew were stood down awaiting postings elsewhere.

The second shake-up soon followed, with the news, on 1st June, that the Squadron was to move to Rivolto, near Udine in Northern Italy, pending a move to the Middle East. On the 3rd W/Cdr Griffiths went to Rivolto to inspect the airfield and to make a bid for a patch of real estate on which to erect the Squadron's tents. The move started on the 5th with Marauders ferrying personnel and equipment between Biferno and Rivolto, prior to the road party leaving on the 8th in a long winding convoy which took four days to reach Rivolto. By the 10th, 39 had said farewell to Campo and had moved into tents at Rivolto. Within a matter of days, a variety of shanty-type buildings, built of 'obtained' items, was evident. At the same time, Nissen huts were begged, borrowed and constructed for use as briefing rooms, ops rooms and messes. Many of the 'comforts' for the Squadron area were obtained by the Adjutant, who toured Italy in a Marauder collecting anything of use. Sergeant Pilot Peter Kennedy remembers one such venture:

'On the 11th we flew the Adj to Marchionese (Naples). He was on the scrounge for anything to make our lives, under canvas again, tolerable. The package was a whopping great drum of goodness knows how many miles of lighting/power cable. The onus being on me to arrange its stowage, I myself endeavoured to lift it into the bomb-bay with the built-in winch gear. I was a big strong lad but all I could do was to wind the aeroplane down onto the drum. Things got a bit too tense and I gave up the idea. The Adj insisted that we just had to have the cable so the only way was to unwind it all and loop it into the bomb-bay. Of course, it occupied

about 50 times its original volume and I got a trifle worried seeing those great festoons getting in amongst control cables and the plumbing generally. Back at Rivolto I beat a hasty retreat and allowed others to unwind it all.'

Although living accommodation at Rivolto was very similar to that at Biferno, the weather was far better - a very pleasant North Italian summer. Flying was limited, and travel opportunities were excellent. Udine, Venice, Milan, Rome and the Dolomites were within range. Furthermore, the atmosphere within Italy was marvellous; now that the war had ended the local people became very friendly. One problem that had developed in the latter days at Biferno continued to plague the Squadron at their new home. A great many of the Squadron personnel had acquired dogs and at Biferno the problem had become so great that a 'shoot' was organised just before the Squadron moved to Rivolto. Shortly after settling in at the new base, the problem arose again and within weeks there were over seventy dogs on 'Squadron strength'. Pete Hatcher recalls the scene:

'The sight and sound that met the eye when Italian civilians cycled through camp had to be seen to be believed. Packs of the animals would rush out, barking, howling and snapping at the wheels and heels of the unfortunate passers by. Woe betide any cyclist that was unable to keep going.'

June ended on a sad note with 39 Squadron having its first accident with the Marauder when R-Romeo crash-landed twelve miles from Biferno on return from a Navex. The pilot when carrying out a feathering exercise had accidently feathered both engines - with the inevitable result. Although the aircraft was a complete write-off, being just a tangle of twisted metal, only two gunners and two airmen were injured, none seriously. The Marauder had proved a hardy, reliable machine for *Trente Nova*, and although some pilots never developed a love for the type as they did with other types, all developed a great respect for the aircraft.

July and August were very quiet months, with transportation of VIPs around Italy to supplement routine training. On 1st September came the order to suspend all training flying pending a move to the Middle East. The question everyone asked was 'where to', and a few days later the question was answered. The destination was to be Khartoum in the Sudan and this news was received with great despondency. Khartoum was looked on as sand, camels and boredom - beyond civilisation. The move was planned for the last two weeks of September, but before departure the Squadron had to 'pension off' a number of aircraft which were not considered worth taking to the Sudan. Crew strengths were also reduced,

The scrapyard at Khartoum became the final resting place for many of the Marauders. 'L' and 'O' are seen here, looking forlorn.

partly due to the reduction in aircraft, but also to the advent of a peacetime crew level of Pilot, Nav and WOP/AG. The first elements of the trimmed down Squadron left Rivolto on 19th September, when Wing Commander Griffiths and Flight Lieutenant Wren and crew left en-route to Bari and El Adem on the first leg of the journey to 'sunny' Sudan.

Shandur, in the Canal Zone, was used as a transit camp. As the first crew left, further news on the fate of the Squadron arrived at Rivolto - 'when established at Khartoum, the Squadron will convert to the Mosquito.'

Throughout September the Squadron packed its goods and chattels and said farewell to Italy. Each Marauder was fully laden, in some cases overloaded, with equipment, tools and personnel. One of the last to leave was Pete Kennedy piloting X - X-Ray who left on 2nd October, with a suitably laden aircraft, for the first refuelling stop, at Bari. Leaving Rivolto, he recalls:

'I felt a bit sad at leaving all that lush greenery in N. Italy and returning to desert conditions. Stories were widespread of the heat and whirl-winds at Khartoum which littered the surrounding countryside with broken aeroplanes. All such thoughts were soon forgotten in the boredom of hour after hour of transit flying: Bari - El Adem - Shandur - Wadi Halfa - Khartoum. A total of 14 hours 10 minutes flying but spread over four days due to an enforced 36-hour stop at Bari as the route across the Med was blocked by violent storms and Bari itself became a sea of mud.'

The rear party left Rivolto on 6th October, which was the same day that the first ground party arrived at Khartoum - after a frightful journey by sea, train and Nile steamer. Thus, by the middle of the month 39 was established at its new home and one of the first tasks was a 'show the flag' formation flight in the Khartoum/ Omdurman area. On the 25th September, 39 Squadron formally came under the command of HQ Middle East (HQME).

The Squadron soon settled down to its new life of scorpions and sand; the football team had to change its tactics somewhat to allow for the change from mud and grass in Italy to baked mud and sand at Khartoum! On the flying side, the programme was one of photo, navigation, formation, a good deal of trooping - mainly to Cairo, and the occasional special task, usually SAR for aircraft lost in the desert. The 1,000 mile Khartoum - Cairo trip became very routine, with a pilot's description of the navigation features thus:

'First the Nile flowing SW, the two hills at Wadi Halfa and the 3rd Cataract, a railway line, the Nile again flowing northish this time, then on to the Delta and the Bitter Lakes. The tarmac at Kasfareet runway could be seen as a tiny black dot in the yellowness a 100 miles away at least.'

To alleviate the boredom, an unofficial competition for the shortest time one way be-came popular. Anything between 4½ hours and 5 hours was considered good going.

A mercy flight was requested on 23rd December because RAF Malakand had run out of beer! Accordingly, on Christmas Eve, two heavily laden Marauders left Khartoum on the mission of mercy - to the great relief of the personnel of Malakand. Thus 1945 came to an end.

The daily routine at Khartoum began early in the morning so that work could cease before the day became too hot. The incredible heat of the afternoon was avoided, either in siesta or at least in the shade. When temperatures cooled down in the evening it was time for sport or for a visit to the outdoor cinema.

A good deal of flying time was spent on photo reconnaissance work, building up a mosiac cover of large areas or covering individual targets. The southern part of the Sudan was the main area being photographed and it was usual on these sorties to refuel at the 'airfield' (if it deserved such a title) at Juba. One pilot recalls Juba:

'I can still vividly recall the sight of several stark naked members of the Dinka tribe clearing wild elephants from the PSP runway so that the aircraft could take-off. The poor blighters had to fill the aircraft fuel tanks, holding 750 gallons, using hand pumps on 45 gallon drums of 100 octane.'

January 1946 saw a continuation of the established routine, although the Squadron was becoming more and more a transport squadron, flying senior military officials around the Middle East - and on one occasion even the Bishop of the Sudan and his entourage on a tour of the Diocese! This latter event being remembered by the crew because the Bishop bought them all a beer at an Arab hostelry in El Fasher.

January also saw the beginning of the end for for the Marauders with the arrival of the first of the new aircraft - a Mosquito FB.VI. New crew members also arrived, primarily navigators as some of the Marauder pilots were scheduled to convert to the new type. Many sad partings of long-established crews took place and sad fare-wells became a feature of the month. By 1st February, the Squadron was the proud owner of thirteen brand new, some slightly soiled by acceptance flying done in January, Mosquitos - a mix of FB.VI and FB.26s.

In conjunction with the increase in Mosquito strength went a reduction in Marauder strength, although a number of the latter stayed on strength as general communications aircraft. The last, F - Freddie (HD719) was still on strength in September 1946. The sad fate of the time-expired and unwanted airframes was a final short taxy to the stretch of desert that was the Khartoum scrapyard. Gradually, bits of Marauders were robbed - officially by the RAF and un-officially by the Arabs, and the eroding sands of the desert did the rest. Within months, the once proud airframes became untidy hulks.

Yet another new era dawned for 39 Squadron.

The semi-remote controlled guns of the rear position with Sergeant 'Hoppy' Hebblewhite the rear gunner of Marauder HD607.

8

Sudan Defence Squadron

39 Squadron had been sent to Khartoum to convert to the Mosquito and then become the Sudan Defence Squadron, with a wide range of responsibilities. The Canadian-built Mosquito Mk.26 fighter-bomber was almost identical to the more common Mk.VI and carried a fixed armament of four 20mm cannon and four .303 machine guns. Underwing hardpoints could take a variety of bombs and rockets, up to a maximum of sixteen RPs.

The changeover was well underway by 3rd February with the thirteen aircraft which had arrived by the end of January being joined by a fourteenth aircraft to bring the Squadron up to its initial establishment in preparation for the intensive conversion course. The Mosquito Conversion Unit arrived at Khartoum from Aden on 8th February, having completed conversion training for the Mosquito squadron at Khormaksar, and on the 11th the task of crew conversion for 39 Squadron began. However, by the second day, problems were encountered with the aircraft, with serious engine overheating. The situation became worse on the 13th with almost every aircraft suffering brake and tyre trouble and boiling glycol in the overheating engines, to add to the problems, many crews began to suffer from heat exhaustion. It later became standard practice for crews to start-up, taxy and take-off after only a minimum of checks, to reduce the time that aircraft and crews were exposed to the fearsome heat of the airfield. This policy was potentially disastrous, with the first full check of the flying controls being done only after take-off. The Squadron battled on for another day, in which time the first two pilots went solo, but by the end of the 14th it was painfully obvious that the situation could not continue as too many of the aircraft were unserviceable and the hard-pressed groundcrew could not keep pace with repairs.

The following day a decision was made to complete the conversion programme at Nairobi in order to ease the strain on the servicing teams at Khartoum and to take advantage of the lower surface temperatures at Nairobi (lower because the airfield was at an altitude of 5,371 feet above sea level) to reduce the problem of engine overheating.

No time was wasted and on the 18th Squadron Leader Elliott flew to Nairobi to set up the detachment headquarters; he was followed two days later by three of the Squadron's Marauders carrying equipment and groundcrew. Two more Mosquitos joined the detachment on the 21st, and the conversion programme began again. The move proved to be a success as intensive flying was possible throughout the day, the aircraft behaving very well. Aircraft were swopped between Khartoum and Nairobi as required, Khartoum being used for major servicing as well as remaining the Squadron HQ. The route Khartoum-Malakal-Juba-Kisma-Narok-Nairobi became familiar as the number of qualified crews increased week by week. Overall Mosquito strength was increased to nineteen with the arrival of two aircraft on the 9th March, with one more promised later in the month. While the courses continued at Nairobi, air tests and ground-runs were the norm at Khartoum. Despite the increase in aircraft and qualified crews, the future of the Squadron was in doubt as overheating was still preventing intensive operations from Khartoum.

The twenty Mosquitos on strength were a mix of dual-control T.Mk.3, Mk.VI and Mk.26; the latter being the most numerous. 39 Squadron was officially part of Middle East Air Force (MEAF) and was assigned to day fighter-bomber duties in the Anglo-Egyptian Sudan and adjacent areas when required. As 'converted' crews arrived back at Khartoum, the routine of peacetime training began, with low flying and navigation exercises as the main occupations. However, training continued to be hampered by the high aircraft unserviceability rate and the consequent large number of air tests as aircraft were returned to the line after repair. The situation improved a little in March as more of the original twenty aircraft were given their acceptance checks and air tests and made available to the Squadron, thus increasing the number of available aircraft from which to choose a 'goer'. Therefore, despite continued problems, by the end of March 1946, the Squadron was gradually building up its strength of operational crews and was beginning to feel established in its new life. The Marauders, of which there was still half a dozen on strength were busy with ferrying personnel and spares between Khartoum and Nairobi and with general ferrying and trooping duties throughout the Command. More often than not a pilot who was both Mosquito and Marauder qualified would find himself flying far more hours in the Marauder than in his new 'love', the Mossie. For many of the Marauder pilots, the Mossie was looked on as the 'nearest thing to heaven to fly' and the first solo was treated like a new lease of life. However, this by no means denigrated the firm respect that they had acquired for the sturdy, reliable Marauder.

Peter Kennedy recalls what life, both social and operational, was like at Khartoum: 'Our clothing consisted of open necked short sleeved shirts, shorts, pants, socks, mosquito boots and a cap of some kind. Although the risk of injury from fire was very great, to wear anything else would have been intolerable. Take-off early in the day was OK but landing around midday, say at Wadi Halfa, was literally like stepping into an oven. Getting back in again was even worse, as all the shading in the world could not have reduced the greenhouse effect in the cockpit. Take-off and climb-away from Wadi Halfa was extremely hard work. The worst clear air up current I expereinced produced a rate of climb of 5,000 fpm with the stick hard forward with, in an instant, a complete reversal. Together with either wing dropping it became quite a game to keep the attitude in some semblance of straight and level. In time it was remarkable that some sixth sense anticipated those violent changes but either way the pilot ended up in cooler air sitting in a pool of perspiration and everything else being saturated. Returning to Khartoum mid or late afternoon not a soul could be seen until the last possible moment when some poor sleepy-eyed erk appeared to guide us to a parking position.

'We had the odd sand storm and one plague of locusts. What the latter found to eat I don't know. The 'rainy' season was grim: most people suffered with a prickly heat rash and frequent cold baths or showers did little to relieve anything. Night-time insects were numerous and lights attracted them in their millions. The only one which was a nuisance was what was termed a piss-beetle. It did something to the unwary which raised a huge blister and if this broke, the fluid raised yet more blisters. It happened to me once when I suppose I must have stuck a knee through the mosquito net one night. The batmen used to make up a bed on the veranda during the hottest time of year leaving bare springs on the bed inside. There were many mess parties attended by the local Civil Servants, wives and daughters, at which the most popular cocktail was the *Atom Bomb*. This consisted of a generous measure of each of the considerable range of liquor held in the Mess. One night I was shaken gently and I came-to many miles out in the desert by the road to Kosti. How I got there I've no idea but I was found by a patrol of the Sudanese Defence Force. The SDF were probably the most smartly turned out group of soldiers in the world at the time but nevertheless marching in bare feet. I must have felt that I couldn't let the side down so I took my shoes and socks off and marched back with them. Arriving eventually at my bungalow, I flopped down inside and no doubt passed out. It was days before my feet recovered and for the marks of the bed-springs to disappear.

'Most late afternoons some of us played tennis but promptly at six a group of us settled down and played lie-dice all evening with a break for dinner at nine. Mostly we drank Rye and Dry and with a round of drinks from the loser of each game, stocks had to be replenished often!

'Most of the air tests I flew on Mosquitos were really acceptance tests of newly delivered planes. The test, such as it was, was to check normal operations, controls, systems, etc, except W/T which was undertaken on a separate flight. Handling characteristics were proved by an ordinary power-off stall, a stall at +4 boost and a high speed dive. The former was a very simple affair, a gentle nodding but with some vibrations and an easy nose or wing drop at the stall recovery was easy with minimum power. The +4 boost stall required a preliminary 4,000 fpm climb at an angle of, I suppose, around 30 degrees: after a time, which seemed endless, the speed at last fell off with the stall only a little more violent than before. The first high speed dive I did was started with a slightly barrelled roll through 180 degrees throttles and stick back further when inverted thence into the dive. The ground appeared to approach with extreme rapidity and the new horizon seemed ages coming down from above - these were quite illusory as I finished the dive well above 5,000 feet. What I had failed to do however was to trim sufficiently forward before the dive. Being inexperienced in such matters, the pressure needed on stick and rudder to correct the characteristic nose-up and left wing down tendency became enormous and I overdid the elevator retrimming to compensate. I could only have moved the trim wheel forward a fraction because instantly both crew endeavoured to part company from the aeroplane in an upward direction. IAS in these dives got to around 370 knots.'

On the 30th April Mosquito KA407 crashed thirty miles north of Khartoum killing both crew members. The cause of the crash was never fully established, but for a few weeks prior to the accident a new problem with the aircraft had come to light. As the surface temperatures rose higher than ever in mid to late April, it was noticed that the glue of the joints which held the 'wooden wonder' together was melting in the heat and that the joints were expanding and twisting the wooden frame. This particular problem brought its own incidents, this one related by Peter Kennedy: 'Someone flying Mossie '162 had left it at Malakal. It had been standing in the sun down there for days and upon learning that I was elected to go down there and fly it back to Khartoum all and sundry treated me with mock (I hoped) sympathy because without doubt, all the glue joints would have opened up and all the wood twisted and torn asunder in the heat. Not without some trepidation we set off in '362 in company with another Mossie crewed by two pilots. On arrival, KA162 was just sitting there, although looking innocent it had an air of malevolence about it. I gave it a thorough pre-flight inspection: things were undone, peered into and put back under close supervision. Every slot in a screwhead lined up properly and everyone thought I was mad when I wanted to check for expansion of control cables. I was at last satisfied but to clinch it I innocently asked if any of the ground crew would like to come on an air test. There was no shortage of volunteers and one, LAC Smith was chosen by his colleagues. I suppose it was rotten of me but on top of flying around a bit gingerly doing this and that, I did a couple of stalls, one each with engines off and on and ended up with a medium paced beat up. After landing I felt perfectly happy with things but a mottled green-faced Leading Aircraftman had to be assisted from the aeroplane. Three Mossies eventually took-off, '162 navigating in the lead with '362 and another being flown solo by the other pilot. I remember particularly the marvellous sight of the other two in circuit echelon with port flaps and wheels down before landing back at base.'

The glue problems plus the engine overheating made it obvious that the Mosquito 26s would never be suited to the Sudan without substantial modifications and, therefore, for a number of reasons it was decided to reduce 39 Squadron to cadre status. This decision took effect on 8th September 1946 when MED/ME Air Order No. 371/46 promulgated the reduction of the Squadron to 'number plate only'. Marauder F - Freddie (HD719) was one of the last aircraft to leave the Squadron. For many of the crews the next move was back to the UK for demobilisation, and 39 entered limbo for a while.

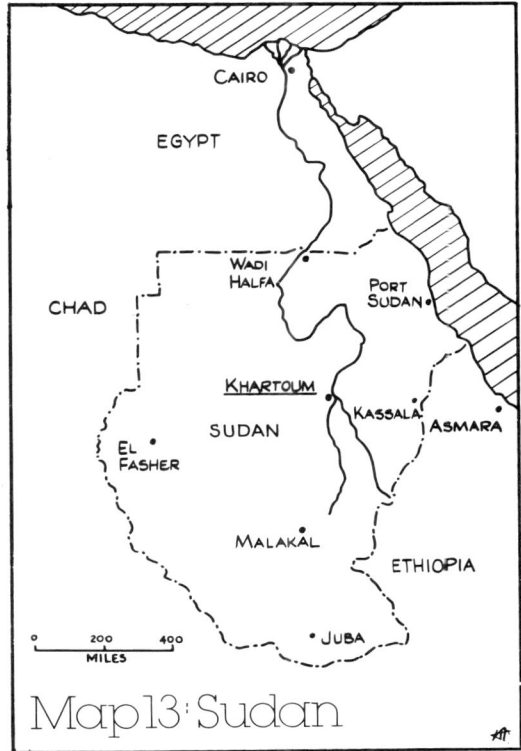

Map 13: Sudan

One of the few photographs of the Mosquito 26 in service with 39 Squadron. The 'wooden wonder' did not like the heat and humidity of the Sudan and after numerous problems the Squadron had to convert to yet another type. (K.J.Salter)

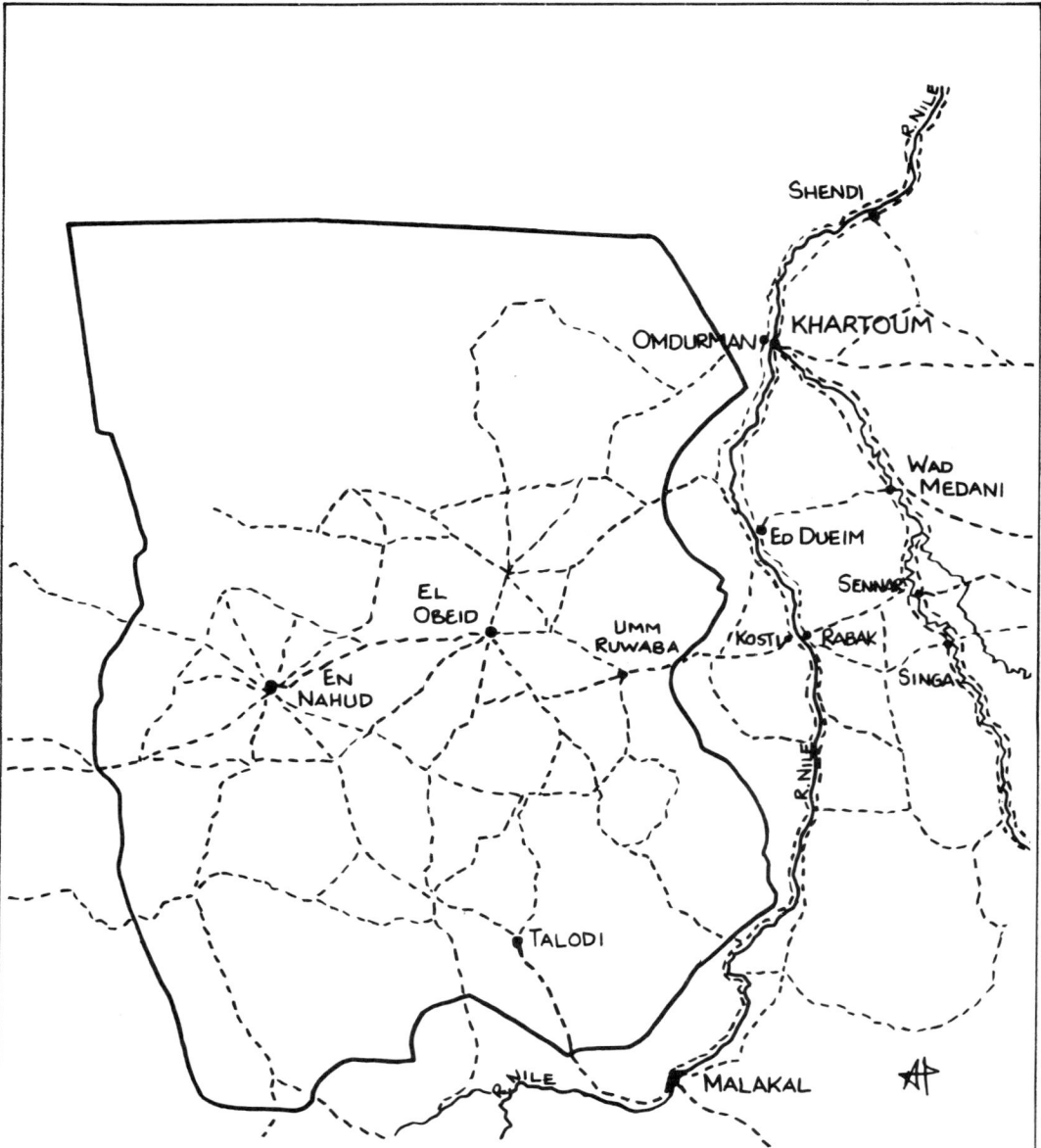

SHENDI

R.NILE

KHARTOUM

OMDURMAN

WAD MEDANI

ED DUEIM

EL OBEID

SENNAR

UMM RUWABA

KOSTI

RABAK

EN NAHUD

SINGA

R.NILE

TALODI

MALAKAL

W. NILE

Map14:Sudan 1946-49

After two years as a number plate only unit, the decision was taken to reform 39 Squadron again as the Sudan Defence Squadron, to be based at Khartoum flying Tempest Mk.VI aircraft.

This was to be a unique period, albeit short-lived, in the history of the Squadron as it was the only period in which the Squadron was equipped with single-seat aircraft. The Tempest had performed well in the latter part of the war as a ground attack aircraft and it was in this role that 39 Squadron was being sent back to the Sudan. The Tempest Mk.VI was powered by a single 2,340 hp Napier Sabre V engine giving a top speed of 438 mph at 17,000 feet. Armament was four 20 mm Hispano Mk.V cannon in the wings, plus hardpoints under the wings which could carry two 1,000 lbs or a variety of rockets, napalm, smoke and oil bombs.

Thus, in June 1948, 39 Squadron was officially reformed, and on the 16th June the new pilots assembled at Manston to collect the eight Tempests allocated to the Squadron. It was a very young set of aircrew that arrived at Manston. The CO, Squadron Leader Steedman, was only 26 and the 'old man' of the Squadron was Bob Butt, the Flight Commander, who was 28. These were the only two experienced pilots, having flown offensive reconnaissance and ground attack; the other six were straight out of training. To start with, no Tempest VIs were available so the pilots flew a few hours on Tempest IIs for familiarisation; eventually the Squadron's eight Mk.VIs turned up and each pilot flew three hours familiarisation on the type in preparation for the long flight to Khartoum.

The Sudan was one of those areas of British involvement where large distances, sparse population and poor communications made military intervention and control difficult. The Government considered that a military presence was needed in the Sudan and based on previous experience of similar situations in Mesopotamia and the North West Frontier, it was decided that the practical solution was a Sudan Defence Squadron, based at Khartoum. The army were also present in small numbers, including the Camel Corps. Until 39 Squadron arrived in July 1948, the defence responsibility was held by 6 Squadron (part of 324 Wing) but they then moved to the Canal Zone.

As the aircraft had been in store, it was feared that they would cause problems on such a long flight and so it proved. The move to Khartoum was not uneventful, as related in the Operations Log: 'The Squadron pilots assembled at Manston on 16th June, 1948, for the purpose of flying out its eight Tempest VI aircraft to Khartoum where the Squadron was reforming after two years on a number only basis. During the period of 16th June 1948 to 29 June 1948,

the aircraft were prepared for the trip and the pilots each flew three hours air experience on type. None of the pilots had flown Tempest VI aircraft before and only one had more than six hours experience on any type of Tempests. Various snags occurred - largely concerned with the 90 gallon overload fuel tanks, it being the first time these tanks had been used in service. These snags delayed the take-off daily, but at 15.00 hours of 30th June 1948 the eight Tempests became airborne behind Mosquito '853 (No.1 Ferry Unit - F/Lt Hanson) which was to be convoy leader. After flying through several storms for two hours 20 minutes, all aircraft landed safely at Istres in S. France (103 Staging Post) where they stayed the night. The pilots were called at 05.30 hours, but minor snags delayed take-off until 13.00 hours. The flight to Luqa (Malta) took two hours 45 minutes and was uneventful. Two aircraft had hydraulic failure on landing and had to use the emergency system and make flapless landings. F/O Baker and P.II Haughey in NX247 and NX282 were the two unfortunates. These snags necessitated a night stop.

'The morning call was for 05.30 hours but the aircraft snags had not been cleared so all the early calls were cancelled except for the CO. The Commanding Officer found out about the snags from F/O Baker when he turned up for breakfast because he couldn't sleep. Together, they walked down to see the aircraft. It was to little avail, however, for take-off was not until 11.00 hours. At 13.20 hours they landed at El Adem. F/O Baker and P.II Haughey experienced the same hydraulic trouble, and once again a night stop was necessary.

'An attempt was made to continue the journey the next day (2nd July) at 09.30 hours, but the same two aircraft developed last minute trouble and although the Mosquito and six Tempests took off, they had to return after orbiting to use up overload fuel. P.II Bell in NX284 had a tyre badly cut and there were no spares at El Adem. His aircraft was temporarily abandoned, and he carried on in NX281 which was F/O Scott's aircraft. F/O Scott remained behind as it was desirable to leave an officer. It had been decided to cut across the desert to Wadi Halfa by-passing Fayid and then to go on to Khartoum in one day, therefore the re-take-off was postponed until dawn on 4th July 1948.

'The convoy of seven Tempests and one Mosquito took off at 08.00 hours and after three hours flying over bare desert (three oases in 840 Statute miles) landed at Wadi Halfa just after 11.00 hours. Here again, with what was becoming monotonous regularity, F/O Baker and P.II Haughey had hydraulic trouble. An attempt was made to patch them up, but when the

Converting from the Mosquito to the Tempest Mk.VI gave the Squadron its only true single-seat aircraft type. 39 was now the Sudan Defence Squadron. NB not a 39 Squadron aircraft.

Squadron took off at 16.00 hours (the Mosquito had gone unserviceable and returned to El Adem) for Khartoum P.II Haughey could not leave dispersal and F/O Baker had to land immediately with complete hydraulic failure. On landing, the full 90 gallon tanks broke away from their rear mountings so only five aircraft carried on the last leg. They were glad to leave Wadi Halfa for the five hours spent there had been the hottest of any of the pilots had known. Five aircraft then landed at Khartoum at 17.35 hours. S/Ldr Steedman had difficulty in lowering his under-carriage and went round again so that F/O Downs landed first. It is a matter for record that he inadvertently landed on the wrong runway, cross wind, and taxied into dispersal collecting all the photographs en route. The reception committee made the arrival pleasant, and it was good to see how pleased the men were to see their aircraft and pilots after so long. They had come from various sources and had been waiting at Khartoum for several weeks.'

With so many aircraft having problems, Squadron Leader Steedman had decided to cut down the flying time by missing out the planned leg via Fayid and flying straight across the desert from Wadi Halfa to Khartoum, having first of all checked that the Mosquito nav leader was confident of finding Khartoum using the direct route. Eventually arriving at Khartoum with just over half the Squadron, Alisdair Steedman recalls the official reaction: 'I had hardly settled in for the night when a signal arrived from Middle East Command asking why I had not called in

at Fayid (HQ MEC), and why I had risked my aircraft by flying across the desert instead of following the coast and then the Nile. I gave my reasons in writing, explaining the reasons for strewing unserviceable aircraft all along the route, and never heard any more about it - presumably my reasons were considered good enough.'

The groundcrew, who had been waiting for some weeks, were relieved when the aircraft and aircrew arrived, as it meant that 39 Squadron was a complete unit once again and could begin the task of settling in at Khartoum and working up to full operational status. It was soon evident that very few of the groundcrew had any experience on the Tempest and the few experienced NCOs had a hectic time putting the other ground-crew through a training course, whilst at the same time supervising the acceptance checks on the aircraft.

At last, on the 10th July, the Squadron flew its first sorties from Khartoum, when NX287 (Squadron Leader Steedman) and NX283 (Flying Officer Davidson) took to the air. However, those who had suffered the problems of Khar-toum two years before could have warned the newcomers of what they faced, especially as the

Tempests had arrived in July with the prospect of four months of oppressive weather ahead of them. When the Squadron had started to come together in England everyone was enthusiastic about the prospect of going to the Sudan; it was a young squadron and the majority were single (of the aircrew only the CO and the Flight Commander were married) and this, combined with the serviceman's love of overseas tours, ensured that morale was high. For the married chaps, there was the possibility of families moving to Khartoum after the Squadron had settled in (it turned out that the Squadron was not at Khartoum long enough for this plan to come into force and it became a twelve month unaccompanied tour). Nevertheless, everyone settled down quickly and found Khartoum generally pleasant. It was hot and dusty, but the working day was from seven in the morning to just after midday so that work was over before the hottest part of the day. For the aircrew, it was a blessing to get airborne as the heat was almost unbearable when sitting in the aircraft on the ground; for the groundcrew trying to service the aircraft when the metal panels were too hot to touch it bordered on the intolerable.

Squadron line-up at Khartoum September 1948. A very young Squadron; the CO, Squadron Leader Steedman, was only 26.

The evenings were the most pleasant times when the heat had reduced to a comfortable level.

Socially Khartoum was well organised. For the officers there was the Sudan Club, a very civilised and well equipped club, as Sir Alisdair Steedman again recalls:

'In Khartoum there was a system of sluices to channel the river through various parts of the city once or twice a week. Thus, people had lush gardens and tennis courts; the Sudan Club had some twelve or so perfect grass tennis courts which were very popular.'

There was an Officers Mess at RAF Khartoum but it was very quiet on the station as 39 was the only squadron there, although from time to time the Boscombe Down trials unit used Khartoum for hot weather trials on new aircraft types (the Valetta was undergoing trials during this period). Otherwise, the only other aircraft were the Station Flight Ansons (usually two) and a Harvard plus support personnel. 39 Squadron quickly formed its football team to take on teams from station sections; swimming was a popular pastime too and there was a pool on the station. For the airmen, the main element of social life was the Airmens Club, but as the majority were fairly young, sport was one of the main pre-occupations. Whenever possible, parties of groundcrew were sent up to the Canal Zone for a day or two as a change from the routine

of Khartoum. There was no organised leave plan to send personnel up to Egypt and so small groups took advantage of 'hitching' rides in transiting aircraft.

The Tempest proved to be a very reliable aircraft. The engine, although liquid-cooled did not suffer the overheating problems of the glycol-cooled Mosquito, despite the atrocious conditions; they were, however, affected by the frequent sandstorms. Nevertheless, intensive training was the order of the day as pilots gained experience of the local area and their aircraft. To assist with this intensive training, 39 Squadron made use of the Station Flight Harvard, particularly for instrument flying and check rides, although it was a difficult aircraft to keep serviceable. Likewise, the Ansons were used for pilot training, and for communications duties and later on anti-terrorist operations.

Throughout July, Tempest strength remained at seven as one aircraft was still unserviceable at El Adem and towards the end of the month weapon training began. This was continued in August with RP and cannon exercises on the range at Jebel Merhijat. By the end of August, most pilots were proficient and the Squadron was declared operational. This was just in time, as the call to arms came shortly afterwards.

In Eritrea the army was engaged in operations against groups of Shifta bandits who were terrorising local villages. A request for air support resulted in three of 39 Squadron's Tempests being detached to Asmara on the 20th August to act as close air support for the army and also to fly armed reconnaissance patrols to dissuade the Shifta bands from further action (similar operations to those flown by 39 on the North West Frontier, although the firepower on one aircraft was now much greater than the whole Squadron in the 1930s). The detachment, led by Flying Officer Downs, eventually returned to Khartoum on 7th September.

The anti-Shifta sorties were primarily reconnaissance sorties looking for groups of Shifta and reporting their strength and positions to the local District Officer (the equivalent of the Political Officers of the India period). On many occasions, the Squadron used the Ansons for this work, especially when operations were in the far south of the country, as they could take the District Officer with them. This was most useful as the DO could often identify the individuals making up the Shifta group - an indication of the low-level nature of the work! Unfortunately, it was sometimes difficult to tell who was Shifta and who wasn't as most natives took to their heels at the sight of an aeroplane.

Once or twice, however, the Squadron was called on to destroy huts or villages. This was the same policy as that used on the North West Frontier. By destroying the livelihood of the people and keeping them away from their homes, tended to persuade them to accede to Government demands. As before, warning notices were dropped forty-eight hours or so in advance of the air strikes. In the Sudan this was a very successful policy in that the naturally warlike natives considered it no loss of honour to give way to something they could not fight, ie aircraft, whereas they would have fought a ground force hammer and tongs.

Despite the difficulties of operating fast, heavy aircraft from an airfield at an altitude of 8,000 feet, and flying low-level sorties at a time of the year when weather conditions often made flying hazardous, the detachment was most successful and the army were full of praise for the air support they had received.

Re-united at Khartoum, the training routine continued with 39 Squadron flying an average of 115 - 130 hours a month in the Tempests. However, the routine was disrupted again when it was learnt that 39 was now to convert to the Bristol Brigand; starting in the latter months of 1948 with a re-equipment programme planned for early 1949. The initial plan was for the CO and two other pilots to return to the UK on 10th November for the Brigand conversion course, and for the rest of the pilots to follow at the rate of two per month in December, January and February. The plan for the Squadron as a Brigand unit was for it to remain at Khartoum as the Sudan Defence Squadron but in the role of light bomber, with no responsibility for air defence - a role which the Tempest equipped squadron was, in theory, to provide alongside all its other roles.

When pilots returned to the UK they first flew a multi-engine refresher on Oxfords before moving on to the Brigand conversion course at Leeming in Yorkshire. Squadron Leader Steedman and the first batch of pilots duly went to Leeming for the course, but while they were away the planned future of 39 Squadron was changed; it was decided to send the Squadron to the Canal Zone and re-equip it with NF Mosquitos as a night fighter squadron. It was further decided not to convert the recently converted Brigand pilots, including the CO, to the Mosquito but instead to post them en masse to 8 Squadron in Aden which was due to convert to the Brigand but had not started. When the changeover eventually came in early 1949, all the aircrew went to 8 Squadron but the majority of the groundcrew stayed with 39 and moved up to the Canal Zone.

Before any of these upheavals took place, the Squadron was back in action again with three aircraft detached to Port Sudan for anti-Shifta operations in the Kwabab Plain. It was only a short detachment, but in the meantime the Squadron had acquired a commitment to keep four aircraft on standby for a possible detachment to Mogadishu. In view of this commitment, normal training was suspended and the tedious job of waiting for orders to deploy became the daily routine. As November approached, and with it the advent of the Sudan winter (equivalent to an English summer), the standby commitment continued, but there was also an increase in the amount of practical training. During November the emphasis was on joint exercises with the army, and saying farewell to the CO and the other pilots who left on 3rd November for the UK.

The following extract from the operations log gives a good idea of the war-time role of the Squadron: 'On Tuesday 23rd November a display of cannon and rocket firing, cab-rank, standby procedure and aircraft control by a contact car was attempted. This was for the benefit of the two battalions stationed at Khartoum and officers and troops of the SDF. Jebel Merhijat range provided the venue. It was planned to use two aircraft but, at the last moment, one became unserviceable - in fact, only one serviceable aircraft was available all day. The aircraft was flown by F/O French. The ALO and F/Lt Butt were on the range with the contact car and the R/T conversation was broadcast to the spectators over a tannoy. The demo went well. The Tempest came over low and everyone got a good view of the eight rockets in position. Four of these were rippled at the target (two tanks) in the first attack and the remainder salvoed the next time round. The aircraft then returned to the cab-rank while an imaginary battle in the target area was described by the ALO. Air support was 'requested' and the Tempest called down to attack with cannon. A number of different attacks were demonstrated, the exercise closing with a display of aircraft control - height, speed, approach etc, directed by the operator in the control car.'

When not on active operations or committed to standby, 39 Squadron flew training detachments to such places as Asmara (Eritrea), Juba (on the border with Uganda), El Fasha and Wadi Halfa. This serves to demonstrate how extensive was the Squadron's area of responsibility.

As the Sudan Defence Squadron, 39 was responsible for air defence, reconnaissance and ground attack, although the air defence role was very much a non-starter as there was no air defence system in the Sudan and no-one on the Squadron had any air defence experience. Therefore, the Squadron concentrated on the ground attack role. In the immediate post-war period there was

no shortage of weapons for training use and 39 made intensive use of the range for live-firing of all sorts of munitions, but mainly the cannons. The CO, from previous experience, had discovered that the closer to the target that you fired the cannon, the greater the chance of causing maximum damage. Thus, 'I set out to teach my chaps to fire short bursts at close range. I took the Squadron out to the range and showed them what I meant, flying race-tracks around the range, diving in on the target, firing short bursts. This was fine as long as you remembered to pull out in good time. Unfortunately, the range at Omdurman was littered with stones and these would be thrown into the air by the impact of the cannon shells, if you pulled-out a little too late you went through a cloud of these stones which caused severe damage to the large, exposed radiator at the front of the engine. This caused lots of problems and we had an enquiry from HQ which resulted in us having to fire from further out than I considered desirable.'

As 1948 drew to a close, the Squadron was still expecting to change-over to the Brigand and remain in the Sudan. It was decided to train pilots for the air defence role and camera-gun recorders were fitted to the aircraft in preparation for air combat training, which began in January. By mid-January the continual standby commitment was beginning to cause severe strain on personnel and aircraft and it was relaxed, but not withdrawn, for the last week of the month.

In a flying accident on 7th January an aircraft crashed during an air test, killing the pilot. The operations log records an aside to this incident:

'The aircraft disintegrated in the air, the two main planes, and the tail unit were recovered in Umm Dumm village. At least one native inhabitant had an escape from death that was little short of miraculous. This character, a rather aged bachelor, had just climbed off his bed and was half way through the door of his house, when crash, through his not over substantial mud roof, plummeted the complete, the port mainplane of a Tempest. The bed was buried in debris and the house wrecked.'

Shortly afterwards, Squadron Leader Steedman and the other 'converted' pilots arrived back at Khartoum. At first it was hoped that they would bring with them a Brigand or two but this proved impossible, although the CO did have a silver model of a Brigand, presented to the Squadron by the aircraft makers.

It was now that the fate of the Squadron became official. 39 was to move to the Canal Zone in the 'near future', hand over its Tempests and prepare to re-equip. In March, 39 Squadron said farewell to its aircraft and aircrew. It was back to Noctuque again.

9

Pyramids by Night

39 Squadron duly arrived at its new home at Fayid, near the Great Bitter Lake, in the Suez Canal Zone in May 1949, and began the job of sorting out resources and accommodation. The target date for the completion of the re-equipment programme was 1st August and the first aircraft arrived in June. The CO, Squadron Leader R D Doleman, had arrived at Fayid on 13th May and in desparation set about organising accommodation and obtaining equipment as Fayid was, to say the least, a little chaotic. Built by German and Austrian POWs in the latter part of the war, Fayid had since mid-1946, been the home of GHQ Middle East after that august body had been forced to leave its previous accommodation (in Cairo) in the face of growing Nationalist fervour amongst the Egyptians. Fayid was a bleak and barren place surrounded by rock and sand and the base itself was very spartan, with tents and huts as working accommodation and communal 'Butlin'-style centres, serviced under protest by NAAFI, as recreation for families.

By the time 39 Squadron arrived in the Canal Zone, there was a renewed determination in Britain that the nation should make no more concessions to the Egyptian Nationalists. The hardening of attitudes, (or strengthening of determination, depending on one's political view of the situation), was possibly due to the basic instability of the area vis-a-vis Israel and the Arab States, and the growing threat of Russian intervention in the area if a political vacuum was left by a major power. The Canal Zone was the focus of attention as it was a vital lifeline for the oil that flowed to Britain and Western Europe. Hence, the arrival of 39 as a night fighter squadron can be seen as one element of this attempt to reverse the weakening of British strength in the area.

The first Mosquito was taken on Squadron strength on 11th June, a dual control T.3, TV610, acquired from No. 107 Maintenance Unit. The first operational aircraft, RL151, an NF.36, and crew did not arrive until 30th June.

The NF.36 was powered by two 1,690 hp Rolls-Royce Merlin 113 engines, giving a maximum speed of 404 mph at 30,000 feet. Armament consisted of the well-tried and reliable quadruple 20 mm Hispano cannon.

During July, the embryo unit built up its strength of groundcrew and equipment, and training began for the few crews who had arrived so far. The T.3 was used for general pilot training during the early weeks while the one or two NF.36s were used for night flying training and night practice intercepts (PIs). The build-up progressed slowly with no more arrivals in August, but there was an addition to the training routine with the commencement of the all-important GCIs (ground controlled intercepts), the bread and butter routine of any modern fighter squadron. September saw the arrival of a further four NF.36s to bring the total to six, plus a T.3. More importantly, the Squadron took part in its first major exercise, Exercise *Bullseye,* when the Mosquitos claimed four kills on the 'enemy' Lancasters.

Following the success of this exercise, 39 was declared operational and was at last beginning to feel and operate, like an established unit. Two more NF.36s arrived in early October, bringing the Squadron up to its full establishment of eight NF.36s and a T.3. Unfortunately, the gremlins which had plagued 39's previous venture into the world of Mosquitos appeared to have moved from Khartoum to Fayid when all the NF.36s were grounded for engine changes. The problem was caused by sludge forming over an oil feed to an impeller bearing, which in turn caused the supercharger to seize. The engines were duly replaced and a local modification was made to try and prevent a recurrence of the problem. However, the net outcome was that three weeks training was lost and the high morale after the *Bullseye* exercise had drifted away during the 'T.3 only' flying period. All was back to normal the following month and intensive training on all aspects of Squadron flying was the order of the day not only to catch up with lost time but also to prepare for a visit by examiners of the Central Flying Establishment who were due to arrive at Fayid in December.

The CFE examining team duly arrived on the 9th December, bringing with them a T.3, NF.38 and a Wellington 'flying classroom' fitted with AI Mk.10 radar to check all the Navigators on their AI techniques. Circuit work was done in the T.3 and NF.38. After this, pilots and navigators had a series of ground lectures and exams. All crews were given good assessments by the team.

Formation flying was continued throughout the month as the Squadron was due to give a formation display during the AOC's Annual Inspection of Fayid in early January 1950. Such displays were fairly common occurrences and on one such display the formation leader had an engine failure which meant that he had to continue on one engine; the other three members of the formation thought this was an unrehearsed part of the display and promptly each shut down an engine!

By the end of the year, the Squadron had overcome most of the teething problems and crews were gaining rapidly in experience, as were the GCI controllers they worked with. Mutual understanding between crew and controller was seen to be vital for night interceptions when it was the job of the controller to get the

fighter into a position from which the crew were able to pick up the raider on their own AI radar and close in for the kill.

Crews averaged twenty hours a month, of which about half was night flying. Most of the day sorties were either gunnery or cine (camera gun) or cross-country navexs. The night sorties, as one would expect from a night fighter squadron, saw more 'business' flying with PIs and numerous exercises. January gave crews their first taste of live firing with the Hispano cannon. On the 10th, the entire Squadron moved to Nicosia, Cyprus, for No.29 Armament Practice Shoot (APS). The groundcrew, equipment and spares were flown over in four Valettas, and a small corner of Nicosia airfield was soon in the hands of 39 Squadron. From 12th January to 20th February, all crews underwent an intensive training course starting with air-to-air cine exercises to check basic techniques. This was followed by air-to-ground firing, high altitude cine and infra-red night cine and, finally, air-to-air firing against towed banners. The overall result was 'good average' for the Squadron, which was a pleasing conclusion to the first live shoot. Back at Fayid the Squadron settled back into its training routine, with particular emphasis on night GCIs and sector patrols, for which an aircraft or pair of aircraft would patrol a designated 'sector' looking for 'customers'.

Re-loading the four 20mm Hispano cannon under the nose.

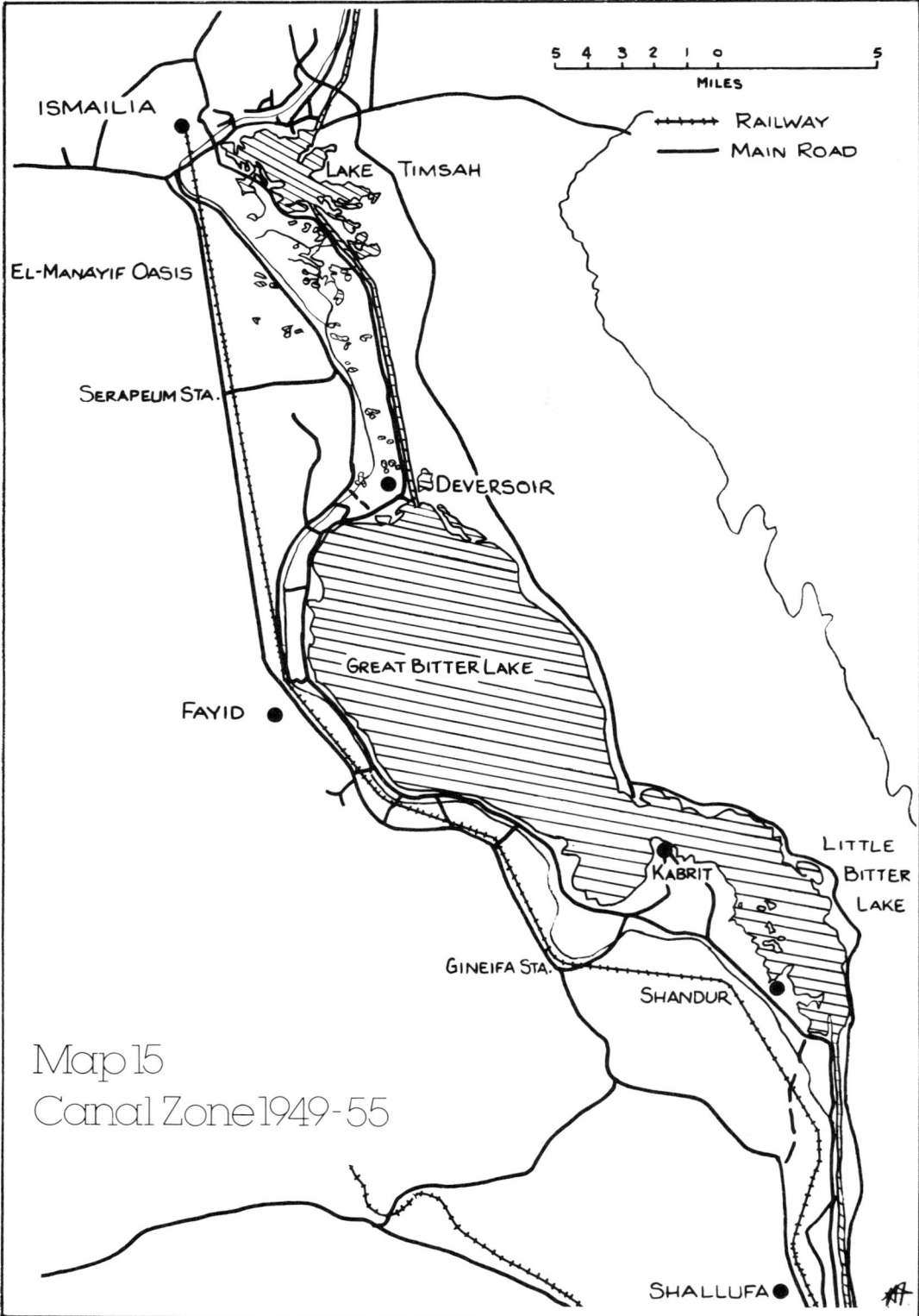

ISMAILIA

Lake Timsah

El-Manayif Oasis

Serapeum Sta.

Deversoir

Fayid

Great Bitter Lake

Kabrit

Little Bitter Lake

Gineifa Sta.

Shandur

Map 15
Canal Zone 1949-55

Shallufa

5 4 3 2 1 0   5
MILES

+++++ Railway
──── Main Road

An unusual exercise in March was Exercise *Groundnuts,* a large-scale army exercise in the desert to the east of the Canal, during which 39 flew night intruder reconnaissance patrols picking out 'enemy' vehicles using the AI radar. After a little practice, most Navigators became quite good at adjusting their AI sets to pick out the small unnatural returns made by vehicles in the flat expanse of the desert.

Ten members of the Squadron were back in the desert the following month, but this time on foot, as participants in Exercise *Hot Foot,* for which they spent forty-eight hours in the desert to test the suitability and efficiency of the aircraft survival kit and the emergency organisation. On return to Fayid, the victims reported it as the most aptly named exercise they had ever participated in!

39 Squadron made its first visit back to the UK since 1928 when, in October, seven aircraft flew, via Malta and Dijon, to Tangmere in Sussex to participate in one of the largest Air Defence exercises ever held over the UK - Exercise *Emperor.* Operating from Tangmere, 39 and 29 Squadrons were responsible for the night defence of the whole of Southern England during the exercise period of 6 - 16th October. The net result was twenty-eight kills claimed by the Squadron and a feeling that the exercise had provided invaluable training.

After the normal hectic Christmas at Fayid, the Squadron was at Nicosia on APS for the first

Above: **Pre 'dogtooth' shot of 151, 973, 113 and 133 in formation over the Canal.**

*Below:***Presentation of the Lloyd Trophy on 21 February 1951 by Air Marshal Sir John Slessor.**

Squadron line-up Kabrit, Suez Canal Zone, 7 March 1951. The bulbous nose of the NF.36 held the Mk.10 AI radar.

five weeks of 1951. From mid-January onwards, a series of detachments were sent to Luqa to provide the Malta GCI controllers and air defence network with practice in the control of night fighters. These detachments, each of two or three aircraft, were sent at monthly intervals.

In February it was announced that 39 was to move from Fayid to the nearby airfield at Kabrit, a little further south on the peninsula between the Great and Little Bitter Lakes. On the 21st February, the Squadron took-off from Fayid for the last time, formed up, and flew over the airfield in farewell salute. Soon after settling down at Kabrit, the Squadron was visited by Air Marshal Sir John Baker, KCB, MC, DFC, C-in-C Middle East Air Force, who presented the Squadron with the Lloyd Trophy. This was awarded to 39 for being the most efficient squadron in MEAF in 1950, a pleasing achievement as it was the first full year with the Mosquitos.

The months passed as the Squadron continued its training routine from Kabrit and Luqa. However, from mid-1951 onwards, the restive fervour of Nationalsim began to stir again in Egypt. Russia began to give verbal support to Egyptian demands for total British withdrawal; in reply, Britain offered gradual evacuation but with the proviso that they could return in an 'emergency' of unspecified nature. The British reply caused increasing anger in Egypt and the mood of Nationalism grew, although at first it was restricted to verbal and printed invective. Britain turned to NATO seeking support for a multi-national force (Turkey, France, Britain, Egypt) to act as equal partners in the Canal Zone. The tension of the summer came to a head in October, when on the 8th, a decree was tabled in the Egyptian Chamber of Deputies abrogating the 1936 Anglo-Egyptian Agreement, by right of which Britain was present in Egypt, and the

Sudan Convention of 1899. The decrees were made law on 15th October and on the 16th rioting, encouraged and supported by the government, broke out in the Canal Zone, especially Ismailia. The rioters looted and pillaged and set houses, buses and cars on fire. A group of army wives and children were besieged in the NAAFI store until they were rescued.

With the news of the proposed decree, British forces in the Canal Zone were put on an increased state of readiness. The outbreak of rioting on the 16th and the fear of worse to come, led to further measures being taken. On the 17th, 39 Squadron was called on to provide daily armed reconnaissance sorties along the borders of the treaty zone, watching for any attempt at intervention by the Egyptian army. The following day, a Squadron aircraft on one such mission discovered a large force of Egyptian infantry, tanks and field guns dug-in astride the Suez-Cairo road near El Ribreigi.

Details of the force were passed to GHQ and 39 was ordered to maintain an overnight watch on the Egyptian position and report any movement. The next day, the 19th, a Lancaster dropped messages from the GOC onto the 'enemy' position and later in the day the Egyptians retired down the Cairo road. During this time the Squadron was required to maintain one aircraft at thirty minutes readiness day and night. Into this situation walked Squadron Leader J C Coghill, DSO, DFC, to take command of the Squadron on the 25th October.

On the same day, a Conservative Government, led by Churchill and with Eden as Foreign Secretary, took power in Britain - with an immediate strengthening of British resolve not to give way over the Canal. The Egyptian Government, however, could not afford a war over the Canal as their army was in a poor state, with the best units concerned with 'watching' Israel. Therefore, they pursued a policy of non co-operation and blockade, with terrorists supplied by Communist and fanatic Moslem groups, and with unofficial support from the Government.

At this time, the British military bases employed some 40,000 Egyptians and these, or most of them, left, in many cases under intimidation from the terrorist groups. At Fayid, the village was almost deserted and troops had to move in to run essential services such as the power and filtration plants. It was the same story at Kabrit and throughout the Canal Zone and the actions of the terrorists made life very uncomfortable. Service families were moved into garrison encampments protected by barbed-wire fences and armed guards. Terrorists occasionally fired pot-shots at the camps and a number of soldiers were killed in civil disturbances in the villages.

At Kabrit, 39 Squadron maintained its state of readiness, and at the beginning of November picked up a new task - daylight armed reconnaissance along the El Adem road - with sorties flown every third day. The high level of tension continued, and on the 13th the Squadron was required to hold all available aircraft (a total of six) at one hours readiness. This was maintained for three days and was then relaxed, although an immediate readiness night standby remained in force. In order to achieve these readiness states, the Squadron was operating from a tented camp adjacent to the aircraft and near the end of the runway. With the sleeping area, briefing rooms and engineering support on the spot, average scramble times were three or four minutes. Once during this period, the entire Squadron was called to thirty minutes armed standby, but soon after was reverted to normal states. No-one on 39 ever found out the reason for the sudden 'panic'.

In late December/early January (1952), the political situation deteriorated and the decision was taken to disarm the troublesome Egyptian police. Unfortunately, this move went badly when fifty policemen were killed during two sieges of police stations. The scale of rioting increased and there were direct threats to 'British lives and property' in Cairo and the Canal Zone. British troops were placed under orders to move on Cairo if the situation became more than just a threat, and a mobile force was concentrated on the Suez road ready to move at short notice. The Egyptian army had two brigades dug-in on the

hills overlooking the road and they were keen to fight. The British commanders were not so keen, but nevertheless planned an air-supported flank attack, which they calculated would enable them to reach Cairo in a matter of hours. 39 Squadron was to act as part of the air support.

Fortunately, the call did not come. The riots subsided, and King Farouk called on the Egyptian army to dispel the rioters, rathers than have the British do it for him. Farouk then sacked his government and an uneasy peace returned to the Canal Zone, although the civil labour boycott continued.

With the return of more peaceful conditions, the Squadron settled down to normal training, although the memory of the recent disturbances lingered on. The Squadron greeted 1952 in the following manner: 'at first light on January 1st, four aircraft gave the station the benefit of some harmonious close formation flying; this was extended to the local army camps but no appreciation of our efforts has been received to date.'

On the 7th, the NF.36s made their debut in new markings - an oblong of yellow and black dog-tooths (interlocking triangles) along both sides of the fuselage. News of further changes came with the visit of the AOC on his annual inspection in March; the AOC announced that the squadron was to convert to the Meteor NF.11 in early 1953. The following month, the Central Flying Establishment team visited Kabrit with two NF.11s, and Squadron Leader Coghill plus two other Squadron pilots who had flown in a Meteor T.7 the previous week, had the chance to try out their future aircraft. All were very enthusiastic, and looked forward eagerly to the re-equipment. As the political situation was reasonably settled, the Squadron went on its annual APS to Nicosia in May, although the name had just changed to APC - Armament Practice Camp. Part of the detachment was an escape and evasion exercise for all aircrew. From the drop-off point, the crews dispersed into the Cypriot countryside and headed for the next check point. Shortly after the start of the exercise, an old Turk shepherd was riding home on his donkey carrying his life savings (about £60) when he saw two lurking figures. His challenge in Greek and Turkish went unanswered so, suspecting the figures to be robbers, he fired his shotgun at them, at close range. The net result was that Pilot Officer Wilson was taken to the British Military Hospital in Nicosia to have some fifty shotgun pellets removed from his buttocks!

The official notification of re-equipment was received in August; 39 was to re-equip with the Meteor NF.13, starting in March 1953. A Meteor T.7 was due to arrive in early December for pilot conversion training prior to the arrival of the NF.13s. The T.7 (WL431) arrived as planned,

145

Below: **A return to the original role of night fighter and another Mosquito, this time the NF.36. 39 Squadron, Kabrit 1951 as part of the Suez Canal Zone defences. The yellow/black dogtooth design was adopted in January 1952.** *Above:* **RK994, RK983 and RL115 break to port.**

and during December five pilots were converted making a total of six qualified pilots on the Squadron.

In January and February 1953, further conversion flying was done in the T.7 and borrowed NF.11s. By early March, most of the Mosquitos were approaching their hours-expired point and were grounded in readiness for the flight back to the UK; the first two leaving for the UK on the 11th March. The available Meteors were now in full use, four NF.13s arrived on the 19th, with a further two arriving on the 20th bringing the Squadron up to its establishment of seven (WM308, 310, 311, 313, 314, 317, 322) and one T.7 (WL431). In an eight day period in late March, the Squadron flew 74 hours and 35 minutes day conversion and 50 hours 25 minutes night conversion and took part in their first exercise with the Meteors, claiming nine 'kills'.

The Meteor NF.13 was basically a tropicalized version of the NF.11 and was specifically built for MEAF. The first aircraft, WM308, flew on 23rd December 1952 and a total of forty were built by Armstrong Whitworth. Powered by two 3,700 lb thrust Rolls-Royce Derwent 8 turbojets the NF.13 had a maximum speed of 541 mph at 30,000 (Mach .8) and a ceiling of 43,000 feet.

Meteor T.7 (WL411) and NF.13s (WM327/E and camera-ship). The 'dogtooth' was dropped when the Squadron converted to Canberras.

Armament consisted of the inevitable four 20 mm cannon in the wings. The distinctive feature of the aircraft was the long thin nose which housed the AI Mk.10 radar.

We must go back in time to mention a major political change in Egypt which occurred in July 1952. King Farouk, following his 'success' with ending the riots earlier in the year, increased his direct involvement in the running of the government. This proved to be an unpopular and not very effective move. By July, this had caused upheaval, and the 'Society of Free Officers', a fiercely nationalistic group, decided to act. In July 1952, Gamal Abdul Nasser led the revolutionaries to power, and King Farouk bowed out and sailed for Europe. Egypt now had a Nationalist government, with Nasser as Prime Minister, but the new regime opened in moderation: 'Egypt will always treasure the friendship of the British people.'

However, attitudes change, and in early 1953 (by which time Nasser felt reasonably well established) the Nationalist Government raised the question of the Canal Zone. Britain replied in the same conditional vein as before and the Egyptians demanded unconditional evacuation, a stand supported by the Americans. Negotiations began but broke down in May. Nasser declared that he would, 'pull down the pillars of the temple' but in fact did nothing. However, the British Government had already reconsidered the wisdom

147

of having 70,000 servicemen in an area that could only be used with Egyptian co-operation. Churchill proposed the withdrawal of Middle East Command to Cyprus but with continued use of the Canal Zone installations for maintenance throughout 1953 and early 1954. Nasser became impatient and decided to hasten the British departure by a mixture of concession and duress; he agreed to the principle of right of return in an 'emergency', and let loose his terrorists in early 1954.

Eventually, agreement was reached, and in October 1954 the Anglo-Egyptian Agreement was signed by which Britain agreed to evacuate all military forces within twenty months with the proviso that civilian technicians were allowed to maintain the bases for immediate re-occupation if any Middle Eastern Country, including Turkey, was attacked. The troops began to move out even before the agreement was signed. However, it was a dead letter as soon as it was made public. The terms were anathema to many right-wing elements in Britain and were considered insulting by the Nationalist and Moslem groups in Egypt. Nevertheless, the withdrawal went ahead and the last British troops left Egypt on 13th June 1956.

In February 1954, Squadron Leader Coghill returned to the UK and Squadron Leader J J O'Meara, DSO, DFC, took command of the Squadron. On the 26th June, 39 was presented with its first Squadron Standard by Air Marshal Sir Claude B R Pelly, KCB, CBE, MC, an ex-Squadron member from the 1923-24 era.

The remainder of 1954 was reasonably quiet, although in December, the Squadron was told that it would be transferred to Malta in January 1955 as part of the Anglo-Egyptian Agreement withdrawal. 39 Squadron said farewell to the Middle East on 10th January after fifteen years

of operating from a multitude of bases throughout the area.

At Luqa, the Squadron soon settled down in what were semi-familiar surroundings after the frequent detachments. It was not long after 39 was taking part in realistic exercises such as that on the 18th/19th February when aircraft were scrambled to intercept a Canberra squadron en route from the UK to Cyprus. The Squadron flew sixteen sorties and claimed eleven kills (the Canberra squadron was intercepted again on its return flight in mid-March).

Although 39 was designated a night fighter Squadron, a tremendous amount of work was also done in the daylight hours, a practical arrangement if one is stationed in the Med! This included exercises and PIs as well as routine flying training, and throughout 1955 the Squadron flew roughly twice as many day hours as night. February was typical for the NF.13s with 154 hours day and 68 hours night. Throughout the year, it was one never-ending round of exercises of various types. In mid-March it was Exercise *Sealance* with the Mediterranean and Home Fleet; 39 flew forty-two sorties and claimed twenty-nine kills. Exercise *Sealance* was typical of the intensive flying required on such exercises. Six aircraft were available on line and were allocated thus:-

2 a/c to Brown Section) together made up
2 a/c to Pink Section) Red Section
2 a/c to Purple Section

The following extract from the log kept by the duty operations officer shows the fast and furious nature of scrambles and QTRs (Quick Turn Rounds): Times are local (GMT + 1 hour):

0845	Red available
0903	Pink and Brown scrambled
0904	Pink and Brown airborne
0908	Purple ready
0921	Purple standby
0942	Purple scrambles
0942.5	Purple airborne
0945	Pink in the circuit
0947	Pink landed
0953	Brown in the circuit
0954	Brown landed
1003	Pink 2 available
1009	Pink 1 available
1009	Pink at readiness
1013.5	Pink standby
1013.5	Brown at readiness
1020	Pink scrambles
1021	Pink airborne
1026	Purple in the circuit
1028	Purple landed
1046	Purple available
1056	Brown standby
1113	Brown scrambled
1114	Brown airborne
1118	Purple scrambled
1119	Purple airborne.....

.....and so on until 1900, when the Squadron was stood down.

This was followed in early April by Exercise *Easter Egg*, a mainly daylight exercise in which 39 had to defend Hal Far airfield, Malta, against an 'enemy' consisting of Sea Hawks, Wyverns and Skyraiders - the net result was twenty-two sorties and eighteen kills. These exercises were the 'bread and butter' of Squadron training and on average there was one such exercise per month. However, in June flying was curtailed when skin cracks were discovered on the upper surfaces of the wings. This problem was cured within days but recurred in December with skin cracks in the engine nacelles and inboard wing area.

July brought the major exercises of the year - *DXM*, Defence Exercise Malta. During this three day exercise (18 - 20 July), to test the defences of the island, 39 was involved in the night phases. Overall, the Squadron flew forty-one sorties (a total of just over thirty-seven hours) and claimed thirty-six kills: twenty-four Lincolns and seven Canberras from Tripoli; three Savages and two Skyraiders from the US Sixth Fleet at Naples. During *DXM*, the Squadron's average scramble time was one and a half minutes with a turn-round time of nine minutes and twenty seconds (refuel and 're-arm').

An exercise on the 23rd/24th November brought the Squadron face to face with opponents using electronic jamming and dropping profuse quantities of 'window'. This was the first time that crews had come up against window but, after a few initial problems, the navigators learnt how to tune their sets to partly overcome the interference.

The first half of 1956 was reasonably quiet, the regular round of exercises plus an APC in Cyprus in March/April and an air to ground shoot in Libya in late May. On the APC the Squadron average was 14 - 28%, although when the 30% 'fiddle factor' was added to compensate for the use of wing guns the average became a respectable 20 - 39%.

However, the peace was not to last. As mentioned before, the last British troops left Egypt on 13th June 1956; Nasser had achieved part of his goal and he now prepared to complete his plans. At a speech in Alexandria on 26th July Nasser showed his hand:

'The Suez Canal was one of the facades of oppression, extortion and humiliation. Today, O Citizens, the Suez Canal has been nationalised . . . and it will be run by Egyptians, Egyptians, EGYPTIANS!'

Even as he spoke, the Egyptian army was taking control of the Canal. The crowds were euphoric. However, the British and French Governments were not so impressed; one Labour MP called it, 'the technique which we got used to in Hitler's day . . . the consequences of not answering force with force until it is too late.' HM Government found it necessary to take 'certain precautionary measures of a military nature' and joint planning with the French began. The decision was taken to use Malta as the main naval base and to build up Cyprus as the main air base (meaning Nicosia airfield as Tymbou was allocated to the French and Akrotiri was hurriedly built during the crisis). The air build up included 39 Squadron, and warning orders were received to prepare for a move to Cyprus 'owing to the grave political situation in the Middle East.' On the 4th August, the Squadron was brought to twenty-four hours readiness to deploy and crews were brought to two hours standby; long-range drop tanks were fitted to all the aircraft. By mid-day on the 4th, the Squadron dispersal at Luqa 'resembled a travelling circus the morning after the last show', but by midnight on the same day all essential items were crated and the NF.13s stood ready on the ORP (Operational Readiness Platform).

Farewells were said to families and the tension on the Squadron was intense, all ranks standing by for the word to go. However, at 8 am the next morning, crews were reverted to twelve hours readiness and remained so until the 9th August when the 'GO' was given and seven aircraft left Luqa for Nicosia (via El Adem). The ground support party had left two days before in Hastings transport aircraft.

The NF.13s arrived at Nicosia at 1300 on the 9th to find the groundcrew settled into a tented camp on one side of the airfield. Les Wisdom recalls the conditions at Nicosia:

'Conditions were atrocious, four men to a tent in a dirty, dusty compound, with only one stand-pipe for drinking water. Toilets were of the ditch variety in unlit tin sheds which, after dark, crawled with enormous cockroaches. The Mess was quite good to start with but became worse as the Nicosia camp complex grew from its normal 1,000 men to over 7,000. Tents were erected in every open space - frequently, nailed to bedrock! When it rained, the water ran in streams across the airfield and through the tents.'

After a period spent in tents and mud huts the officers 'negotiated' for themselves two of the abandoned married quarters and proceeded to set up home away from the chaos of the Officers' Mess. Further negotiations led to aircrew ration allowances being 'swapped' for food supplies from the Catering Section. Ian Welch (now Squadron Leader) recalls that this was a great system as they catered for themselves, living on steaks, and were thus able to make life reasonably comfortable. When the crisis ended the detachment that remained at Nicosia continued to make use of the houses.

The Squadron was not at full status until

Above: **Nicosia 1956. 39 Squadron tented area.**

Opposite: **Refuelling at Nicosia, note yellow/ black 'invasion' stripes.** *(Both L.Wisdom)*

the end of August due to teething problems in setting up GCI sites around the island. However, by the end of the month, 39 Squadron was flying an average of eighteen sorties per night, plus a number of day PIs, sector reconnaissance and cine work. The move to Nicosia and the operational nature of the deployment had brought about a marked improvement in morale and efficiency, both of which had begun to suffer at Malta from a 'flying-club' atmosphere generated by the endless routine of training flying.

Soon after arrival at Nicosia, the aircraft were adorned with yellow and black Suez 'invasion' stripes on the wing roots and rear fuselage, the latter stripes partially obscuring the black/yellow dogtooth.

Throughout the military build-up of late summer 1956, 39 Squadron sharpened its readiness by refining and practising interception techniques with the GCI stations and by running an air-to-air gunnery programme using two Meteor 8s from the APC unit.

By October, Anglo-French planning for 'intervention' in Egypt was well advanced, although subject to frequent major alterations which threatened to bring disaster to the whole project.

The air defences of Cyprus were fully established by early October and 39 took part in a major exercise to test the efficiency of the defences. These defences existed to counter the threat from the Soviet-equipped Egyptian Air Force.

With the Israeli attack in Sinai and the proposal by Britain and France to 'intervene to separate the belligerents and protect the Canal', units on Cyprus came to full standby. On the 20th, 39 Squadron came to armed standby with four crews at immediate readiness at the dispersals for the period 1700 to 0700, plus a further two crews in the Mess at thirty minutes readiness. On the first day, the Squadron flew three armed patrols under the GCI control. The high level of standby was continued for the period 20 - 30th October with an average of twelve sorties per night, most of which were directed against unidentified 'contacts' - all of which proved non-hostile, the majority being Allied aircraft which had strayed from their flight-planned routes. The 31st October saw the start of the Anglo-French intervention and so the whole Squadron was brought to standby. On the 25th, Squadron Leader A J Owen, DFC, DFM, took command of the Squadron, and all day flying by Valiants and Canberras from Malta and Cyprus was suspended because of the high level of night standby commitment. In early November, the Egyptian Air Force and nearly all of its aircraft were bombed out of existence , thus neatly removing the immediate threat which they had posed to Cyprus.

On 6th November, the initial seaborne landings of Operation *Musketeer* took place and the Anglo-French forces advanced to secure the Canal. During this critical phase, 39 Squadron kept six crews on standby at dispersals, although on the 6th November this was reduced to four standby and two at thirty minutes in the Mess; there was a further reduction on the 29th to two at dispersal and two in the Mess.

During November, the Squadron made seventy-five interceptions including twenty-two Constellations, twelve Noratlases, four Shackletons, six Yorks, ten Valettas and a Viscount.

Meanwhile, the Suez 'war' was being heavily criticised in the UN and although the invasion was progressing reasonably well, the political pressure, unpleasant comments from the Americans and threats from the Russians, led to the opening of negotiations for a UN peace-keeping force. By 13th November, the advance party of UN troops had arrived, and by the 20th the UN Emergency Force was on the Canal in strength. Negotiations continued, and in December the Allied forces began to withdraw, 'helped' on their way by Egyptian terrorists. The entire Anglo-French force had left by the 22nd and 'intervention' was over.

For 39 Squadron, early December brought a reduction in the standby commitment and a consequent reduction in operational flying, with only nine operational sorties and four interceptions. Therefore, there was an increase in the

amount of continuation training flying, including the use of an air-to-ground firing range at Larnaca. from the 11th-22nd December the Squadron kept one crew at dispersal and one in the Mess, but with the end of the withdrawal on 22nd December the Squadron was stood down. Tragically, about this time, WM314 crashed while making an approach to Nicosia in bad weather, killing both crew members.

The day before the stand down, AVM A L Patch, CB, CBE, visited the Squadron to congratulate all ranks on their efforts during the crisis and especially during the period of the Port Said landings.

Over the Christmas period, married personnel were sent back to Malta on leave. The relaxed atmosphere of post-Suez did not last long as on the 29th an unidentified aircraft was picked up on radar, and it was thought that this aircraft was dropping supplies to EOKA forces. Thus, on the 30th the Squadron resumed armed standby, with one crew at dispersal and one in the Mess.

The EOKA (Ethniki Organosis Kyprion Agoniston - National Organisation of Cypriot Fighters) forces, led by 'General' Grivas, had been active in Cyprus since 31st March 1955, that being the date of the first EOKA bomb attacks - in Nicosia, Larnaca and Famagusta. As early as July 1952 a secret committee for the 'liberation' of Cyprus had met in Athens under the guidance of Archbishop Makarios. Between July 1952 and March 1955, sabotage plans were made and arms bought and shipped to Cyprus, the first boatload arriving in March 1954. Grivas arrived in November of that year and made his final plans for a terror campaign to start in early 1955. The aim of EOKA was 'Enosis', the union of Cyprus with Greece, and to achieve this aim - or at least bring pressure on the British authorities, Grivas planned a terrorist campaign of sabotage and murder. Sabotage groups were formed to attack government buildings, barracks and police stations, while the murder squads attacked civilian officials and soldiers. The campaign lasted for two years, with a peak during the Suez crisis, which provided EOKA with plenty of good targets made easier to attack by the confusion which reigned in the large temporary camps.

EOKA is dealt with here in some detail for two reasons: first, the direct involvement of 39 Squadron in trying to prevent aircraft dropping supplies to the terrorists; and, secondly, because of the effect on 'social life' and conditions that the EOKA campaign had on all British personnel in Cyprus. As Les Wisdom recalls:

'I can recall the time when a time-pencil[1]

bomb blew up and destroyed a 92 Squadron Hunter right before our eyes! At Nicosia we were very much confined to camp because of EOKA gunmen. Airmen were only allowed into town in fours, in uniform and armed. Since wearing uniform made one an obvious target we tended to stay in camp. One could chance it by going in civvies but had to travel everywhere by taxi. Trips by coach, with an armed guard, were sometimes run to the beaches at Kyrenia or places of historical interest such as Salamis or St Hilarion castle. The most popular entertainments were the open-air cinema and drinking in the various messes.'.

In view of the events of November/December 1956, the standby commitment continued in January 1957 with eighteen operational sorties resulting in eight intercepts, all of which proved non-hostile. However, as a safety precaution, aircraft were flown with the guns disarmed and crews were briefed to intercept, identify and if necessary force down any suspect aircraft. On the 14th, an NF.13 was scrambled to intercept a suspect Dakota which had approached the island at low level and did not respond on radio. When intercepted, the Dakota took evasive action and was therefore thought to have been working with EOKA. Flight Lieutenant Derek Lewis picked up the aircraft on his AI set and directed Master Pilot Christie towards the contact. They turned to approach the aircraft from the rear for a visual ident but went past it without seeing anything. As the 'blip' vanished from the screen Derek Lewis called his pilot to turn around, and soon picked up the contact again, it seemed likely that their prey had switched off all its lights and descended low over the sea. They closed again with Lewis calling out the ranges. All of a sudden there was an almighty BANG; the pilot thought he had hit a ship so he pulled up and headed back to base. Taking stock of the situation the crew discovered that the airbrake was jammed out, there was no indication on the starboard engine and the undercarriage had come down. After landing at Nicosia, the true extent of the damage could be seen. The starboard jet pipe was missing and the turbines were exposed; also the ventral fuel tank had been ripped off. The crew had been very lucky - they had hit the sea but at such a shallow angle that they had skipped off again like a stone! However, subsequent diplomatic enquiries revealed that it was an Israeli aircraft on a 'training' flight.

It was the same story in February, eleven sorties and thirteen intercepts, including a Persian Air Services Avro York which was intercepted three times and was subsequently reported for overflying the island without clearance!

However, in March the Squadron was ordered to prepare to move back to Luqa leaving an

---

(1) In early 1956 attacks on aircraft at Nicosia were made by civilian employees planting time-pencils.

operational detachment of two aircraft, started as three NF.13 WM313, 339, 327 and a T.7 WH201, and three crews at Nicosia 'for the foreseeable future'. The detachment moved into permanent accommodation as Nicosia was returning to normal in the post-Suez run down, and the advance party of the main body of the Squadron left for Malta on the 20th.

Following a UK negotiated cease-fire, EOKA disturbances virtually ceased in 1957 although there was the occasional flare-up again before the final cease-fire of March 1959. Nevertheless, the Battle Flight, as it was now called, at Nicosia flew an average of twenty operational sorties a month, although all targets proved non-hostile. Aircraft and crews were rotated between Nicosia and Luqa, although in late June the Squadron was re-united at Luqa for Exercise *Rosie Rosie,* a NATO exercise to test the air defences of Southern Europe, and the air defence exercise *Maltex.*

The remainder of the summer saw the main element of the Squadron engaged in its routine training while at Nicosia the Battle Flight maintained its standby commitment. However, the political situation in the Mediterranean was on the boil again in November with tension between Syria and Turkey and so an additional two aircraft were sent from Luqa to strengthen the Battle Flight. This was short lived as by the 14th the extra element had returned to Luqa, just in time to take part in Exercise *Red Epoch* - to intercept a force of Canberras at 40 - 43,000 feet, much higher than usual for intercepts.

A major change in the fortunes of the Squadron was announced in March 1958 when it was confirmed that the Squadron would disband on 30th June that year. The misery which greeted this news was soon overshadowed when, on the 15th May, a state of emergency was declared in the Lebanon. The Battle Flight was joined by the rest of the Squadron and 39 again stood at full armed readiness at Nicosia, with eight NF.13s in position by the 19th.

It was hoped by many on 39 that these events would postpone the day of disbandment, but on the 5th June it was announced that the Squadron would return to Luqa to disband as planned on the 30th. However, 39 Squadron would live again with the re-numbering of 69(PR) Squadron on the 1st July. This decision was to a large extent due to negotiations between the COs of the two Squadrons. Over a period of time the CO of 69 Squadron was persuaded that a re-numbering was in everyones best interest. This

1 July 1958, Luqa, Malta. Farewell to the Meteor and hello to the Canberra PR.3 as 39 Squadron disbands and 69 Squadron renumbers as 39 Squadron.

was then put to the Air Ministry who, having no objection, agreed! Thus, on the 15th 39 handed the standby duties to 153(AW) Squadron and three days later was back at Luqa preparing for the various ceremonials.

When 39 left Nicosia they were sent the following message by C-in-C MEAF: 'Now the 39 Squadron detachment has finally left us and that the Squadron will soon be disbanding, I would like to express my appreciation of their work in Cyprus over the past two years. The disbandment of a Squadron is naturally a sad occasion for its members, but it is also time for looking back with pride at past achievements. They have had a thankless job involving long hours of standby with little activity; they have had to endure continuous family separation and indifferent accommodation at Nicosia. In spite of this, they carried out their duties efficiently and without complaint and I am sure that His Excellency the Governor and the Director of Operations would wish me to include with mine their sincere thanks for a vital job well done under difficult circumstances.'

Thus, on 1st July 1958 it was farewell to 39 'Night Fighter' Squadron and hello to 39 'Photo Recce' Squadron. It was also the start of 39's Canberra era as the box of four Meteor NF.13s flew over the parade followed by a box of four Canberra PR.3s.

10

Smile Please!

When 69(PR) Squadron became 39(PR) Squadron there was no transfer of personnel between the squadrons. The 're-formed' 39 consisted of ten Canberra PR.3s, one Canberra T.4, twenty-seven officers and ninety-seven airmen. The number of airmen was lower than normal for a full-size squadron because only routine (1st Line) servicing was done by Squadron personnel; detailed periodic servicing and repair was done by Luqa station personnel and the Maintenance Unit (MU) at RAF Safi.

The stated war role of 39 Squadron was 'Pre-strike recce in support of the Supreme Allied Commander Europe's (SACEURs) nuclear retaliation to aggression.' Effectively, this meant that the Squadron had a Strategic Recce (SR) role, flying high-level missions to cover large areas of territory, a very similar role to that which the Squadron had in 1941/42 with the Marylands. In the English Electric Canberra PR.3, 39 Squadron acquired a high performance, high-level, long-range aircraft ideally suited to perform this role, although the PR.3 was in fact a modified B.2 bomber. The two 6,500 lb thrust Rolls-Royce Avon RA3 engines gave a maximum speed of 570 mph at 40,000 ft, with a service ceiling of 48,000 ft and an excellent range. The 'tools of the trade' were a fan of six 36-inch focal length F52 cameras plus a single F49, which were reliable and efficient cameras and produced good results. However, the hot Mediterranean sun beating down on the concrete aircraft dispersals at Luqa made changing the heavy magazines an exhausting and sweaty job, particularly during exercises when 'speed was of the essence' for a quick aircraft turn-round.

It was not only the 'Moles' (camera tradesmen) who suffered from the heat. The aircrew faced the serious problem of heat exhaustion when they climbed into aircraft which had been sitting on dispersals baking in the sun. A shower-bath was installed in the Squadron buildings to help alleviate the problem of heat exhaustion. The greenhouse effect produced by the non-opening bubble canopy posed a problem that defeated sunshades and even mechanical coolers in hot

climates. The best solution was to get airborne as soon as possible after climbing into the aircraft and let Nature cool the aircraft, and its occupants, as the aircraft climbed into levels of lower ambient temperature (average summer temperatures in the Central Mediterranean at 10,000 ft are 10°C).

69 Squadron had been well established as a reconnaissance squadron in Germany, part of 2 Allied Tactical Air Force (ATAF), and so in mid-1958 when it became 39 Squadron the latter was immediately experienced! This enabled 39 to become operational very quickly. To meet the strategic reconnaissance role, the emphasis on photographic training sorties was on high level photography of point targets (designated pinpoints) of things like airfields, town, bridges, power-stations etc, or rectangular areas to cover a line on the ground (designated feature lines) which followed a coast-line, railway line, river or road. The Squadron's primary area of operations was the Mediterranean and its bordering countries to the east of Malta; the main training areas being Italy, Sicily, Turkey, Greece, Libya and Cyprus.

The Squadron was declared to NATO, ie., made available to NATO Commanders for operations, and became part of Sixth Allied Tactical Air Force (6 ATAF). As a NATO-assigned Squadron, 39 was subject to short notice or no notice evaluation exercises by NATO inspection teams. An exercise would be announced by a code-word passed by telephone, or by the sudden appearance of an evaluation team. One aircraft was held on Quick Readiness Alert (QRA) with a full war fit of cameras and this aircraft had to be airborne within thirty minutes, but usually got off the ground in less than twenty. Meanwhile, the rest of the Squadron would be arriving at the Squadron following the summons 'to action' (often by a telephone call along the lines of 'get your knickers on, we're off to war') and would be getting themselves and the aircraft ready for tasking. Within hours of the exercise being called, the Squadron would probably have six or seven aircraft airborne over various parts

Camouflaged PR.3, WE144 at Luqa. One of the camera doors can just be seen below the jet pipe.

of the Mediterranean, each one working flat out to get the photography necessary to satisfy the task and get back to base with the results, so that the Photographic Interpreters (PIs) could analyse the film.

The Squadron was also allocated Forward Operating Bases (FOBs) in Turkey and Greece from which to operate 'as and when the tactical situation demanded'. Ground equipment was pre-stocked at Eskishehir in Turkey and Larissa in Greece to speed up deployment, and since it was necessary for personnel to become familiar with operating from both FOBs, regular visits to Turkey and Greece took place. These two-week detachments continued until 1970 when 39 Squadron eventually left the Mediterranean theatre. As well as regular full Squadron detachments, it was common for individual aircraft to be tasked for a two or three day deployment to one of the FOBs. Deployment to these bases was often included as part of an exercise, as with Exercise *Flashback* on 21st September 1960 when six aircraft scrambled from Luqa on simulated war missions and landed at Eskishehir (commonly known as Eski).

On pre-planned major detachments, ground-crew were flown out to support the aircraft. When deployed to Eski all Corporals and below received acting rank of Sergeant, as this entitled them to be accommodated in beds as opposed to tin bunks used by the 'conscripted' Turkish airmen! Eskishehir airfield had a standard NATO layout, which included having aircraft dispersals (pans) in a variety of remote locations - a situation which caused certain problems, as Brian Howett recalls:

'The dispersal area was a wild and desolate area of the airfield and the last aircraft to land was to use a pan half a mile or so across scrub land. So at 7 pm, Jock Bald and I set off jogging across to the pan as the aircraft taxied in. As we passed a hollow in the ground several dogs got up and ran across the airfield. We thought no more about it and duly put the aircraft to bed. On returning to the hangar, which always had an armed guard, we spoke to the Turkish liaison officer to suggest that it was dangerous to allow dogs loose on an active airfield. To our amazement, he explained that they were not dogs, they were wolves down from the mountains! By putting out corned beef from our rations we were able next day to photograph the animals.'

By mid-1959, the Squadron establishment had increased to eleven PR.3s. This was further increased to fifteen aircraft by early 1960, and included a replacement for WF926 which crashed into the sea on a night sortie in January killing both crew members. All the aircraft from Laarbruch were in standard 2 ATAF green/grey upper surface camouflage finish, and in early 1960, some of the aircraft were re-painted silver. With the re-spraying programme, the Squadron's most famous aircraft (WE139) lost its name-plate, 'The Winner'. This aircraft had won the London and New Zealand Air Race in October 1953. Fortunately, this aircraft has been preserved and can now be seen in the RAF Museum with its name-plate restored.

Shortly afterwards, the aircraft were given *Green Satin* doppler equipment which transmitted beams ahead and behind the aircraft and used the doppler shift of the returning signals to provide an accurate indication of drift and groundspeed, an important factor in accurate navigation. It was early 1961 before the majority were fitted with this navigation aid, and in May 1961 accuracy trials were conducted on the *Green Satin* sets by re-setting them over known positions and recording the errors. These trials were in preparation for night photography trials as it was anticipated that 39 Squadron would soon acquire a night PR role. Some months earlier, selected crews had completed a bombing course at RAF Lindholme, Yorkshire, the principles of bombing and 'flashing' being the same.

During October 1962, the Squadron was involved in preparations for a complete vertical photographic survey of Aden in the latter half of the month, and also with plans for a re-equipment programme. The Aden survey was notable for the unprecedented achievement of the aircraft involved flying 100 hours between 18 - 30th October without any major unserviceabilities.

In the last week of October, a number of aircrew and groundcrew went back to the UK, to Wyton, to convert to the Canberra PR.9 under the tender mercies of 58(PR) Squadron, who had been the first squadron to receive this Mark. By the beginning of November, 39 had received the first five of its new aircraft - giving the Squadron an establishment of five PR.9s, six PR.3s and a T.4.

Built by Short Brothers of Belfast, the PR.9 was the latest and most powerful mark of the Canberra and its two 11,250 lb thrust Avon 206 engines gave it a performance far superior to all previous marks of Canberra, (the engines being almost twice as powerful; 6,500 lb thrust for the PR.3 against 11,250 for the PR.9 - for each engine). Designed originally as an ultra high level strategic recce (SR) aircraft, the design was modified to allow the aircraft to fly at low level at speeds up to 450 knots. It was not unknown for aircraft to fly at 500 knots plus (low level) when the occasion demanded, either to meet a target time or to get back for bar opening time!

One of the many unique features of the PR.9 was the arrangement of the crew compartments. The pilot sat under a bubble canopy in a position off-set to one side of the upper fuselage and the navigator sat in a self-contained compartment in the nose; the nose of the aircraft being hinged to allow access to this position. The navigator sat on an ejection seat, facing forward and then the nose was closed; this compartment had often been referred to as 'the black hole of Calcutta'. When shut-in the navigator had a small window on either side for observation and natural light and a periscopic sextant which could be adjusted to look straight forward or at any angle downwards, back as far as being able to see the underside of the fuselage. This was primarily designed for use in the vertical mode for accurate vertical tracking during survey photography.

Squadron T.4 (WH861) at Luqa, Malta. Yellow and black Squadron markings on the tip tank. The port engine cowling has been removed. (*J.D.R.Rawlings*)

XH170 on Aden survey, 1967. The Canberra PR.9 with its unique cockpit arrangement of bubble canopy and hinged nose. *(P.C.A.Major)*

Thus, the aircraft is unique for a Canberra in having a maximum of two seating positions.

Throughout its existence, the PR.9 has had a reputation as an exhilarating but unforgiving aircraft, a reputation which started during the development trials. The prototype PR.9, a converted PR.7, first flew on 8th July 1955; WH793 was given the larger RA24 engines and a larger wing area by increasing the chord of the wing between the engines and the fuselage and extending the wing span by approximately six feet. This aircraft went on to have a long, distinguished career with RAE at Farnborough and Bedford and was eventually broken up at Farnborough in August 1975. Canberra PR.9 XH129, the first production aircraft, also underwent flight trials and on 9th October 1958, in the structural demonstration, designed to test the airframe under its worst conditions, the aircraft went out of control and crashed into the sea. When recovered, the wreckage revealed that the addition to the wing section between the engines and the fuselage had made the section too rigid and the load on the wing caused the outer wing to break. The designers had given the aircraft powered rudders to handle the asymmetric power that was possible and it became clear that the ailerons needed to be powered to handle the secondary effects of rudder application. There followed a period of re-design but by early

January the basic flight trials had been successfully completed and the aircraft was ready for the final stage, the structural demonstration. This time there were no problems and the PR.9 moved to its next stage, evaluation trials at Boscombe Down. Although the engines, power controls and wing section made the PR.9 quite different from all other spring tab variants, the aircraft was treated as another mark of Canberra and so entered service shortly afterwards. A total of twenty-three aircraft were built, with the production run ending in 1961. By 1976, 39 Squadron had acquired a monopoly on the PR.9 when it received the last of four aircraft from XIII(PR) Squadron (although there was one other, XH132, in use with RAE Bedford as the SC.9). However, in early December 1962, the Squadron establishment was eight PR.9s, four PR.3s and one T.4, and the hectic conversion programme instigated in November continued unabated in order to get the whole Squadron combat ready as soon as possible. With the PR.3s, 39 had mainly operated in the airspace band 2,000 - 5,000 feet with the long focal length F52 cameras. A major change in operational role with the PR.9 was an increased emphasis on tactical low level targets using the three F95 cameras in the nose. The F95 camera used four or eight frames a second and was normally fitted with a 500 exposure magazine. One camera was mounted on the port side of the nose compartment, at a 15° depression angle with a second camera mounted in a similar position on the starboard side and a third, at an angle of 10° in the nose as a forward-looking sensor. A four-inch focal length lens was the standard fit but this could be changed for a twelve-inch lens.

The remaining PR.3s continued with the Squadron's task commitment through November and December 1962, but by the end of January there were only two aircraft left on strength and the last of these, WE135, was ferried back to the UK in April 1963 leaving the Squadron with nine PR.9s and a T.4, WH861.

Thus, by early 1963 the Squadron was at full strength and rapidly gaining experience with the new aircraft and the low level role. A low level training cell was set up to assist crews to learn the demanding and complex task of target reporting. Up until this time the only low level flying area had been in Libya, but in early June, a low level route around Sicily became available, a short route but much more interesting and realistic terrain than the desert wastes of Libya. Furthermore, the CO, Wing Commander F G Agnew, went to Naples to discuss with AF South the Squadron's role in war and peace. This was a necessary prerequisite for establishing the type and intensity of training for crews.

The outcome of the discussions was to make 39 a strategic and tactical recce squadron asssiged to the Southern Flank of NATO, using FOBs in Turkey and Greece. Basically, this continued the previous commitment but added the low level tactical role, thus giving 39 Squadron four main roles:

1 Day low level recce.
2 Day medium/high level recce - vertical and oblique.
3 Air survey - vertical photo for map production or updating.
4 Shipping recce.

By the end of June, the Squadron establishment was ten PR.9s, which it was to remain for some years, plus one T.4 (although the Squadron actually had two - WH861 and WT481) plus one PR.3 on loan.

Low level training facilities were still inadequate, so the Squadron began to negotiate for use of the low flying system in Germany. Agreement was eventually obtained, and the first crews deployed to Laarbruch on 6th November for a three week detachment in which thirty-three low level sorties were flown. In the period up to the 19th December, nine crews had completed the 'course' of low flying in Germany, and were considered to be low level qualified. The standard was set at a minimum of nine effective sorties to be classified as low level 'combat' qualified. This left only four crews to complete the course; 39 was rapidly gaining experience in the tactical low level role.

In the meantime, 39 Squadron had carried out its first major exercise - *Southex 63* - in which a command post was set up at Eskishehir to co-ordinate Squadron flying effort in Turkey. In the event, for the first half of the exercise most of the sorties were flown from Luqa and it was only in the second half that aircraft flew high and low level sorties out of Eski.

Eskishehir, situated 120 miles west of Ankara, had an extra long runway, 12,000 feet, because the Turkish squadrons were flying the desperately underpowered RF-84 and the slightly better F-100 and therefore needed every available foot of runway. Despite the poor facilities available to 39, the Squadron was well supported by the Turks both operationally and socially. In view of the tight flying restrictions in the RAF, some aircrew recall the 'refreshing' approach the Turkish Air Force had to operating aeroplanes. There was one occasion when an F-100 landed in the undershoot, wiped off its undercarriage and burst into flames on the end of the runway. Accordingly, the first 1,000 feet of runway, covered in F-100 and flaming fuel, was declared unusable and the rest of the F-100 Squadron landed over the top of the flames!

There was a healthy and friendly rivalry between the F-100 fighter squadron at Eski and 39. Under normal circumstances, the PR.9 was far more manoeuvrable than the F-100, but to the great delight of the Turkish fighter pilots, they learnt that the PR.9 was not so nimble on one engine. Indeed, on the occasion that Malcolm Swinhoe returned to Eski with an engine failure, the Turks beat hell out of the stricken aircraft during his transit to Eski, not breaking away until the aircraft landed.

At Luqa, a QRA aircraft was maintained at thirty minutes readiness both day and night. Crews did a twenty-four hour stint on QRA and the idea was to get airborne in less than thirty minutes and then fly a pre-planned sortie. Thus the QRA aircraft could be called to deploy to Turkey, Greece, Italy or Cyprus with tasking provided on arrival. A room was allocated in the Officers Mess for the QRA crew, who would be called out by Station Ops to leap into the QRA Land Rover, with its blue light, and belt the three-quarters of a mile from the Mess to the Squadron area and thence to the aircraft. On most occasions, practice call-outs were terminated as the aircraft lined up on the runway when a code word was broadcast. On one occasion, the controller could not find the code word in time to stop the aircraft taking off with a full fuel load. Some impressive times were turned in - such as John Clemons and Dick King with eleven minutes from in the Mess to ready for take-off. The crew did admit later that neither was strapped in, the pilot was still soaking from his unfinished shower and the Nav was clothed in flying suit and boots - but nothing else! On another

The front panel of the Navigators station before the mod programme of the late 1970s. Bottom right — Green Satin doppler, left — GPI Mk.IV. The object in the centre is the periscopic viewer.

occasion, a crew broke the magic ten minute barrier from Mess to take-off point. When the Station Commander asked what held them back, the pilot is reported to have said that he had to finish his beer before running to the vehicle!

From late 1963, the number of aircraft available was reduced because of a modification programme whereby aircraft were returned to Shorts at Belfast to have TACAN fitted. This greatly improved the navigation fit of the PR.9, and TACAN, radio compass (Marconi sub miniature type), *Green Satin* doppler and GPI (Ground Position Indicator) Mk.IV was to remain the basic fit of the PR.9s until the late '70s when the fit was brought up to date with the introduction of the Decca TANS system.

Despite the increased importance of the low level role, a large proportion of the Squadron's task remained medium level and high level photo. The PR.9 carried a variety of cameras for these roles, ranging from the 6-inch or 12-inch focal length F96 vertical camera at the rear of the aircraft, to the F96 split-pair (ie two F96

cameras looking slightly out from the vertical), the 'fan' of four F96 cameras, and a 24-inch or 48-inch focal length oblique camera usually fitted as a Port Facing Oblique (PFO). Thus, the camera fit and focal length could be altered to suit a particular task and the permanent camera fit of the aircraft gave a capability from ground level (F95) to over 50,000 feet (F96). Compared with its predecessor, the F52, the F96 was a modern sophisticated camera which incorporated Image Movement Compensation (IMC) to compensate for the aircraft moving over the ground by moving the film and thereby producing a sharp image.

The tasks which required these cameras ranged from the pinpoints and feature lines of the PR.3 era to vertical survey and high level long range oblique photo. The air defence environment had changed around the time that the PR.9 had entered service with the advent of the Surface to Air Missiles (SAMs) capable of knocking down targets above 60,000 feet. They largely negated the intended application of the PR.9 as an aircraft that could fly above air defences. This was graphically demonstrated on the 1st May 1960, when the Soviet Union shot down an American Lockheed U-2 spy plane which had been flying at a height 'in excess of 55,000 feet.'

Nevertheless, the role remained practical for SR of areas of threat and build-up, during a period of tension. This means of monitoring an enemy has been particularly useful in containing the threat posed by minor incursions into friendly territory. Many of Britain's allies have benefited during the life of the PR.9 from the ability of the large oblique cameras to produce evidence of troop concentrations.

The vertical survey role whereby a land area is photographed to a precise scale in conditions of little or no cloud, is the role which took the Squadron worldwide. Usually, the requirement was for photography to update, or complete, existing maps, but occasionally new areas were covered. Over the years, 39 Squadron has carried out surveys of Hong Kong, Belize, Denmark, Germany, Fiji, Malaysia, Bermuda, Borneo, Cyprus, Malta, and many other Commonwealth and allied territories. This role is retained by the PR.9 with No.1 Photographic Reconnaissance Unit (PRU) at RAF Wyton being the successor to 39 Squadron.

The survey role was one of the most demanding for the Navigator. The area to be photographed was divided up into parallel flight lines, spaced so that there is a 30% overlap between adjacent lines - to allow for lateral error and providing link information for adjacent frames. It was the job of the pilot to line up the aircraft and then to maintain height, speed and heading as directed by the Navigator. As soon as the pilot was roughly 'on line', the Navigator took over, and from that moment on, parameters were very precisely defined - changes of heading by as little as half a degree and of speed by two or three knots. Using the periscope viewer in the vertical position the Navigator then map read along the flight line adjusting heading, height and speed as necessary. The camera (either the F96 Vert or, for survey, the more sophisticated F49 Mk.IV survey camera - a podded unit which fitted in the flare bay) would have been set-up on the approach run for aperture, shutter speed and time interval, the latter setting being the number of seconds between each picture, which depended on the height and speed of the aircraft, usually for a 60% overlap from frame to frame. Furthermore, IMC was necessary to allow for movement of the aircraft over the ground and

Below: **Villafranca detachment July 1967 — XH171 with an RF-84 of 132 Gruppo, Italian Air Force.** *Opposite:* **In transit over Italy, a mix of camouflaged and original silver finish aircraft.**

therefore the movement of the image across the film. The intense concentration, particularly for the Navigator, could last on a single flight line from thirty miles to 300 miles, up to an hour or so without a break!

The number of 'customers' dropped in the late 1970s as it became more economical for countries to hire private survey firms with low fuel consumption aircraft and modern camera equipment. Nevertheless, 39 Squadron still undertook regular survey tasks of a military nature or on behalf of allied Governments. The success or failure of a survey was greatly influenced by the weather because of the requirements for no cloud, in practice a maximum of one eighth of cloud. In May 1980 the weather was so good over a five day period that three aircraft were able to photograph the whole of Denmark; the year before, however, a survey of part of Germany was rained off for almost the whole of its three week stay.

It was a notable feature of the Squadron that only on very few occasions was the whole Squadron together in the same place at the same time. Apart from 'major' detachments of two or more aircraft, 39 always had a commitment to despatch single aircraft 'rangers' to various parts of the world. This often led to the Squadron being scattered between two or three bases worldwide.

This was particularly true of the years when the Squadron was in Malta; in the mid-1960s, 39 maintained almost continuous detachments in Aden (Khormaksar) and Bahrein (Muharraq) on reconnaissance duties over the Persian Gulf and surrounding areas - as well as regular detachments in various parts of Africa and from late 1963 rangers to Livingstone, Zambia. Add to this the QRA commitment which kept one aircraft grounded at Luqa, and the nine PR.9s were kept incredibly busy.

In the middle of this 'peaceful' scene, SACEUR could decide to call an exercise to test the readiness of the Squadron! These could be called at the most inconvenient of times, as on the 26th June 1964 when the exercise was called in the middle of the RAF Luqa Officers Mess Summer Ball. Unceremoniously abandoning drinks - and wives - the aircrew rushed off to the aircraft and, while trying to sober up, got ready to fly. Fortunately, the exercise was halted before any of the crew tried to take-off!

1964 saw yet another role added to the list, that of night photography using the F97 double camera system, artificial light being provided by 1.75 inch photo flares. This was a low level system, up to 5,000 feet in practical terms, which relied on the aircraft flying straight and level over the target, dropping flashes. The nav would

Denmark survey detachment Karup 1980. XH165 with aircrew supporting the groundcrew. Standing l to r: Pete Horrocks (J Eng) Stu Wilson, Ian Roberts, Mal Young, Al Summerside, Ken Delve, Dick Jennison, ?, ?, ?, Sqn Ldr Ed Elton, Wg Cdr Robin Phipps, CT Ted Hanby.

set the camera for the number of flashes he wanted to use on the run, usually five or seven, with a switch-on point calculated so that the aircraft would be overhead the target when the middle flash of the sequence exploded. The flashes were stored in the flare bay (bomb bay) and were thrown out below and behind the aircraft. When the flash exploded, the light illuminated the target and triggered a photo cell which closed the shutter of one camera and opened the shutter of the twin camera to await the next flash. Most training sorties were flown over Fifla Island, just off mainland Malta. Because of the anti-social nature of the explosion and flash of light, and the possibility of duds hitting the ground unexploded, crews later flew rangers to the UK, being based at Wyton, to fly low level flashing sorties on the UK military training ranges.

On one of these UK-based flashing sorties, a crew, who shall remain nameless, was tasked to photograph a target on the Salisbury Plain ranges. At each range in the UK an easily identifiable point, such as a unique group of lights, had been selected as the Initial Points (IPs) for flashing runs - to ensure that no-one dropped flashes outside of the range. The crew duly ran in on the target from their Initial Point, dropped their flashes and returned to Wyton. Unfortunately, the IP had been mis-identified and the crew had a superb picture of a village just outside the range! It is reported that a lorry driver who was driving through the village thought the end of the world had come with the loud bangs and intense light, stopped his lorry and opted to lie underneath it for protection!

In November 1964, crews began training in high-level night flashing. The intention was to use the normal day camera and so a very powerful light source was needed to turn night into day.

This was provided by huge World War Two photoflashes of 8-inch diameter and about five feet long, which produced 4,250 million candlepower! These mini-suns were dropped from 40,000 feet and ignited, by a barostatic fuse, at 20,000 feet, producing a tremendous amount of light and noise. The PR.9 carried five of these monsters which were normally dropped as a single stick with a time interval of twenty seconds between each flash. They were very unreliable and quite often only two or three would ignite, the others falling intact onto the range at El Adem, the normal venue for this type of training. The original intention was for each crew to fly one high level flash sortie every six months but the problems and hazards of the role led to the experience being limited to three crews in each six-month period. The first crew to visit the range carried inert flares so that they could check all the procedures before taking live rounds into the air; they dropped three concrete flares and were severely shaken when the release was followed by a muffled explosion within the aircraft. The crew returned to Malta for the most gentle landing the pilot had ever made. Subsequent investigation showed that an eddy current in the release mechanism had fired the explosive suppresion system in the No.6 (belly) fuel tank. The engineers solved the problem by removing the fuses for the explosive suppression system before the next drop! One of the biggest problems was safety as it was theoretically possible for the flashes to become live as the aircraft went through 20,000 feet, the fusing height, if the safety devices were defective; this meant that there was a danger of the flashes igniting when the aircraft descended back through 20,000 feet! Fortunately, this never happened although crews were informed of the possibility when they were briefed on the role. The intended application of this role was for night reconnaissance of enemy airfields, or similar large targets, or surveillance of the battle area. Over the next five years, the Squadron tried hard to keep current with the role but it was abandoned when Libya, and the El Adem range, were closed to the RAF when Colonel Qaddafi seized power in Libya in 1969.

So, on 39 Squadron in Malta there was never a dull moment; 'have cameras will travel' would have made a good Squadron motto. Prior to the loss of Libya, the Squadron was flying low level sorties in Libya, Italy, Sicily, Greece and Turkey - and the UK where 39 took part in a number of army exercises. May 1965 was so busy that the Squadron flew nearly 450 hours in the month, an unusually high total. Tragedy followed in June when T.4 WT481 crashed into the sea off Malta killing all three crew, although this was not attributed to the heavy work load of the previous weeks.

Only rarely was operational flying called for. For the first six months of 1966, PR aircraft from Malta were detached to Tengah, Singapore to assist 81(PR) Squadron during the period of confrontation in Borneo. 39's first involvement was to send one aircraft and crew as part of a XIII Squadron detachment in February/March 1966. However, when the detachment returned, the Squadron sent three aircraft and four crews to Tengah for the period April - early June. Most operational sorties were survey flights of parts of Borneo.

A year later there was political upheaval in Malta with a disagreement between the UK and Malta on the proposed run down of British Forces. The Maltese Government refused supplies of duty-free fuel and 39, along with other units, was grounded apart from air test flying. This situation prevailed for only the first week of February and then the Squadron started normal flying again using Naval Avcat Fuel. The dispute was solved by April and things returned to normal. The remaining years at Malta followed the pattern of low and high level PR, both day and night, including numerous exercises. Of the latter, probably the most important were the NATO TACEVAL (Tactical Evaluation), designed to test all aspects of the Squadron's operations and its effectiveness for war. TACEVAL usually involved the Squadron in deploying to its FOB, Eskishehir. Although these detachments to Tur-

key were hard work and conditions on base were primitive there were compensations. The Turkish Officers Club at Eski had burnt down in the mid-1960s and so the Turkish Air Force had commandeered a luxury hotel which had just been built. The new Officers Club, the Ordu Evi, was very plush and westernised. John Clemons recalls social life at Eski:

'There was very little to do in town, apart from shopping, there were a few night clubs but it wasn't thought safe to be out at night except in groups - and this led to the sport of chariot races! In town there were two types of taxi, the Mercedes and the horse-drawn carriage; the latter were four-seater jobs pulled by flea-bitten, broken-down nags. The Squadron aircrew would fall out of a night club en masse and pile into two of these carriages, seven or eight to each. All it then took was a promise of double fare to the winner and we were off! The drivers often became caught up in the excitement and we would career down the streets back to Ordu Evi, sometimes line abreast, with cars and people scattering before us and with us sobering up rapidly and hanging on for dear life!'

Back in Malta, 39 Squadron had a pair of mascots and in May 1969 one of them had a fatal disagreement with an MT vehicle. As one of the few PR ducks in captivity it was laid to rest with due ceremony and reverence and the Squadron went into mourning until a replacement could be found. Fortunately, the following month, a new 'crew' of ducks was posted in and duly went through the PR conversion course under the watchful eye of the one remaining qualified duck. They duly passed the course and all three remained on Squadron strength until 39 left for the UK in October 1970. It is said that with the departure of the Squadron the ducks were broken-hearted and leapt onto a Maltese dinner table. In November 1969 news was received of a move back to the UK 'sometime in 1970'. The long sojourn in the Mediterranean, and 39 Squadron's forty-one years of service outside the UK were to come to and end. The destination was one that was familiar to the Squadron from its rangers to the UK; it was to be RAF Wyton. Early in the new year it was announced that the move would take place on 1st October. In early September, the CO passed on the unwelcome news that only eight of the officers would go to Wyton with the Squadron and that the rest of the aircrew strength would be drawn from 58(PR) Squadron, already at Wyton and which was due to disband in December 1971.

39 Squadron maintained the QRA commitment and remained fully operational until the 24th September, when all commitments to AFSOUTH were relinquished so that the Squadron could make preparation for the move to

Wyton. General Sforza, Vice-Chief of the Italian Air Staff, not only arranged an impressive farewell party but also presented the Squadron with a wrought iron 'gremlin' for 'services rendered' to AFSOUTH; this object thereafter occupied a corner of the aircrew crewroom at Wyton. After numerous, and exhausting, farewell celebrations, five aircraft left Luqa as planned on 1st October. XH170 followed shortly afterwards but XH169 had to be shipped back; the eighth aircraft was already in the UK. On arrival back in the UK, the Squadron was given an excellent reception at their new base. Families were flown from Malta to Brize Norton by Britannia and then by road to Wyton to meet up with their husbands; the biggest surprise of all was to find that the Married Quarters were fully prepared, beds made and fires burning. Thus, everyone settled down ready for an English winter! After a period of familiarisation flying, 39 flew its first photo sortie from its new home on the 27th October - the Squadron had arrived.

However, the task commitment could not be met because of a shortage of aircraft and two Canberra PR.7s (WT532, WT825) were acquired to supplement aircraft strength until the establishment of PR.9s could be brought up to a reasonable level. The PR.7s arrived on 15th October and were only used for high level work, particularly survey, being flown by some of the ex-58 Squadron crews who were PR.7 qualified. In May 1971 these two aircraft undertook a very successful survey of Singapore. By December of that year only one PR.7 was held by 39 and that left in February 1972.

Although 39 had moved from the Southern flank of NATO, the Squadron continued to be a NATO-assigned unit and soon after its arrival in the UK it was allotted, through SACEUR, to the Northern Region (Norway and Denmark). In this respect, the main area of operation for 39 became Norway, with the Royal Norwegian Air Force base at Oerland as an FOB. As the Squadron's home in Norway, Oerland was used for two full-strength Squadron detachments each year, nominally one in winter and one in Spring or Summer. The first rangers to Norway began in early 1971 and in May that year Wing Commander O'Brien went to Oerland to finalise arrangements for the first full Squadron detachment. This deployment, Exercise *Applaud*, took place in September/October 1971 and is remembered for the quality of the beer and fish! It became a feature of Oerland detachments that all and sundry tried their hand at becoming the 'Fishermen of England!' The first NATO TACEVAL for 39 Squadron in its new theatre took place in April the following year. The area of operations extended from South Denmark to North Norway with tasks covering the full range of Squadron roles from pre-hostility SR to day and night TR and shipping reconnaissance. The PR.9 was an ideal aircraft for this theatre because of its excellent radius of action and the capability of crews to operate with a minimum of ground support if required.

At Oerland, 39 operated as a self-contained unit and each two-week detachment was an intensive period of training for aircrew and groundcrew. For at least part of the period, the Squadron operated on a full war posture with twenty-four hour operations. In winter, the snow, ice and freezing wind presented a massive challenge to maintaining operational readiness and it reflected great credit on the groundcrew that aircraft were kept serviceable in such appalling conditions: to see a huddled figure crouching on top of the wing in a raging snowstorm trying to repair an aircraft for a sortie taught the aircrews to respect the hard work of the groundcrew. The PR.9s sat outside in all weathers and at times the task of digging out aircraft from snow banks was almost a full-time one. Added to this was the problem of actually flying off snow and ice, a thing that the RAF when at home in the UK is reluctant to do. However, in Norway they do not, for obvious reasons, try to clear all snow and ice from the concrete surfaces of runways and taxiways; instead, they burn and grit the surface of the compacted snow/ice with a machine affectionately referred to as 'the dragon'. This gave a very good operating surface. Unfortunately, the same treatment was not given to the aircraft parking areas and these circular pans were often like skid pans.

Soon after arrival at Oerland, the aircrew were briefed by a Norwegian officer on local flying regulations; with emphasis on the danger of low flying in the fjords, the danger of power cables slung across the fjords - power cables that were almost impossible to see as you approached them at 300 knots plus. The rule was simple - keep out of the fjords. At times it was a hard rule to follow as the fjords could be invitingly beautiful. Indeed, both in winter and summer, Norway was a beautiful country to fly over and a two hour low level sortie was always a mixture of marvelling at the scenery, interspersed with

XH171 in formation with two Saab F35 Drakens of 729 Esk, RDAF Karup, Denmark survey 1979. This highlights the top tanks fuel group filling caps (black squares) on the right hand side of the fuselage.

periods of intense concentration on the target runs. When flying over the high snow fields it was not unusual to see the tracks of a lone skier in the middle of nowhere, and sometimes the lone skier himself - probably annoyed that the peace of his white world had been disturbed.

Of course, detachments had their social side. In winter, this included the 'aircrew survival course', for which the aircrew took themselves off to 'svartsvanhutte', a hut in an idyllic setting in the mountains beside the Trondheim fjord. Survival training took the form of sessions of 'downhill kamikaze' on borrowed skis and instruction on survival techniques including building snow shelters, making snow shoes and lighting fires on snow - a tricky manoeuvre! Lessons over, everyone repaired to the hut to try to survive the night in the primitive facilities. The hut had no water, other than that available from the frozen lake, no power and no light, but with a roaring log fire and the aid of a few crates of beer it became a veritable palace. It was tradition to hold a Dining-In Night at svartsvanhutte, usually with an impressive menu:

No.39 SQN DINING-IN
SVARTSVANHUTTE, 2 JAN '78
-- -- --
Crême de Tomate Soup
-- -- --
Fillets Poissons à la Clemons
Haricot vert
Pommes de terres instant
-- -- --
Poires avec crême
-- -- --
Bord de fromage
Café
-- -- --
VIN: Teachers vin de l'Écosse 1977
Gordons vin blanc 1977
Mckewans vin-chaud

Operationally, Squadron aircraft ranged the length and breadth of Norway and Denmark on sorties of from one hour to three and a half hours, depending on the nature of the target, ie high level or low level, the aircraft could refuel at another base in Norway or Denmark and be re-tasked from there. All sorties were flown by single aircraft as 39 had no formation role; it was common for six or seven aircraft to be airborne at the same time with some over the tundra area of Northern Norway and others over the Jutland peninsula of Denmark. No other reconnaissance aircraft in NATO could have offered the same flexibility in role.

In recent years, every unit has had its 'zap' maniacs who deem it a point of honour to stick their Squadron symbol or badge on any non-Squadron object, stationary or moving. 39 was no exception and throughout recent history the profession of 'zapper' was well upheld. One campaign deserves mention as a classic example of the art. In September 1980, the Squadron sent a detachment to Exercise *Teamwork 80,* a NATO land, sea and air exercise in the fjord and mountain area to the South-West of the Trondheim fjord. The 39 Squadron detachment was based at Oerland along with 2,500 American Marines and their aircraft (Phantoms, Broncos, Hueys, Hueycobras, and A-7s of the Air National Guard). Life started peacefully enough with the 39 resident bagpipe team playing a tune for the Americans - by marching up and down the lines of tents at 4 am playing 'Halls of Montezuma'! Full credit to the Marines, they responded to their tune by leaping out of bed and forming up outside their tents. Having thus established friendly relations, the real 'work' began. By day two the 'zap' team had prepared their tools - a large cardboard stencil of the Squadron's winged bomb emblem, plus a plentiful supply of yellow paint. Predictably, yellow winged bombs began to blossom on everything in sight, aircraft, trucks, cars, tents, flying suits, you name it and the lads

'zapped' it. Reactions amongst the recipients of this loving attention were mixed; the comments of the Air National Guard Commander being unrepeatable. However, some took it better and accepted it as a challenge. One Phantom crew resorting to putting a guard on their aircraft until the aircraft was taxying. However, as soon as the aircraft moved and the guard relaxed, the 39 Squadron boys sprang from the bushes and 'zapped' the taxying aircraft. Similar aircraft guarding also failed to protect the OV-10 Broncos from their 'destiny'; the captain of one of the aircraft was so impressed with the skill and determination of the 'zappers' that he presented them with a bottle of whisky!

The *pièce de résistance* was, however, saved until the end of the detachment. Two supply ships were anchored outside the local harbour at Brekstad and sights were set on these 'targets'. While any watchers on the ships were kept busy with a bagpipe serenade the 'zappers' went into action. After this final great achievement the

Comparison of low-level optical and infra-red photography. Opposite, an F95 nose photo taken on a target search for troops and AFVs (Armoured Fighting Vehicles). A number of vehicles can be seen, arrowed, around the wood and in the open land beyond. It was standard practice to run the vertical IRLS at the same time as the F95 and the photo right shows the IRLS view of the target area. The same two vehicles (A & B) can be seen on the edge of the wood but this shows a further 5 AFVs around the edges of the wood plus a group of troops (small white spots) in the centre of the wood.

stencil and paint was reverently laid to rest and the Marines breathed again. On all counts, social and operational, it was an outstanding detachment.

In the early 1970s a decision was taken to update the equipment of the PR.9, and in the period 1976-80 twelve of the aircraft were fitted with the Decca TANS Nav system and associated Sperry Gyro platform, plus an RWR (Radar Warning Receiver), UA60 comms box and the IRLS (Infra Red Line Scan) camera system.

This fit brought the PR.9 into the 1980s, or at least the late 1970s. Four of the aircraft were not modified: this was reduced to three when one more was modified following the loss of two aircraft between 1977-78 (XH137 in May 1977 and XH176 in May 1978). The unmodified aircraft continued to carry the *Green Satin*/GPI fit. Obviously, the new fit brought about changes in techniques and capability. Capability was also improved with the IRLS system replacing the very limited photo flash system. As well as being the only night sensor, it was also of great tactical use by day against likely camouflaged targets, and other targets such as airfields as the heat picture revealed details that an optical sensor would not register. It was able to do this because it was a thermal sensor which picked up the temperature differences between objects over which the aircraft passed but also registered objects which had recently been there; the classic example is that of an aircraft dispersal where the thermal 'shadows' of aircraft which have recently left the dispersal appear in varying degrees of clarity depending on the length of time which has passed since their departure. This is a very simplified 'picture' of the capability of the IRLS system, which can best be appreciated by looking at the photographs below.

The main advantage of the Decca TANS system, apart from greater accuracy and reliability was the tactical freedom it gave crews. The system as fitted to the PR.9 comprised a Decca TANS computer, a Sperry Gyro platform

(SGP 500) and the Decca Doppler 72M, plus a number of other inputs. Although on daylight sorties the system was available either as a prime aid or as a back-up to visual navigation, at night it was the only aid in a war situation where visual reference from ground lights is unlikely. At low level the lateral cover of the IRLS was small and accuracy of navigation essential; equipment calibration trials were flown on a regular basis to try and ensure that the system could meet the stringent requirements. Nevertheless, the greatest difficulty remained that of keeping the system updated at regular intervals, there being no nav aid in the PR.9 accurate enough for this task. Without doubt, the system greatly reduced the navigational workload and allowed both crew members spare mental capacity to concentrate on the tactical situation, with particular emphasis for the Navigator on monitoring the EW information from the RWR.

We have now looked at four of 39 Squadron's roles, day and night low level tactical reconnaissance, medium/high level photo, and aerial survey which leaves only one role to consider - shipping reconnaissance. The Squadron had such a role for the whole of its Canberra period but with the rapid improvement in shipborne air defence systems it became largely impracticable as a war role, although it remained viable for peacetime intelligence gathering.

As Britain withdrew from her overseas involvements so the world-wide requirement for Strategic Reconnaissance reduced. This, and other factors, led to an overall reduction in the demand for high level photography. For the past five or six years, low level tactical reconnaissance amounted to 60-70% of Squadron flying time, and up to 80% in winter months. Much of the low level flying was completed in poor weather and much time was spent in learning to operate in nuclear, biological or chemical warfare conditions. Combined with the improvements in aircraft fit, this increased level of training made 39 a very viable tactical reconnaissance Squadron dedicated to the Northern Flank of NATO.

It was intended that the PR Canberra force would remain operational until replaced by the Tornado reconnaissance aircraft in the mid-1980s. However, the defence moratorium of 1979 led to the decision to phase out the PR Canberra force two or three years earlier than originally planned. Thus, XIII Squadron disbanded at the end of 1981 and 39 Squadron was reduced to half strength as a preliminary to disbandment on 31st May 1982. The Squadron was superceded by a small flight of Canberra PR.9 (No.1 PRU) aircraft which will provide high level photography to meet national requirements.

The future of the Squadron is less certain. Present policy is for 39 to reform as the second Tornado Reconnaissance Squadron, but with the timescale involved, it is possible that another nameplate will be given to the Tornado Reconnaissance Squadron. If past record has anything to do with this decision, then 39 should be at the head of the queue and maybe this book will help to put the record straight.

In July 1981 the Squadron reached a peak of tactical and operational effectiveness and achieved an 'excellent' rating during Evaluation Exercises in Oerland. Two months later the Squadron was presented with a new Standard; many old members came back to see their old Squadron, and none were disappointed by the occasion. In June 1982, the Squadron faced closure but not death. It cannot be long before 39 Squadron adds another aircraft type to the inventory and so begins another Chapter in a quite remarkable record of achievements.

This view of XH174 shows the offset canopy and the black 'Frangible' hatch. *(S.G.Richards)*

Appendix A

List of Commanding Officers

Command From:			
19.4.16	Major T C R Higgins	11.9.42	W/Cdr M L Gaine AFC
13.6.16	Major W C H Mansfield	12.6.43	W/Cdr N B Harvey
27.6.16	Major A H Morton	19.6.44	W/Cdr A R De L Inniss DFC
20.3.17	Major R G H Murray	1.3.45	W/Cdr D Griffiths DFC
7.7.17	Major C C Halahan	23.3.46	W/Cdr C J O'Donovan
9.8.17	Major W H D Ackland	30.6.48	S/Ldr A McK S Steedman DFC
20.11.17	Major G Allen	21.4.49	S/Ldr R D Doleman DSO, DFC
24.4.18	Major W T Holland	25.10.51	S/Ldr J C Coghill DSO, DFC
1.7.19	S/Ldr P Babington	.2.54	Sqn Ldr J J O'Meara DSO, DFC
1.4.21	S/Ldr T S Impey	.10.56	Sqn Ldr A J Owen DFC, DFM
18.1.22	S/Ldr A A B Thompson	.7.58	Wg Cdr V C Woodward DFC
8.2.23	S/Ldr J T Whittaker	.8.59	Wg Cdr R L Wade DFC
6.3.25	S/Ldr H V Champion de Crespigny	.12.60	Wg Cdr W L McD Scott
28.4.30	S/Ldr S B Harris	.12.62	Wg Cdr F G Agnew AFC
14.3.33	S/Ldr S D Culley	.6.65	Wg Cdr H A Caillard
9.11.35	S/Ldr J H Butler	.3.67	Wg Cdr T P O'Brien
11.3.37	S/Ldr S H V Harris	.6.67	Wg Cdr A McI Cobban
9.12.38	S/Ldr A F MacKenna	.6.69	Wg Cdr C H Foale
	W/Cdr Brookes	.4.71	Wg Cdr T P O'Brien
2.8.39	S/Ldr A McD Bowman DFC	.4.73	Wg Cdr F Allen
4.9.41	W/Cdr R B Cox	.6.75	Wg Cdr B Higgs
17.12.41	W/Cdr A I Mason DFC	.12.77	Wg Cdr L S Frame
.8.42	W/Cdr R P M Gibbs DSO, DFC	.12.79	Wg Cdr A R P Phipps
		6.11.81	Wg Cdr C Adams AFC

Appendix B

List of Aircraft Types and Serials

B.E.2c	April 1916 — 1917
B.E.2d	April 1916 — 1917
B.E.2e	April 1916 — 1917
B.E.12	April 1916 — 1917
Bristol Fighter	1917 — November 1918
D.H.9a	July 1917 — 1928
Westland Wapiti II	1928 — November 1931
Hawker Hart II (India)	November 1931 — August 1939
Bristol Blenheim I, IV	August 1939 — January 1941
Martin Maryland	January 1941 — January 1942
Bristol Beaufort I, II	August 1941 — June 1943
Bristol Beaufighter X	June 1943 — January 1945
Martin 179 Marauder III	December 1944 — September 1946
DH Mosquito VI (Canadian-built Mk.26)	Jan 1946 — September 1946
De Havilland Mosquito T.3	January 1946 — September 1946
Hawker Tempest VI	June 1948 — March 1949

De Havilland Mosquito T.3, NF.36	June 1949 — March 1953
Gloster Meteor T.7, NF.13	March 1953 — June 1958
English Electric Canberra PR.3	June 1958 — April 1963
English Electric Canberra PR.7	October 1970 — February 1972
English Electric Canberra T.4	June 1958 — June 1982
English Electric Canberra PR.9	November 1962 — June 1982

Other types associated with No.39 Squadron : Avro 504 (April 1921), Hawker Audax K4862 (1932), Miles Magister P2401 (January 1941 for comms duties), Hawker Hind K6826 (January 1941 for pilot training), Junkers Ju 87 Stuka HK 827 (late 1941-early 1942), Hawker Hurricane (prob.1944), Avro Anson (1948-49 for comms.), N.A.Harvard (1948-49 for pilot training) and Gloster Meteor F.8 (borrowed when necessary, e.g. if own T.7 unserviceable).

Appendix C

Locations

As a result of the loss of certain documents during the history of the Squadron, not every detachment base is included in this list.

15 Apr 1916	Hounslow
	Detachments: Hounslow, Northolt, Hendon, Chingford, Hainault Farm, Sutton's Farm, Joyce Green, Farningham, Croydon, Wimbledon.
Jul 1916	HQ Woodford Green
	'A' Flight - North Weald Bassett
	'B' Flight - Sutton's Farm
	'C' Flight - Hainault Farm
Sep 1917	North Weald Bassett 1.12.17 to 31.12.17. Detachment at Biggin Hill - 'D' Flight
1 Jul 1919	Biggin Hill
20 Dec 1919	Uxbridge
12 Apr 1920	Kenley
12 Mar 1921	Spittlegate
9 Jan 1928	Bircham Newton
22 Jan 1929	Risalpur
Aug 1939	Kallang
19 Apr 1940	Lahore
13 May 1940	Sheikh Othman
2 Dec 1940	Helwan
22 Jan 1941	Heliopolis
21 Mar 1941	Shandur
May 1941	Wadi Natrun
	Detachments: Burg-el-Arab and Edku.
15 Oct 1941	Mariut
	Detachments: Maaten Bagush and Fuka
27 Dec 1941	Sidi Barrani
	Mobile base at El Gubbi (Tobruk)
	Detachment: Bu Amud

21 Jun 1942	Detachment to Malta
1 July 1942	Shandur
	Detachment: Gianaclis
Aug 1942	Luqa
1 Oct 1942	Shallufa
	Detachment: Gianaclis
Dec 1942	Shallufa - ground personnel only aircraft at Luqa
28 Feb 1943	Gianaclis - ground personnel only aircraft at Luqa
2 Jun 1943	Protville
19 Oct 1943	Sidi Amor
	Detachment: Grottaglie
16 Nov 1943	Reghaia
	Detachment: Marrakesh
19 Feb 1944	Algherro
	Detachment: Grottaglie from 12.6.44
12 Jul 1944	Grottaglie
13 Jul 1944	Biferno
	Detachment: Athens 16.12.44 to 18.1.45
8 Jun 1945	Rivolto
25 Sep 1945	Khartoum
Sep 1946	Reduced to a cadre unit
16 Jun 1948	Reformed at Manston
Jun 1948	Khartoum
Mar 1949	Fayid
21 Feb 1951	Kabrit
Jan 1955	Luqa
Aug 1956	Nicosia
Mar 1957	Luqa - detachment at Nicosia until June 1958
Jun 1958	Luqa - main detachment base at Eskishehir, Turkey.
1 Oct 1970	Wyton - main detachment base at Oerland, Norway.
1 Jun 1982	Disbanded at Wyton

Battle Honours and Decorations

Decorations
This list is an extract of entries in the F540 Operational Record Books of the Squadron and will therefore be incomplete as it is inevitable that not all awards were recorded. If anyone can provide additional information or first-hand knowledge of the incidents leading to an award then would they please contact me.

1916-1929
Sep 1916 Lt W Leefe Robinson - VC
Sep 1916 Lt F Sowrey - DSO
            2nd Lt A de B Brandon - DSO
Oct 1916 2nd Lt W H Tempest - DSO

1929-1939 (India)
North West Frontier 23 Apr - 12 Sep 1930:
S/Ldr S B Harris DFC, AFC - bar to DFC
F/Lt S McKeever - DFC
Sgt J E Wren - DFM
LAC R W Ellis - DFM
NWF 28 Jan-6 Feb, 6 Mar - 18 Mar 1932:
S/Ldr S B Harris DFC, AFC - 2nd bar to DFC
Cpl R W Ellis - bar to DFM
Chitral Relief Sep-Oct 1932:
F/Lt J Collingwood - DFC
Cpl R Wright - DFM

1939-1945
Oct 1940 S/Ldr A McD Bowman - DFC
            Sgt S W Sills - DFM
Jul 1941 Sgt R D Mohr - DFM
Mar 1942 F/Lt A M Taylor - DFC
Jun 1942 W/Cdr A I Mason - DFC
            S/Ldr Gibbs - bar to DFC
Jul 1942 F/Lt Strever - DFC
            P/O Dunsmere - DFC
            Sgt Wilkinson - DFM
            Sgt Brown - DFM
Sep 1942 W/Cdr R P M Gibbs - DSO
            F/O Marshall - DFC
            F/O J C Creswell - DFM + DFC
                Grant - DFC
                L Wordsell - DFC
            F/Sgt H Watlington - DFM
            Sgt L Tester - DFM
            Sgt G Sanderson - DFM

Oct 1942 Lt D P Tilley - DFC
            Sgt W C Stephens - DFM
Dec 1942 F/Lt R A Lenton - MC
            Sgt E R Cereley - MM
Feb 1943 P/O J G Miller - DFM
            P/O J Featherstone - DFM
Jul 1943 S/Ldr S R Muller-Rowland
            - bar to DFC
            P/O R E Dodd - DFC
            F/Sgt J D Anderson - DFM
Oct 1943 F/O N D Cox - DFC
Apr 1944 F/O H H Deacon - DFC
            F/O C L Heide - DFC
May 1944 F/O M C Hyslop - DFC
            F/O D A Derby - DFC
Jun 1944 W/Cdr N B Harvey - DSO
            P/O W A G Hook - DFC
Sep 1944 F/O N D Cox - bar to DFC
            W/O W K Patterson - DFC
            F/Sgt V J Kyrke-Smith - DFM
Sep 1944 F/Sgt S S Campbell - GCM
Oct 1944 S/Ldr T H Curlee - DFC
            S/Ldr I D Charles - DFC
            F/Lt H W Wheeler - DFC
            F/Lt J P Browne - DFC
Jan 1945 F/O E H Pitman - DSO
Apr 1945 S/Ldr T B Marshall - DFC

Battle Honours
The following list details the Battle Honours of 39 Squadron and all, except North West Frontier 1930-31, Mohmand 1933, North West Frontier 1935-39, appear on the Squadron Standard. Squadron Leader Coghill selected the honours to appear on the Standard as he was CO in 1954 when the first Standard was presented.

            Home Defence 1916-18
            North West Frontier 1930-31
            Mohmand 1933
            North West Frontier 1935-39
            East Africa 1940
            Egypt and Libya 1940-43
            Greece 1941
            Mediterranean 1941-43
            Malta 1942
            North Africa 1942-43
            South East Europe 1944-45

Appendix E

Analysis of Operational Flying

This appendix details all operational sorties flown by No. 39 Squadron in the period 1940-45 and is reconstructed from the operational returns in the Squadron ORB. The nature of some of the roles performed by the Squadron in this period was such that a large number of single aircraft sorties were mounted, often with three or four aircraft attacking the same target either over a period of hours or spanning a whole day. On such occasions I have recorded the number of aircraft/sorties per target per day rather than list each sortie. This applies mainly to the Blenheim period.

The following abbreviations are used:

Target/Type of Operation

AR	- Armed Reconnaissance (see Intruder)
ASP	- Anti-submarine patrol
ASR	- Air Sea Rescue Search
B	- Bombing

Intruder/Rover - Armed search for targets of opportunity

LG	- Landing Ground
OFP	- Offensive Fighter Patrol, targets of opportunity (aircraft)
OS	- Offensive Sweep (see Intruder)
PR	- Reconnaissance and photo-reconnaissance
RP	- Rocket Projectile attack
SP	- Stopper Patrol, to attack specific target (aircraft)
SR/SS	- Sea reconnaissance, Shipping Search

Trapper One/Dolphin - as OFP

TS	- Torpedo Strike

Losses

SD	- Shot Down	Di	- Ditched
CL	- Crash Landed	Dam	- Damaged

Remarks

D	- Destroyed
Dam	- Damaged
nf	- not found
MT	- Motor Transport
MV	- Merchant Vessel
CX	- Cancelled
RTB WX	- Returned to base before completing mission, because of bad weather.
loco	- locomotive
nro	- no results observed

Date	Target/Type of Operation	Number of acft/sorties	Losses/Remarks
	BLENHEIM		
1940			
12 Jun	B - Diredawa airfield	7	
13 Jun	B - Assab airfield satellite	5	
14 Jun	PR - Assab; B - Macaaca airfield	1	
15 Jun	B - Diredawa airfield	6	One CR.42 shot down

172

Date	Target/Type of Operation	Number of acft/sorties	Losses/Remarks
16 Jun	PR - Assab	1	
17 Jun	Inspect LG at Little Aden	2	
19 Jun	B - Diredawa rail junction	5	Set fire to petrol dump
21 Jun	B - Macaaca airfield	4	
22 Jun	B - Diredawa airfield	3	
22 Jun	B - Diredawa airfield	6	L4920 CL British Somaliland; LAC Olley killed.
25 Jun	B - Assab (Macaaca bomb dump)	6	
26 Jun	PR - Assab	1	
26 Jun	B - Assab (Macaaca bomb dump)	4	
27 Jun	B - Assab	1	
28 Jun	B - Barracks and bomb dump Macaaca	2	
29 Jun	PR - Assab	2	
1 Jul	PR - Assab	1	
2 Jul	B - Macaaca	4	Co-op with Gladiator
7 Jul	B - Macaaca	3	Cancelled
8 Jul	PR - Macaaca	1	
9 Jul	B - Macaaca	6	
10 Jul	B - Assab	2	
12 Jul	B - Petrol dump at Assab	6	
13 Jul	Search for missing Gladiator	1	
15 Jul	B - Diredawa HQ building	4	
16 Jul	PR - El Bah	1	
19 Jul	PR - Macaaca	1	
19 Jul	B - Diredawa	1	
22 Jul	B - Diredawa	6	three landed at Djibouti
24 Jul	B - Macaaca	1	
26 Jul	PR - Raheita	2	
27 Jul	B - W/T Station Raheita	1	
29 Jul	B - Naval barracks at Assab	2	
1 Aug	B - Chenile airfield	5	one S.81 shot down
2 Aug	ASP	1	
2 Aug	B - Chenile airfield	3	
6 Aug	B - Hargesia - Jiggiga road	3	
7 Aug	B - Diredawa airfield	4	
7 Aug	B - Macaaca	1	
8 Aug	B - Hargesia - Oadweina LG	3	one damaged by Gladiators
10 Aug	B - troops north of Dubato	5	
12 Aug	B - Turargon gun positions	4	
13 Aug	B - troops at Biyo, Fogo, Zeilah	3	
14 Aug	B - Zeilah	1	
15 Aug	B - Zeilah, Bulhar	1	MT convoy
15 Aug	B - Biyo, Fogo, Zeilah	1	MT
15 Aug	B - Darborik	2	
16 Aug	B - Bahun Dera	1	MT
17 Aug	B - Hargeisa	1	L8384 ditched near HMS *Ceres*
17 Aug	B - Hargeisa W/T station	2	
17 Aug	B - Hargeisa	1	
17 Aug	B - Bulhar - Zeilah road	1	MT
17 Aug	B - Berbera road	1	Gun positions
17 Aug	B - Laferug	1 with 11 Sqn	MT
18 Aug	B - Bul - Zeil road	1	
18 Aug	B - Lubbage (guns), Hargeisa road	2 with 11 Sqn	Guns and MT
20 Aug	B - Diredawa	4	L8474 crashed in flames (P/O Jago, Sgt Wilson and Cpl Wintle
25 Aug	B - Dessye MT repair yard	3 with 11 Sqn	
27 Aug	B - Harar barracks and MT	3 with 11 Sqn	

Date	Target/Type of Operation	Number of acft/sorties	Losses/Remarks
1 Sep	B - Assab harbour	8	
3 Sep	B - Assab dock	1	
5 Sep	B - Assab dock	3	
6 Sep	B - Berbera airfield	1	
9 Sep	B - Dessye	3	
15 Sep	B - Assab naval barracks	3	
17 Sep	B - Diredawa airfield	1	
18 Sep	B - Diredawa airfield	2	
19 Sep	B - Diredawa airfield	2	
23 Sep	B - Zeilah town and harbour	2	
23 Sep	B - Diredawa airfield	1	
25 Sep	B - Berbera town	1	
26 Sep	PR - Mille	1	
27 Sep	B - Macaaca power house	3	
2 Oct	B - Assab naval barracks	2	
3 Oct	B - Aisha rail station	3	
8 Oct	B - Assab naval barracks	2	
8 Oct	B - Assab piers and workshops	1	
10 Oct	B - Assab piers and workshops	1	
10 Oct	B - Assab warehouses	2	
13 Oct	PR - British Somaliland	1	
14 Oct	B - Diredawa	2	
15 Oct	B - Chenile LG	3	
18 Oct	B - Diredawa airfield	2	
19 Oct	B - Diredawa airfield	2	
19 Oct	B - Chenile	1	
23 Oct	PR - Assab and Macaaca	1	
24 Oct	B - Alomata, aircraft	1	
25 Oct	B - Assab oil tanks	1	
31 Oct	B - Dunale rail station	2	
3 Nov	B - Assab underground oil tanks	2	
6 Nov	B - Assab supply depot	1	
11/12 Nov	B - Chenile LG	2	
14 Nov	B - Harrawa, bridge	1	
14 Nov	B - Diredawa, rail buildings	1	
19/20 Nov	B - Assab area	4	
9 Dec	B - Sollum airfield	2	
10 Dec	B - El Gubbi LG	2	
10 Dec	B - Sofafi camp	1	RTB WX
11 Dec	B - El Gubbi LG	1	
11 Dec	B - Halfway House, SE of Sollum	2	
12 Dec	B - El Gubbi LG	1	
12 Dec	B - Menastir LG	1	
13 Dec	B - El Gubbi LG	1	
13 Dec	B - Bardia	1	
14 Dec	B - Bardia	1	
15 Dec	B - Gazala LG	1	
15 Dec	B - Tobruk west LG	1	RTB WX
15 Dec	B - El Adem LG	1	RTB WX
15 Dec	B - Bardia	2	
16 Dec	B - El Adem	1	
17 Dec	B - MT north-west of Bardia	2	
19 Dec	B - Bardia	1	
24 Dec	B - El Tmimi LG	2	
29 Dec	B - El Gazala LG	1	
31 Dec	B - Bardia	1	

Date	Target/Type of Operation	Number of acft sorties	Losses/Remarks
1941			
1 Jan	B - El Gazala LG	2	
2 Jan	B - MT west of Bardia	4	
3 Jan	B - Gazala No.2 LG	1	
3 Jan	B - Tobruk west LG	1	
3 Jan	B - Gazala No.1 LG	2	
4 Jan	B - Tobruk	3	
6 Jan	B - Tobruk	2	
8 Jan	B - Tobruk	1	

No Operational Flying for February, March or April 1941 due to changeover from the Blenheim to the Maryland. Records for Maryland are very poor in May and June.

MARYLAND

May/ June — Almost daily PR of Al Agheila - Derna and Giarabub - Capuzzo, plus Malta, Aegean and Ionian Islands. From 20 May the Squadron was involved in PR and other operations over Crete and a number of Ju 52 transports were shot down or damaged.

Losses May/June:

5 May	One aircraft missing (S/Ldr Mills)
8 May	Two aircraft missing (Lt Campbell and P/O Best)
13 June Crete	One aircraft missing (Lt Coetsee)
14 June Crete	One aircraft missing (P/O Brine)

From July 1941 to January 1942 the Marylands operated in the strategic reconnaissance role, flying a single aircraft over the main areas of interest - the Western Desert, Crete and the Greek Islands. The table below denotes the number of aircraft sorties per month over each area with notes when appropriate. There are few details of losses but the narrative Operations Record Book records that losses were fairy heavy.

	JUL	AUG	SEP	OCT	NOV	DEC	JAN
Western Desert	53	69	12	—	—	2	—
Crete	4	17	1	6	12	2	—
Greek Islands	10	13	14	20	—	—	—
Sea Reconnaissance	—	—	—	—	15	5	2
Notes	1	2,3,4		5			

Notes:
1. Three sorties Greek mainland
2. Two sorties Greek mainland
3. 7 August one aircraft bombed camp ½ miles south of Bir Rusgh
   27 August one aircraft PR shipping Eastern Mediterranean
4. 28 August '384 shot down (F/Lt Halliday, Sgt Wakeling, Sgt Williams, Sgt Fourane)
5. 29 October search for Italian destroyers.

Last Maryland operation 19 January 1942

BEAUFORT

From 17 September 1941 the Squadron was flying Beaufort ops as well as Maryland ops. The majority of the former were 'Sea Reccos' (PLUG) of the area south and west of Crete (Sep - Nov) and Libya - Crete - Southern Greece (Dec) with a period in mid-September of anti-submarine patrols between Alexandria and Haifa. Most sorties were by single aircraft or pairs. The table overleaf gives details of aircraft/sorties per month.

	SEP	OCT	NOV	DEC	JAN
Sea Reconnaissance	8	38	48	26	8
Anti-submarine patrols	7	—	—	—	—
Notes			1,2	3,4,5	

Notes:

1. 22 November one aircraft search for damaged ship off Egyptian coast.
2. 27 November pair shipping search off Matapan.
3. 5 and 6 December PR Navarin - Libya - Crete - Southern Greece.
4. 12 December search for MV off Benghazi.
5. 16 December search Barrani - Sollum.

On the 23 January 1942 the Squadron made its first torpedo attack. Numbers of aircraft refer to a formation unless otherwise stated.

Date	Target/Type of Operation	Number of acft/sorties	Losses/Remarks
1942			
23 Jan	TS - convoy	3	2000-ton MV hit, prob sunk
	Note: During January, one Beaufort (P/O Saunders and crew) was lost but no details.		
16 Feb	SS - tanker, Gulf of Sirte	3	nf
17 Feb	SS - tanker, west of Navarin	2	nf, attacked MV at Sapienza
22 Feb	SS - convoy	4	nf
28 Feb	SR - SW Greece	4	
1 Mar	SR - SW Greece	4	
4 Mar	SR - SW Greece	5	
9 Mar	TS - convoy, 3325N 1746E	8	nf
17 Mar	TS - convoy	8	nf
22 Mar	TS - convoy	6	RTB, out of range
27/28 Mar	Escort Hurricanes to Malta/RTB-SR	1	
	Note: 10 March one aircraft SD by 109s on RTB from Sidi Barrani (Sgts Elliot, Flett, Bloomfield, Hopkins)		
4 Apr	TS - Convoy, Gulf of Sirte	6	nf; landed Malta
5 Apr	SR - RTB	3	landed LG05 and Bu Amud
6 Apr	SR - RTB	3	landed LG05
12 Apr	TS - Convoy 3517N 2030E	3	attacked, no result (nro)
14 Apr	Locate convoy	1	nf landed Malta
14 Apr	TS - Convoy 3458N 1558E	8	1166 SD, 1100 SD nr Malta; 1169 FTR, 8923 FTR; 1186 Di nr Malta. Attacked, nro
15 Apr	RTB	1	landed Bu Amud
26 Apr	TS - Convoy	2	one MV attacked, nro
8 May	TS - Convoy	3	one MV attacked, nro
17 May	TS - Convoy	2	nf
3 Jun	ASP - Coast - LG86 - Barrani	3	
4 Jun	TS - Convoy	2	nf
10 Jun	ASP - LG86 - Barrani	3	
12 Jun	ASP	11	
13 Jun	ASP	2	
15 Jun	TS - Italian Battle Fleet	12	AW352 SD near Derna; DD955 FTR. Attacked 250 miles East of Malta, no hits
16 Jun	ASP - RTB	11	
17 Jun	ASP	1	
20 Jun	ASP - LG86 - Barrani	7	
21 Jun	ASP	6	DD976 missing

Date	Target/Type of Operation	Number of acft sorties	Losses/Results
10 Jul	Locate convoy	1	found North of Tobruk
10 Jul	TS - Convoy	5	nf
15 Jul	TS - Convoy	1	nf
17 Jul	TS - Convoy	6	attacked, nro
20 Jul	Search for missing aircraft	1	Blenheim nf, but found a Wellington
24 Jul	SS	3	nf
27 Jul	SS	2	nf
28 Jul	SR	1	nf
30 Jul	SR	2	nf

Malta Detachment

Date	Target/Type of Operation	Number of acft sorties	Losses/Results
23 Jun	TS - Convoy East of P. Stilo	5 (+ 217 Sqn)	6518 SD, DD976 FTR Two MVs hit
3 Jul	TS - Convoy	3 (+ 217 Sqn)	nf
3 Jul	TS - Convoy, North of Navarino	2 (+ 217 Sqn)	One MV hit
21 Jul	TS - Convoy near Alphaonia	2 (+ 217 Sqn)	MV sunk, small cruiser hit
28 Jul	TS - Convoy, Sorprinza	2 (+ 217 Sqn)	MV hit
6 Aug	ASP - Base - Malta	6	
7 Aug	ASP - Base - Malta	1	
10 Aug	ASP - Base - Malta	3	
11 Aug	ASP - Base - Malta	1	
19 Aug	ASP - Malta - Shandur	3	
21 Aug	ASP - Malta - Shandur	1	
20 Aug	TS - Convoy Toe of Italy	12	'T' and 'F' FTR. Attacked, no hits
21 Aug	TS - Tanker near Corfu	9	'V' FTR. Three hits on tanker
24 Aug	TS - Tanker near Corfu	9	'S' FTR. Explosion seen but no hits claimed
27 Aug	TS - Convoy Benghazi	9	MV sunk
30 Aug	TS - Convoy South of Taranto	9	tanker sunk, 1 Ju 88 probable, 1 MC.200 shot down
3 Sep	SR	1	attacked nro
3 Sep	SS	3	L9875 cr in sea. Attacked nro
4 Sep	SS - Off Cotrono	7	nf
6 Sep	TS - South of Taranto	13	'Q' and 'R' FTR. Probable hits on MV. 1 Ju 88 damaged, 1 MC.200 SD, 2 damaged
22 Sep	TS - Convoy	9	'M' FTR. One hit on MV
24 Sep	TS - Convoy	3	no hits
27 Sep	TS - Convoy	3	no hits
26 Oct	TS - Convoy North West of Tobruk	5	no hits
12 Nov	Mines - Tunis	5	
13 Nov	Mines - Tunis	5	
20 Nov	OS	4	2500-ton MV damaged
21 Nov	OS	6	
21 Nov	OS	6	
22 Nov	B - Linosa Island	4	4 x 250 lb bombs
22 Nov	TS - Convoy	3	nro
23 Nov	TS - MV Tunisian coast	3	nf
23 Nov	B - Lampedusa	3	12 x 250 lb
24 Nov	Mines - Bizerta	8	
26 Nov	TS - Convoy, Bizerta	5	one drop, nro
27 Nov	Mines - Bizerta	9	
28 Nov	Mines - Bizerta	3	
28 Nov	TS - Convoy	3	one drop, nro

Date	Target/Type of Operation	Number of acft sorties	Losses/Results
28 Nov	Mines - Tunis	8	
29 Nov	Mines - Palermo	8	'H' FTR
30 Nov	Mines - Bizerta	8	'S' and 'Y' FTR

Egypt Detachment

Date	Target/Type of Operation	Number of acft sorties	Losses/Results
2 Nov	OS	3	
2 Nov	TS - Convoy Tobruk	6	one Di, one FTR. 5-6000-ton sunk, one dam. 1 Ju 88 SD
3 Nov	OS	2	
20 Dec	Mines - Homs, Misurata	5	
24 Dec	Mines - Homs, Misurata	2	

Malta Detachment

Date	Target/Type of Operation	Number of acft sorties	Losses/Results
7 Dec	ASP - Support own convoy	3	
8 Dec	SS - Tanker	7	nf
10 Dec	ASP - Support own convoy	2	
13 Dec	ASP - Support own convoy	3	
15 Dec	SS	3	nf
18 Dec	ASP - Support own convoy	3	4 depth charges dropped. nro
20 Dec	ASP - Support own convoy	1	
21 Dec	ASP - Support own convoy	2	
30 Dec	OS	3	two MVs bombed, nro
31 Dec	ASP	1	
1943			
1 Jan	ASP	1	
6 Jan	Mines - La Goulette	4	'P' FTR
10 Jan	ASP	1	
12 Jan	Mines - Melita Island	4	
14 Jan	ASP	3	4 x 250 lb depth charges dropped sub damaged, sunk by destroyer
14 Jan	Mines - Kerkennah	3	
15 Jan	Mines - La Goulette	4	
16 Jan	Mines - La Goulette	4	
17 Jan	Mines - Sousse	4	
17 Jan	SS - Sicilian Channel	2	attacked, no hits
18 Jan	TS - Convoy	2	attacked, no hits
19 Jan	Mines - La Goulette	3	
20 Jan	SS - North of Cap Bon	2	MV hit
21 Jan	TS - North of Cap Bon	1	attacked, no hits
22 Jan	ASP	1	
22 Jan	Mines - Kerkennah	5	
23 Jan	SS	5	MV damaged. Destroyer hit with bombs
27 Jan	SS - Mantimo - Cap Bon	5	nf
27 Jan	Mines - Sfax	3	
28 Jan	ASP	3	
29 Jan	Mines - Kerkennah	5	
31 Jan	TS - North of Sicily	3	nf
1 Feb	ASR	1	nf
1 Feb	Mines - Tropan	7	
2 Feb	ASP	1	
2 Feb	Mines - Sfax	4	
3 Feb	SS	3	nf
3 Feb	Mines - Rasaboudia	2	
9 Feb	Mines - Tropania	6	
10 Feb	ASP	2	

Date	Target/Type of Operation	Number of acft sorties	Losses/Results
14 Feb	ASP	3	
14 Feb	Rover	4	
15 Feb	SS - Sicilian Straits	3	
15 Feb	TS - Convoy	7	attacked, nro
17 Feb	Search	4	nf
18 Feb	Rover	4	
19 Feb	Search	5	nf
20 Feb	SS - Convoy	4	attacked, nro
21 Feb	TS - Convoy	5	attacked, nro
21 Feb	TS - South West of Martino	6	7-10,000-ton tanker sunk
23 Feb	OS	6	attacked destroyer, no hits
23 Feb	OS	3	nf
24 Feb	Rover	3	AW349 FTR. Attacked MV and destroyer, nro
25 Feb	SS - Same convoy	3	DD910 FTR. 8000-ton MV sunk
26 Feb	TS - South of Naples	5	attacked MV, nro
27 Feb	OS	4	nf
28 Feb	Search	5	attacked, nro
3 Mar	SS	5	DD899 FTR. nf
9 Mar	SS	8	recalled
12 Mar	OS	6	DD928 and DD934 FTR One MV damaged
13 Mar	OS	3	nf
17 Mar	SS - Pt. Stilo	9	DD902 FTR. 10000-ton tanker sunk
18 Mar	Search	2	nf
20 Mar	OS	3	nf
22 Mar	Search	5	attacked MV, nro
23 Mar	OS	2	nf
23 Mar	Search	4	5000-ton MV hit
24 Mar	OS	2	nf
24 Mar	OS	2	nf
25 Mar	OS	3	nf
27 Mar	SS - Sfax	2	AW348 FTR. MV attacked, but nro
1 Apr	SS - Maritimo	2	nf
3 Apr	Search for missing MTBs	1	
5 Apr	Mines - Trapani	6	
10 Apr	OS	3	
11 Apr	ASR	1	
11 Apr	OS	4	DD892 FTR
14 Apr	SS - Martimo	2	nf
15 Apr	Search - Sicilian Channel	5	MV attacked, nro
23 Apr	TS - Maritimo	4	MV sunk
2 May	ASR	1	
7 May	ASR	1	
7 May	Mines - Trapani	10	
9 May	B - Marsala	4	
10 May	Search	3	nf
10 May	B - Marsala	4	
11 May	Search	6	Destroyer attacked, nro
12 May	Rover	3	
13 May	Rover	3	attacked train ferry, nro
14 May	Search	3	
15 May	OS	3	DD936 FTR
16 May	Search	3	
18 May	OS	3	MV attacked, nro

Date	Target/Type of Operation	Number of acft sorties	Losses/Remarks
18 May	Search	4	2 x 300-ton schooners strafed
20 May	Search	2	nf
21 May	OS	3	
21 May	ASP	3	
21 May	Rover	3	1500-ton schooner strafed
24 May	Mines	8	

BEAUFIGHTER

Date	Target/Type of Operation	Number of acft sorties	Losses/Remarks
2 Jul	ASR	2	
3 Jul	ASR	1	
11 Jul	TS	6	JM408 SD. 4000-ton MV and destroyer damaged
12 Jul	TS	8	12000-ton MV and destroyer hit
13 Jul	TS - Troopship	6	nf. Ferries strafed
14 Jul	TS	8	JM399 SD. 5000-ton tanker blew up, 1500-ton tanker burning
18 Jul	Offensive Rover	8	
20 Jul	TS	10 (incl af)	nf
21 Jul	TS	6 (incl af)	LX790 FTR. MV and destroyer hit
23 Jul	TS	8	nf
25 Jul	TS	8 (incl af)	nf
26 Jul	TS	8 (incl af)	nf
28 Jul	TS	8	nf
30 Jul	TS	8	one 5000-ton MV sunk, destroyer on fire
1 Aug	TS	4 + 4 af	nf. Small schooner strafed
3 Aug	TS	4 + 4 af	nf
8 Aug	TS	4 + 4 af	nf. He 115 damaged
10 Aug	TS	4 + 4 af	one 3500-ton MV hit
12 Aug	TS	4 + 4 af	LX862 SD. nf
16 Aug	TS	4 + 4 af	two MVs and destroyer hit
23 Aug	TS	4 + 4 af	nf
5 Sep	TS	4 + 4 af	nf
7 Sep	TS	6 + 4 af	one 2500-ton MV sunk - Swiss marks
10 Sep	ASR	2	
15 Sep	TS	6 + 5 af	JM386 SD, JM387 SD, LX785 Di Tanker attacked, nro
15 Sep	ASR for LX785	2	nf
16 Sep	ASR for LX785	2	homed rescue services
16 Sep	ASR for LX785	2	homed rescue services
16 Sep	ASR for LX785	1	escort to rescue Walrus
23 Sep	OFP	4	three SM.82 SD
23 Sep	OFP - North East Corsica	4	one Ju 52 and one SM.82 SD; three Ju 52s damaged
23 Sep	OFP - Bastia	2	JM411 SD. two Ju 52 SD
24 Sep	OFP - Pianosa	4	LX792 Di. one Ju 52 SD
24 Sep	OFP - South East Bastia	4	three Ju 52 SD
24 Sep	OFP - South West Elba	5	LX779 FTR, LX903 Di two Ju 52 SD, one Ju 52 dam
24 Sep	OFP - Bastia	6	LX799 FTR. Two Ju 52 SD, one probable, four damaged
25 Sep	ASR - drop supplies to S/Ldr Petch	2	LX911 SD
30 Sep	ASR	4	
30 Sep	ASR	4	
Oct	No operational flying in October		
1 Nov	ASR	1	

Date	Target/Type of Operation	Number of acft sorties	Losses/Remarks
2 Nov	ASR	1	
5 Nov	TS	6	one 4500-ton MV hit
13 Nov	TS	5	nf
21 Nov	TS	5	
22 Nov	ASP	1	
23 Nov	ASP	4	
26 Nov	Stopper	4	
29 Nov	Stopper	4	
30 Nov	Stopper	6 (3 pairs)	
2 Dec	Stopper	5 (2 pairs + 1)	Ju 88 SD
3 Dec	Stopper	6 (3 pairs)	
4 Dec	Stopper	8 (4 pairs)	
5 Dec	Stopper	2	
5 Dec	Stopper	4 (2 pairs)	
6 Dec	Stopper	6 (3 pairs)	
7 Dec	Stopper	6 (3 pairs)	
8 Dec	Stopper	6 (3 pairs)	
9 Dec	Stopper	6 (3 pairs)	
19 Dec	Stopper	2	
20 Dec	Stopper	2	
23 Dec	Fighter patrol	10 (5 pairs)	
24 Dec	Fighter patrol	2	
26 Dec	Convoy Fighter patrol	8 (4 pairs)	
27 Dec	PR	2	
1944			
10 Jan	OFP - Ibiza - Spanish mainland	5	One Ju 88 damaged
11 Jan	OFP - Ibiza - Spanish mainland	8 (4 pairs)	
12 Jan	OFP - Mallorca - Minorca - Ibiza	4 (2 pairs)	
17 Jan	Escort to VIP C-47	6	
19 Jan	OFP - NW Mediterranean	14 (7 pairs)	
23 Jan	Convoy fighter patrol	2	
24 Jan	OFP	10 (5 pairs)	
25 Jan	OFP - Mallorca - Minorca	13 (4 pairs; 5 formation)	
26 Jan	PR - gun positions Minorca	3	
30 Jan	OFP - Mallorca - Minorca - Ibiza	8 (4 pairs)	
30 Jan	PR - Minorca	1	
1 Feb	SP - Formentera Island	6	'F' NE412 (F/Sgt Cooper) SD; 'C' NE371 (Sgt Brindle) CL two Ju 88 SD; three Ju 88 Dam
2 Feb	OFP - Minorca	4	
2 Feb	ASR Search (for NE412)	4	Located dinghy
2 Feb	ASR Search (for NE412)	2	
23 Feb	Search for missing aircraft	2	
23 Feb	ASR Search	1	
4 Mar	SP - Mallorca - Minorca	4	
4 Mar	SP	2	
10 Mar	RP - MW 20 miles West of Marseilles	4+4 af	3000-ton MV damaged
11 Mar	RP - MV 40 miles West of Marseilles	4+4 af	nf
11 Mar	SP - 3944N 0417E	3	
12 Mar	RP - MV Cap Tortosa	4+4 af	3700-ton *Killisi* damaged
12 Mar	RP - South of Barcelona	4+4 af	3500-ton Spanish MV damaged
15 Mar	RP - Cap San Sebastian - Cap Salan	4+4 af	nf
16 Mar	Rover Palamos - Cap de Creuz	5+4 af	
16 Mar	RP - Gulf of Fos	5+4 af	5000-ton + 3000-ton on fire
25 Mar	RP - Marseilles - Cap Capat	5+4 af	'V' LZ494 missing (F/O York and F/O Mathias)

Date	Target/Type of Operation	Number of acft/sorties	Losses/Remarks
27 Mar	RP - 4321N 0340E	5+4 af	
27 Mar	ASR Search (for LZ494)	4	nf
28 Mar	ASR Search (for LZ494)	6	nf
28 Mar	ASR Search (for LZ494)	3	nf
29 Mar	ASR Search (for LZ494)	2	nf
29 Mar	Rover - Nouvelle - Sete	4+4 af	
31 Mar	ASR Search (for LZ494)	3	nf
1 Apr	RP - North of Cap Creus	4+4 af	nf
6 Apr	RP - Cap Creus	4+4 af	1200-ton hit, attack stopped - international markings
9 Apr	RP - Convoy. Sete - Gulf of Fos	10+12 af	nf
10 Apr	RP - 20 miles West of Marseilles	5+ af	nf
11 Apr	RP - 4237N 0310E	5	nf
11 Apr	SP - Minorca	5	
13 Apr	SR - Cap Creus	2	attacked a Me 210
18 Apr	Rover - Mars - Cap Couronne - Port Vendres - La Nouvelle	6+ af	
19 Apr	Rover - Gulf of Lyons	6+ af	'C' NE371 hit sea and exploded (F/Sgt Hewitt, F/Sgt Garnett) 2000-ton damaged
20 Apr	RP - 4230N 0309E	4	600-ton damaged
22 Apr	RP - Torreille	6+ af	2000-ton on fire
28 Apr	SR - Cap Tosa - Cap Creus	1	sighted 2500-ton off Cap Bagur
28 Apr	RP - Cap Bagur	6	nf
28 Apr	ASR Search	1	
29 Apr	AR - Sete	1	
29 Apr	AR - Port Vendres	1	
1 May	Dolphin - Cap Bagur	2	one Ju 188 shot down
1 May	Trapper One - Minorca	6	
2 May	Trapper One - Minorca	6	
2 May	Dolphin - Cap Bagur	2	
6 May	RP - Shipping Sete harbour	6+6 af	1500-ton damaged
10 May	Trapper One	12	
11 May	Dolphin	2	
11 May	Dolphin	2	
11 May	Trapper One	2	
11 May	Trapper One	5	
12 May	ASR escort	6	
13 May	ASR escort	3	
14 May	Rover - Impena - Sap Serrat - Lerins Is.	5	
14 May	Dolphin	2	
15 May	Rover - Nice - San Remo	6	
18 May	RP - Cap Camarat radar	4+6 af	
20 May	RP - Cap Mele radar	4+4 af	RTB WX
20 May	RP - Cap Antibes radar	4+4 af	RTB WX
21 May	Dolphin	2	
21 May	Dolphin	2	
22 May	Dolphin	2	
22 May	Dolphin	2	
22 May	Trapper One	6	
25 May	RP - Cap Mele radar	4+4 af, +4 bomb	
26 May	RP - Cap Camarat radar	4+4 af, +4 bomb	
27 May	RP - Cap Antibes radar	4+4 af, +4 bomb	
29 May	Dolphin	2	
29 May	Dolphin	2	
29 May	Dolphin	1	

Date	Target/Type of Operation	Number of acft/sorties	Losses/Remarks
30 May	Dolphin	6 (3 pairs)	
30 May	Trapper One	6	
1 Jun	AR - Savona	1	
1 Jun	AR - Impenia	1	
1 Jun	AR - Nice	1	
1 Jun	AR - Marseilles	1	2000-ton exploded
1 Jun	AR - San Remo	1	
3 Jun	Night Intruder - north of Rome	6 (singles)	
4 Jun	Rover - Genoa - Leghorn	1	two ships damaged
4 Jun	Rover - Leghorn - San Stefano	1	500-ton damaged
4 Jun	Rover - Leghorn	1	attacked jetty near Leghorn
4 Jun	Rover - Leghorn - Lividonia	1	
5 Jun	Rover - Toulon - Nice	1	
5 Jun	Rover	1	RTB ASV u/s
5 Jun	Rover - Ombro	1	attacked TLC at Ombro, inland MT
5 Jun	Rover - Genoa - Elba	1	two ships attacked
5 Jun	Rover - Grosseto Island	1	1000-ton damaged
5 Jun	Rover - Genoa - Elba	1	two ships attacked
5 Jun	Rover - Florence	1	rail bridge Monte Pescali
6 Jun	Rover - Florence	1	
6 Jun	Rover	2 (singles)	RTB WX
6 Jun	Rover - Leghorn - La Rocca	1	MT + rail bridges
6 Jun	Rover - Genoa - Leghorn	1	800-ton damaged
6 Jun	Rover - Genoa - Leghorn	1	
6 Jun	Rover - Leghorn - La Rocca	1	800-ton damaged
6 Jun	Rover - Genoa - Leghorn	1	700-ton damaged
6 Jun	Rover - Leghorn - La Rocca	1	Bridge Castiglione
6 Jun	Rover - Genoa Leghorn	1	
6 Jun	Rover - Leghorn - La Rocca	1	
7 Jun	Rover - Spezia - Leghorn	1	
7 Jun	Rover - Elba - Lividonia	1	attacked Tarquinia airfield
7 Jun	Rover - Spezia - Elba	1	road/rail junction San Vincenzo railway
7 Jun	Rover - Elba - Montaltodi Castro	1	
7 Jun	Rover - Spezia - Elba	1	road/rail bridge San Vincenzo
7 Jun	Rover - Elba - Lividonia	1	two ships attacked
7 Jun	Rover - Spezia - Elba	1	
7 Jun	Rover	1	RTB engine failure
8 Jun	Rover - Genoa - Spezia	1	'W' NE385 missing (F/O Griffiths and F/O Atkin)
8 Jun	Rover - Genoa - Spezia	1	1500-ton tanker attacked of a convoy
9 Jun	Rover - Spezia - Elba	1	Road bridge over River Mass
9 Jun	Rover - Spezia - Elba	1	'S' LZ143 missing (S/Ldr Curlee and W/O Adam
9 Jun	Rover - Spezia - Elba	1	500-ton damaged
9 Jun	Rover	1	one MV attacked
10 Jun	Rover - Spezia - Elba	1	RTB WX
10 Jun	Rover - Genoa - Cannes	1	
10 Jun	Rover - Genoa - Spezia	1	
10 Jun	Rover - Genoa - Spezia	1	
10 Jun	Rover - Spezia - Elba	1	
14 Jun	AR - Trieste - Pola	2	
14 Jun	AR - Venice coast	2	
15 Jun	AR - Istrian coast and Ficime	2	ex Yugoslav cruiser beached at Dalmacija, attacked

Date	Target/Type of Operation	Number of acft/sorties	Losses/Remarks
16 Jun	AR - Istrian coast and Ficime	2	'X' LX486 lost (F/Sgt Spence and F/Sgt Barnes). Two schooners, and 700-ton damaged.
17 Jun	AR - Venice - Triests	2	
17 Jun	AR - Salonika	2	'L' NE415 (F/O Greenburgh and F/O Oakes). Trains
18 Jun	AR - North Adriatic	2	200-ton schooner sunk
18 Jun	AR - North Adriatic	2	
20 Jun	AR - Fano - Venice	2	
21 Jun	RP - Fano - Venice	2	2000-ton, flak too heavy
21 Jun	RP - Pola	2	80-ton coaster sunk
22 Jun	RP - Maestra Point	2	One barge sunk, 3 damaged, one tug and one schooner damaged
22 Jun	RP - Pola	2	1000-ton hit, 80-ton
23 Jun	AR - North Adriatic	2	schooner damaged
23 Jun	RP - 4425N 1227E	2	30-ton coaster damaged
24 Jun	RP - 4518N 1225E	2	tug and barge hit
24 Jun	RP - North Adriatic	2	700-ton sunk (?) plus fishing vessel sunk
25 Jun	RP - Rimini	2	
27 Jun	Intruder - Salonica	1	Rail junction
27 Jun	Intruder - Salonica	2	One RTB
28 Jun	AR - Salonica	2	Rail
28 June	AR - Salonica	2	Rail
29 Jun	RP	2	
30 Jun	Offensive Sweep - Salonica	2	Rail
1 Jul	OS - Salonica	2	Amyntaion station
2 Jul	AR - North Adriatic	2	60-ton schooner sunk, 30-ton coaster damaged
2 Jul	Intruder	1	
3 Jul	AR - North Adriatic	2	100-ton tug attacked
3 Jul	Intruder - Salonica	1	RTB WX
4 Jul	Intruder - Salonica	1	Rail
4 Jul	AR - North Adriatic	2	
5 Jul	OS - Corfu - Strophades Island	1	two 20-ton ships attacked
5 Jul	OS - Corfu - Strophades Island	1	
5 Jul	AR - North Adriatic		1500-ton sunk, 90-ton damaged
6 Jul	OS - Salonica	2	
6 Jul	AR - North Adriatic	2	
7 Jul	OS - Salonica	2	Rail and MT
7 Jul	AR - North Adriatic	2	50-ton damaged, 'E'-Boat damaged
7 Jul	OS - Salonica	1	RTB WX
8 Jul	OS - Salonica	1	Rail
8 Jul	AR - Salonica	2	
9 Jul	OS - Stamphani Island - Arta	2	
9 Jul	AR - North Adriatic	2	
10 Jul	AR - North Adriatic	2	300-ton probably sunk
11 Jul	AR - West Coast Greece	2	
11 Jul	AR - North Adriatic	2	
14 Jul	OS - Railway north of Belgrade	4+4 Must	'O' LZ480 lost (F/O Chandler and F/O Lamb). Rail target [see note 1]
15 Jul	OS - River Sala	3+4 Must	Rail
16 Jul	OS - River Sala	1	RTB no escort
18 Jul	AR - Podgorski Channel	2+2 Must	two 100 ft schooners sunk
19 Jul	OS - Vincovci - Novska	2+4 Must	one a/c dam, CL in Yugoslavia; Rail
19 Jul	RP - Chrome mine, Dhomokos	4	one CL Foggia

Date	Target/Type of Operation	Number of acft/sorties	Losses/Remarks
20 Jul	AR - Podgorski Channel	2+2 Must	200-ton attacked
20 Jul	OS - Railway Pec - Pristiria	2+3 Must	Rail
21 Jul	Intruder - Verria	2	'S' NE598 lost (F/O Clifford and F/O Williams). Rail
23 Jul	Intruder - Lama - Larissa	3+4 Must	Rail
2 Aug	SR - Zirje Island	3	nf
3 Aug	SR - Fiume area	3	nf
4 Aug	RP - Power station 4354N 1559E	4+4 Must	14 hits
5 Aug	SR - Fiume	4+4 Must	nf
7 Aug	SR - 4442N 1444E	4+4 Must	one 120 and 20 sunk in harbour
8 Aug	OS - Fiume	2+4 Must	
9 Aug	RP - Jablanac fuel/ammo dump	3	9 hits, burning
10 Aug	RP - Sisak oil refinery	3	already destroyed
10 Aug	RP - Bebar barracks	4+3 Must	24 hits, on fire
11 Aug	SR - 4 schooners 4507N 1450E	4+4 Must	attacked camouflaged area
12 Aug	RP - oil refinery 4339N 2034E	4+4 Must	hit tanks and buildings
13 Aug	RP - observation post 4450N 1510E	4	
13 Aug	SR - two Siebel ferries, Jablanac	3	nf. One soft schooner damaged
14 Aug	RP - 500-ton MV in Senj harbour	4+4 SAAF	11 hits, smoking. [note 2]
15 Aug	RP - Paracin barracks	4+4 Must	numerous hits
16 Aug	RP - Prilep rail sidings and ammo dump	6	explosions, burning
17 Aug	RP - Railway rolling stock, Rajnic	4	trucks burning
18 Aug	ASR	1	nf
19 Aug	AF escort for 16 Sqn. Barracks at 4805N 2032E	2+4	RTB WX. [note 3]
20 Aug	AF escort for 16 Sqn. Medari railway	2+4 (16 Sqn)	
21 Aug	RP - Flak ships Zaganthos harbour	4+3 SAAF	16 hits
21 Aug	RP - Power station Zadvarje	4+4 (16 Sqn)	14 hits
22 Aug	SR - Gulf of Venezia	4	nf
24 Aug	SR - Gulf of Venezia	4	Coastal freighter
24 Aug	RP - Barracks 4104N 2032E	4+2 (16 Sqn)	17 hits, smoke
25 Aug	OS - Salonica	4	RTB WX
26 Aug	SR - Corfu	4+4 SAAF	nf
26 Aug	RP - Bebar barracks	6	smoke
27 Aug	RP - Medari warehouse	4+2 SAAF	22 hits smoke
28 Aug	SR - Levka - Preveza	4	'X' NT990 RTB early and CL at base. nf
28 Aug	RP - German-held monastery at 4407N 1538E	4	smoke
29 Aug	RP - 1000 oil trucks 4547N 1728E	6+4 Must	sidings empty
29 Aug	RP - 500-ton MV 4459N 1404E	6	nf; attacked jetty area
30 Aug	Night Rover - Gulf of Venezia	2 singles	
2 Sep	RP - Rolling stock, Sunja	4	24 hits, smoke
3 Sep	SR - Pola - Salvore Point	4	
5 Sep	RP - Pontoon bridges at positions 4514N 1633E and 4523N 1632E	4	RTB WX
6 Sep	RP - Pontoon bridge, Dobrljin	4	nf; rail bridge destroyed
6 Sep	Intruder - South east of Sisak	2	2 locos D, 25 boxcars and 44 trucks damaged.
7 Sep	Intruder - Zivaja area	2	1 loco D, 10+ box cars damaged
7 Sep	Intruder - Salonica	4	
7 Sep	RP - Landing barges 4313N 1639E	4	'K' LX877 ditched Brac Island (F/Sgts Kyrk-Smith, Campbell)
8 Sep	ASR for 'K'	2	nf
8 Sep	RP - 51000-ton liner *Rex*, Capodistria	6	48 hits, listing, burning
9 Sep	Intruder - Agrinion area	4	1 armoured car D + 5 damaged, 5 trucks D + 9 dam. Road bridge dam

185

Date	Target/Type of Operation	Number of acft/sorties	Losses/Remarks
10 Sep	SR - Istrian coast	6	nf. One hospital ship seen
11 Sep	RP - Coastal guns 4335N 1555E	3	explosions
11 Sep	RP - Coastal guns 4111N 1510E	5	
12 Sep	SR - Preveza - Zante	4+4 SAAF	'P' NE297 CL Grottaglie. Siebel ferry attacked
13 Sep	AR - Railway 4403N 1612E - 4422N 1608E	2	
14 Sep	Intruder - Drnis - Bihac	2	
14 Sep	Intruder - Brod - Novi Gradiska	4	P/O Orme killed. Trucks damaged
16 Sep	RP - Barracks Knin	4	smoke
17 Sep	RP - Barracks Valjevo	8+2 SAAF	Burning
18 Sep	RP - Railway 2 miles east of Novigradiska	6	one loco destroyed, six box cars damaged
20 Sep	RP - Coastal guns Novi	6	explosions
20 Sep	PR - Damaged to MT park Amyntaion	2	PR+ one tank destroyed
21 Sep	RP - Railway east of Dubrovnik	4	RTB WX
22 Sep	RP - Railway east of Dubrovnik	5	12 box cars D, other damaged
24 Sep	SR - Fiume Islands	4	
25 Sep	RP - Gun positions, Aikatenni	8	explosions
27 Sep	AR - Podgorski Channel	4	RTB WX
4 Oct	RP - Sunja rail station	3	damaged, lines cut
4 Oct	AR - Dalmation Islands	5	
7 Oct	RP - Preko harbour (Uljan Islands)	6	RTB WX
9 Oct	RP - Preko harbour	4	20 small boats damaged
9 Oct	Rover - Zara - Fiume	6	
10 Oct	RP - Kris barracks and rail	6	one Do 217 SD; 30 box cars dam
11 Oct	RP - Corvette and E-boats, Levrera Isl.	6	'F' NT889 dam, CL at Ancona. nf, one schooner on fire
11 Oct	RP - Observation post 12 ml SE Tirana	3	RTB WX
12 Oct	SR - Dalmation Islands	8	
13 Oct	SR - Ewoia Channel	8	'I' LZ460 ditched, engine trouble (S/Ldr Payne, F/Sgt Potts) picked up by ASR aircraft.
16 Oct	SR - Gulf of Salonica	6	600-ton boom laying MV sunk
18 Oct	RP - Railway Sarajevo - Visegrad	8	RTB WX
20 Oct	SR - Dalmation Islands	8	One small MV sunk
21 Oct	SR - Gulf of Fiume	8	'W' NE724 dam, CL Canne; 3000-ton MV hit
23 Oct	SR - Podgorski Channel	8	RTB WX
25 Oct	RP - Rolling stock, Novska	5	
31 Oct	RP - MT near Knin	8	nf
3 Nov	SR - Fiume area	8	nf
5 Nov	SR - Dalmation Islands	7	nf
7 Nov	RP - King Zog's Palace, Tirana	7	smoke
15 Nov	RP - King Zog's Palace	11	burning
16 Nov	RP - King Zog's Palace	9	CX
19 Nov	RP - Zegat village	6	Damaged
19 Nov	RP - Ostrozar village	6	Damaged
20 Nov	RP - Railway near Novska	8	300 trucks attacked, explosions
23 Nov	RP - Danilovgrad village	12	Damaged [note 4]
27 Nov	Weather Recce	2	
30 Nov	Weather Recce	2	
2 Dec	Weather Recce	2	
2 Dec	RP - Bjlovar	12+16/19 Sqns	RTB WX
2 Dec	Transport two army officers to Yugoslavia and RTB	1	

Date	Target/Type of Operation	Number of acft/sorties	Losses/Remarks
3 Dec	RP - Coastal guns, Lussin Piccolo	11	10 guns attacked
4 Dec	RP - Troop concentrations Gracac	12+16/19 Sqns	
6 Dec	RP - Castle at Gracac	11	10 hits
15 Dec	Weather Recce, Bihac	2	
15 Dec	PR - Berane - Bioce	2	
17 Dec	RP - Power station, Lussin Island	6	18 hits
18 Dec	RP - MT Bioce	6	21 on fire, 40+ damaged
20 Dec	Weather recce, Sarajevo	2	
21 Dec	Ferry trips to Niksic and Belgrade	5	
23 Dec	Weather recce, Lujunjana	2	

1945
4 Jan	Weather recce, Trebryne - Lussin Piccolo	2	

Athens Detachment [note 5]

1944
Date	Target/Type of Operation	Number of acft/sorties	Losses/Remarks
16 Dec	RP Athens radio station	2	Destroyed
17 Dec	KKE HQ	6	
17 Dec	ELAS ammo dump	2	
17 Dec	ELAS HQ	2	
18 Dec	Gun positions	2	Destroyed
18 Dec	Gun positions	2	Destroyed
18 Dec	Position near Athens stadium	4	
19 Dec	Strongholds	6	
20 Dec	AAA position, Galatsi	4	
20 Dec	ELAS HQ, Galatsi	2	
21 Dec	Strongpoint (Athens jail)	5	Destroyed
21 Dec	AFQ interrogation room	1	Destroyed
22 Dec	Strongpoints	2	
22 Dec	Ammo dump, Piraeus	3	Destroyed
23 Dec	Strongpoints	4	
23 Dec	Ammo dumps, North Athens	4	
23 Dec	Strongpoint	4	
24 Dec	Strongpoint, Piraeus	2	
24 Dec	Petrol store	2	
24 Dec	ELAS billet	2	
24 Dec	ELAS HQ	3	
25 Dec	ELAS HQ	2	
25 Dec	Petrol dump	2	
25 Dec	Strongpoint	3	
26 Dec	ELAS HQ, Piraeus	3	
27 Dec	Ammo dump, North Athens	2	
28 Dec	Strongpoint	4	
29 Dec	Storage area	4	
29 Dec	Strongpoint, monastery	3	
29 Dec	ELAS conference site	4	Destroyed
31 Dec	Strongpoints, Piraeus	4	

1945
1 Jan	8th State School	4	
3 Jan	Gun positions, North Piraeus	4	
3 Jan	ELAS HQ	4	
4 Jan	PR Milos	1	
5 Jan	Demonstration Flight, N. Patras	4+108 Sqn	
5 Jan	Artillery spotting for Army	1	
6 Jan	PR Milos	1	

Date	Target/Type of Operation	Number of acft/sorties	Losses/Remarks
8 Jan	PR Milos	1	
10 Jan	PR Milos	1	
12 Jan	ASR	4	
13 Jan	Army co-operation, Patras	2	One train destroyed
13 Jan	PR Volos	1	
14 Jan	PR Evvoia Gulf	1	

MARAUDER   [note 6]
1945

Date	Target/Type of Operation	Number of acft/sorties	Losses/Remarks
7 Feb	Senj harbour	12	
8 Feb	HQ 21/22 Mountain Corps, Brinje	11	
9 Feb	Konje marshalling yards	11	two RTB early
10 Feb	Coaling wharf Arsa Channel	10	
13 Feb	Bihac rail station	11	
15 Feb	Oil installation, Banova Jaruga	12	one RTB early
16 Feb	Novska marshalling yards	6	RTB WX
18 Feb	Kraljevica slipway	12	RTB WX
20 Feb	Kraljevica	4	
21 Feb	Jetty, Arsa Channel	12	
24 Feb	Rolling stock Bunova Jaruga	10	two RTB early
25 Feb	Jablanac	8	two RTB early
26 Feb	Banova Jaruga	4	
26 Feb	Sunja	4	
27 Feb	Rail bridge Zenica	8	
27 Feb	Sisak marshalling yards	12	
28 Feb	Weather recce	1	
11 Mar	Gun positions Stojan Point (Rab Island)	10	
12 Mar	Gun positions Stojan Point (Rab Island)	8	
13 Mar	Gun positions Stojan Point (Rab Island)	8	
14 Mar	Road bridge Gospic	10	
18 Mar	Gun positions, Kristofor Point (Rab)	6	
19 Mar	Strongpoints Bihac	12	
20 Mar	Novahepella marshalling yards	12	three RTB early
21 Mar	Oil installations Banova Jaruga	12	
22 Mar	Gun positions Stojan Point	10	
23 Mar	Kostajnica rail station	12	
24 Mar	Railway Nova Gradiska area	12	
25 Mar	Nova Gradiska marshalling yards	12	
26 Mar	Railway Nova Gradiska area	12	one RTB early
30 Mar	Leaflet dropping, Lussin Piccolo area	1	
1 Apr	Popovaca marshalling yards	12	
2 Apr	Medari marshalling yards	12	two RTB early
3 Apr	Nova Gradiska marshalling yards	12	missed but hit ammo dump
5 Apr	Nova Gradiska marshalling yards	12	
5 Apr	Banova Jaruga marshalling yards	6	
8 Apr	Gun positions Chistopher Point	13	
9 Apr	Kutina marshalling yards	12	
10 Apr	O'Rucani marshalling yards	12	
10 Apr	Gun positions Lussin Island	6	
11 Apr	Rail line Brod - Zagreb	12	
11 Apr	Rail line Brod - Zagreb	14	
12 Apr	Lipovljani marshalling yards	12	
12 Apr	O'Rucani marshalling yards	6	
14 Apr	Banova Karunga marshalling yards	11	one RTB early
16 Apr	Rail line Brod - Zagreb	12	
16 Apr	Gun positions Krk Island	5	

Date	Target/Type of Operation	Number of acft/sorties	Losses/Remarks
17 Apr	Rail line Novska - Brod	10	
18 Apr	Rail bridge Banova Jaruga	7	
19 Apr	Gun positions Lussin Island	6	
19 Apr	Gun positions Lussin Island	6	
20 Apr	Gun positions Cherso Island	6	one RTB early
20 Apr	Rail line Rajic	5	
21 Apr	Banova Jaruga marshalling yards	6	
23 Apr	Rajic marshalling yards	6	
24 Apr	Rail bridge RK 982736	6	
24 Apr	Rail line Kutina - Popovaca	6	
24 Apr	HQ, Porto di Brione	6	
25 Apr	Gun position 333414	12	
26 Apr	Popovaca marshalling yards	11	
4 May	Popovaca marshalling yards	12	

Notes:

1. Must - air escort of Mustangs of 213 Squadron
2. SAAF - Beaufighters of 19 Squadron SAAF (a/f and/or RP)
3. 16 Sqn - Beaufighters of 16 Squadron SAAF (a/f and/or RP)
4. With Beaufighters of 19 Squadron and eight aircraft of 16 Squadron, plus Spitfires
5. Destroyed targets are those confirmed as Destroyed, others suffered various degrees of damage. All sorties RP unless otherwise specified
6. All sorties formation bombing unless otherwise stated

Appendix F

Serials of Aircraft Operated by 39 Squadron

This list is compiled from the ORBs (F540 and F541), the official aircraft record cards and the logbooks of Squadron personnel. N.B. World War I serials are representative only, not a complete list.

B.E.2c 2092 (crashed on take-off 16.9.16); 4112
B.E.2e 7151; B4482; B4453; B4481
B.E.12 A6326
Bristol Fighter A7265; B1350
D.H.9a J7037; J7039; J7041; J7058; J7061; J7067; J7073; J7316; J7792; J7812; J7818; J7819; J8096; J8133; J8137; J8143; J8144; J8147; J8159; J8169; J8170; F1641; F2851; E876; E948; H3552
Westland Wapiti IIA All aircraft were delivered to the Air Depot, RAF Drigh Road, Karachi, between 16.1.29 and 1.12.29 before being sent on to the Squadron. J9288; J9380; J9381; J9383; J9386; J9388; J9389; J9393; J9395; J9396; J9397; J9399; J9481; J9400; J9484; J9493; J9495; J9830; J9889.
Hawker Audax K4862
Hawker Hart II (India) All aircraft were delivered to the Air Depot, Karachi, between 24.10.31 and 31.12.31 before being sent on to the Squadron: K1417; K2084; K2085; K2086; K2087; K2088; K2089; K2090; K2091; K2092; K2093; K2096; K2098; K2099; K2100; K2101; K2102; K2104; K2105; K2106; K2110; K2113; K2114; K2115; K2116; K2117; K2118; K2119; K2122; K2123; K2124; K2126; K2128; K2129; K2130; K2131; K2132; K3921; K3922; K8627; K8628; K8629; K8630; K8631.

From 1939 onwards the record cards are generally more complete although 39 Squadron spent most of its time in overseas Commands and unit transfers within a command are not usually recorded. In the Canberra period record cards of aircraft still in service are not available. For other periods some cards are missing for one reason or another. The symbol * indicates 39 Squadron on record cards.

Serial/Code	Delivery date to Sqn or operating area	Previous unit/ Command	Last sortie or transfer details	SOC date
Bristol Blenheim I				
L1434	15.8.40	Aden		13.4.41
L1498	27.4.39	AD		12.6.41
L1533	20.4.39	Aden - 8 Sqn		1.1.47
L1546	6.7.39	India		
L4834	31.12.39	Aden		21.8.40
L4910	10.40	Aden		27.7.44
L4920	7.39	India	CL British Somaliland 24.6.40	
L4921	3.8.39	India		
L8374	8.4.40	Aden		28.12.40
L8384	27.4.39	AD	Di Red Sea 17.8.40	
L8385	27.4.39	AD	To Greek Govt 1.4.41	
L8387	27.4.39	AD		19.9.40
L8402	27.4.39	AD		19.9.40
L8381	27.4.39	AD		12.12.40
L8474	8.40	Aden	Cr Diredawa 20.8.40	
L8543	15.4.40	Aden		12.12.40
L8612	18.10.39	AD		21.4.41

Bristol Blenheim IV From 2.10.40 combat reports state Mk.IV in use but no serials are given

Serial/Code	Delivery date to Sqn or operating area	Previous unit/ Command	Last sortie or transfer details	SOC date
Martin Maryland				
AX227			(no card)	
AX689	20.1.41	Takoradi	'Blue Pencil' Cr 4.41	5.4.41
AH282*	3.3.41	Takoradi		16.9.41 (39 Sqn)
AH284	3.3.41	Takoradi		last entry 20.2.44
AH286*	3.3.41	Takoradi		1.8.43
AH287	3.3.41	Takoradi		17.11.41
AH288*	15.6.41	via South Africa		16.7.41 (39 Sqn)
AH291	3.3.41	Takoradi	to ME 1.11.41	
AH292	3.3.41	Takoradi	to Malta 31.8.42	
AH295	3.3.41	Takoradi	with 203 Sqn 23.2.42	
AH297*	3.3.41	Takoradi		12.8.41 (39 Sqn)
AH298	3.3.41	Takoradi		15.4.42 (203 Sqn)
AH299*	3.3.41	Takoradi		24.6.41 (39 Sqn)
AH300*	3.3.41	Takoradi		15.6.41 (39 Sqn)
AH307*	15.6.41	ME		30.5.41 (39 Sqn)
AH312	3.3.41	Alexandria		9.8.42 (203 Sqn)
AH349	3.3.41	Alexandria		1.2.44 (21 Sqn)
AH359*	.41	Alexandria		4.12.41
AH358*	.41	Alexandria		28.2.43
AH361*	.41	Alexandria		25.8.41 (39 Sqn)
AH367*	.41	Alexandria		3.9.41 (39 Sqn)
AH390	15.6.41	via South Africa		1.8.41
AH384	14.12.41	Takoradi	SD 28.8.41	
AH425	1.8.41	via South Africa	with 21 SAAF 24.11.41	
AR709	10.41	ME	to Malta 11.41	
AR711	10.41	ME		6.4.42 (69 Sqn)
AR749	15.5.41	ME		1.1.47 PSOC
BS776	6.6.41	ME	to Malta 11.41	

ORB records five aircraft lost May/June 1941 but gives no serials. Probably AH299, AH300 and AH307 by their SOC dates but no other SOC dates fit the loss dates.

Serial/Code	Delivery date to Sqn or operating area	Previous unit/ Command	Last sortie or transfer details	SOC date
Bristol Beaufort I/II				
DD875/S	31.8.42	ME	missing 30.11.42	
DD878/W	17.8.42	ME		27.2.43
DD882/W	27.2.43	ME		1.4.44
DD887/R	10.2.43	ME		27.7.44
DD892/N*	6.3.42	ME	FTR 11.4.43	
DD896/G	6.3.42	ME		27.7.44
DD898/I*	1.9.42	ME		1.11.43
DD899/Q*	10.9.42	ME	FTR 3.3.43	
DD902/D*	1.2.43	Malta	FTR 17.3.43	
DD910/G*	1.2.43	Malta	Hit sea 25.2.43	
DD911/J*	18.8.42	ME		27.7.44
DD927/F	1.9.42	ME		27.7.44
DD928/C	1.12.42	Malta	FTR 12.3.43	
DD934/N	31.12.42	ME	FTR 12.3.43	
DD935/T*	23.8.42	ME		PSOC 1.1.47
DD936/N*	15.4.43	ME	FTR 15.5.43	
DD906/C	26.2.43	ME		27.7.44
DD940/H	27.2.43	ME		7.44
DD943/A*	1.2.43	Malta	Dep ME 1.7.43	
DD949*	13.5.42	ME	CL Malta 15.6.42	
DD950	24.5.42	ME	India 30.9.42	
DD951*	29.5.42	ME	Cat 3 24.7.42	24.7.42
DD952/V*	24.5.42	ME	CL 13.1 43	14.1.43
DD955	23.5.42	ME	missing 15.6.42	
DD974	29.5.42	ME	CL 15.6.42	1.12.42
DD975	13.5.42	ME	CL (Malta) 15.6.42	18.6.42
DD976	24.5.42	ME	missing 23.6.42	
DD986*	7.7.42	ME	CL Gianaclis 6.8.42	31.8.42
DD992	2.7.42	ME		30.9.42
DD993	3.6.42	ME	CL Malta 3.7.42	18.10.42
AW219	4.5.42	ME	India 1.12.42	
AW240	19.3.42	ME	FTR 3.7.42	
AW284/Y	27.7.42	ME	FTR 30.11.42	
AW290	3.6.42	ME	FTR 24.8.42	
AW297	14.4.42	ME	SD Derna 15.6.42	
AW295	23.6.42	ME	FTR 20.8.42	
AW300/B	1.5.42	ME		27.7.44
AW305	27.7.42	ME	FTR 6.9.42	
AW348/M*	6.4.42	ME	FTR 27.3.43	
AW350	27.7.42	ME	FTR 22.9.42	
AW352	20.4.42	ME	SD Derna 15.6.42	
AW337	30.3.42	ME		18.6.42
AW349/R	18.8.42	ME	FTR 24.2.43	
AW358	6.4.42	ME		22.5.42
AW353	16.8.42	ME	FTR 21.8.42	
AW359	31.12.42	22 MU	to 44MU 7.3.43	
AW362/E	29.7.42	ME		1.9.43
AW374/M	22.3.43	ME		27.7.44
N1024	6.4.42	ME	with 5 METS 23.10.42	1.12.42
N1033	15.12.41	ME		1.12.42
N1035	20.10.41	ME		13.4.42
N1091	16.10.41	ME		31.12.41
N1092	16.10.41	ME		1.2.??
N1094	16.10.41	ME		4.6.42
N1098	28.10.41	ME		23.11.41

39 SQUADRON
BRISTOL BEAUFIGHTER
CODE & SERIAL ALLOCATIONS
1943 - 1945

Code	1943 Jul	Aug	Sep	Oct	Nov	Dec	1944 Jan	Feb	Mar	Apr	May	Jun	Jul	Aug	Sep	Oct	Nov	Dec	1945 Jan
A	LX785	LX785	LX785		LX877	LX799	NE466	NE466	NE466	NE466	NE466	NE291		NV218	NV218	NV218	NV218	NE291	
B	LX791	LX791	LX789		LX789	LX789	LX789	NE378	NE378	NE378	NE378	NE378	NE378	NV271	NV271	NV271	NV271	NV271	NV271
C	JM399			LZ236	NE371	NE371	NE371	NE371	NE371	NE371									
D	LX790			N															
F	JM413	JM413	JM413	O	LZ119	LZ119	NE412	NE412	NE412	NE412	NE412	NE412	NE383	NT889	NT889	NT889	NT998	NT998	
G	LX792	LX792	LX792									LZ338	NE549	NE549	NE360	NE360	NV311	NV311	NV311
H				D	LX154	LX154	LX154	LX154	LX154	LX154	NE415	NE415	NE581	NE581	NE581	NE581	NE581	NE581	
I	LX788	LX788	LX788	E	LX788	LX788	LZ484	LZ460	LZ460	LZ460	LZ460	LZ460	LZ460	LZ460	LZ460	NV150	NV150	NV150	NV150
J	LX810	LX810	LX810	T	LX810	LX810	LZ484	NE362	NE362	NE362	NE362	NE362		NE581	NE581	NE581	NE581	NE581	
K	LX871	LX871	LX871	A	LX909	LX909	LX909	LX909	NE410	NE410	NE410	NE410	NE410	LX977	NE291	NE291	NE291		
L			LX850	I	LX786		LX154	LX154	LX154	LX154	NE415	NE467	NE467	NE581					
N	JM387	JM387	JM387	L	LX786						NE467	NE467	NE467	NV273	NV273	NV273	NV273	NV273	
O	LX790			S			LX154	LX154	LZ338	LZ338	LZ338	LZ338	LZ480	NV250	NV250	NV250	NV250	NV250	NV250
P	JM404	JM404	JM404			JM404	LZ460	LZ460	NE297	NE297	NE297	NE297	NE297	NE297	NE297	NV597	NV597	NV597	NV597
Q		JM386	JM386																
R	JM417	JM417	JM417		JM417	JM417		NE385	NE521	NE521	NE521	NE521	NE521	NE521	NV124	NV124	NV124	NV124	NV124
S	LX867	LX867	LX862		LX999	LX999	LX999	LZ143	LZ143	LZ143	LZ143	LZ143	NV242	NV123	NV123	NV123	NV123	NV123	
T	LX793	LX903	LX903		LX882	LX882	LX882	LZ521	NE322	NE322	NE322	NE322	NE322	NV209	NV209	NV209	LX788	LX788	
U			JM411																NE581
V	JM415	JM415	JM911		LX914	LX914	LZ494											NV135	NV135
W	LX907	LX907	LX907		LX907	LX903	LZ140	LZ140	LZ140	LZ140	NE385	NE385	NE528	NE724	NE724	NE724	NE474	NV474	NV474
X	JM316	JM316	LX779		LZ142	LX779	LZ484	LZ486	LZ486	LZ486	LZ486	LZ486	LX788	LX977	NE291	NE291	NV117	NV117	NV117
Y	JM408										NE249	NE249	NE249	NE249	NT990	NE249			
Z	LX862	LX862			LX898	LX878	LX878											NV135	NV135

Remarks: NE291 also noted as 'A' in 5.44   NE385 also noted as 'N' in 5.44

NV218 noted in use 12.44 and 1.45 but no code is recorded   NV311 also noted as 'G' in 11.44

Serial/Code	Delivery date to Sqn or operating area	Previous unit/ Command	Last sortie or transfer details	SOC date
N1100	19.3.43	ME	SD 14.4.42	
N1153	15.3.42	ME		1.1.44
N1165	15.12.42	ME	with 5 METS 19.10.42	1.12.42
N1166	8.2.42	ME	SD 14.1.42	
N1167*	1.9.42	ME		1.1.44
N1169*	15.2.42	39 Sqn	SD 14.4.42	
N1170	11.2.42	ME		1.1.47 PSOC
N1186	15.2.42	ME	SD 14.4.42	
W6488*	1.9.42	39 Sqn		27.7.44
W6495	15.12.41	ME		1.1.47 PSOC
W6504	8.41	ME	with 450 Sqn 9.12.41	16.3.43
W6505	8.41	ME		1.1.44
W6506	8.41	ME		30.9.42
W6518	9.41	ME	Crashed 23.6.42	
W6519	23.3.42	Malta		1.9.43
W6520	8.41	ME	FTR 2.1.42	
X8923	15.12.41	ME	FTR 14.4.42	
X9824	19.3.42	ME		1.11.43
L8924			(no card)	
L9875	9.41	ME	Crashed in sea 3.9.42	
DE114	7.7.42	ME		16.4.43
DE116/O	30.9.43	ME		27.7.44
DE122/D	30.7.42	ME		??.1.44
DW802/P	1.8.42	ME	FTR 6.1.43	
DW817/H*	4.9.42	ME	FTR 29.11.42	
DW835/Z	19.10.42	ME		PSOC 1.1.47
DW836/K	31.12.42	ME		27.7.44
DW880/X	2.11.42	ME		25.5.43

From August 1942 the Malta element sorties and losses are recorded by serial letter only, as follows: 20.8.42 'T' and 'F' FTR - possibly AW295 and one other; 21.8.42 'V' FTR; 24.8.42 'S' FTR - possibly AW290; 6.9.42 'W' and 'R' FTR - possibly AW305 and one other; 22.9.42 'M' FTR - possibly AW350.

Bristol Beaufighter X

Serial/Code	Delivery date to Sqn or operating area	Previous unit/ Command	Last sortie or transfer details	SOC date
LX779/X*	31.7.43	NA	SD, Elba 24.9.43	
LX785/A*	31.7.43	NA	Di, Cap Carbonara 15.9.43	
LX788/I	31.7.43	NA		6.9.45
LX789/B	1.7.43	ME		14.6.45
LX792/G*	31.7.43	NA	Di Pianosa Island 24.9.43	
LX791/B	14.6.43	ME	Missing 21.6.43	
LX790/O	24.7.43	NA	SD by flak E.Corsica 21.7.43	
LX793/T	31.7.43	NA		31.7.43
LX799/A*	23.7.43	ME	SD Bonifacio 24.9.43	
LX810/J	6.7.43	ME		31.5.45
LX850/L	23.7.43	NA		24.9.43
LX862/S	4.7.43	ME	CL near base 24.9.43	
LX877/K	31.8.43	NA	Di Nrac Island 7.9.44	
LX878/Z	31.8.43	NA		6.12.44
LX882/T	6.8.43	ME		31.5.44
LX903/T	13.7.43	ME	SD Elba 24.9.43	
LX907/W	31.7.43	NA		29.2.44
LX909/K	31.7.43	NA		1.1.47
LX911/V	8.8.43	ME	SD Chiappa Point 25.9.43	
LX999/S	3.9.43	ME		14.6.45
JM316/X	1.7.43	NA		1.1.47
JM386/Q*	29.5.43	NA	SD Elba 15.9.43	

Serial/Code	Delivery date to Sqn or operating area	Previous unit Command	Last sortie or transfer details	SOC date
JM387/N*	31.7.43	NA	SD Elba 15.9.43	
JM399/C*	14.6.43	NA	SD by flak E.Corsica 14.7.43	
JM404/P	12.6.43	ME		Cat 3 1.11.43
JM408/Y*			SD 11.7.43	
JM411/U	31,7,43	NA	SD Bastia 23.9.43	
JM412*	6.6.43	ME	Missing 12.7.43	
JM413/F	31.7.43	NA		Cat 3 1.11.43
JM415/V	3.6.43	en route India		29.2.44
JM417/R	31.7.43			31.5.44
LZ140/W	19.9.43	ME		
LZ143/S	19.9.43	ME	Missing 9.6.44 (recorded as 29 Sqn)	
LZ154/N	8.9.43	ME		
LZ338/H	31.10.43	NWA		13.9.45
LZ460/I	30.11.43	NA	Di 13.10.44	
LZ480/O	15.3.44	ME	Missing Belgrade 14.7.44	
LZ484/I	7.12.43	ME		31.5.44
LZ486/X	30.11.43	NA	Crashed Novalja 16.6.44	
LZ494/V	30.11.43	NA	Missing 25.3.44	
LZ521	31.12.43	ME		13.9.45
NE291/K	7.2.44	ME		19.7.45
NE297/P	1.3.44	ME		31.3.45
NE249/Z	3.2.44	ME		18.8.44
NE322/T	25.3.44	ME	CL Brindisi 21.7.44; back to service	
NE362/J	21.1.44	ME		31.5.44
NE371/C	28.1.44	ME	Hit water, exploded Espinguette Pt 19.4.44	
NE378/B	9.5.44	ME		28.2.45
NE383/F	21.2.44	ME		??.8.44
NE385/W	28.1.44	ME	Missing 8.6.44	
NE410/K	6.2.44	ME		12.1.45
NE412/F	13.2.44	ME	SD 3820N 0015E 1.2.44	
NE415/L	12.2.44	ME	Crashed Salonica 17.6.44	
NE466	12.2.44	ME		31.5.44
NE467	9.4.44	ME		31.3.45
NE518/J	12.2.44	MAC		1.1.47
NE521/R	4.2.44	MAAF		13.12.45
NE528/W	9.3.44	ME		26.12.44
NE549	7.3.44	ME		24.2.45
NE598/S	15.3.44	ME	Crashed Koritsa 21.7.44	
NE615/X	21.4.44	ME		28.8.44
NE724/W	21.7.44	ME	CL Canne 21.10.44	
NT889/F	10.7.44	ME	CL Ancona 11.10.44	
NT905/P	21.8.44	ME	CL Brindisi 13.10.44 (back to service)	20.9.45
NT990/X	20.7.44	ME	CL base 28.8.44 (back to service)	25.10.44
NT998	15.9.44	ME		28.2.45
NV123	4.8.44	ME		20.9.45
NV124	3.8.44	ME		31.5.45
NV117	15.9.44	ME		10.9.45
NV135/Z	4.10.44	ME		31.3.45
NV150/I	24.9.44	NWA		31.5.45
NV209/T	28.7.44	MAAF		1.1.47
NV218/A	10.2.44	MAAF		31.5.45
NV242/S	29.7.44	MAAF		31.3.45
NV250/O	23.7.44	MAAF		6.9.45
NV271/B	23.7.44	MAAF		14.6.45

Serial/Code	Delivery date to Sqn or operating area	Previous unit/ Command	Last sortie or transfer details	SOC date
NV273/X	16.7.44	MAAF		11.12.44
NV311/G	24.10.44	NWA		13.12.45
NV374/W	27.9.44	NWA		20.7.45
NV597/P	8.10.44	NWA		20.9.45

Martin Marauder III

Serial/Code	Delivery date to Sqn or operating area	Previous unit/ Command	Last sortie or transfer details	SOC date
HD458	30.6.44	MAAF		6.46
HD531	30.6.44	MAAF		6.46
HD558	21.6.45	MAAF		6.46
HD570	30.11.44	MAAF		3.46
HD581	29.9.44	MAAF		3.46
HD606	28.9.44	MAAF		3.46
HD607	28.9.44	MAAF		3.46
HD610	28.9.44	MAAF		6.46
HD611/A	28.9.44	MAAF		6.46
HD619	28.9.44	MAAF		6.46
HD625/R	27.10.44	MAAF		5.7.45
HD636/S	27.10.44	MAAF		6.46
HD639	28.9.44	MAAF		3.46
HD640	28.9.44	MAAF		6.46
HD644	27.10.44	MAAF		7.46
HD674	25.1.45	MAAF		8.46
HD691	25.1.45	MAAF		14.3.46
HD719/F	22.2.45	MAAF		26.9.46

One aircraft 'R' crashed in June 1945. Other codes known are 'B', 'G', 'I', 'J', 'K', 'L', 'N', 'P', 'Q', 'O', 'R', 'S', 'T', 'W', 'X'. Many aircraft were left on the scrapyard at Kharthoum.

de Havilland Mosquito 26

Serial/Code	Delivery date to Sqn or operating area	Previous unit/ Command	Last sortie or transfer details	SOC date
KA136	6.12.45	MED ME		28.9.46
KA154	28.2.46	MED ME		28.9.46
KA162	31.1.46	MED ME		28.9.46
KA164	10.1.46	MED ME		28.9.46
KA165	11.4.46	MED ME		28.9.46
KA175	31.1.46	MED ME		31.12.46
KA190	28.3.46	MED ME		26.9.46
KA284	14.2.46	MED ME		26.9.46
KA298			To Canadian authorities 17.11.45	
KA309	28.3.46	MED ME		31.12.46
KA349	31.1.46	MED ME		26.9.46
KA354	14.2.46	MED ME		26.9.46
KA362	28.2.46	MED ME		26.9.46
KA364	14.3.46	MED ME		26.9.46
KA407	28.2.46	MED ME	Crashed 30.4.46	
KA464			(no card)	
KA282	11.4.46	MED ME	Crashed 20.12.46	

Hawker Tempest VI

Serial/Code	Delivery date to Sqn or operating area	Previous unit/ Command	Last sortie or transfer details	SOC date
NX172*	15.6.48	Manston		
NX197			(no card)	
NX264*	29.7.48	Manston		31.3.49
NX247*	8.7.48	Manston	Crashed 7.1.49	24.1.49
NX282*	8.7.48	Manston	to 107 MU 10.3.49	
NX283*	8.7.48	Manston	to 107 MU 10.3.49	
NX284*	8.7.48	Manston	to 107 MU 10.3.49	
NX285*	8.7.48	Manston	to 107 MU 10.3.49	
NX287*	8.7.48	Manston		31.3.49

Serial/Code	Delivery date to Sqn or operating area	Previous unit/ Command	Last sortie or transfer details	SOC date
de Havilland Mosquito NF.36				
RL113*	8.9.49	Fayid	to 109 MU 25.5.51	
RL115*	9.7.52	Kabrit	to 38 MU 30.3.53	
RL123*	16.7.52	Kabrit	to 38 MU 30.3.53	
RL130*	22.10.51	Kabrit	Cat 5 1.7.52	1.7.52
RL133*	8.9.49	Fayid	to 38 MU 30.3.53	
RL151*	14.7.49	Fayid	to 109 MU 28.12.49	
RL202*	19.6.51	Fayid	to UK 29.10.52	
RL211*	4.12.51	Kabrit	Cat 5 20.5.52	
RL229*	22.12.50	Kabrit	Cat 5 25.9.51	
RL233*	24.11.49	Fayid	Cat 5 26.9.51	
RL234*	9.12.49	Fayid	Cat 5 12.8.52	
RL235*	12.11.52	Fayid	to UK 20.4.53	
RL236*	23.5.52	Kabrit	to UK 30.3.53	
RL237*	15.6.51	Kabrit	Cat 5 12.2.52	
RL240*	24.11.49	Fayid	Cat 5 1.6.51	
RL241*	11.8.49	Fayid	to UK 16.11.50	
RK973*	8.9.49	Fayid	Cat 5 2.5.52	
RK975*	24.10.52	Fayid	Cat 5 28.11.50	
RK976*	29.9.49	Fayid	to 15 MU 12.3.53	
RL983*	24.10.52	Fayid	to 15 MU 12.3.53	
RK994*	24.10.52	Fayid	to 19 MU 23.3.53	
Also in use Mosquito T.2 VT610				
Gloster Meteor NF.13				
WM305			(no card)	NF.11 for AdlA
WM308*	19.3.53	Kabrit	to 109 MU 23.12.54	
WM310*	19.3.53	Kabrit		11.3.57
WM311*	10.1.55	Kabrit	to 20 MU 7.7.58	Scrap 12.58
WM313*	10.1.55	Kabrit	to 20 MU 7.7.58	Scrap 12.58
WM314*	23.3.53	Kabrit	Crashed 12.56	
WM315/F*	23.3.53	Kabrit	to 20 MU 7.7.58	Scrap 12.58
WM318*	6.5.57	Kabrit	to 20 MU 3.7.58	Scrap 2.59
WM317*	20.3.53	Kabrit	to MU Safi 18.4.58	Scrap 2.59
WM322*	20.3.53	Kabrit		Scrap 12.58
WM323*	15.8.53	Kabrit	to 20 MU 7.7.58	Scrap 2.59
WM327/E*	6.1.55	Kabrit	to 20 MU 3.7.58	Scrap 12.58
WM329*	2.6.56	Kabrit	to HQ MEAF 3.11.56	Scrap 2.59
WM333			(no card)	To Syria .54?
WM363	15.6.55		to MU Safi 3.4.58	To Syria .54?
Gloster Meteor T.7				
WL431	12.52		w/o 13.5.53	
WL411	24.8.54		17.5.57	
English Electric Canberra PR.3				
WE135*	3.5.60	EE mods	to 33 MU 23.4.63	
WE137/A*	1.7.58	69 Sqn	Dafi 3.9.62	
WE138/B*	1.7.58	69 Sqn	to 15 MU 10.12.62	
WE139/C*	1.7.58	69 Sqn	to 231 OCU 19.12.62	
WE144/D*	8.8.58	Takali	Bassingbourn 30.11.62	
WE148	11.8.60	MEAF	to 15 MU 29.8.61	
WE159			(no card)	
WE167			(no card)	
WE168/E		69 Sqn	via 231 OCU to 8049M 13.5.69	
WE169/G*	1.7.58	69 Sqn	to 231 OCU 11.6.63	

Serial/Code	Delivery date to Sqn or operating area	Previous unit/ Command	Last sortie or transfer details	SOC date
WE173*	1.7.58	69 Sqn	to 231 OCU 16.11.62	
WE174/H*	23.11.59	EE mods	SAF 22.10.62	
WE175		58 Sqn	(no card) to 231 OCU	13.5.69
WF922/J*	23.7.59	EE	to EE 27.10.60	
WF924/K*	1.8.58	ex Special Flt	to 231 OCU 22.2.63	
WF927/O*	4.2.59	EE mods	to 231 OCU 26.11.62	
WD950			(no card)	
WJ629			(no card)	
WF926		69 Sqn	crashed in sea 1.60	

English Electric Canberra T.4

Serial/Code	Delivery date to Sqn or operating area	Previous unit/ Command	Last sortie or transfer details	SOC date
WT478		Akrotiri Stn Flt	(no card) to 13 Sqn	
WT480			(no card)	
WT481*	10.4.62	EE mods	crashed in sea 6.65	
WH861/L*	14.11.61	Safi	to Akrotiri Stn Flt 22.6.66	

English Electric Canberra PR.9

Serial/Code	Delivery date to Sqn or operating area	Previous unit/ Command	Last sortie or transfer details	SOC date
XH131				
XH132			became SC.9 with RAE at Bedford	
XH133				
XH134	.62		to No.1 PRU 6.82	
XH135				
XH136				
XH137*	28.9.70	13 Sqn	crashed	10.5.77
XH165			to No.1 PRU 6.82	
XH166*	18.10.76	Shorts	sold 15.10.82 (Chile)	
XH167*	5.11.62	58 Sqn	sold 15.10.82 (Chile)	
XH168	.62			
XH169	.11.62		to No.1 PRU 6.82	
XH170/E				Wyton gate guard
XH171				
XH172*	18.12.62	58 Sqn		
XH173	4.12.62	58 Sqn	to St Athan 5.1.82	
XH174			to No.1 PRU 6.82	
XH175	.11.62		to No.1 PRU 6.82	
XH176	.62		crashed 5.78	

ASV Mk 2

Aircraft to Surface Vessel (ASV) Mk.2 was the earliest form of ASV to be put into operation, its purpose was to 'detect ships from aircraft at greater ranges than is possible by the eye and under conditions of poor visibility'. The system consisted of a transmitter to irradiate the surface of the sea in front of the aircraft and a pair of Yagi aerials as a receiver. The information displayed on a Type 96 Indicating Unit.

The System incorporated a beacon facility providing a valuable homing device. Typical ranges for the equipment were:
1. On a ship   — Up to 20 miles
2. On coastline   — 50 - 70 miles
3. On beacons   — 80 - 90 miles

In use with 39 Squadron:
Fitted to Beaufighter II: April 1942 - June 1943.
Fitted to Beaufighter X: October 1943 onwards.

Extract from AP.2544A Section 5, Chapter 1

OPERATING INSTRUCTIONS
FOR ASV Mk. 2

1. In order to obtain the best results from the equipment close co-operation between the pilot, the navigator and the operator is essential. It is therefore necessary that these members of the crew should be thoroughly trained in the operation of the equipment and in the interpretation of the indication on the screen.

2. The strongest echoes are given by coast lines with high cliffs or by large vessels and weak echoes are returned from low coast lines, small islands, small ships and partly submerged submarines. By the selection of a suitable range on the indicating unit the distance is indicated on the scale on the cathode ray tube and some conception of the nature of the object can be obtained from the strength of the returning echo. The indications, however, may vary due to a number of reasons, for instance large variations in echo amplitude will result according to the aspect that the target presents to the searching aircraft. A ships which is in line ahead of in line astern to the aircraft gives a very much less powerful echo than one which is abeam. It is also important to note that echoes of exceptional strength might conceivably return from portions of the detected aircraft which happens to have physical dimensions which cause them to resonate at the transmitted frequency.

3. The following procedure should be adopted when using the apparatus in flight.

    (i) Switch ON at the control panel, and verify that the blower in the transmitter is working by placing the hand momentarily over the intake. It should now be possible to see the glow of the transmitter filaments through the louvres in the cover. Since the control panel supplies the power for the receiver no further control switch is employed in this unit or in the indicating unit.

    (ii) Allow about one minute after switching on at the control unit, then switch on the high-tension switch on the transmitter. The milliammeter on the transmitter should show a value of 4 to 4.5 mA. The value of 8 to 10 mA indicates a very high pulse recurrence frequency and higher values than those indicate either continuous oscillation or no oscillation at all. Such values are very harmful to the valves and the transmitter should be immediately switched off if a reading higher than 8 mA is obtained.

    (iii) Approximately three minutes is required by the valves to warm up fully in the receiver and indicating unit. A luminous vertical line should appear on the viewing screen of the indicating unit; if this is not visible, adjust the BRIGHTNESS control until the line appears. Now adjust the FOCUS control until the line is sharp and clear. With the GAIN control advanced, horizontal lines should now be seen on both sides of the vertical time base line.

Fig.1: TYPICAL INDICATION

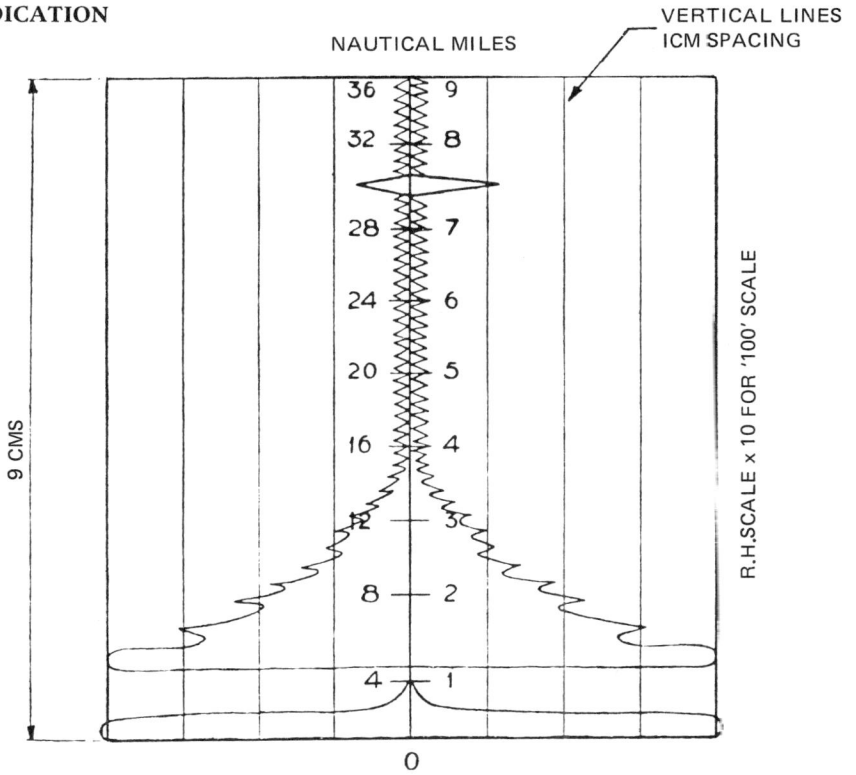

NAUTICAL MILES

VERTICAL LINES
ICM SPACING

9 CMS

R.H. SCALE x 10 FOR '100' SCALE

0

Fig.2: INDICATING UNIT TYPE 96

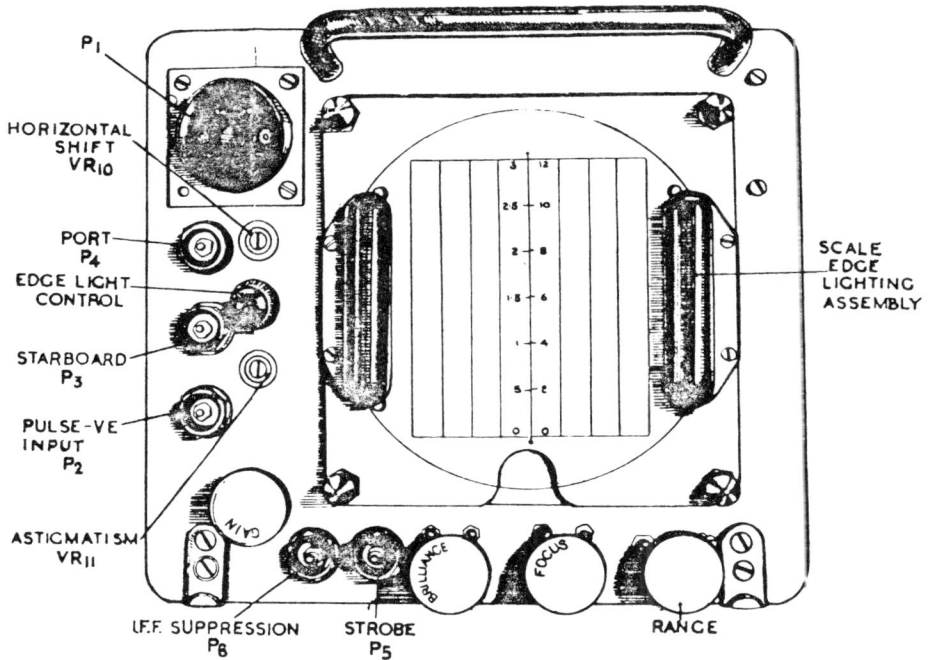

P₁

HORIZONTAL
SHIFT
VR₁₀

PORT
P₄

EDGE LIGHT
CONTROL

STARBOARD
P₃

PULSE-VE
INPUT
P₂

ASTIGMATISM
VR₁₁

SCALE
EDGE
LIGHTING
ASSEMBLY

GAIN

I.F.F. SUPPRESSION
P₆

STROBE
P₅

BRILLIANCE

FOCUS

RANGE

The tuning control on the receiver panel should now be adjusted so that the returning echoes are of maximum amplitude. In the case of aircraft which are fitted with 'local' and 'remote' indicating units, the gain control switch on the receiver should be first put in the LOCAL position, so that the operator can observe the screen of the local indicating unit while he tunes the receiver. The gain switch may then be put over to the REMOTE position to allow the navigator to control the gain of the receiver whilst observing the screen of the remote unit. Along the time base line small horizontal lines of continually varying amplitudes will be seen due to 'noise' in the receiver, see fig. 1. Towards the zero end of the scale will be seen echoes from the waves, if flying over the sea, or echoes from buildings, trees, etc., when flying over land. The echoes from ships will show themselves as indications, which appear as blips along the base line, as illustrated in fig. 1. In this diagram the horizontal returns at the zero end of the scale are due to the direct pulse from the transmitter to the receiver. The first large return is due to the reflection from the sea vertically below the aeroplane. It will be seen from the diagram that the aeroplane in this case was flying at about 6,000 ft. At low altitudes the first sea return merges with the direct ray from the transmitter and there will be no distinct gap between the two. The echoes shown up to nearly 4 miles are due to the uneven surface presented by the waves. A ship is shown at 7½ miles and, since the right-hand echo is greater than the left, the ship is to starboard of the searching aeroplane.

(iv) The BRIGHTNESS control should not be turned up more than is necessary for clear observation.

4. When a ship has been located, the echo will usually appear more strongly to one side or the other of the vertical time base line. If the indication occurs equally on both the starboard and port sides, the navigator should tell the pilot to maintain his course. The indications should now move towards the zero end of the time base and increase in strength as the aeroplane approaches the ship. If the echo shows greater amplitude to the starboard, or port of the vertical line the course should be altered until the echo lies symmetrically about the line. The vertical lines on the scale, spaces 1 cm. apart, are used to estimate the relative amplitudes of the port and starboard echoes. As the target is approached the appropriate time base is selected by the range switch, in order to give the most accurate estimate of the distance of the target. During the last stages of approach the amplitude of the echo will increase rapidly and the gain control will have to be turned back to keep the indications at a reasonable size, say 3 cm., to avoid saturation of the receiver, which would destroy the D/F ratio. This will also reduce the amplitude of the sea echoes, thus making the echo from the ship more easily distinguishable, and allowing the navigator to obtain directional indications as long as possible. Finally, sea echoes become of amplitude comparable with that of the ship and no further D/F indications can be obtained.

5. In aircraft fitted with broadside aerial arrays, a lane of sea to both port and starboard of the aircraft is 'searched' by the A.S.V. equipment. On observation of an echo a decision may be made to investigate the ship concerned more closely. The range of the ship should be read from the engraved scale superimposed on the screen of the cathode-ray tube, and since the equipment only detects ships when they are abeam of the aeroplane its approximate position is known. The aircraft should now be turned through 90 degrees until it is flying towards this position. During the manœuvre the echo on the screen will disappear, for the ship will no longer be within the lane which is searched by the transmission from the broadside arrays.

6. During the 90-degree turn of the aircraft the homing aerials should be substitued for the broadside arrays by means of the aerials changeover switches. A remote H.T. switch should be located in the vicinity of the aerial changeover switches and it is most important to SWITCH OFF H.T. TO THE TRANSMITTING VALVES BEFORE OPERATING THE AERIAL CHANGEOVER SWITCHES. After switching the aerial changeover switches to 'HOMING' it will be necessary to switch H.T. againto the transmitter before carrying out the homing procedure as described in para. 4.

7. The maximum range of the equipment with the homing aerials connected is rather less than the operational range when searching the broadside lanes, therefore it may be necessary for the aircraft to fly for some time on the homing aerials before again picking up the ship which was originally located on the broadside arrays. When the ship has been investigated and it is required to resume broadside searching. the aerial changeover switches should be switched back to 'LONG RANGE'.

Index